# OUT OF THIS CENTURY

Ata B. Olson

# OUT OF THIS CENTURY

Confessions of an Art Addict

Peggy Guggenheim

Foreword by Gore Vidal

Introduction by Alfred H. Barr, Jr.

ANDRE DEUTSCH

First published in Great Britain in 1979 by
André Deutsch Limited 105-106 Great Russell Street London WC1B 3LJ

Paperback edition first published in 1983
Second impression 1985
Third impression 1987
Fourth impression 1987

ISBN 0 233 97601 9

Printed in Great Britain by
Ebenezer Baylis and Son Ltd, Worcester

# To James Johnson Sweeney

Apropos of the dedication of this book the following telephone conversation occurred:

*Peggy Guggenheim:* Sweeney, I have something very embarrassing to ask you. Would you mind if I dedicated my memoirs to you?

*James Johnson Sweeney:* On the contrary, I would be flattered and delighted.

*Peggy Guggenheim:* I hope you will not live to regret it.

*James Johnson Sweeney:* I hope you mean I'll live but not regret it.

# Contents

| | | |
|---|---|---:|
| | Foreword by Gore Vidal | xi |
| | Introduction by Alfred H. Barr, Jr. | xv |
| 1 | Gilt-edged Childhood | 1 |
| 2 | Virginity | 16 |
| 3 | Marriage | 27 |
| 4 | End of My Life with Laurence Vail | 78 |
| 5 | My Life with John Holms | 86 |
| 6 | Hayford Hall | 113 |
| 7 | Death of John Holms | 123 |
| 8 | My Life with Garman | 130 |
| 9 | Yew Tree Cottage | 139 |
| 10 | Communism | 151 |
| 11 | Guggenheim Jeune | 159 |
| 12 | My Life During the War | 207 |
| 13 | My Life with Max Ernst | 230 |
| 14 | End of My Life with Max Ernst | 278 |
| 15 | Peace | 287 |
| 16 | Life in the Duplex | 300 |
| 17 | Art of This Century | 314 |
| | Interlude | 321 |

18  Venice and the Biennale                             325
19  Palazzo Venier dei Leoni                            333
20  Ceylon, India and Venice Again                      349
21  New York Revisited                                  358
    Conclusion                                          365
    Appendix: Venice                                    379
    Index                                               386

# List of Illustrations

BETWEEN PAGES 76 AND 77
Benita and Peggy Guggenheim, 1903
Myself in 1908
Peggy, Hazel and Benita Guggenheim, 1908
Benita Guggenheim
Myself in 1912        Curtis Bell
Myself in 1913
My Jacoby School graduating class
Laurence Vail: The King of Bohemia, 1922; On our honeymoon, 1922;
  In Egypt, 1923
Myself in my Poiret evening dress, 1924        Man Ray
Sindbad Vail, 1926        Berenice Abbott
Pegeen Vail, 1926        Berenice Abbott

BETWEEN PAGES 140 AND 141
Myself with Sindbad and Pegeen, 1934        Barbara Kerr-Seymot
Pegeen, 1937        Humphrey Jennings
Emma Goldman        Bettmann Archive
Emily Coleman
John Holms
John Holms and myself, 1931
Douglas Garman, 1936
Myself with my mother, 1938
Myself with Yves Tanguy, 1938
Peggy
Peggy and Milton Waldman
John Tunnard
Humphrey Jennings
E. L. T. Mesens and Henry Moore
Samuel Beckett and Geer van Velde, 1938
Herbert Read
Constantin Brancusi, Marcel Duchamp and Mary Reynolds, 1929
Jacqueline Breton and Victor Brauner, 1940

BETWEEN PAGES 204 AND 205
Antoine Pevsner  Alexander Liberman
Jean Arp  Alexander Liberman
Max Ernst  Leonar
Jimmy Ernst
Leonora Carrington
Djuna Barnes  Berenice Abbott
Marcel Duchamp  Sidney Waintrob
Piet Mondrian
Yves Tanguy  Man Ray
Myself at Art of This Century
Frederick Kiesler  Renate Ponsold
Surrealist Gallery, Art of This Century
Abstract and Cubist Gallery, Art of This Century
Kenneth McPherson
John Cage  James Klosty

BETWEEN PAGES 268 AND 269
Tanguy, *Le Soleil dans son écrin*
Tunnard, *PSI*
Hélion, *Large Volumes*
Dali, *The Birth of Liquid Desires*
Ernst, *The Anti-Pope* (2 versions)
Delvaux, *The Break of Day*
Hirshfield, *Two Women in Front of a Mirror*
Pollock, Mural
Pegeen, one of a series of oils and pastels
Myself on my marble chair

BETWEEN PAGES 332 AND 333
Palazzo Venier dei Leoni
The view from my roof  Jerome Zerbe
With Pevsner's construction  Roloff Beny
With my Lhasa terriers and Calder's bedhead, 1956  Cacco
With Vittorio Carrain, c. 1954
In my gondola
The two Sir Herberts and Raoul Gregorich  Cacco
With Edmondo Bacci and Tancredi in my garden  Cacco
The celebration of my 80th birthday, 1978  Interpress Photo
Myself in the center hall of my palazzo, 1978  Nino Leto
Myself in 1978  Nino Leto

# Foreword by Gore Vidal

In the winter of 1945–46 I was a Warrant Officer in the Army of
the United States, stationed at Mitchell Field, Long Island. I had
just finished a first novel, *Williwaw*, based on my experiences as
the first mate of an army freight supply ship in the Aleutians.
Before I enlisted in the army at seventeen, I had lived in
Washington, D.C. My family was political-military. I give these
little personal facts to set the scene for my first meeting with
Peggy Guggenheim.

In the early part of that winter I had met Anaïs Nin. I was
twenty. She was forty-two. Our long and arduous relationship, or
Relationship, began in the cold, as the sweet singer of Camelot
would say. Anaïs was a shining figure who looked younger than
she was; spoke in a soft curiously accented voice; told lies which
for sheer beauty and strangeness were even better than the books
she wrote—perhaps because what she wrote was always truthful
if not true while what she said was intended only to please—
herself as well as others.

"I shall take you to a party, *chéri*," she announced. We were in
the five-floor Greenwich Village walk-up where she lived with her
husband (a banker who made movies and engravings and helped

Anaïs play at being a starving Bohemian). Anaïs always called me
*"chéri"* with a slightly droll inflection. Since I had not yet read
Colette, it was several years before I got the joke. But then she did
not get all my jokes either. So *"chéri"* and Anaïs went to Peggy
Guggenheim's house (described on page 259) and *"chéri"* has never
forgotten a single detail of that bright, magical (a word often used
in those days) occasion. In a sense, like the character in *Le Grand
Meaulnes,* I still think that somewhere, even now, in a side street
of New York City, that party is still going on and Anaïs is still
alive and young and *"chéri"* is very young indeed, and James Agee
is drinking too much and Laurence Vail is showing off some
bottles that he has painted having first emptied them into himself
as part of the creative process and André Breton is magisterial and
Léger looks as if he himself could have made one of those bits of
machinery that he liked to paint; and a world of color and humor
is still going on—could be entered again if only one had not
mislaid the address. Recently I came across an old telephone book.
I looked up Anaïs's number of thirty-five years ago. Watkins
something-or-other. I rang the number; half-expected her to
answer. If she had, I'd have asked her if it was still 1945 and she
would say, Of course. What year did I think it was? And I'd say,
No, it's 1979, and you're dead. (*"Chéri"* was never noted for his
tact.) And she would laugh and say, Not yet.

Not yet. Well, "yet" is here. And so is Peggy Guggenheim.
When I first saw her she was smiling—a bit sleepily. I remember
something odd hanging about her neck . . . Barbarous jewelry?
My memory's less perfect than I thought. Actually, I remember
Agee's red-rimmed drinker's eyes and Vail's white streaming hair
rather more vividly than I do Peggy, who drifted effortlessly
through her own party, more like a guest than a hostess.

There. I am getting, as it were (as Henry James would say),
something of Peggy's aura then and now. Although she gave
parties and collected pictures and people, there was—and is—
something cool and impenetrable about her. She does not fuss.
She is capable of silence, a rare gift. She listens, an even rarer
gift. She is a master of the one-liner that deflates some notion or
trait of character or person. As I write this, I am trying to think of
a brilliant example; and fail. So perhaps it is simply the dry tone—
the brevity with which she delivers her epitaphs—that one
remembers with pleasure.

Peggy never liked Anaïs. For some reason, to this day, I have never asked her why. Last year, shortly before Peggy's eightieth birthday, we were sitting in the *salone* of her *palazzo* on Venice's Grand Canal (writing that sentence I begin to see Peggy Guggenheim as the last of Henry James's transatlantic heroines, Daisy Miller with rather more balls), and Peggy suddenly said, "Anaïs was very stupid, wasn't she?" It is the artful making of statements in the form of a question that sets apart Peggy's generation from the present age where there are no questions, only thundering self-serving assertions.

"No," I said. "She was shrewd. And she got exactly what she wanted. She set out to be a legendary figure." Legend was a word that Anaïs always used with reverence. "And she lived long enough to see herself a sort of heroine to the women's liberation movement."

"That may be shrewd," said Peggy—in the late afternoon light the sleepy narrow eyes suddenly shone like cats' eyes—"but it seems a stupid thing to want to be."

Now Peggy has been transformed by time (with a bit of help from her own shrewd nature) into a legend of the very same variety that Anaïs had in mind, a high romantic Murgeresque mind. Yet, at eighty, the legendary Peggy keeps a sharp eye on a world that is declining rather more rapidly than she is. After all, Venice is sinking, literally, beneath her unfinished white *palazzo*. If the ultimate dream of the solipsist is to take the world with him when he dies, Peggy may very well end by taking Venice out of this world and into her own world where that party still goes on and everyone is making something new and art smells not of the museum but of the maker's studio.

Last summer I asked, "How are you?" Polite but real question: she'd been in considerable pain with some disturbance of the arteries. "Oh," she said, "for someone dying, not bad."

It seems to me that these two memoirs—artful rather than artless, though the unknowing will not get the point to the art— reflect a world as lost now as the Watkins number that did not ring for lack of a digit. But since the prose in this volume is all Peggy's own, something has been salvaged. One hears in these lines the brisk yet drawling voice; sees the sudden swift side-long glance that often accompanies her swift judgments; takes pleasure if not in her actual self, in its shadow upon the page.

I last saw Peggy looking very shadowy on Italian television. Venice was celebrating her eightieth birthday; or at least that part of Venice which has not sunk into sloth as opposed to the Adriatic.

The camera came in for a very close shot of Peggy's handsome head. An off-camera voice asked her what she thought of today's Italian painters. The eyes shifted toward the unseen questioner; the half smile increased by a fraction. "Oh," she said, "they're very bad." Then always the Jamesian heroine, she added, "Aren't they?"

Consternation throughout Italy. The heroine of *The Golden Bowl* had shattered the bowl—and prevailed once again.

# Introduction by Alfred H. Barr, Jr.

Courage and vision, generosity and humility, money and time, a strong sense of historical significance, as well as of esthetic quality—these are factors of circumstance and character which have made Peggy Guggenheim an extraordinary patron of twentieth-century art. On ground rocked by factionalism, she has stood firm, taking no sides, partisan only of the valuable revolution. Consequently we find in her collection works which are diametrically opposed in spirit and form, even though they may seem to be alike in their radical strangeness.

The collection is Peggy Guggenheim's most durable achievement as an art patron, but it is quite possibly not her most important. I have used the threadbare and somewhat pompous word "patron" with some misgivings. Yet it is precise. For a patron is not simply a collector who gathers works of art for his own pleasure or a philanthropist who helps artists or founds a public museum, but a person who feels responsibility toward both art and the artist together and has the means and will to act upon this feeling.

Peggy Guggenheim had no early interest in modern art. In fact, she loved and studied Italian Renaissance painting, particularly that of Venice. Berenson's books were her guide, and perhaps they confirmed that sense for the history of art which she carried into the twentieth century, the very point in time and taste at which her mentor stopped.

Then in the late 1930s, largely as an amateur's diversion, she opened an *avant-garde* gallery in London. Marcel Duchamp was her chief adviser (the same who in New York twenty years before had counseled Katherine Dreier in her creation of the pioneering *Société Anonyme*). Guggenheim Jeune, as she humorously called the enterprise, gave several excellent exhibitions, among them England's first one-man shows of Kandinsky, the first abstract expressionist, and Yves Tanguy, the surrealist painter. At the same time, the gallery gave their first exhibitions to young artists such as John Tunnard, the best of the new English abstract painters of the period. Yet these achievements seemed to her too impermanent.

Early in 1939 Peggy Guggenheim "had the idea of opening a modern museum in London," a project which must have seemed urgent, the director of the Tate Gallery having not long before declared for customs purposes that sculptures by Calder, Arp, Pevsner and others, which Guggenheim Jeune was importing for a show, were not works of art at all.

With her usual flair for enlisting the ablest help, she asked Herbert Read, later Sir Herbert, to become the director of this projected museum. Read, generally considered the leading English authority on modern art, was persuaded to resign his editorship of the highly respectable *Burlington Magazine* in order to assume his new and adventurous position. The patron and the director drew up an ideal list of works of art for the new museum—a list which was also to serve as the basis for the opening exhibition. A building was found, but before the lease could be signed World War II began and the dream faded, or better, was suspended.

In Paris during the winter of the "phony war" Peggy Guggenheim, only a little daunted, kept on adding to the collection, "buying a picture a day" with the advice of her friends Duchamp, Howard Putzel and Nellie van Doesburg. She even rented space for a gallery in the Place Vendôme, but meanwhile the cool war turned hot. The Brancusi *Bird in Space* was bought as the Germans were nearing Paris.

During the first year of the German occupation the collection was safeguarded in the Grenoble museum; but it was not shown there because the director feared the reprisals of the collaborationist Vichy régime. Finally, in the spring of 1941, the collection and its owner reached New York.

Thanks largely to the influx of refugee artists and writers from Europe, New York during the war supplanted occupied Paris as the art center of the Western world. Later, most of the Europeans returned, particularly to France; yet, in the postwar world, Paris seems clearly less preeminent and New York remained a contestant partly because of the rise of the most internationally respected group of painters so far produced in the United States. In their development, Peggy Guggenheim, as patron, played an important, and in some cases a crucial, role.

She had been frustrated in London, in Paris and in Grenoble, but in New York, thanks to its distance from the conflict, she was able temporarily to realize her vision. With the advice of the Surrealist painter Max Ernst and the poet André Breton, she continued to add to her collection and published a brilliant catalogue, *Art of This Century*, the title she also gave to her new gallery.

Art of This Century immediately became the center of the vanguard. Under the influence of Duchamp, Ernst and Breton, the surrealist tradition was strong but never exclusive. The great abstract painter, Piet Mondrian, was also welcome and took an active part as a member of the juries which chose the recurrent group shows of young American artists.

In the first "Spring Salon," 1943, three young painters stood out: William Baziotes, Robert Motherwell and Jackson Pollock. Within a year all three were launched by the gallery with one-man shows. Pollock's exhibition, with an enthusiastic catalogue preface by James Johnson Sweeney, won special admiration. Then, again with remarkable prescience, Art of This Century gave shows to Mark Rothko, Clyfford Still and others. I say prescience because although their work had not come to full maturity at that time, Rothko, Still, Baziotes, Motherwell, Pollock and two or three others are now recognized in the United States and increasingly in Europe as the chief pillars of the formidable new American school.

Early pictures by these painters, bought by Peggy Guggenheim out of their shows in the 1940s, may be seen in her collection today. Jackson Pollock, the most renowned of them, is represented by several works, though not by his largest, a mural commissioned by his patron for the lobby of her New York residence. Pollock she also helped financially, and when in 1947 Art of This Century closed she helped to place the artists in other galleries.

Today, in Venice, Peggy Guggenheim, her collection and her exhibition gallery continue to work. Visitors who study the collection with the sounds of the Grand Canal in their ears should know something of the history of the collector as patron—particularly Americans, who owe a special debt to their countrywoman, Peggy Guggenheim.

# OUT OF THIS
# CENTURY

# Chapter 1

# Gilt-edged Childhood

I have no memory. I always say to my friends, "Don't tell me anything you don't want repeated. I just can't remember not to." Invariably I forget and I repeat everything.

In 1923 I began to write my memoirs. They began like this: "I come from two of the best Jewish families. One of my grandfathers was born in a stable like Jesus Christ or, rather, over a stable in Bavaria, and my other grandfather was a peddler." I don't seem to have gotten very far with this book. Maybe I had nothing to say, or possibly I was too young for the task which I had set myself. Now I feel I am ripe for it. By waiting too long I may forget everything I have somehow managed to remember.

If my grandfathers started life modestly they ended it sumptuously. My stable-born grandfather, Mr. Seligman, came to America in steerage, with forty dollars in his pocket and contracted smallpox on board ship. He began his fortune by being a roof shingler and later by making uniforms for the Union Army in the Civil War. Later he became a renowned banker and president of Temple Emanu-El. Socially he got way beyond my other grandfather, Mr. Guggenheim the peddler, who was born in Lengnau in German Switzerland. Mr. Guggenheim far surpassed

Mr. Seligman in amassing an enormous fortune and buying up
most of the copper mines of the world, but he never succeeded in
attaining Mr. Seligman's social distinction. In fact, when my
mother married Benjamin Guggenheim the Seligmans considered
it a *mésalliance*. To explain that she was marrying into the well
known smelting family, they sent a cable to their kin in Europe
saying, "Florette engaged Guggenheim smelter." This became a
great family joke, as the cable misread "Guggenheim smelt her."

By the time I was born the Seligmans and the Guggenheims
were extremely rich. At least the Guggenheims were, and the
Seligmans hadn't done so badly. My grandfather, James Seligman,
was a very modest man who refused to spend money on himself
and underfed his trained nurse. He lived sparsely and gave
everything to his children and grandchildren. He remembered all
our birthdays and, although he did not die until ninety-three, he
never failed to make out a check on these occasions. The checks
were innumerable, as he had eleven children and fifteen grandchildren.

Most of his children were peculiar, if not mad. That was
because of the bad inheritance they received from my grandmother. My grandfather finally had to leave her. She must have
been objectionable. My mother told me that she could never invite
young men to her home without a scene from her mother. My
grandmother went around to shopkeepers and, as she leaned over
the counter, asked them confidentially, "When do you think my
husband last slept with me?"

My mother's brothers and sisters were very eccentric. One of
my favorite aunts was an incurable soprano. If you happened to
meet her on the corner of Fifth Avenue while waiting for a bus,
she would open her mouth wide and sing scales trying to make you
do as much. She wore her hat hanging off the back of her head or
tilted over one ear. A rose was always stuck in her hair. Long
hatpins emerged dangerously, not from her hat, but from her
hair. Her trailing dresses swept up the dust of the streets. She
invariably wore a feather boa. She was an excellent cook and made
beautiful tomato jelly. Whenever she wasn't at the piano, she
could be found in the kitchen or reading the ticker-tape. She was
an inveterate gambler. She had a strange complex about germs
and was forever wiping her furniture with Lysol. But she had
such extraordinary charm that I really loved her. I cannot say her

husband felt as much. After he had fought with her for over thirty years, he tried to kill her and one of her sons by hitting them with a golf club. Not succeeding, he rushed to the reservoir where he drowned himself with heavy weights tied to his feet.

Another aunt, who resembled an elephant more than a human being, at a late age in life conceived the idea that she had had a love affair with an apothecary. Although this was completely imaginary, she felt so much remorse that she became melancholic and had to be put in a nursing home.

My most attractive uncle was a very distinguished gentleman of the old school. Being separated from his wife who was as rich as he, he decided to live in great simplicity in two small rooms and spend all his money on fur coats, which he gave away to girls. Almost any girl could have one for the asking. He wore the *Légion d'honneur* but would never tell us why he had been decorated.

Another uncle lived on charcoal which he had been eating for many years, and as a result his teeth were black. In a zinc-lined pocket he carried pieces of cracked ice which he sucked all the time. He drank whiskey before breakfast and ate almost no food. He gambled heavily, as did most of my aunts and uncles, and when he was without funds he threatened to commit suicide to get more money out of my grandfather. He had a mistress whom he concealed in his room. No one was allowed to visit him until he finally shot himself, and then he could no longer keep the family out. At the funeral my grandfather greatly shocked his children by walking up the aisle with his dead son's mistress on his arm. They all said, "How can Pa do that?"

There was one miserly uncle who never spent a cent. He arrived in the middle of meals saying he didn't want a thing and then ate everything in sight. After dinner he put on a frightening act for his nieces. It was called "the snake." It terrified and delighted us. By placing lots of chairs together in a row and then wriggling along them on his stomach he really produced the illusion. The other two uncles were nearly normal. One of them spent all his time washing himself and the other one wrote plays that were never produced. The latter was a darling and my favorite.

My other grandfather, Meyer Guggenheim, lived happily with his stepmother's daughter to whom he was married. They brought up an even larger, if less eccentric, family than the Seligmans.

There were seven brothers and three sisters. They produced twenty-three grandchildren. When my grandmother died my grandfather was looked after by his cook. She must have been his mistress. I remember seeing her weep copious tears because my grandfather vomited. My one recollection of this gentleman is of his driving around New York in a sleigh with horses. He was unaccompanied and wore a coat with a sealskin collar and a cap to match. He died when I was very young.

I was born in New York City on West Sixty-ninth Street. I don't remember anything about this. My mother told me that while the nurse was filling her hot water bottle, I rushed into the world with my usual speed and screamed like a cat. I was preceded by one sister, Benita, who was almost three years older than I. She was the great love of my early life, in fact of my entire immature life. But maybe that has never ended.

We soon moved to a house on East Seventy-second Street near the entrance to the Park. Our neighbors were the Stillmans and the Rockefellers. Opposite us lived President Grant's widow. My father remodeled this house and made it very elegant. Here my second sister Hazel was born when I was almost five. I was fiendishly jealous of her.

There is nothing about this house that does not still arouse my most poignant memories. In fact for years I dreamed about it. To enter our new domain you had to pass not one but two glass doors with a vestibule in between. Then you found yourself in a little marble entrance with a fountain. On the wall was a stuffed eagle with chains. My father had shot it himself, though it was a legal offense. He had done this in the Adirondacks, where we had a camp and went in the late summer.

Behind this hallway, which had a marble staircase, there was a door which led to the elevator. In 1941, when I returned to New York after an absence of many years, I went back to this house to visit an aunt who lived there. When we were in the elevator my daughter of sixteen, who was accompanying me, suddenly burst out with, "Mama, you lived in this house when you were a little girl?" I modestly replied "Yes," and to convince her added, "This is where Hazel was born." My daughter gave me a surprised look and concluded with this statement: "Mama, how you have come down in the world." From then on the butler, who was ushering us upstairs, looked upon me with suspicion and rarely admitted me to the house. However, my memories alone warranted my admission.

On the reception floor there was a high-ceilinged dining room with panels and six indifferent tapestries. In the back was a little conservatory filled with plants. In the center of this floor was a reception room with a huge tapestry of Alexander the Great entering Rome in triumph. In front of it was a double-trayed tea table with a monstrous silver tea set. It was in this room that my mother gave a weekly tea party to the most boring ladies of the haute Jewish bourgeoisie, which I was forced reluctantly to attend.

In the front of the house was our Louis Seize parlor with huge mirrors, tapestries on the wall and tapestried furniture. On the floor was a bearskin rug which had an enormous red mouth and a red tongue. Sometimes the tongue broke loose, and, when it was detached, it had the most revolting appearance. The animal's teeth were forever being mended as they also came out. There was also a grand piano. One night I remember hiding under this piano and weeping in the dark. My father had banished me from the table because, at the tender age of seven, I had said to him, "Papa, you must have a mistress as you stay out so many nights."

The center of the house was surmounted by a glass dome that admitted the daylight. At night it was lit by a suspended lamp. Around this was a large circular winding staircase. It commenced on the reception floor and ended on the fourth floor where I lived. I recall the exact tune which my father had invented and which he whistled to lure me when he came home at night and ascended the stairs on foot. I adored my father and rushed to meet him.

The third floor belonged to my parents. In the front was a library with red velvet paneled walls and large glass bookcases that contained the classics. Here there was another fur rug, a tiger skin. On the walls were portraits of my four grandparents. This room, as well as every room in the house, had cream colored lace curtains at the windows.

It was in this room that I sat at a large Louis Quinze table with a glass top and was fed by a maid whose sole duty at that time was to see that I ate. I never had any appetite. When my tears were of no avail, I protested by vomiting and the feeding came to an end.

In the back of the house my mother had her room. It was preceded by a little alcove containing cupboards, which space she needed for her large wardrobe. The bedroom was covered with pink silk and had twin beds. The furniture was mahogany with brass incrustations. On her bureau, which was much too high for her to use as a dressing table, was a set of silver brushes and bottles. There was a long cheval glass, in front of which my mother sat to have her hair brushed by her French maid or by a special hairbrusher who came in for that purpose. This was the hour that I was allowed to play in my mother's room. Behind her room was my father's dressing room.

Upstairs my sisters and I had a whole floor to ourselves until my grandfather Seligman came to live with us. My room was next to a steep and dark staircase that led up to the servants' quarters. It frightened me and I had nightmares about it.

I also have poignant memories of the servants' quarters which were less than adequate, and seemed to be distinctly in contrast to our elegant rooms. The men-servants' rooms were the worst of all. They were not on the top floor, which was bad enough: they were in the back of the house on queer little landings along the servants' back stairs. The kitchen was below the ground floor and, in consequence, very dark.

My mother gave many dinner parties and I remember on one of these occasions the nurse rushed downstairs to call my mother away from the table. She had heard a baby cry in the kitchen-maid's room and upon investigating the matter she had found a newly born infant hidden in a trunk, strangled in its own navel cord. The girl had come to our house only a few days before to take refuge. She had given birth alone and then murdered her illegitimate offspring. Our family doctor declared her insane to save her from prison.

My childhood was excessively unhappy: I have no pleasant memories of any kind. It seems to me now that it was one long protracted agony. When I was very young I had no friends. I didn't go to school until I was fifteen. Instead I studied under private tutors at home. There was one period when I took lessons with a girl called Dulcie Sulzberger. She had two brothers who fascinated me, one in particular, Marion.

My father insisted that his children be well-educated and saw to it that we acquired "good taste." He himself was keen on art and bought a lot of paintings. In Munich he had us painted by

Lenbach but since I was only four at the time I do not remember anything about it now. My memory goes back only to Hazel's birth. Lenbach painted me in a Vandyck costume and, for some strange reason, gave me brown eyes instead of green, and red hair instead of chestnut. With Benita he was less fanciful. Perhaps because she was so beautiful, he portrayed her as she really was, with brown hair and brown eyes. I have two portraits, one of myself, and the other one of Benita and me, in which I appear with golden hair. These are the greatest treasures of my past.

The only toys I can remember were a rocking horse with an enormous rump and a doll's house containing bearskin rugs and beautiful crystal chandeliers. The doll's house must have left me with a fearful nostalgia, because for years I tried to reproduce it for my daughter. I spent months papering walls and buying objects to furnish her house. In fact I still can't resist buying toys. I immediately give them away to children but I must buy them for my own delight. I also remember a glass cabinet filled with tiny hand-carved ivory and silver furniture, which had an old-fashioned sculptured brass key. I kept the cabinet locked and allowed no one to touch my treasures.

My strongest memories are of Central Park. When I was very young my mother used to take me driving there in an electric brougham. There was a certain rock on the East Drive that resembled a panther about to spring. I called it "the cat," and whenever we passed it, I pretended to telephone to it to say hello or to warn it of our arrival. For a telephone I used the speaking tube of our brougham. Later I rode in the Park in a little foot-pedaled automobile. The Mall was the perfect place for this. In the Ramble I climbed rocks all by myself, while my governess waited below. In the winter I was forced to go ice skating, which caused me to suffer agonies. My ankles were too weak and my circulation much too bad. I shall never forget the excruciating pain I felt from the thawing of my toes, when returning from the lake I clung to a stove which was in a little cabin intended for skaters.

All this left me with such painful memories that I have carefully avoided the Park ever since. In fact I refused to visit it when I came back to New York in the early 1940s. However, one hot summer night Alfred Barr insisted on taking me there. I tried to find all the haunts of my childhood, but everything was changed. Only the Ramble with its old castle remained, true to my childhood memories.

Not only was my childhood excessively lonely and sad, but it was also filled with torments. I once had a nurse who threatened to cut out my tongue if I dared to repeat to my mother the foul things she said to me. In desperation and fear I told my mother and the nurse was dismissed at once. Also I was not at all strong and my parents were perpetually fussing about my health. They imagined I had all sorts of illnesses and were forever taking me to doctors. At one period of my life, when I was about ten, they decided I had some intestinal disturbance and found a doctor who ordered me to have colonic irrigations. These were administered by Hazel's nurse and, as she was quite unqualified for her task, the result was catastrophic. I got an acute attack of appendicitis and was rushed off to the hospital at midnight and operated on. For days I was kept in ignorance of the operation, since they thought I was too young to be told. However, I did not believe their silly stories and insisted that my stomach had been cut open.

Soon after this, my sister Benita developed the whooping cough and we had to be separated lest I catch it and cough open my newly healed, and let me add, enormous wound. My mother took a house in Lakewood, New Jersey, for herself and Benita, and I was sent to a hotel with a trained nurse. Needless to say I passed a lonely winter and only occasionally was I permitted to speak to Benita on the street and from a great distance. My mother had several nieces who were marriageable and she was perpetually giving house parties for them while she shut poor Benita up in a wing of the house. As a result Benita became melancholic. I must have been very precocious and spoiled, since I was allowed to visit my mother and entertain her visitors. I fell in love with one of them. His name was Max Rossbach and he taught me to play pool.

Not long after this I had a bad accident while riding in Central Park. As I passed under a bridge some boys on roller skates overhead made such a noise that my horse bolted. My lady riding teacher was as incapable as I of stopping the beast. I lost my seat, fell to the ground and was dragged for quite a distance. I could not disengage my foot from the stirrup and my skirt caught on the pommel. Had I been riding astride this never would have occurred. I not only hurt my foot but I seriously injured my mouth. My jaw was broken in two places and I lost a front tooth. A policeman, finding the tooth in the mud, returned it to me in a letter, and the next day the dentist, after disinfecting it, pushed it up into its original position. This did not end my troubles. My jaw had to be set. During the operation a great battle took place among the attending surgeons. Finally, one of them triumphed over the other and shook my poor jaw into shape. The vanquished dentist, who was called Buxbaum, never got over this. He felt he had superior rights over my mouth, as he had been straightening my teeth for years. The only good that came out of all this was that it put an end to the agonies I had been suffering in the process of being beautified. Now that had to end. The first danger incurred was the possibility of being blood-poisoned. When that passed, the only risk I ran was of getting hit in the mouth and losing my tooth again before it was firmly implanted. In those days my sole opponents were tennis balls, so that when I played tennis I conceived the bright idea of tying a tea strainer in front of my mouth. Anyone seeing me must have thought I had hydrophobia. When it was all over, my father received a bill for seven thousand five hundred dollars from the dentist who had never admitted his defeat. My father persuaded this gentleman reluctantly to accept two thousand.

In spite of all the trouble I went through to preserve the tooth, I knew it could not remain with me for more than ten years, after which time its root would be completely absorbed and the tooth would have to be replaced with a porcelain one. I was prophetic in gauging its life, may I say, almost to the day. After ten years I made an appointment to have it replaced before it fell out, which it did exactly two days before the dentist expected me.

One of my first great passions was for the actor William Gillette. I went to all his matinées and virtually screamed to warn him when I thought he was going to be shot by an enemy in the play *Secret Service*.

I had taken to riding again as soon as I was allowed to after my accident, but this time I took no chances. Not only did I have a male teacher but I also learned to ride astride. At fourteen I fell in love with my riding teacher. He was a fascinating Irishman who flirted with all of his pupils.

Benita was the only companion of my childhood and I therefore developed a great love for her. We were perpetually chaperoned by

French governesses, but they were always changing, so that I can barely remember them. Hazel, being so much younger, had a nurse and lived a distinctly separate life. I don't remember my mother at all at this age.

When I was five or six my father began to have mistresses. A certain trained nurse lived in our house in order to massage my father's head, since he suffered from neuralgia. According to my mother, this nurse was the cause of all her troubles in life as she somehow influenced my father for the bad, without actually ever having been his mistress. It took my mother years to rid herself of the poisonous presence of this woman in our household, for my father depended on her so much for the massage. However, we finally got rid of her, but it was too late. From then on my father had a whole series of mistresses. My mother took it as a great offense that my aunts remained friendly with this nurse and had long feuds with them for befriending her. All this affected my childhood. I was perpetually being dragged into my parents' troubles and it made me precocious.

My father always called me Maggie; only much later did I become Peggy. He had beautiful jewelry made for us which he designed himself. In honor of my name, Marguerite, he once presented me with a little bracelet that looked like a daisy chain, made of pearls and diamonds. My mother received more substantial presents, among them a magnificent string of pearls.

I adored my father because he was fascinating and handsome, and because he loved me. But I suffered very much as he made my mother unhappy, and sometimes I fought with him over it. Every summer he took us to Europe. We went to Paris and to London where my mother visited hundreds of French and English Seligmans. We also went to fashionable watering places. My mother was very mean about tipping and on one occasion I remember to my great embarrassment seeing all our luggage chalked with crosses. When we were leaving Trouville the hotel porters had marked them as a sign of warning to the porters of the next hotel, our future victims.

My father engaged a lady called Mrs. Hartman to teach us art. We brought her to Europe with us and it was her duty to make us cultured. She took us to the Louvre, to the Carnavalet and to the châteaux of the Loire. She taught us French history and also introduced us to Dickens, Thackeray, Scott and George Eliot. She

also gave us a complete course in Wagner's operas. I am sure Mrs.
Hartman did her best to stimulate our imaginations, but personally, at that time, I was more interested in other things. For one, I
was infatuated with my father's friend Rudi. He was a typical
roué and I can't imagine now why he fascinated me. I was so
much enamored of him that I wrote mad letters about my passion,
in which I said my body was nailed to the fire of the cross. When
Rudi married one of my cousins whom my mother had brought to
Europe with her, and whose unfortunate marriage I fear she and
my father arranged, I wept bitter tears and felt completely let
down. I complained, saying he had no right to trifle with the
affections of two women at once. At this time I must have been
about eleven.

Besides this exalted life which I seem to have led, I had a hobby
for something much more material—I collected elegant little wax
models and dressed them in the most fashionable of clothes,
which I created and executed myself. This was inspired by the
fact that we were summering in Trouville where all the ladies and
the courtesans were so chic.

One day when I was having tea with Benita and my governess
at Rumpelmeyer's in Paris, I found myself fascinated by a woman
at the next table. I could not take my eyes off her. She seemed to
react in the same way to us. Months later, after I had been
tormenting my governess to tell me who my father's mistress was,
she finally said, "You know her." Like a flash the face of the
woman at Rumpelmeyer's came to my mind and when questioned
my governess admitted I was right.

This woman was called the Countess Taverny. She was neither
pretty nor young. I never understood my father's infatuation for
her. But she had the same agreeable quality (maybe sensuous) of
his trained nurse. The Countess was dark and resembled a
monkey. She had ugly teeth which my mother used to refer to
with contempt as "black." We met this woman everywhere in
Paris. It was most awkward. One day at the dressmaker Lanvin,
my mother, accompanied by Benita and me, walked into a room
where Countess Taverny was seated. My mother rushed out of
the room and we followed her. The Lanvin staff, with correct
French understanding, gave us another *salle* to ourselves.

The Countess, as we used to call her, or C.T. as my father
referred to her for short, meaning Countess Taverny, wore the

most elegant clothes. She had one suit which was made entirely of
baby lamb fur. One day when we were taking our morning walk in
the Bois on the Avenue des Acacias, we met the Countess wearing
this costume. My mother protested to my father regarding his
extravagance. To console her he gave her money to have the same
suit made for herself. Being a good business woman she accepted
the money but instead she invested it in stocks and bonds.

Countess Taverny had been preceded by another lady. This
lady, whom I never saw, nearly succeeded in marrying my father.
In fact my mother had come to the point of divorcing him. But the
whole Guggenheim family came in groups and individually,
begging her to reconsider her decision. We had streams of visitors
all day long. Their one idea was to avoid this catastrophe. Finally
my mother gave in. I don't know when the affair ended, but I do
know that the disappointed mistress received a large consolation
prize and for many years part of my income went to her regularly,
twice a year.

Countess Taverny did not last long and was followed by a young
blond singer. She was with my father when he was drowned on
the *Titanic* in 1912 and was among the survivors brought back to
New York.

In 1911 my father had more or less freed himself from us. He
had left his brothers' business and had his own in Paris. This was
a move he doubtless made to be able to live a freer life, but its
consequences were more far-reaching than he ever realized. By
leaving his brothers and starting his own business, he forfeited his
claims to an enormous fortune. He had an apartment in Paris and
was interested in or owned a concern which built the elevators for
the Eiffel Tower. In the spring of 1912 he was finally to return to
us after an eight months absence. He had a passage on some
steamship which was canceled because of a strike of the stokers.
By this mere accident of fate he was to lose his life: he booked a
place on the ill-fated *Titanic*.

On April 14th, as people came out of the Metropolitan Opera
House, they were greeted with shouts of "Extra!" announcing the
dramatic sinking of this gigantic liner on her maiden voyage. In
order to make a record trip for the White Star Line, Bruce Ismay,
the president of the company, who was himself on board, and the
captain ignored the warning of icebergs and forged their way
ahead completely disregarding the danger. The *Titanic* rushed to

her doom. The first iceberg she encountered ripped her bottom open. Within an hour she sank, stern and bow going under together after a terrific explosion which split her in two. There were only enough life boats for a quarter of the people on board. Others who could swim were frozen in the icy water before Captain Rostrom of the S.S. *Carpathia* could come to their rescue. Seven hundred people were saved out of twenty-eight hundred. The world was shaken by this disaster. Everyone waited breathlessly for the *Carpathia* to dock to find out who were the lucky survivors. We wired Captain Rostrom to find out if my father was on his ship. He wired back, "No." For some reason I was told this while my mother was kept in ignorance until the last minute. Then two of my cousins went down to meet the survivors. They met my father's mistress.

With my father there died a lovely young Egyptian, Victor Giglio, who was his secretary. He had had a hard time in the past and was happy to have been engaged by my father, thinking his troubles were ended. I was attracted to this beautiful boy, but my father did not approve of my ardor. A steward of the *Titanic*, a survivor, came to see us to deliver a message from my father. He said that my father and his secretary had dressed in evening clothes to meet their death. They had wanted to die as gentlemen, which they certainly did, by gallantly giving their places to women and children.

My father's body was never recovered and was therefore not buried in Halifax with those that the sea washed up. Many other well-known men were lost on the *Titanic,* among them Harry Elkins Widener, John B. Thayer, John Jacob Astor, Edgar Meyer, and Isidor Straus with his wife who refused to leave him. In those days before World War I and before the sinking of the *Lusitania,* the sinking of the *Titanic* was considered a worldwide tragedy. Naturally there was an inquest, but the captain had committed suicide, or rather he had had the decency to go down with his boat. From then on we avoided the White Star Line like the plague.

At the time of my father's death we were living in the St. Regis Hotel—we had rented our house to one of my aunts—where we had enormous apartments. In those days the St. Regis Hotel was the stronghold of the Guggenheim family. My uncle Daniel had a whole floor beneath us. Every Friday evening there was a family reunion, when my uncles would get together to talk business while my aunts retired to a corner to discuss clothes. Needless to say they had plenty to recount on this score, since they all went to the most expensive dressmakers in New York.

After my father's death I became religious. I attended the services in Temple Emanu-El regularly, and took great dramatic pleasure in standing up for the *Kaddish* (the service for the dead). My father's death affected me greatly. It took me months to get over the terrible nightmare of the *Titanic,* and years to get over the loss of my father. In a sense I really have never recovered, as I suppose I have been searching for a father ever since.

When my father died, he left his business affairs in an awful muddle. Not only had he lost a vast fortune by discontinuing his partnership with his brothers, but the money he should have had, some eight million dollars, he had lost in Paris. The small amount that was left was tied up in stocks that were yielding no interest and were at such a low ebb that they could not be sold. However, my mother did not know this and we continued living on the same scale. My uncles, the Guggenheims, very gallantly advanced us any funds we needed, keeping us in supreme ignorance. Finally my mother discovered the truth and took drastic steps to end the false situation. To begin with she started spending her own personal fortune. We moved to a cheaper apartment with fewer servants. She sold her paintings, her tapestries and her jewelry. She managed very well, and although we were never poor, from that time on I had a complex about no longer being a real Guggenheim. I felt like a poor relative and suffered great humiliation thinking how inferior I was to the rest of the family. My grandfather Seligman died four years after my father, and then my mother inherited a small fortune from him. We immediately reimbursed my father's brothers. After seven years my uncles settled my father's estate. They had finally put things into such shape that by advancing their own money my sisters and I each inherited four hundred and fifty thousand dollars and my mother slightly more. Half of what I received was placed in trust and my uncles insisted that I voluntarily do the same with the other half.

Of course we went into mourning. I felt important and self-conscious in black. In the summer, to my great relief, I was allowed to wear white. We went to Allenhurst on the New Jersey coast, which was the summer resort of most of the Jewish families we knew. Not actually Allenhurst but the places next to it, Deal Beach, Elberon and West End, were all built up with the homes of the Jewish bourgeoisie. It was the ugliest place in the world. Not one tree or bush grew on this barren coast. The only flowers I remember were rambler roses, nasturtiums and hydrangeas, and since then I have not been able to endure them. My grandfather had a family mansion in West End, in which all his children were born, including my mother, the youngest. It was in this hideous Victorian house that my grandfather, at the age of ninety-three, died during World War I.

My Guggenheim uncles all owned the most magnificent houses on this coast. One uncle had an Alsatian wife and with her French taste they built a house which was an exact copy of the Petit Trianon at Versailles. Another uncle had a magnificent Italian villa with marble Pompeian inner courts and beautiful grottoes and sunken gardens. Compared to these my grandfather Seligman's house was a modest affair. It was completely surrounded by two porches, one on each floor. The porches were covered with rocking chairs where the entire family sat and rocked all day. It was so ugly in its Victorian perfection that it was fascinating. The culminating point was the family portraits. My mother and her two sisters and five brothers had all been painted as children, in costumes of the period made of black velvet with white lace collars. In their hands they carried birds, Bibles or hoops. They looked so heavy-eyed in these portraits that they were unmistakably Semitic.

As most of this coast was inhabited by Jewish families, it became a sort of ghetto. In Allenhurst, which was anti-Semitic, there was a hotel opposite us that would not admit Jews. During the summer, to our great delight, it burned down while we stood watching. Every summer that we did not spend in Europe we spent on this horrible coast. We bathed in the Atlantic in the wild breakers and played tennis and rode horses. However, I much preferred Europe and the next year, 1913, we persuaded my mother to take us back.

When war broke out in 1914 we were again in England, visiting one of my mother's cousins, Sir Charles Seligman. I remember shocking him very much by my careless and extravagant appetite. He was worried about the lack of food that would result from the war, and I had asked for some more beef to finish up my mustard.

# Chapter 2

# Virginity

During my sixteenth summer I became conscious of sex. It was very upsetting and frightening. It began pleasantly when I fell in love with Freddy Singer, a nephew of the Singer Sewing Machine people. We were all living in a hotel in Ascot. His brother fell in love with Benita, so we had great fun dancing and playing tennis together. But after that I had a disagreeable fright about sex. I was visiting one of my Seligman grand-aunts in Kent. In her household was a young medical student from Munich, who was an American by birth and therefore not interned. I felt he wanted to seduce me and I think he was amused by my fear and played up to the role of seducer. I have never been so terrified in my life. Later when I met him in New York he resumed his role again, but this time he wanted to marry me. I convinced him to marry my cousin instead. She was my best friend and he seemed to be in love with both of us. I was then in school and my cousin was a mature woman fifteen years older than our suitor. The marriage was successful and they had lovely twin daughters.

During the war I finally was sent to school. The Jacoby School was a private school on the West Side for young Jewish girls, and I would walk there every day through Central Park, since we lived

in an apartment on Fifth Avenue and Fifty-eighth Street. But
after a few weeks I developed whooping cough and bronchitis, and
had to spend the winter in bed. I was lonely and neglected, as it
was the year of Benita's début, and my mother was very busy with
her. Somehow I managed to do all my homework alone and kept
up with the school course and passed all my exams. I am not at all
intellectual and it was a great effort. But I did like reading, and I
read constantly in those days. I read Ibsen, Hardy, Turgenev,
Chekhov, Oscar Wilde, Tolstoy, Strindberg, Barrie, George
Meredith and Bernard Shaw.

My second year at school was slightly more fortunate than my
first. I managed to attend regularly, with the exception of a short
period when I contracted the measles. We had a busy winter
preparing to produce *Little Women* as our graduation play. Mrs.
Quaife, our wonderful dramatic teacher, conceived a life-long
affection for me, introduced me to Browning's poems and gave me
the rôle of Amy in the play. When I left school I renounced the
idea of going to college. This was due to Benita's influence. She
talked me out of it, she said I had done the same to her. For years
I regretted it.

During my second school year I began to have a social life. I
organized a little dance club with my schoolmates and some other
girls. To cover the expenses of a monthly ball, we all contributed
money. We were permitted to invite one or two boys to come and
dance with us. We made a list of the desirable young men in our
Jewish circles and then I held a mock auction sale and auctioned
them off to the highest bidder, who then had the privilege of
inviting him. These parties were gay and really not at all stuffy.

About the time I graduated from school I began a great
friendship with a beautiful girl called Fay Lewisohn. She
resembled Geraldine Farrar, which was most appropriate, as her
home was the center of gatherings of the Metropolitan Opera
Company. My feeling for Fay was much greater than hers for me
and I now think that mine was unconsciously of the order of
*Mädchen in Uniform*. Maybe Fay suspected this. In any case she
was interested in young men.

Fay's mother, Mrs. Adele Lewisohn, and her grandmother,
Mrs. Randolph Guggenheimer, were charming hostesses. They
entertained lavishly not only singers, but also all the intellectuals
of New York. Unfortunately Fay and I were too young to take

part. Or rather, Fay hated this as much as I hated being dragged into my mother's social life. They lived on Fifth Avenue in a house with a strange balcony on the top floor bearing stone figures of women resembling caryatids. Mrs. Lewisohn admired me, as I did her; and years later when I met her in Paris she told me how suitable a friend she had considered me for Fay and regretted that her daughter did not appreciate me as much as she did. She considered me a serious-minded girl compared with Fay who loved only pleasure.

During the summer of 1915, I received my first kiss. It was from a young man who took me out driving every night in my mother's car. He invariably borrowed our automobile to drive home afterward and would bring it back every morning at seven on his way to the station, when he went to New York to his job. My mother disapproved of my suitor because he had no money. She controlled herself until the night when he kissed me for the first and last time. We were in the garage and as he leaned over me, by mistake he put his arm on the horn. This awoke my mother. She greeted us with a storm of abuse and screamed at us,"Does he think my car is a taxi?" Needless to say, I never saw the young man again. My mother felt triumphant, but several years later Fate proved her, according to her standards, entirely in the wrong, as this young man fell heir to a million dollars.

After graduating from school I was rather at a loose end. I continued reading with my voracious appetite and studied courses in history, economics and Italian. I had one teacher called Lucile Kohn, who had a stronger influence over me than any other woman has ever had. In fact, because of her, my life took a completely new turn. It didn't happen suddenly; it was a gradual process. She had a passion for bettering the world. I became radical and finally emerged from the stifling atmosphere in which I had been raised. It took me a long time to liberate myself, and although it was not for several years that anything occurred, the seeds that she sowed sprouted, branching out in directions that even she never dreamed of. Her interests were entirely political and economic. She had complete faith in Woodrow Wilson. But when she was disappointed by his inability to carry through his program she joined the labor movement. I did not follow her, being by then in Europe, but I sent her vast sums of money. Later she told me that I had altered her life, too, by sending her this

19

money. She acquired an important standing in the labor movement and worked fervently for it after that time.

During the war I learned to knit. Once I started, I never stopped. I took my knitting everywhere with me, to the table, to concerts, even to bed. I became so adept I could make a sock in one day. I remember my Grandfather Seligman greatly disapproving of my speed, which he claimed made me spend too much money on wool. I fear his parsimoniousness surpassed his patriotism.

As we could not go to Europe during the war, my mother took us up to Canada one summer. We motored all the way. During the entire trip I knitted and missed most of the beautiful scenery. However, I managed to look up occasionally and felt well recompensed for my sacrifice. In Canada we made great friends with the Canadian soldiers who were stationed near Quebec. Benita and our friend, Ethel Frank, and I had great fun with them. On the way home we were politely but firmly turned out of a hotel in Vermont for being Jewish. As the state law forbids hotel keepers to refuse lodgings overnight, we were allowed to remain until morning and then we were informed that our rooms were rented. This gave me a new inferiority complex.

Later I went to a business school to learn stenography and typing. I thought I might get a war job. However, I was too stupid to keep up with the girls who were all of the working class and who made me feel like a rank outsider. I soon gave it up.

In 1916 I made my début. I gave a big afternoon Leap Year party in the Ritz Tent Room. From then on I went to many parties and was taken out in the evening by young men. I found this sort of life idiotic, though I was a good dancer and loved dancing. The whole thing seemed to me artificial and I never met anyone I could talk to seriously.

Eventually, we moved to 270 Park Avenue. My mother permitted me to choose furniture for my bedroom, and I was allowed to charge it to her. But unfortunately I disobeyed her and went shopping on the sacred Day of Atonement, the great Jewish holiday *Yom Kippur*. I had been expressly warned not to do this and I was heavily punished for my sin. As a result my mother refused to pay for the furniture. I was left stranded with this large debt which I had to take out of my allowance. Benita came to my rescue and supported me for weeks. Among many other things, I remember going for a beauty treatment to Elizabeth Arden's at Benita's expense.

Ever since my earliest childhood every day at twelve sharp a sad old lady with a lisp called Mrs. Mack came to our house. She was a shopper and had a little book in which she would note any object that was required in our household. One day it was three yards of lace, a bottle of glue or six pairs of stockings. Another day it might be a box of soap, sewing silk or a green feather for a hat. At Christmas time she was most occupied when she came with a much larger notebook and found out confidentially, in turn, what each of my sisters and I would like for presents from Mrs. Dan, Mrs. Sol, Mrs. Simon, Mrs. Murray, etc., as she called my Guggenheim aunts. Then she proceeded to the shops where she had charge accounts and received ten percent discount on her purchases. As she invariably bought everything wrong, most of her life was spent in exchanging things. When we shopped for ourselves we did much better and she benefited just the same because we charged everything to her.

In 1918, I took a war job. I sat at a desk and tried to help our newly-made officers buy uniforms and other things at reduced rates. I had to give advice and write out many cards of introduction. I shared this job with my friend Ethel Frank, who had been my most intimate school companion. When she fell sick, I did all her work and mine, and the long hours proved too strenuous for me. I collapsed. It began by my not sleeping. Then I stopped eating. I got thinner and thinner and more and more nervous, I went to a psychologist and asked him if he thought I was losing my mind. He replied, "Are you sure you have a mind to lose?" Funny as his reply was, I think my question was quite legitimate. I used to pick up every match I found and stayed awake at night worrying about the houses that would burn because I had neglected to pick up some particular match. Let me add that all these had been lit, but I feared there might be one virgin among them. In despair my mother engaged Miss Holbrook, my dead grandfather's nurse, to look after me. She accompanied me everywhere. I wandered around, revolving in my brain all the problems of Raskolnikov, thinking how much I resembled this hero of Dostoevsky's *Crime and Punishment*. Finally Miss Holbrook, by sheer force of will, made me think of other things. Little by little I became normal again. During this period I was engaged to a flying officer who was still in this country. I had several fiancés during the war as we were always entertaining soldiers and sailors.

In the spring of 1919 Benita married Edward Mayer, a young American aviator who had just come back from Italy. The whole thing was most unfortunate. Since 1914 she had been in love with a Russian baron she had met in Europe. For some reason or other, which I could never make out, this Russian, although he seemed to love her, never came to the point of actually proposing to her. During the war he was attached to his legation in Washington and we saw him often in New York.

However, in a moment of weak-mindedness, she married the flier because he threatened to commit suicide if she didn't. Peggy, our best friend, and I were witnesses at City Hall. As soon as the marriage was over we came back and told my mother. She was all for having it annulled, and Benita seemed to agree. But in the end she went off with the aviator on a honeymoon and they settled down together. To me he was completely unworthy of her. He was handsome in a flashy way, but superficial with no depths of passion. He was melodramatic. I was madly jealous and unhappy. I missed her presence in our house beyond words, and I was left alone with my mother, for Hazel was at boarding school. My mother's one idea was to sacrifice her life to her children and she had done nothing else since the death of my father. We wished that she had married again instead.

In the summer of 1919, I came into my fortune. I was an heiress and I was independent. My mother was greatly upset. She could no longer control me. The first thing I did was to make an extensive trip all over the United States. I invited my brother-in-law's cousin to chaperon me. We went from Niagara Falls to Chicago and from there to Yellowstone Park, all through California, down to Mexico, up the coast to the Canadian Rockies. At that time Hollywood was just born. It was so small that it was almost nonexistent. I had a cousin there who introduced me to some movie people. They all seemed quite mad. On the way home we visited the Grand Canyon. Then we returned to Chicago, where I was met by my aviator fiancé; who had been demobilized. He introduced me to his family, who were all Chicagoans, but I did not make a hit. I complained too much about the provincialism of Chicago. As I was leaving on the Twentieth Century, he told me it was all off. I was very unhappy because I thought I was in love with him and was patiently waiting for him to make a fortune in the loose-leaf paper business so that he could marry me. His name was Harold Wessel.

In the winter of 1920, being very bored, I could think of nothing better to do than have an operation performed on my nose to change its shape. It was ugly, but after the operation it was undoubtedly worse. I went to Cincinnati where there was a surgeon who specialized in these beauty operations. He made you choose a plaster model of the nose you preferred. He never was able to give me what I wanted, a nose "tip-tilted like a flower," something I had read about in Tennyson. During the operation (performed under a local anesthetic), when I was suffering the tortures of the damned, surrounded by five nurses in white masks, the doctor suddenly asked me to choose again. He could not do what he had planned. It was all so painful I told him to stop and leave things as they were. As a result of the operation my nose was painfully swollen for a long time and I didn't dare set foot in New York. I hid in the Middle West waiting for the swelling to go down. Every time it rained I knew it beforehand, because my nose became a sort of barometer and would swell up in bad weather. I went to French Lick, Indiana, with a friend and gambled away nearly another thousand dollars, the operation having cost as much.

A short time later Margaret Anderson came to me and asked me if I would give her some money for *The Little Review*, and an introduction to one of my uncles. She said that if people believed in preventing wars the best possible thing to do was to subscribe to the arts. Being young and innocent, I hoped I had put off the next World War for several years by contributing five hundred dollars to *The Little Review*. I sent Margaret to my fur coat uncle and if she did not succeed in getting five hundred dollars out of him (I can't recall now) I trust at least that she got a fur coat.

If Lucile Kohn was responsible for my radical beliefs, my actual liberation came about quite differently from any manner she might have foreseen. One day when I was at my dentist's, I found him in a predicament. His nurse was ill and he was doing all his work alone. I offered to replace the nurse as best I could. He accepted my help, for which he paid me $2.35 a day. I opened the door and answered the telephone. I held instruments for him and boiled them. I also learned which of my acquaintances had false teeth. Of course I was recognized by the patients, who asked Dr. Scoby in great surprise if it wasn't Miss Guggenheim who admitted them into the office. All this soon came to an end when the real nurse returned.

I now felt in need of a job so I offered my services to my cousin, Harold Loeb. He had a little radical bookshop near Grand Central Station. I became a clerk and spent my afternoons on the balcony writing out checks and doing various boring jobs. I was permitted downstairs only at noon, when I had to replace the people who went to lunch, at which time I sold books. When I complained of my fate to Gilbert Cannan, who came often and sat for hours in the bookshop, he said to me, "Never mind, Lady Hamilton started out as a kitchenmaid."

Though I was only a clerk, I swept into the bookshop daily, highly perfumed, and wearing little pearls and a magnificent taupe coat. My mother disapproved of my working and came often to see what I was up to and to bring me rubbers if it was raining. This was embarrassing. My rich aunts also came and literally bought books by the yard to fill their bookcases. We had to bring out a tape measure to be sure the measurements coincided with their bookshelves.

In the bookshop I met many celebrities and writers and painters, among them Marsden Hartley and my future husband, Laurence Vail, as well as Leon Fleischman and his wife Helen, who later married James Joyce's son.

Although I received no salary in the Sunwise Turn Book Shop, Harold Loeb and his partner, Mary Mowbray Clarke, allowed me a ten percent reduction on all the books I bought. In order to have the illusion of receiving a big salary, I bought many books of modern literature and read them all with my usual voracity.

The people I met in the Sunwise Turn fascinated me. They were so real, so alive, so human. All their values were different from mine. I loved Mary Mowbray Clarke. She became a sort of goddess for me. Eventually she sold the bookshop to Doubleday Doran, having bought out Harold Loeb long before.

Marsden Hartley impressed and terrified me. So did Gilbert Cannan. I was much less afraid of Laurence. He was about twenty-eight at this time, and to me he appeared like someone out of another world. He was the first man I knew who never wore a hat. His beautiful, streaky golden hair streamed all over as the wind caught it. I was shocked by his freedom but fascinated at the same time. He had lived all his life in France and he had a French accent and rolled his r's. He was like a wild creature. He never seemed to care what people thought. I felt when I walked down the street with him that he might suddenly fly away—he had so little connection with ordinary behavior.

The Fleischmans became my great friends. They practically adopted me. I was so unhappy about Benita that I was delighted to have a new home. I fell in love with Leon, who to me looked like a Greek God, but Helen didn't mind. They were so free.

One day Leon took me to see Alfred Stieglitz. They put the first abstract painting I had ever seen in my hands. It was painted by Georgia O'Keeffe. I turned it around four times before I decided which way to look at it. They were delighted. I didn't see Stieglitz again until twenty-five years later, and when I talked to him I felt as though there had been no interval. We took up where we left off.

Soon after, I went to Europe. I didn't realize at the time that I was going to remain there for twenty-one years, but that wouldn't have stopped me. My mother went with me and she brought my Aunt Irene Guggenheim's cousin, Valerie Dreyfus, to help look after me. I was already too much of a handful and my mother knew she couldn't keep up with me. As much as I could, I dragged these two ladies all over Europe with my usual speed and my usual enthusiasm. Soon my mother got tired and handed me over to Valerie. *She* could keep up with me. In fact she encouraged me. She was a wonderful guide, had been everywhere before and was a very smart traveler. We went to Holland, Belgium, Spain and Italy. With my mother we had already been to Scotland, all over England and through the Loire country.

In those days my desire for seeing everything was very much in contrast to my lack of feeling for anything. That was born, however, as a result of my other frenzy. I soon knew where every painting in Europe could be found, and I managed to get there, even if I had to spend hours going to a little country town to see only one. I had as a great friend Armand Lowengard, the nephew of Sir Joseph (later Lord) Duveen. He was a fanatic about Italian painting. Seeing what a good subject I was, he egged me on to study art. He told me that I would never be able to understand

Berenson's criticism. This remark served its purpose. I immediately bought and digested seven volumes of that great critic.
After that I was forever going around looking for Berenson's seven
points. If I could find a painting with tactile value I was thrilled.
Armand had been wounded in the war and was rather badly done
in. My vitality nearly killed him and though he was fascinated by
me, in the end he had to renounce me, as I was entirely too much
for him.

I had another boyfriend, Pierre. He was a sort of cousin of my
mother's. I felt wicked because I kissed both him and Armand on
the same day. He wanted to marry me but I merely wanted to have
as many suitors as I could collect. Soon I wanted more than that. I
had a great friend, Fira Benenson, a Russian girl. We lived in the
Crillon Hotel in Paris and tried to outdo each other in collecting
proposals. We dressed in the most elegant French fashions and I
am sure we were idiotic.

I didn't see the Fleischmans again until I returned to America
for a brief visit in the spring to attend Hazel's wedding to Siggy
Kempner. I then persuaded the Fleischmans to come and live in
Paris. As they had a child and little money, Leon having resigned
as a director of Boni and Liveright's publishing house, it was all
very complicated. But they came. It changed their life as much as
they had changed, and were still to change, mine.

Through the Fleischmans I again met Laurence Vail. Helen
Fleischman was a friend of Laurence's. She was having a little
affair with him into which Leon had pushed her. It excited him.
She told me that she wanted me to come to dinner with Laurence
and then she told Laurence not to pay too much attention to me
because Leon would be offended. I think Leon must have been, as
Laurence and I got quite friendly.

A few days later Laurence took me out for a walk. We went to
the tomb of the Unknown Soldier and then we walked along the
Seine. I was wearing an elegant costume trimmed with kolinsky
fur that I had designed for myself. He took me into a bistro and
asked me what I wanted. I asked for a porto flip thinking I was in
the kind of bar I was used to. In those days I led only the most
expensive sort of life and had never set foot in an ordinary café
and had no idea what to order.

At this time I was worried about my virginity. I was twenty-
three and I found it burdensome. All my boy friends were disposed

to marry me, but they were so respectable they would not rape me. I had a collection of photographs of frescos I had seen at Pompeii. They depicted people making love in various positions, and of course I was very curious and wanted to try them all out myself. It soon occurred to me that I could make use of Laurence for this purpose.

Laurence lived with his mother and his sister Clotilde in a very bourgeois apartment near the Bois. When his father was not in a sanatorium having a *crise de nerfs*, he was living at home upsetting his entire family. Laurence's mother was an aristocratic New England lady. His father was a painter of Breton ancestry, half French, half American. He had been neurasthenic for years and his family had no idea what to do about him. They had tried everything but he was the world's great incurable neurotic.

Laurence wanted to get away from home again. His mother gave him a small allowance of one hundred dollars a month and, considering her income was ten thousand dollars a year, she wasn't over-generous. But she preferred to spend it on her husband, whose capital had long since vanished paying doctor's bills. He had been in every sanatorium in Europe. Laurence might have taken a job but he didn't like working. He was a writer of considerable talent but as yet unknown.

He now told me he was about to take a little apartment, and I asked if I could pay half the rent and share it, hoping by this maneuver to get somewhere. He said yes, but soon changed his mind. The next time I saw him he told me he had taken a hotel room in the Rue de Verneuil on the left bank, in the Latin Quarter. He came to see me at the Plaza-Athénée Hôtel where I was living and started to make love to me. When he pulled me toward him, I acquiesced so quickly that he was surprised by my lack of resistance. However I told him that we could not do anything there as my mother might return at any moment. He said we would go to his hotel room sometime. I immediately rushed to put on my hat, and he took me to the Rue de Verneuil. I am sure he had not meant to. That was how I lost my virginity. It was as simple as that. I think Laurence had a pretty tough time because I demanded everything I had seen depicted in the Pompeian frescoes. I went home and dined with my mother and a friend gloating over my secret and wondering what they would think of it if they knew.

# Chapter 3

# Marriage

Laurence was considered the King of Bohemia. He knew all the American writers and painters and a lot of French ones too. In those days they met at the Café de la Rotonde in Montparnasse. But Laurence had a row with a waiter or the manager of that café and he made everybody move opposite to the Dôme. After that they never returned to the Rotonde. Laurence gave wonderful parties in his mother's apartment. The first one I went to was very wild. I took with me a bourgeois French playwright, and in order to make him feel at home in the midst of Bohemia, I sat on his lap most of the evening. Later I received a proposal (I can hardly say of marriage) from Thelma Wood, the girl who was to become the well-known Robin of *Nightwood*. She got down on her knees in front of me. Strange things were happening everywhere. Laurence's father was at home and was very annoyed by the confusion the party caused. In desperation he retired to the toilet where he found two delicate young men weeping. He retired to another bathroom where he disturbed two giggling girls. He liked to be the center of attraction. If there was anything going on he wanted to be the star himself. After he had made a scene he felt better. Even if no one else paid much attention to him, at least his wife must have.

I soon met two great friends of Laurence: Mary Reynolds and' Djuna Barnes. They had both been his mistresses. They were very beautiful women. They had the kind of nose I had gone all the way to Cincinnati for in vain. Mary was dark with a beautiful figure. She was tall and elegant and had soft eyes. Her widow's peak was her great attraction. She was the only person in Bohemia with any money, and yet she was always broke because she lent it or gave it all away the minute it arrived from America. She was a war widow. She was waiting for some man called Norman to join her in Paris, but first he had to disentangle himself from his wife.

Djuna was quite different. She was already a well-known writer. Leon had borrowed a hundred dollars from me to help pay her passage to Europe. Later she did journalistic jobs. She rushed around Europe interviewing famous people. She wrote articles about celebrities for which she received enormous prices. At this time she was not rich.

Helen Fleischman told me to give Djuna some underwear. A disagreeable scandal ensued as the underwear I gave was Kayser silk and it was darned. I had three distinct categories of underwear: the best, which I had decorated with real French lace and which I was saving for my trousseau; my second best that was new, but unadorned, and that which I sent to Djuna. After she complained, I sent her the second best sets. I went to visit her. She was sitting at the typewriter wearing the second best underwear. She looked handsome with her white skin, her magnificent red hair and her beautiful body. She was very much embarrassed to be caught wearing the underwear after all the rows that had been made. Anyhow I apologized about the first lot I had sent her, and she forgave me. When Helen gave Djuna presents she just opened her cupboards and said, "Help yourself." I felt I should be less mean, so I gave Djuna my favorite russet cape and my favorite hat. It was adorned with a cock's tail feathers and when she wore it she looked like an Italian soldier.

One day I took Djuna to the Musée du Louvre and gave her a lecture on French art. I think she was bored. We met Mary Reynolds there and all three of us went to lunch. All through the meal I could not talk to them. I had a lot of homework to prepare. In those days I was studying Russian because I did not like Fira Benenson to have secrets from me. All her friends were Russian and I felt left out of their conversations, so I decided to study their language.

When Laurence told Helen about our affair she took it very well. But Leon was furious. Anyhow that ended Laurence's affair with Helen and from then on he belonged to me. I decided really to go in for my love affair in a big way, so I convinced my mother to go on a little trip to Rome with one of her nieces. She left Valerie Dreyfus behind to chaperon me. Poor Valerie had no idea what was going on, but she took a room in the Hôtel Plaza-Athénée where I was living and tried to look after me. Laurence came nearly every day.

One day Laurence took me to the top of the Eiffel Tower and when we were gazing at Paris he asked me if I would like to marry him. I said "Yes" at once. I thought it was a fine idea. As soon as he had asked me, he regretted it. In fact, from then on he kept changing his mind. Every time I saw him look as though he were trying to swallow his Adam's apple I knew he was regretting his proposal. He got more and more nervous about our future and one day he ran away to Rouen to think matters over. Laurence's mother, Mrs. Vail, insisted on sending Mary Reynolds with him (she even paid her train fare), hoping that this would cause sufficient trouble to end the engagement. But when they got to Rouen they did nothing but fight, and soon Laurence wired that he still wanted to marry me.

As we were more or less engaged I decided to warn my mother. She came rushing back from Rome to stop the marriage. She thought she should get references of Laurence's. She asked him who would give any. Laurence had a wide circle of acquaintances and at St. Moritz he had once met the King of Greece, so to tease my mother he gave the king's name. My mother carried a little notebook and inscribed names in it. She was quite puzzled and even asked me how she could communicate with the King of Greece. Of course no one thought that we should marry. Leon went to my mother and told her how much of a catastrophe it would be, and Marion, an old friend, the brother of Dulcie Sulzberger, begged me to give up the project. He said, "Do anything, come and live with me as a sister, but don't marry Laurence." Of course I did marry him. It was all the fault of a lawyer called Charlie Loeb. We went to him to find out how it could be done and before we knew it he got all the papers and posted the bans and drew up a *séparation des biens* to protect my rights.

After the bans were posted I began to think we might really marry, but suddenly Laurence decided to go to Capri with his sister Clotilde and postpone the wedding. I was to return to New York, where he would join me in May if we still felt like marrying. One afternoon, when he was all packed, he went to buy the tickets for his trip. My mother, Mrs. Vail and I sat in the Hôtel Plaza-Athénée, each with her private feelings about the future. Suddenly Laurence appeared in the doorway, looking as pale as a ghost and said, "Peggy, will you marry me tomorrow?" Of course I said, "Yes." After that I was still not at all sure that Laurence would not run away, so I decided not to buy a dress for the wedding. I bought a hat instead.

The morning of the wedding Laurence's mother phoned me to say, "He's off." I thought she meant Laurence had run away. He hadn't. She merely meant that he was on his way to fetch me. We went in a tramcar to the Mairie of the Seizième Arrondissement at Avenue Henri-Martin, where the ceremony was to take place.

We had all invited lots of friends. There were four distinct elements among the guests. First of all, Laurence had invited all his Bohemian friends, but as he was rather ashamed of marrying me, he had written them *petit bleu* notes briefly asking them to be present, as though he were asking them to a party, and he did not even mention who the bride was to be. My mother invited all her French Seligman cousins who lived in Paris, and all her bourgeois friends. Laurence's mother invited the American Colony, of which she was herself a well known hostess. I invited all my friends. They were very mixed at that time. They were writers and painters, mostly from a very respectable milieu, and of course there was Boris Dembo, my Russian friend, who came to the wedding and wept because I wasn't marrying him. Helen Fleischman was my witness and Laurence's sister was his. My mother nearly cried because she was not asked to sign the register, so we had to let her add her name to the others. We made her provide lots of champagne and she gave us a big party at the Plaza-Athénée after the ceremony.

When we had all drunk a lot of champagne and danced for hours, someone suggested that Laurence take me away on a

honeymoon. We were going to Italy in three days but Laurence
did not seem to be in the slightest hurry about ending the wedding
party. He was tied up with his sister and hated leaving her. He
felt that his marriage in some way would break up his relationship
with her. To console him I said she could join us in Capri, where
we were going on our honeymoon. I then asked my Russian
teacher, Jacques Schiffrin, to come too, but Laurence objected,
and I had to disinvite him. Finally Betty Humes, a friend of
Laurence who was in the consulate service, persuaded him to take
his bride away. We went to a hotel on the Rue de Rivoli and then
to bed. We soon got up, however, as we had invited many of our
friends to come to a second wedding party at the little Boeuf sur le
Toit in the Rue Boissy d'Anglas. On the way there we went to
Prunier's and ate a lot of oysters.

The next morning my doctor came to administer a *piqûre*, as I
was recovering from the flu. He was Proust's doctor and had
looked after him all that winter, when he was dying. He now
seemed elated by my marriage and told me I was entering into a
marvelous new life. I was surprised as I felt depressed and said,
"Do you really think so? I don't."

As soon as I found myself married, I felt extremely let down.
Then, for the first time, I had a moment to think about whether
or not I really desired the marriage. Up to the last minute
Laurence had been in such a state of uncertainty that I had been
kept in suspense and never questioned my own feelings. Now that
I had achieved what I thought so desirable, I no longer valued it so
much.

We went to have lunch with my mother. She was curious about
what she imagined was my introduction to love and I was
boastfully apologetic about the smell of Lysol which I was carrying
around with me. My mother, thinking she would catch me, asked,
"How often did you use it?" I was disgusted with her indiscretion
and refused to answer her question. All the waiters in the Pláza-
Athénée looked at me as though they too were curious.

Two days later we went off to Rome. My mother came to the
station with an emergency passport for me bearing my new name,
Marguerite Guggenheim Vail, in case I felt the need of running
away from Laurence, as I was now on his passport.

In Rome we looked up my cousin Harold Loeb, who was
publishing *Broom* magazine with Kitty Cannell. Harold was

shocked by Laurence's sockless feet in sandals. I wanted to retain my independence so I looked up my former beaux in Rome, and Laurence found some former girl friends. I still felt distinctly let down by my marriage and somehow thought it ought to be much more exciting.

Laurence chose an ideal place to take me for our honeymoon. He had lived in Capri before and while I had spent a few brief hours there with Valerie on one of our hasty trips, I had no idea what it was like. I had merely visited the Blue Grotto in a boat. Now we settled down and rented a villa on the Tiberius side of the island, very high up. As we walked down to the sea every day for our swim we found the climb back very trying in the heat. We swam at different beaches but our favorite one was the Piccola Marina. At the Grande Marina we rented little boats called sandolas which were manipulated with a double oar. First you used it on one side and then on the other. We rowed out to meet the steamboat that came from Naples every day. It was all exciting and new to me. I had never been in such a natural place and the beauty of this simple life delighted me.

Capri itself is like an enchanted island. Once you have come there it is very difficult to leave. Most of the inhabitants are *queer* but the beauty of the place and its marvelous setting in the blue Bay of Naples are too good to be true. It is a small rocky island that rises high out of the sea. Above is another town called Anacapri, and below are little fishing villages. The main town, Capri, is the center and has its intense social life on the piazza like all Italian towns. There was a café called Morgano's where one met and made friends. The walks around Capri are extremely beautiful and in parts the vegetation resembles the moors of Scotland.

There were no cars on the island and very few carriages. There was a funicular which took people up from the boat landing to Capri. One's life depended more or less on the supplies brought over by the boat. For days one could be cut off from the mainland by the rough seas. One had absolutely no sense of responsibility, the whole atmosphere reminding one of an *opéra bouffe*. The following year I was to fathom the depths of intrigue here and then I really got to know Capri much better. But that comes later.

We had many strange neighbors. Our nearest one was a Swedish count who lived a mile farther up our road on the way to the ruins of Tiberius's villa. The count, who was a descendant of Marie Antoinette's faithful lover Fersen, lived with a goatherd he had adopted. In order to hold him, he first had him educated, and then he taught him to smoke opium. They were a handsome young couple. Capri was full of such people.

There was one old lady who sold coral in the streets. She was reported to be the ex-mistress of the Queen of Sweden.

Krupp had built himself a magnificent villa here with his war profits. Mrs. Compton Mackenzie had a wonderful villa overlooking the rocks called the Faraglioni, while Mackenzie had built a little stone hut up in the heath at the very top. The year before I came, the Marchesa Casati roamed about the island with a leopard.

I soon found that I had married into a strange family. My mother-in-law was fussy but she was a fine woman of the old school. She was a D.A.R. and behaved like one. Even though she had not approved of the marriage, once it was accomplished she accepted me wholeheartedly. I think she really liked me, and she was the first person I ever met who admired my looks. I had been brought up to believe that I was ugly, because my sisters were great beauties. It had given me an inferiority complex. When Mrs. Vail met Benita and Hazel, she claimed that I was better looking than either of them. Imagine how this surprised and pleased me. Mrs. Vail accepted me as a daughter-in-law, but she never permitted me to call her "Mother."

If Mrs. Vail accepted me, I cannot say the same for her daughter Clotilde. She was the thorn in my marriage. She adored her brother with a passion one could not fail to admire and which he reciprocated. (They gave one the feeling that they were made for incest; and by not indulging in it they augmented their frustrated passion.) Everything was "my brother" with Clotilde. She did not relinquish one inch of him to me. She always made me feel that I had stepped by mistake into a room that had long since been occupied by another tenant, and that I should either hide in a corner or back out politely. She was a very strong character and I soon found her trying to run my household. My life was doubly complicated by the fact that she was excessively attractive, and was perpetually having love affairs. At first I was shocked, but later I outgrew my puritanical prejudices. Every time she had a new lover Laurence became wildly jealous and, as I was his

whipping boy, I suffered very much from it all. Clotilde was three
or four years older than I, and completely mature while I was a
baby. That also put me at a disadvantage. She had a very beautiful
mezzo-soprano voice and had been studying for years to be a
singer. Clotilde had long blond hair the color of Laurence's. They
looked exactly alike as they both had their mother's beaky Roman
nose. But Clotilde was small.

As soon as we were settled in Capri, or rather after three
weeks, Clotilde joined us. She did allow us to be alone for that
short period. She brought with her an Italian friend called Elaine
Le Bourg, which helped a lot, but when Laurence and Clotilde
stalked together on the Piazza at the hour when everyone
collected, I was made to feel nonexistent.

I did not have any responsibilities in Capri because our house
was run by four Italian sluts, who made love every night with
soldiers in our garden. Teresina, the mother of an illegitimate
baby, and her three little sisters looked after us. Their salary was
minute and only two of them were paid, but they made up for it by
cheating us outrageously when shopping and by taking home half
of the food. In Italy this was more or less taken for granted by
Americans, and when Elaine, as a good Italian woman, wanted to
put a stop to it Laurence as a foreigner would not hear of it. The
sluts were charming. They sang Neapolitan songs for us all day
long and they even brushed and combed my hair which was too
long for me to cope with. They served good meals and we
considered ourselves lucky to have them in our household.

Laurence was snobbish about my family. He did not like the
Guggenheims, and was perpetually making fun of them. One day
after my Aunt Rose had arrived at our house riding a mule, as she
could not walk up the hill, he told me that it was extremely
appropriate, since it appeared to be quite in keeping with the Old
Testament. Another day he told me he would like to throw all my
uncles over the cliff where Tiberius had killed his enemies. I was
so offended I burst into tears.

In the late summer we left Capri for St. Moritz. We motored
through Italy and stopped in Arezzo and San Sepolcro to see the
Piero della Francesca frescoes. I enraged Laurence by looking for
Berenson's seven points instead of enjoying the paintings for
themselves. We went to Venice, Florence and Milan and finally
ended up in a little train that zigzagged up to the Engadine.

I had never been to St. Moritz before and was much impressed by the social life there; not that we took much part in it. As a matter of fact we led a quiet family life with Mrs. Vail and Clotilde and a few friends of mine from England and New York who showed up. Laurence and I played a lot of tennis and we won a tournament. We played well together for he was very strong at the net and I backed him up. I accepted his directions and never let him down.

In the fall I went to New York to see Benita. I had planned this trip long before my marriage and nothing in the world could interfere with it. Laurence went off with Clotilde to the Basque country on a motorbike that Benita had given him for a wedding present.

Benita had settled down with her husband and they seemed quite happy. There was still terrible jealousy between him and me, and Benita was like a rose between two thorns. Before I left New York I signed a contract with a publisher who wanted to publish a novel that Laurence had written long before.

After a short time I realized that I was going to have a baby. I was quite sick but very happy, and I wired Laurence in order to warn him. My beautiful aunt, Irene Guggenheim, took me back to Europe with her in her stateroom, because I was so sick and she wanted to look after me. I was in bed for the whole trip. Laurence met us at Southampton, and we were very happy to be together again.

We had to plan our future about the birth of our child. We immediately called him Gawd Guggenheim Vail and decided he must be born in London. We did not want him to be a French citizen, which he would be if he were born in Paris. Both Laurence and his father had been born there and the third generation would be claimed by the French and forced to do military service. Laurence had an American passport and had served as a liaison officer in the American Army with the heavy artillery in the last war.

Aunt Irene's daughter Eleanor, who had married the Earl of Castle Stewart, a psychoanalyst, took me to her doctor in London. She had just had a baby and she was very pleased with Dr. Hadley's care. He told me when to expect the birth of Gawd and we decided to go back to France for the winter and return to London in May.

We went down to Sussex to visit Eleanor and I remember her husband telling me what an exciting life I was going to have with Laurence, instead of the dull one Eleanor was leading with him. I don't know why everyone thought my future was to be so thrilling. It certainly was, but I wonder how they all knew it before I did.

Laurence was a dynamic person. He had an amazing personality and he was handsome. He had great charm which he was forever turning on people successfully. He always made me feel inferior. I was inexperienced when I met him and I felt like an awful baby in his (what I considered at the time) sophisticated world. Laurence was always bursting with ideas. He had so many he never achieved them because he was forever rushing on to others. He just tossed them off the way most people toss off clichés. It was extraordinary. His vitality was fantastic. He could stay up three nights running. I could never do without my sleep, and when I lay in bed waiting for him to come home, knowing he was drunk and apt to be in trouble, I had no rest. He brought me into an entirely new world and taught me a completely new way of life. It was all thrilling, often too thrilling.

It is difficult to remember now how Laurence and I began fighting. We had one quarrel before we were married, in the Plaza-Athénée Hôtel, caused, I think, by something Valerie Dreyfus said. Laurence made a scene and stalked out in a fury. However, it never dawned on me that this was a sample of what I might expect perpetually in the future. Laurence was very violent and he liked to show off. He was an exhibitionist, so that most of his scenes were made in public. He also enjoyed breaking up everything in the house. He particularly liked throwing my shoes out of the window, breaking crockery and smashing mirrors and attacking chandeliers. Fights went on for hours, sometimes days, once even for two weeks. I should have fought back. He wanted me to, but all I did was weep. That annoyed him more than anything. When our fights worked up to a grand finale he would rub jam in my hair. But what I hated most was being knocked down in the streets, or having things thrown in restaurants. Once he held me down under water in the bathtub until I felt I was going to drown. I am sure I was very irritating but Laurence was used to making scenes, and he had had Clotilde as an audience for years. She always reacted immediately if there was going to be a fight. She got nervous and frightened, and that was what

Laurence wanted. Someone should have told him not to be such
an ass. Djuna tried it once in Weber's restaurant and it worked
like magic. He immediately renounced the grand act he was about
to put on. As a result of these displays of anger he got into an
awful lot of trouble with the public authorities and was often
arrested. One of the first big fights I can remember was in a
theatre when we went to Raymond Roussel's play, *Locus Solus*.
Everybody was hissing it and of course Laurence was for it. He
made a demonstration and a royal battle followed, and being
pregnant I did not want to be involved. Laurence's opponents
were numerous and they got him down on the floor. The
*Commissaire de Police* was sent for and came to his rescue. Later
he gave us his box so that we might see the rest of the play in
safety.

The next big fight I remember was in the Hôtel Lutétia. It was
brought on entirely by my lack of tact. I had resumed my Russian
lessons with Jacques Schiffrin, and I announced to Laurence that
I was in love with my teacher. Laurence picked up an ink-pot and
hurled it at the wall. It broke the telephone and spattered the
room with ink. The room had to be repapered. To remove the
spots on the floor I found a miraculous little deaf man who came
every day for weeks. He squatted on the floor bringing out from a
bag an array of bottles which he applied one by one until the spots
completely vanished. Schiffrin, in the meantime, borrowed money
from me to pay his printing bill. He was launching his *Editions de
la Pléiade* and ran short of funds. In return he gave me six
hundred copies of his first beautiful book, *La Dame de Pique*. I
went to all the book shops of Paris to dispose of my six hundred
volumes. I was not very successful as a saleswoman and soon
Schiffrin, who was well on the way to success, bought them back
from me.

Because of my money I enjoyed a certain superiority over
Laurence and I used it in a dreadful way, by telling him it was
mine and he couldn't have it to dispose of freely. To revenge
himself he tried to increase my sense of inferiority. He told me
that I was fortunate to be accepted in Bohemia and that, since all
I had to offer was my money, I should lend it to the brilliant
people I met and whom I was allowed to frequent.

When we started living in Paris I was quite sick because of my
pregnancy and I took some medicine every day. Bob Coates,

having no idea what was wrong with me, and as he himself was suffering from some stomach disturbance, insisted on trying my medicine. At that time he was a young writer living a Bohemian life in Paris and he was one of our best friends.

Laurence loved big parties and we never missed a chance to give one. He liked me to dress extravagantly and he took me to Paul Poiret and made me buy elegant clothes, but my fast advancing waistline was not very attractive and I did not look very chic in these wonderful costumes. Hazel joined us in Paris. She was already divorced and that winter she married Milton Waldman.

In the middle of the winter we went down to the Riviera. We found a little villa at Le Trayas and rented it for two months. One of my cousins in the automobile business sold me an old second-hand Gaubron, whose cut-out was perpetually open and it made a terrible noise. We hired a chauffeur and Laurence learned to drive the car. Our life here was very simple. We had only one maid, and we stayed in the villa most of the time. But Laurence bathed in the sea all winter and went to the markets to bring home food. Since I was ill I spent weeks reading all of Dostoevsky. Of course we had our fights to pass the time. What we fought about in Le Trayas and what took up two weeks of our time before we finally signed a truce was the fact that Bob Coates wanted to borrow $200 from Laurence in order to go back to America. For some reason I took this badly and would not let Laurence have the money. He had to refuse it to Bob. Finally Clotilde came down to visit us, and we ended our battle.

In March Benita came to Europe for she wanted to be with me for the birth of Gawd. When she discovered my Bohemian life, she was shocked and was much against it. Benita was extremely conventional and her husband made her more so. It was difficult for her to make a bridge between two such different ways of life.

At the end of April I went to London with Fira Benenson to look for a house. Laurence was to follow with the new car we had just bought, a Lorraine Dietrich. The Gaubron had collapsed. I looked as if Brancusi's egg had been superimposed on my slender person.

I rented a beautiful house with a garden in Kensington up on Campden Hill. We were very comfortable and there was plenty of room for guests and nurses when the moment arrived. Mary Reynolds stayed with us for a while but left to join Norman when he finally came from America. Benita and her husband were living at the Ritz, with my mother. We did not want my mother to know when Gawd was expected. She fussed so much it was nerve-racking. We had managed to keep her in ignorance of his existence for a long time. Now she thought he was much younger than he was.

Actually, on the night of his birth, there was none of my family about. I had left Benita at seven o'clock in town and I was not feeling too well, but I came home to a dinner party Laurence and I were giving. Our guests were Mary Reynolds and Norman, and Tommy Earp and his wife, and an old friend of Laurence from his Oxford days and his wife, and Bob McAlmon. During the dinner we drank the health of someone under the table, meaning Gawd. Tommy Earp, who had no suspicions, began looking for a dog. Soon after dinner the wife of Laurence's Oxford friend threw a pillow at me and that seemed to have an immediate effect. To my great embarrassment the waters broke and I retired upstairs. Mary got hysterical and wanted to put me to bed. Laurence rushed off in the car with Earp to fetch the nurse. She had been actually engaged for that day, but was waiting to be called. When she arrived she took everything in hand and made me do the right things. All I can remember is the most dreadful pain that came in waves and that got worse and worse. Each time I felt as though I could not endure any more. Mary sat on the steps with Laurence. Finally the nurse allowed him to go and fetch Dr. Hadley. When he arrived I was suffering the most excruciating pain. He asked me if I wanted an anesthetist and by then naturally I said "Yes." I felt as though wild horses were dragging me apart, and I had come to the end of my strength. When the second gentleman in a top hat, who took ages to put on his white spats, arrived, my troubles ended but the doctor's didn't. The chloroform worked so well that Gawd refused to budge and had to be taken by forceps. He arrived at eight in the morning just in time for breakfast, and Mary and Laurence saw him before I did, for which I never forgave her. When I came to and was told I had a boy I felt embarrassed to think that I had harbored a male creature inside my being for so long.

Laurence phoned my mother. She thought it was a joke and she would not believe that she had a grandchild. We had fooled her so well that she did not appear until the evening, and then was completely surprised to learn that Gawd was really there. He was born on May 15, the anniversary of Benita's wedding and the day after Mrs. Vail's birthday. We named him Michael Cedric Sindbad Vail. Mary named him Cedric in honor of Cedric Morris, a great friend of hers, a painter. Sindbad (from the Arabian Nights) was Laurence's choice; mine was Michael. He was darling, but very ugly. He had a wrinkled little red face, a lot of black hair, enormous protruding ears, and heavenly feet and hands. The day nurse was a sort of dragon, but the night nurse was an angel. So we postponed all our fun until the night.

I nursed Sindbad for one month. After that I had no milk. Nursing was painful and for some reason I was an unnatural mother and could never give my breast to my children without the assistance of a nurse. If the babies had had to depend on me they would have starved. Dr. Hadley made me stay in bed three weeks. I was bored and read George Moore and Henry James to amuse myself.

It was at this time that Peggy came to stay with us. I don't know what else to call her throughout this book, for she changed her name so often. She first came into my life at school, but as she was one class ahead of me, I never knew her well. Then she married my cousin Edwin Loeb. That didn't work, and Benita and I made her get a divorce. When she came to London she was just recovering from her divorce. She had not as yet got into any further trouble. Laurence loved her, and I was delighted as she was my oldest friend. She is hard to describe, because she was so elusive. If you ever pinned her down to anything you would find out the next day that she had told someone else the exact opposite of what she had told you. She saw around and into everything, and therefore had no *parti pris;* consequently we always called her double-faced. But she was the only really intelligent woman I have ever met. She had the logical brain of a man. She looked like a Cheshire cat because she had an enormous mouth which was perpetually grinning. She was extremely stubborn. She seemed to know what she wanted in life, but she didn't at all really know what was good for her. For some strange reason she always had the wrong husband, and she had three of them. As a mother she was a great success, and had lots of pleasure from her three children. However, at this stage she had no children. Peggy never failed to appear at the crucial moments in my life. I felt all I had to do was to bring out my Aladdin's lamp and Peggy would pop up and help me.

We all went back to Paris for the fourteenth of July as Laurence always celebrated that festival by dancing in the streets for three nights. I couldn't keep up with him.

After Paris we went to Villerville in Normandy and rented a place for the summer. It was a hideous old house, with a bathtub in the cellar; it greatly resembled my grandfather's house, but this one had a beautiful garden with a studio where we all painted, even I. Clotilde and Peggy were with us, and Mina Loy. Louis Aragon, who was Clotilde's boyfriend at the time, came for a visit. So did Harold Loeb and Kitty Cannell and Man Ray and his remarkable hand-painted Kiki. One day James Joyce and Nora walked in. They were looking for their daughter who was in a boarding school somewhere on the coast.

Benita had gone back to America and I was unhappy without her again. I watched the French Line steamships go out to sea from Le Havre, past our house, and wished I were leaving too.

In the fall we went back to Capri. Peggy and Mary and Clotilde were with us. This time we stayed in a little hotel in the center of town. My cousin Eleanor Castle Stewart had found me a nurse called Lilly, whom we had brought back to the continent with us. She was so dark that she looked more like a foreigner than like an English girl. Men were always running after her. She was completely innocent and unsophisticated and excited about traveling. Lilly took good care of Sindbad as she had been trained in a hospital, and she was naturally conscientious.

Soon after we were in Capri Laurence got into trouble. He was jealous of a new lover of Clotilde's. This little Italian, whenever he spent the night away from his wife, pretended he had been to the Caccia or to shoot little birds up on the heath. We used to tease Clotilde and ask her if she had been to the Caccia when she spent the night with him. She did not like the fact that Captain Patuni, as he was called, refused to be seen in public with her. Because of his wife he had to hide Clotilde. One night at dinner she complained bitterly about this and got Laurence, who was drunk, all worked up. He rushed into a private club where Captain Patuni was playing cards with some men and threw all the cards he could seize into Captain Patuni's face. A battle followed. A policeman had his thumb broken. Laurence was put

in chains and lay on a table waiting to be carried off to jail. He had
as an enemy the *sindaco* of Capri, whom he had once mocked, and
as a result this man was his sworn enemy. Laurence was forced to
spend ten days in jail awaiting trial. He was in a damp cell, and
we were told to send him meals from the hotel. We also sent him
wine and whiskey and lots of books. He was guarded by a
wonderful jailer who had lost his job temporarily for allowing his
prisoners out every night. When they were out they went on with
their profession and brought their booty back to jail. He was
reinstated but without salary.

This jailer accompanied the judge, who was blind, on his walks
to and from the courthouse. He told me that he had the judge's
consent for me to go to the prison to visit Laurence, but that I
should get the permission myself. I went to the judge and fell on
my knees, pleading my baby's ill health as an excuse to talk to my
husband. I even wept. The judge was noncommittal, but soon
after that the jailer came to see me. He told me to wear black and
to come to a certain corner of the road where a big black dog would
be waiting for me and would conduct me to the prison. I was
terrified, and if Clotilde hadn't forced me to go, I would certainly
have backed out. When I got to the prison, where I soon went
every night, I fell asleep, exhausted by my worries and my
attempts to rescue Laurence. Everyone on the island had a new
scheme to free him. All the schemes involved enormous bribes,
and they seemed dangerous and uncertain.

Finally Mary found the solution. She was picked up by a
lawyer, Signor Tirelli, who had come from Rome for the day and
who thought she was Clotilde. Having heard about the scandal he
offered his services, which we accepted. Mary went with him to
Rome to see the American Consul-General, who was a great
friend of the Vails, hoping he would help us, but all he said
referring to Laurence was, "That boy was always crazy." Signor
Tirelli was the lawyer of the American Consulate. He was a clever
old thing, and came over one day to prepare the case, the date of
the trial finally having been set. He went around the island and
collected enough witnesses to prove that Laurence was drunk and
had meant no harm. When the trial came up on the tenth day, the
barman of the Quisiana Hotel, where we had started out our
evening, testified that we had not only had eight cocktails, but
that they were gin, which in Italy is not usual, and that after

dinner we had drunk large quantities of Veuve Clicquot champagne. Captain Patuni was called as a witness, but refused to appear. He was forcibly brought by two soldiers and had nothing unpleasant to say against Laurence. The policeman was bribed to be silent. Laurence was released and we left Capri that day on Tirelli's yacht for Amalfi. I insisted on this. Laurence did not like it, but I made him go. Before leaving he stalked around the piazza with Clotilde to show that he was not beaten. Tirelli charged us the modest sum of one thousand dollars, the voyage on his yacht thrown in. After that he charged us another five hundred to have Laurence's name removed from the records of crime.

I was rather ashamed to think that my husband had been in prison, and whenever the matter came up I tried to explain quickly what the offense had been.

When we said goodbye to the jailer, who had become our dear friend, we gave him a large tip. He immediately lost it or said he had, and had to be given another. He told Laurence his only desire in life would be to serve someone like him by guarding his fortune. He said he would have liked to sit and watch a large pile of money which should be placed on the floor in a room, and which would be safe with him.

Amalfi was as beautiful as Capri, but in quite a different way. It did not have the charm of an island. We took walks in the sloping countryside which was covered with vineyards. There were also several towns in this vicinity and we had to drive to get to them. One was a long way off and very high up. It was called Ravello and had a most beautiful twelfth-century building with cloisters covered in Virginia creeper. I wanted to buy the house, which was called Casa Rodolfo, but I could not produce the sum necessary because all my money was tied up in trust.

After Amalfi we decided to go to Egypt for the winter, but Clotilde and Peggy went back to Paris. Our dragoman took us everywhere, and saw to it that we bought everything. It wasn't difficult because Laurence and I were fascinated by the souks of Cairo. We found wonderful earrings for virtually nothing, and bought dozens of them to take back to Paris, since Clotilde, Mary and I were all frantic collectors. We also bought materials and Laurence had suits made with Egyptian cloths of all colors. He bought me perfumes, little coats and a cape from the Sudan, and he bought himself the oddest little rag dolls, beautiful Persian

prints and a water pipe. We ate only in Arab restaurants where
the chief food is lamb. There was one restaurant where we ate
out-of-doors, but it was an ordeal, because during the meals,
whole streams of beggars and vendors of food solicited us in turn.
It would have been possible to buy our entire meal from these
passers-by. The Arabs called me "Princess" to flatter me, thus
hoping to get larger *bakshish*. I have never seen such shameless
people. They were just like flies. One brushed them away merely
to have them return the next minute.

We were admitted to the mosques, but not at the sacred hour of
prayer when the male Arabs would squat in the courtyards around
fountains washing their private parts and urinating before they
turned their faces toward Mecca and the setting sun to invoke
Muhammad.

We spent days in the souks shopping and drinking Turkish
coffee, the thickest and sweetest coffee in the world. It is served
to you by all the shopkeepers if they have hopes of selling you
something expensive. One could never buy anything immediately.
Shopping in Cairo involved days and days of bargaining. It just
had to be done in the traditional way, tiresome as it was.

In the evenings we went to the Arab quarter. This was
considered low and incorrect for foreigners, especially for ladies.
Laurence went everywhere he saw a sign, "Out of bounds for
British officers and soldiers." I remember a beautiful Nubian girl
who did a *danse de ventre*. She so much resembled Hazel, in spite
of being as black as could be, that I called her my sister. Laurence
was fascinated by her and I decided to give him an evening off to
be with her. At that time we were living in the desert in Mena
House, next to the Pyramids of Giza. One evening, when we had
been shopping in Cairo, I left Laurence and went back alone to
Mena House. Considering my sacrifice he might have been nicer
to me. When he put me on the bus he purposely threw all my
packages about or dropped them in order to embarrass me, for he
was annoyed at having had to carry them all afternoon. He
returned late that night, and by chance I followed him into the
bathroom and saw that something was wrong. He had to admit the
truth. Suddenly I was angry when I thought what I might have
been exposed to, and refused to make love to him for days. He told
me that the girl wore white underwear and had a very high bed.
When he could not climb up to it she took him under the armpits
and lifted him up like a doll.

The next day we went camping in the desert. This is not at all what it sounds like. Nothing could be more luxurious. It entails a complete caravan of camels and attendants, a cook and tents and furniture and food all being brought along. It was certainly worth it because it is the only way to see the desert.

The desert is a vast sea of sand which rolls in all directions and in all shapes. It is mountainous and sometimes rocky. Occasionally there is a mirage or an oasis and often you meet other caravans. Otherwise you would feel completely lost. Nothing is more uncomfortable than riding a camel. The jerking and swaying motions drive you mad and exhaust you. You can't rise in a trot or gallop. You just sit in agony. Later I took to riding donkeys instead, and that turned out to be marvelous fun. They have a wonderful little gait, almost better than that of a horse.

We decided to take a trip up the Nile and all the dragomen of Cairo began running after us trying to rent us a *dahabeah*. We were invited to the home of one dragoman in the desert where he gave us a sumptuous meal of thirteen courses. Finally in desperation we ran away to Luxor where we rented a modest boat that depended entirely on the whimsical moods of the Nile winds and on a crew of eight to pull us if necessary. When the winds failed the crew got out and walked on the shore and drew the boat along by ropes. Laurence and I became so impatient that often we got out and walked along the banks, waiting for the boat to catch up with us.

Geographically Egypt is a strange country. It depends entirely on the Nile for its existence; otherwise it would merely be desert. Egypt varies much in width. At its widest point it covers many miles (as in the Delta land) and at other places it shrinks to about one foot. Its cultivated land exists only where the Nile has watered it. Along the banks a system of irrigation is in continuous motion. The lovely singing noise of the revolving wheel that turns as a camel walks in circles to propel it, greets one at regular distances. Buckets of water are attached to this wheel, and as they come out of the Nile full they disgorge their contents into a trough which feeds the channels dug for irrigation. Sometimes there were no camels and human energy replaced them with a simple hand derrick.

All along the banks were little villages of mud huts. The women of the town would come down to the water's edge carrying pitchers on their heads to fetch the water. Laurence insisted on bathing in the Nile, in spite of the dangers of crocodiles and germs, and one day he frightened away a whole bevy of women who screamed as he emerged naked from the water.

The people of Egypt are mostly Arabs, and they are very poor. We tried to learn their language from the dragoman who came on the *dahabeah* with us but he spoke perfect English. He drank a bottle of whiskey a day. The captain was very handsome and I conceived a slight passion for him. He played Arab music for us on a tom-tom.

Once you get on the Nile, you must give up all sense of time, but I couldn't. I became so impatient that I almost went mad. Laurence spent hours below in a cabin writing a book. He had a Puritan conscience, and he was a writer. Sindbad and Lilly were left behind in the hotel in Aswan at the First Cataract. I got bored, and to amuse myself I bought a pregnant goat. I had hoped to see it give birth. However, it fooled me by choosing the one short hour I was absent, visiting some friends on a Cook's steamboat. The captain sent a sailor to fetch me, but it was too late. Soon after that the whole boat reeked of goat smells and we could not endure it. I gave it to the captain. We also had two sheep on board. They were affectionate and sat on our laps. Eventually we were supposed to eat them, since all our food consisted of mutton courses. Sometimes we had as many as five in one meal, all prepared in different fashion. But I could not bear to think of eating the sweet sheep, so we gave them to the captain, too.

We went right up to the Second Cataract of the Nile at Wadi Halfa. We thus saw all the best temples as well as the Valley of the Kings with its gigantic twin statues. It was just before Tutankhamun's tomb was opened. The strongest impressions I have of Egypt proper have nothing to do with the Arabs and their civilization. What the Egyptians stood for was something so cruel, so subtle and so dignified. The carvings of the Egyptians on all the tombs were exquisite and the temples so overwhelming in size that one felt like a midget. Some of the temples were under water at this time because of the machinations of the dam at Aswan. We went in a rowboat through the courtyard of Kimombo Temple which was half under water and we saw only the top half of the Phalaes Temple.

At Wadi Halfa we were entertained by the governor. It was rare

that people got that far on a *dahabeah* and he wanted to honor us.
The British ruling class were pretty awful in their colonies. We
did not relish this visit.

On the way back we picked up a steamboat and were tugged
part of the way. It was strange seeing Egypt fly past in the
moonlight instead of having it unroll itself like a slow-motion film
in the sunlight. It was also exciting to recognize all the spots we
had passed before.

When we left the boat after three or four weeks, the men
expected a tip. We didn't know what to give them. I suggested a
pound each, but they were not very pleased. Then we added
another pound to each and they were very happy and cheered us.
In those days I was very mean, and Laurence had a hard time
arranging things with my money as I always tried to interfere.
Finally he tipped the dragoman with his own money. Much later I
told Benita how badly I behaved to Laurence and she wept for
him.

When we got back to Cairo we left Sindbad and Lilly in Mena
House and went to Jerusalem. For the first time in my life I felt
ashamed to have married outside my faith. The Jews of Jerusalem
looked upon me askance. Palestine was a young country in those
days in spite of its extreme age. It was in its infancy as it had just
been given back to the Jews. It didn't seem to be working any too
well. There were terrible fights among the Muslims, the Jews and
the Christians. They all wanted to own the key to the Holy
Sepulchre. Jerusalem itself was little built up. Most of the
activities were concentrated on farming. The only thing that
really impressed us was the Wailing Wall. It mortified me to
belong to my people. The nauseating sight of my compatriots
publicly groaning and moaning and going into physical contortions
was more than I could bear, and I was glad to leave the Jews
again.

We returned by a different steamship line, disembarked at
Genoa and from there we took a night train to Paris. As soon as
we arrived I dispatched Laurence and Lilly and Sinbad, and
decided to face the customs on my own. Everything we had bought
in Cairo was concealed between my dresses in my Innovation
trunk. It was very ingenious because not only were there
innumerable Sudanese clothes for Clotilde, Mary and me, but also
an odd collection of embroidered tablecloths and pillow slips. The

worst offense was the Turkish tobacco that we were bringing into France. This was not allowed. At the last minute Laurence ripped open an enormous rag doll that he had bought and filled it with about four hundred cigarettes. Nothing was found and I retired with my booty. When I got to the Hôtel Lutétia and began to unpack I could hardly believe my eyes. I felt as if I were a magician bringing things out of a hat. We gave a cocktail party every Sunday and showed our wonderful Arab treasures to our guests.

The rooms in the Lutétia were not big enough for us now that we had Sindbad, so we took an apartment on the Boulevard Saint-Germain for six months. It was Proustian and we did our best to make it cozy. We horrified the Vicomte de Cambon, our landlord, by buying rustic French furniture and installing it in the place of his *Louis Seize meubles,* which we hid in the backroom. We brought all of Laurence's library here and had all the books I had received as wedding presents from my family in America. When we moved from the apartment we caused a scandal on the Boulevard Saint-Germain by throwing all our books out the window and catching them in sheets below in order to remove them.

We gave fantastic Bohemian parties in this flat. Laurence made me buy a cloth-of-gold evening dress at Poiret's. Now I was so thin again it suited me perfectly. I also wore a headdress made by a Russian lady who was Stravinsky's fiancée. It was a tight net gold band that made my skull look like Tutankhamun's. Man Ray photographed me in this costume with a long cigarette-holder in my mouth. It was sensational. In those days I never drank, and I was bored at these parties where everybody got tight. I hated people being sick in my house, and I especially hated people making love on my bed. Once a lady left her corsets behind and called for them later. After the guests would leave I went around, like my aunt, with a bottle of Lysol. I was so afraid of getting a venereal disease.

To one of these parties I invited one of my mother's nieces who happened to be in Paris on her honeymoon with her second husband, after she had got rid of the roué whom I resented her marrying over my head at the age of eleven. When she arrived at this party she was fascinated by a couple of beautiful young men who were dancing closely, locked in each other's arms. I made her sit and guard the silver all evening, telling her that I had no idea who half of my guests were as Laurence picked up odd people in bars when he was tight and invited them all to our house. We kept open house every Sunday evening. At another one of these parties, Kiki, Man Ray's mistress, hit him in the face and called him a dirty Jew. My mother was present and was outraged. She told Kiki what she thought of her.

My mother was much more conventional than I, and she was forever inviting Laurence and me to the Ritz to her parties. On the other hand, she seemed to enjoy our Bohemian parties as well. She had made great friends with Mrs. Vail and was dragged into the American Women's Club which was Mrs. Vail's stronghold. My mother was probably at her best at this time, because she could at last have a life of her own. She was no longer tormented by father's infidelities, and all her children were married. But she never actually relinquished her daughters. She used to phone me every morning and tell me it was cold or raining and that I should wear a warm coat or rubbers, as the case might be. This drove me frantic, but what I hated most of all were the conventional parties at the Ritz and being perpetually told that I led the wrong kind of life. Anyone who was not rich she referred to as a beggar, and any woman who had a lover she called N. G., meaning no good. She was greatly disappointed that I had not married a Jewish millionaire. Nevertheless, she liked Laurence because he flirted with her. She herself had had various proposals, which she turned down. One was from a Sicilian duke, who wrote to ask her to lend him a return ticket to America, at the same time lamenting the fact that although he would like to marry her he regretted that he was not rich enough "to keep her in her usual luxury stand." She was, I am afraid, a one-man woman and, after the bad luck she had encountered with my father, she put all her energies into making matches for other people.

She had a strange habit of repeating everything three times. Once when we were dining with her at the Ritz, Laurence tickled her leg under the table; her only comment to this was, "Shush, Peggy will see, Peggy will see, Peggy will see." Once when she went to a milliner to order a hat with a feather, she said, "I want a feather, feather, feather." She is reported to have received a hat that bore three feathers. In New York when finally at the age of fifty she learned to drive a car, she was stopped by a policeman in a one-way street for going against the traffic. Her reply, if inconsistent, was correct. She said, "I am only driving one way, one way, one way." She not only repeated everything three times, but she also always carried three coats with her which she was perpetually changing. In a heat wave she wore two silver foxes and fanned herself to keep cool. She always carried three watches, one was a wristwatch, one she wore around her neck as a necklace, and the third one formed part of a lorgnon. The latter she could not use as she could see only with the lorgnon. Therefore it was impossible to benefit by this double arrangement. She was very generous to her children although she had a phobia about spending money. She gave me a fur coat or an automobile every year and was forever putting money in trust for me, but when it came to tipping everything went wrong, and one had to be perpetually on the lookout or be frightfully embarrassed. She was an inveterate gambler and very secretive about the size of her income.

During the course of this winter Mary, who also wore a Poiret evening dress I had ordered for her, led a wild life. She usually ended up in bed in this dress with several people. One night she lost her key and she went home with Marcel Duchamp. That started what one might designate as the Hundred Years' War. The next morning she came to us for taxi fare to go home because she was scared to ask Marcel for more than ten francs. At that time she lived near the Eiffel Tower in a little apartment she had made beautiful with maps she pasted on the walls and with earrings hung as décor instead of paintings.

Marcel was much sought after. It was very difficult to attach him, and in any case he disapproved of the mad life Mary led in the Boeuf sur le Toit with homosexuals. Her great friend was Moises who gave her credit in his nightclub, and as a result she spent fortunes there.

Marcel was a mysterious man. He hadn't painted since 1911, the days of the *Nude Descending a Staircase*. That had made him famous. Now he only played chess, and was on the French chess team. He also bought and sold Brancusis. Marcel was a handsome Norman and looked like a crusader. Every woman in Paris wanted to sleep with him. His particular vice was ugly mistresses. Mary was really much too beautiful for him, but in the end she managed to get him anyhow. It took years, but that probably made it more exciting. He was forever coming and going. At one time he even married a hideous heiress to please Picabia. It was during a period when Mary and he were not on speaking terms, but immediately after the wedding he went to find Mary and they had a reconciliation. Marcel soon divorced his wife.

In the spring of 1924, Comte Etienne de Beaumont organized and financed the *Soirées de Paris*. He rented the Cigale, a famous music hall in Montmartre, and engaged all the best talent of Paris to write music, dance and paint scenery for him. Stravinsky and *Les Six* composed music, Lifar, Riabouchinska, Lopokova, Borovansky, Toumanova, Massine, Danilova and other famous stars danced. Picasso, Ernst, Picabia, Chirico and Miró did décors for him. It was all very exciting because the artists collaborated with the Comte de Beaumont instead of just accepting orders as was the case with the Russian Ballet.

This also was the beginning of the social aspect of the ballet. It became very chi-chi and between acts we went into the bar where we met all our friends. It was, incidentally, the last good ballet ever produced.

This was a pleasant change and quite an improvement on our usual routine of life. We generally spent every night in cafés in Montparnasse. If I were to add up the hours I have whiled away at the Café du Dôme, La Cupole, the Select, the Dingo and the Deux Magots (in the Saint-Germain quarter) and the Boeuf sur le Toit, I am sure it would amount to years.

There were not only ballets but plays. Cocteau wrote *Roméo et Juliette* and Tristan Tzara wrote *Le Mouchoir de Nuage*.

During the winter I got the idea of bobbing my hair. Clotilde and I were the only women left in our world with long hair. Laurence adored it that way, but I was awfully sick of the struggles I had with brushing and combing it, and from the headaches it gave me. I must say it was beautiful. It was chestnut colored and very long and wavy. One day I went and had it cut off. When I came home I did not dare face Laurence. I tried to hide my head under a hat. When he finally caught me he was so furious he threw me under the dressing table. I conserved my mane, but I could no longer consider it part of myself.

In the spring Benita and her husband came to Europe again. She was more shocked than ever by our wild Bohemian parties. Benita and her husband left for Italy and my mother and I without

Laurence joined them in Venice. I considered myself an efficient guide, since this was my fourth visit to Venice, and I knew where all the churches and paintings were. I did not yet know Venice on foot, but I was soon to learn that, too. Laurence had given me an inkling of the existence of another life in Venice, when he had taken me for walks on a few of the best known highways of communication that zigzagged around Venice. But when we were there it was too hot to do much walking and we had spent our few days bathing at the Lido. He had initiated me in the use of the steamboat, called a *vaporetto,* which replaced the tramcars of other cities. Before that, I had traveled only in gondolas, like the idle rich and tourists, who never really get to know Venice. The following fall I was to learn every inch of my adored city for we were to live there for three months. But that comes later.

When I left Benita I promised to spend the summer with her in St. Moritz. Laurence was a faithful husband, but during my absence in Venice he had had an affair with a beautiful girl called Katherine Murphy: The affair ended as soon as I came back, but nine months later I went with Laurence to see Katherine's baby. We never knew if it was Laurence's, Katherine's husband's or Bob McAlmon's.

One night Bob McAlmon, who was one of our best friends, gave a big party in a restaurant in the Champs Elysées. He had as guests Louise Bryant and her husband William Bullitt, who was later our ambassador to France. We happened to be sitting at the next table, and Bob, finding himself short of funds, asked us to cash a check so that he might pay his bill. I was annoyed that he should have left us out of this party, and told Laurence not to help Bob in any way. Laurence was furious with me and when we got back to Mrs. Vail's flat where we were staying at the time, we had a dreadful row. In the middle of it Clotilde, who was in the room next door, overheard us and came in to take Laurence's part. I told her it was none of her business and that she should keep out of married people's fights. Clotilde told me to leave the apartment and I was so upset I began rushing around the flat as I was, quite naked. Mrs. Vail took the situation in hand and said to me, "This is my apartment, not Clotilde's, and you are not going to leave." She really was always a good mother-in-law to me.

In the summer we set out for Karesee in the Austrian Tyrol. We drove there over the Stelvio, the highest pass over the Alps and which was used by the Italians for auto races. The road zigzags in hairpin bends up to eleven thousand feet. At every corner we had to stop and back-up our car and turn, for the chassis was much too long for this road which had been built for little racing cars. It was terrifying as we thought each time we might go over the side and drop into the valley below. Our engine couldn't stand the strain of going up in first gear and the water boiled over. We discovered a little mountain stream and carried water back in our bathing caps. When we got to Bolzano we found only one room. Clotilde was with us and Sindbad was to follow with Lilly, by train. We spent a miserable night, Laurence making scenes without end because I wanted to join Benita for the summer and he did not want to go to St. Moritz where we were to meet her, since she would not come to Karesee. Clotilde and I were exhausted by morning, but we continued our trip.

The Austrian Tyrol is the loveliest country in Europe. It doesn't frighten one like the Engadine. Its scenery is less imposing and much more acceptable. Laurence did a lot of rock-climbing with guides. He was good at this and had been brought up to walk on glaciers and climb the highest mountains of Europe. Mrs. Vail was one of the first women mountain-climbers of the Alps. Personally I hated even walking uphill and was terrified the only time that the Vails took me on a glacier, the Diavolezza, near St. Moritz. I thought we would fall into every crevasse, and we came pretty near being killed at one moment, but that, it seems, is part of the excitement required to spur people on to this unnatural sport. They claim that when they reach the top of a mountain some thousands of feet high and see the sun rise they are recompensed for all the hours of hard work and danger they have put into it. They certainly deserve their reward.

In the end Laurence gave in and took me to St. Moritz. I don't think he liked being with my family, but I was always with his. After St. Moritz we went to Lake Como with Benita and her husband and stayed at Tremezzo. Mrs. Vail and Clotilde were with us too. We swam in the lake, we played tennis and I tried to learn to play golf to keep up with the Vails. I was so bad that I felt I had killed my teacher as he soon died, and I gave up this sport forever. Benita and her husband taught us to play Mah Jong. It became a vice. In the evenings we danced.

By this time Sindbad could walk and talk, and he had become

very beautiful. His black hair had turned into thick blond curls
and he had quite a few teeth and wonderful rosy cheeks. I was
quite mad about him, as were all the members of my family.
Benita adored him too as she had no child of her own, having had
many miscarriages. Laurence hadn't wanted a baby, but once
Sindbad arrived he was crazy about him. He really wished to have
a girl, so I promised him I would give him one. I said I would
never stop until I had produced one. So we tried to make a
daughter. In the beginning we couldn't make anything. We were
disappointed for three months. At that time Sindbad was eighteen
months old.

Benita and her husband returned to America, and Laurence
and I remained with his family in Tremezzo for the late summer.
Even Mr. Vail was with us for a while, but he soon went back into
a sanatorium.

We went down to Milan where Clotilde was to join an opera
company. She was to sing in the provinces somewhere in Italy.
Laurence and I left her to go to Venice where we settled down for
three months. We took rooms in a depressing old-fashioned hotel
on the Riva, which was modest in price. Up to then I had lived
only in the more elegant hotels. Laurence had a workroom with a
large stove. The smell that emerged from it was so disagreeable
that he couldn't work. Finally we investigated and found it was
packed with French letters. After the burning rubber was
removed he was able to continue the novel he was writing.

Mary was with us. She loved Italy and spent several months out
of each year in an old castle at Anticoli, near Rome. She was
almost a native by now, and felt great sympathy with the people.
She conversed with everyone in rather good Italian. My Italian
became more fluent after awhile. I had studied the language for
years but it had never seemed real till I lived in Italy. Reading
D'Annunzio's plays and novels in New York was most unreal.

Laurence found an old friend, Favai, in Venice. He was an
Italian Jew, who looked like an El Greco, with his long face and
black beard. His profession was to make false old masters, which
were sold to the unsuspecting public. He gave up his job
temporarily to help us buy the antique furniture with which I had
decided to furnish our home. Not that we had a home, but I knew
that if we bought the furniture we would eventually have one.

Shopping in Italy was almost as tiresome as shopping in Cairo. The question of bargaining was the all-important thing. It became dreadfully boring to have to go back to the same shop six or seven times in order to reduce the price asked to something normal. Favai discovered some wonderful objects that really should have been in museums. Then there was the added trouble of getting them out of Italy, since export of real antiques was prohibited by the government. We found a beautiful fifteenth-century oak buffet which required four men to carry. It looked Spanish as it had once been decorated with red velvet, and little bits of this remained around its metal incrustations. In an attic in Treviso, Favai discovered a beautiful thirteenth-century chest. It had wonderful carvings depicting a baptism and a woman fainting. Of course we bought it, and later I found its sister in the Victoria and Albert Museum in London. We found eleven three-legged oak chairs, all with different carvings. The astute shopkeeper told us that he could have a twelfth one made for us. After ordering it we found dozens of these chairs at many of the other antique dealers.

It was a lot of fun, but what I enjoyed most was getting acquainted with Venice on foot. Laurence had lived there as a child for his father had always gone there in the autumn to paint. Laurence knew every stone, every church, every painting in Venice; in fact he was its second Ruskin. He walked me all over this horseless and autoless city and I developed for it a lifelong passion. Everything in Venice is not only beautiful but surprising. It is very small, but so complicated because of the S-shaped Grand Canal that you are forever getting lost in its little streets. You always come out eventually on the Grand Canal, but not at all where you expect. Nothing is more tiring than these promenades, however, because they involve walking over endless bridges with steps.

The Piazza San Marco with its wonderful soap-bubble-domed Byzantine cathedral and its seventeenth-century arcades is one of the most beautiful squares in the world. It would be pleasant to walk there because there are no automobiles or horses, but the tourists are almost as objectionable. Sitting in cafés around the side or listening to music produced by a brass band in the evening is less dreary. What I really preferred were all the other piazzas that I discovered on my walks about the town. These are unknown to all but the Venetians, as tourists never get any farther than the Piazza San Marco. However, every parish of Venice has its piazza.

It is unnecessary to go into the foul odors of Venice. They fade away or become unimportant compared with the overwhelming beauty of a city that still bears the architecture of ten centuries. Needless to say I wanted to buy a *palazzo*, but I was again handicapped by the foresight of my uncles who had made me put all my money in trust.

While we were in Venice, Lilly got pneumonia and I looked after Sindbad every day instead of on Thursdays, as was my habit. I got so tired carrying around this enormous child, who did not like crossing the bridges with all their steps, that I engaged a little maid to help me. To my great shame she turned out to be about fourteen years of age, and not much bigger than Sindbad, but I presume she was used to looking after a large family of younger brothers and sisters. We often used to take him to the Piazza where he sat and fed the pigeons.

In the winter, there were no tourists to feed the pigeons and they were virtually starving. We felt it incumbent on us to supplement the rations allowed them by the municipality of Venice. Every day at noon we arrived in the Piazza with our five kilo bags of grain. The flutterings of the hungry creatures were alarming, and the wind caused by their flight almost blew us away.

Because of Laurence's exhibitionism he dressed rather eccentrically. Besides never wearing a hat and having golden hair streaming over his face, he attracted attention in various other ways. He wore white, azure blue, terracotta or beige overcoats. His shirts were made from the materials that were designed for entirely different purposes. They were of all colors, but what he liked best was to find an odd material, intended for drapes or furniture covering, at Liberty's in London. These gay, sometimes flowered patterns, he took to the most conservative shirtmakers on Half Moon Street and insisted (to their surprise) on having them made into shirts. He wore sandals rather than shoes. His feet turned in like a pigeon's. I believe he had some kind of a shoe complex because every time he went into a shoe shop he became hysterical and made a scene which often ended by his rushing out without buying anything. His jackets and trousers were a rare assortment. He wore the most conspicuous trousers he could find. They too were of all colors. At one time he had a brown corduroy suit made by one of the smartest tailors in London, but later he preferred to wear ordinary French workingman's blue-velvet trousers that he found in the markets of Toulon. In addition, he had a large collection of weird ties.

In Venice Laurence got the silly idea that he wanted me to have a sable cap made for him to protect his ears from the cold while driving. I think it represented a symbol of power. I refused to gratify this very extravagant wish. Instead, after many fights, I had made to order for him an Italian officer's black cloth cape with a velvet collar. At first he did not like it, but soon he realized how handsome he looked in it with his beautiful blond hair, and from then on he favored it.

When the rainy season finally drove us out of Venice we went to Rapallo. There at least we had sun, but we paid for it. What a horrible dull little town it was! We met Ezra Pound there and joined his tennis club and played every day. Ezra was a good player, but he crowed like a rooster whenever he made a good stroke. Later when I met him in Paris and told him how much I hated his beloved Rapallo, he said, "Maybe you have unpleasant personal memories of it." There was every reason why I should have. Besides my being very bored there, Laurence upset life considerably by terrible rows.

On New Year's Eve we attended a party in a private nightclub. Laurence got jealous of a man who asked me to dance, and went over to his table and insulted him. A big fight ensued. I was taken by the shoulders and hurled against the wall. I did not in the least relish this treatment because I was pregnant again. In the end we were forcibly evicted from the night club and were looked at askance in the tennis club.

One night Laurence and I had a bad private fight. It started by his calling Benita a bore, and to retaliate I said Clotilde was a whore. This so infuriated Laurence that he smashed to pieces a new tortoise-shell dressing-table set I had bought that very day, after months of bargaining in the Italian fashion. He knew just what this meant to me. I had a complex about toilet sets ever since I had regarded with horror my mother's silver brushes and combs. As a child I had spent all my savings on collecting a set of twenty-three ivory pieces in Paris on the Boulevard Haussmann to decorate my dressing table. It was a sort of fetish and I had had "Peggy" engraved on each piece. Ever since I had gone to Italy with Valerie I had dreams of acquiring a tortoise-shell set to replace this ivory one, which had long since vanished.

Laurence's destruction of it was to me more than painful. After he did it he dragged me down to the sea where, though it was a cold night, he rushed in with all his clothes on. After that he insisted on taking me to the cinema where he sat shivering in his wet clothes. No wonder Ezra thought my memories of Rapallo may possibly have been unpleasant.

We motored along the coast and on our way to Paris we found ourselves in an enchanting place called Le Canadel. It was little known at that time and quite unexploited. It was half way between St. Raphael and Toulon on the Côte des Maures. There was a long unpeopled sand beach edged by a forest of pine trees. We stayed at a very dull *petit bourgeois* hotel, but down below was the café and inn of Mme Octobon. It was primitive, but the food was delicious, and people drove there for meals from miles away. We decided to live in this part of the world and began to ask if there were any houses for sale. We were told there was one about a mile away. It was an inn called La Croix Fleurie, where Cocteau stayed every winter with Raymond Radiguet. It was just above the sea and had its own beach extending about a mile toward Cap Nègre. This beach was the first place the American troops landed in 1944, in their invasion of the south of France.

The house itself was not inviting but it was a nice little white plaster building in the Provençal style. It had a double exterior staircase ascending to a balcony which gave access to three spacious rooms. There were another three rooms and a bath in the back. Since this house was so small the owner had added a wing, which made the place not only possible but attractive. The wing consisted of one large room with a huge fireplace and three French windows that reached to the high ceiling and gave out on a lovely terrace with orange trees and palms, forty feet above the sea. There was a kitchen with a primitive coal stove and two other rooms and a toilet on the ground floor. There was neither telephone nor electric light. But there was plenty of sun and pine trees and the sea with a private beach. What more could one want? On the other side of the road there was a double garage with three servant's rooms. About three-quarters of an acre of

land went with the house. It was uncultivated and was covered
with pine trees to the left of the house, and in this tiny forest was
a green wooden cabin.

We bought the house and immediately, as the French do, our
landlord clinched the affair by producing the *notaire* from Cogolin,
who happened to be present, and we signed a promisory document.

However, when I got home and considered my rash act I
regretted it. Not that I did not like the place, I loved it; but I
realized how much too much we had offered to pay for it, not only
offered but actually agreed in writing in the presence of a *notaire*.
I consulted with Laurence, and we decided to go back and tell
them that we had cabled to America for the money and that it was
not forthcoming, as it was all in trust. We said we were going to
New York in a few months, and that we would do our best to raise
some funds. The landlord was so scared that he reduced the price
by one third, which approached what he should have asked in the
beginning, and in order to save his face he declared that, since we
were not intending to use it as a hotel and were relinquishing
those rights, we were entitled to a reduction. We thereby forfeited
forever the privilege of calling our villa by the charming name of
La Croix Fleurie and we found ourselves in the position of not
being allowed ever to make a hotel on these premises or to sell
them as such.

We were not to take possession of our new home until the
summer. We expected the birth of our daughter in August, so we
knew we would not live there until the fall. We now signed the
real *acte de vente* at Cogolin, the official head of the *commune,* and
celebrated with a bottle of champagne. Then we found some local
builders, and Laurence ordered a little house to be built for him as
a studio on the other side of the road.

After that we left for America, but not to raise the funds,
because I did have just the amount necessary. I went, of course,
to see Benita. At the last minute Laurence came with me,
although he hadn't meant to. He was writing a novel, and did not
want to do any more traveling.

We arrived in March, and Laurence chose as our residence the
Brevoort Hotel. Sindbad was a year and ten months old; he had
had a great success with everyone on the boat, the *France*. But not
as much success as a wonderful conversationalist named Esther

Murphy (later Mrs. Chester Arthur III), who held everyone
spellbound for a week by her endless and fascinating talk. She
seemed never to stop, and I wondered how anyone could know so
much and sleep so little.

Mina Loy, who was not only a poetess and a painter, was always
inventing something new by which she hoped to make her
fortune. She had just created a new, or old, form of *papier collé*—
flower cut-outs which she framed in beautiful old Louis Philippe
frames she bought in the flea market. She asked me to take these
to New York for her and sell them. Laurence gave them the
wonderful title Jaded Blossoms. I arranged to have an exhibition
in a decorator's on Madison Avenue. They were to take one-third
commission, which is normal, but I provided all the clients. When
it came to hanging them Laurence assisted us. He was so
Bohemian and temperamental that the lady in charge of the shop
wanted me to send him away, but when I explained that he was
my husband she could not refuse his help. The exhibition was a
great success, and I sold the Jaded Blossoms everywhere. Benita
bought two which she offered to the Metropolitan Museum, but
they were refused. I looked up all my old friends, hoping to sell
them Jaded Blossoms. I became so obsessed by this that I went all
over New York carrying them on my fast-growing stomach. My
poor daughter was perpetually buried under them.

When I felt I had sold enough, Laurence and I began to look for
a house for the summer. We had no idea as yet where Pegeen was
to be born. We got more and more depressed at the prospect of a
summer in America, and finally in desperation went back to
France on the *Aquitania,* with my mother. We thought we had
fooled her again about the date of the birth of our daughter, but
one day she walked into the bathroom when I was having a bath
and informed me that surely I had made a mistake.

In order to avoid giving another soldier to France we decided to
go to Switzerland just in case Pegeen turned out to be a boy. So at
the end of July we went to Ouchy on Lake Geneva just below
Lausanne. Mrs. Vail found us a doctor. As her husband knew
almost every neurologist and psychologist in Switzerland this was
easy. The doctor said Pegeen would be born between the first and
eighteenth of August. I decided not to have chloroform this time,
and a midwife was engaged to look after me. She came on the first
of August and we added another room to our suite in the

enormous Beau Rivage Hôtel. The nurse turned out to be
handsome. She resembled a Leonardo da Vinci Madonna, and I
was greatly attracted to her. She became bored with nothing to do
and every time she said good-night, she begged me to give birth
before dawn. After two weeks I began to lose faith in ever giving
birth again in my life. There was a head-waiter in the hotel whose
wife was also expecting a child, and every day we politely inquired
about each other's future prospects. On the seventeenth day of
August Laurence pulled a terrific scene in the dining room. I have
no idea now what it was all about, but I remember his throwing a
whole dish of beans in my lap and then later rushing around in
our apartment, throwing all the furniture about and breaking a
chair. Maybe this stirred Pegeen because the next day I began to
feel queer. The midwife sent me on a long walk with Laurence
along the lake. It was extremely painful and we had to stop every
now and then when the birth pains became too awful. Toward
evening we took out Sindbad's cot and dressed it up in curtains.
That of course settled it for my mother. She had the tact to
pretend that she had not noticed it, but she sat up all night with a
paper upside down in her hands in an adjoining room with
Clotilde. About ten o'clock we sent for the doctor. This time
Laurence was very happy for he was not banned from the room, as
he had been in England at the birth of Sindbad. In fact he was
permitted to hold one of my legs. As the pains got more and more
unendurable I regretted my decision not to take chloroform.
When I felt the wild horses dragging me apart I begged for a few
whiffs. The midwife had some ready and every time the pain
started she held it to my face. All I remember is her saying to me,
"*Poussez, madame!*" And in the end evidently I did not do my bit
and just as they were about to take Pegeen with forceps she
relented and came by herself at eleven-thirty.

The whole performance was so quiet that our neighbor in the
hotel could not believe a baby had been born. I never screamed
once. I held a handkerchief in my hand throughout the entire
birth. In some strange way it must have given me a feeling of
safety. When the pains got too bad I dug my nails into my palms
hoping to vary the agony. I also clutched onto the railings of the
brass bedstead.

This time I had made Lilly promise that no one would see my
baby before I did. The minute she was born Lilly hid her and

waited for me to come to before showing her. She was brought to
me in a towel. Instead of being covered with blood as I had
expected, Pegeen was covered with what seemed to be cold cream.
She was all white. She looked exactly the way Sindbad had looked
in every other respect. She had black hair and blue eyes. As she
was a girl I knew then that I would never have another child. I
had kept my promise to Laurence.

The afterbirth pains lasted for days. On the eighth day I was
put on a chaise longue and soon after I was allowed to get up. One
day when the midwife was out and I was alone with Pegeen, she
began to cry. I could hardly walk across the room to her and I felt
as if all my insides would fall out. I nursed her for a month and
then I couldn't any more. It happened this way.

Laurence and I decided we had endured Ouchy long enough
and we wanted to go to our new home in the south of France.
Laurence started ahead in the car, and I went by train with the
two babies, Lilly and the midwife. When we arrived in Lyons we
were told we had three-quarters of an hour to wait. I rushed out
with Lilly and Sindbad in order to get them some lunch. When we
got back to the train it had left. Pegeen and the midwife and all
the luggage had disappeared. I was quite frantic as I thought I
would never see my baby again. The midwife had no idea where
we were going and had never traveled before. Instead of losing my
head, I had the presence of mind to go to the *chef de gare*. He
immediately wired to the next station the train was to stop at and
asked that the midwife and Pegeen and the fifteen suitcases be
taken off the train. Then Lilly and Sindbad and I were put on
another train. We remained at the next station for only about two
minutes, but just time enough to recover Pegeen, the nurse and
the suitcases. As a result of the shock I lost my milk. Luckily we
had some powdered milk with us, for Pegeen was already getting
one bottle a day.

Our new home was in a place called Pramousquier. My mother
always mispronounced it Promiscuous. It wasn't a village or a
town. It merely possessed a railway station and a few houses. A
little train passed eight times a day, four going from St. Raphael to
Toulon and four from Toulon to St. Raphael. It took about four
hours to get to these destinations, so we naturally preferred our
car. Once when there was a strike on this line Laurence
suggested that I give the strikers a thousand dollars to keep them

going. He preferred this to Lucile Kohn's causes, where a lot of my money went. As a result of my gift we were the only people who were served on the line during the strike, and we continued to receive ice and other packages. When the strike was won we were allowed to ride free on the railroad. We used this little train to go to the neighboring village of Cavalière, where there was a small shop, and to Le Canadel where we drank Pernod at Mme Octobon's. However, most of my life was not spent on this little train, which looked like a toy and made a noise like an express, but was spent in a Citroën car chasing around the coast buying food. I raced this little train for many years, carefully avoiding it at the most dangerous crossings where people were often killed. Our house painter had lost his son in this way. He was run down on his motorbike. The painter received my condolences with tears at the same time, and in the true French manner he tried to sell me the motorbike.

We had no electricity for years, and at first we had no telephone. We had an old ice-box and we received our ice by the train every morning. It was thrown off on the railway line, and often I had to chase to Cavalière where it got thrown off by mistake. The country was grassless, cowless, and therefore milkless. Our nearest real town was Le Lavandou. It had a post office from which the postman came on a bicycle every day. I am surprised he brought us our mail because we had a wild sheep dog who leaped on and bit anyone in a uniform. She had been left one day by Gabrielle Picabia. We found Lola tied to an orange tree, and although she was ferocious, we could not do other than accept her as a gift. Anyway, she was very sweet to everyone not in uniform. All my frustrated desires to witness a birth were satisfied finally by Lola, who gave birth on our couch in the sitting room. She was completely unconscious of the fact that she was about to be a mother, and her surprise was touching. I forced her to accept and look after her babies. We kept three or four of them and they became ferocious. They rushed about the countryside with Lola, eating all the chickens. We were perpetually having to pay fines for chickens killed, and even once for those that might have been born. Later we had nine cats whose kittens the dogs sometimes ate at birth.

We had an Italian gardener called Joseph. With the help of Laurence he laid out beautiful gardens, but the dogs were forever tearing them up, and Joseph wanted to be rid of them. In order to encourage us to give them·away he used to collect all their *merde* every morning with a shovel and place it on the terrace around our breakfast table. We were puzzled for months wondering why the dogs chose this spot for their convenience until it finally occurred to me that Joseph had plotted this himself.

All our maids were Italian, and as a result our kitchen and larder were filthy. It is a miracle we did not all get poisoned from the rotting of food in the heat and the excessive filth. By degrees we made ourselves a comfortable existence, or rather Laurence did. We furnished our house with all the beautiful Venetian furniture, but Laurence insisted on buying some comfortable sofas and chairs. He rebuilt the house and made a lovely little library. After that he ordered a big studio over the garage for Clotilde. In the end we had four houses, for we had another one built on the extreme end of our property for Bob and Elsa Coates.

Pramousquier was a real home and it grew perpetually in every way. We really felt we belonged to the country. Laurence being almost French we were rooted there. By degrees more and more people came to visit us.

One of our first guests was Mina Loy, who came with her daughters, Joella and Faby. Mina painted a fresco in her bedroom. She conceived lobsters and mermaids with sunshades tied to their tails. We had good food finally by engaging *cordon bleu* cooks in Paris and buying a whole set of copper pans to bribe one to stay with us. We had a wine cellar and Laurence saw to it that it was well filled. However, in the early stages I remember one maid pouring all the wine left in bottles together. The only discrimination she had made was between red and white.

That winter we went up to Wengen to ski. Laurence loved this sport but I never dared to try it, my sense of balance being as weak as my ankles. Since my painful experiences in my childhood I carefully avoided anything that I knew would be unpleasant. Naturally I got bored waiting all day alone in the hotel with the babies. One day I took Sindbad out on a sled and cracked a rib. I decided to go to Paris and leave Laurence with Clotilde. I intended secretly to lead a wild life, and enjoy my freedom of ten days.

I gave a big cocktail party in Laurence's studio. It was a dirty old workshop in an *impasse* or *cul de sac* but ideal for Bohemian parties. This was the first party I had given without Laurence in Bohemia, and I was very pleased with myself.

After this party I found what I wanted, but I was excessively tight and was almost unconscious of it. When Laurence came back he sensed at once that I had been up to something, but it was so harmless that he need not have taken it so badly. The night he arrived without any warning I was with my friend Boris Dembo. That certainly was perfectly innocent, but Boris left at once because Laurence was in a state of frenzy. He immediately proceeded to give a demonstration in the Hôtel Lutétia where I was living. He rushed around tearing up the whole place and throwing all my clothes in the middle of the room. My shoes went out the window. Then he tried to get into the babies' room. Fortunately our new nurse, who had just replaced Lilly, had locked herself in, and she did not have the pleasure of seeing him in this state. Laurence then found my hair which I had so carefully conserved in a drawer and taking it with him, kissing it, he rushed out, only to return in a few hours to begin the scene all over again.

This was not the end. It went on for days and it ended up by producing an unknown husband for Clotilde. I admitted to Laurence that I had been untrue to him, but I lied about who it was. He suspected some nonexistent person who lived on Avenue de la Bourdonnée. One night when we were having dinner in a little bar in Montparnasse, Laurence, who was still chafing over my infidelity, suddenly arose and hurled four bottles into the corner just over the heads of four Frenchmen who were peacefully eating their dinner. Naturally they took this very badly, and the police came and removed Laurence in a pushcart. I fainted on the bar, and when I came to, Laurence was in prison.

Clotilde, who was with us, suggested that we go and get Marcel Duchamp to help us out of our troubles. He told Clotilde immediately to get the four Frenchmen to withdraw their complaints. They all agreed except one, and another one fell in love with Clotilde and later married her. He was a handsome Vendéen and although completely out of our world, belonging to an old French military family, he managed to enjoy himself in our midst. If he started off this way he certainly could stand anything.

Marcel and I wandered around Paris all night longing to go to bed together, but we did not consider it an appropriate moment to add to the general confusion.

The next morning I went to the police and escorted Laurence to the *Commissaire*. Laurence was covered in blood and wore no tie, and we were guarded on this walk through the streets by several policemen. It was very romantic. Then Laurence was freed and he thought his troubles were over, but they were not.

The fight continued, and one night when Laurence and I were still at it, he dragged me to the Gare de l'Est and said we were going to Provence overnight. We sat in a double-decker train waiting for it to leave when he suddenly changed his mind and took me out. Then we walked in the streets and to my great surprise, offering me a glass of beer, he pushed me through an unknown door. To my amazement fifteen naked girls greeted us, begging us each to choose one of them as a partner. I was so surprised I chose the ugliest one. We sat and talked and Laurence's choice, who was quite pretty, told him she knew who he was. She had read about his goings-on in the paper and had recognized him from the description. This was not my first admittance to a brothel. I had been to one in Venice, but this time the girl seemed to want to continue the friendship. I gave her my address. One day much later she appeared in a car at Pramousquier. She waited at the gate, uncertain as to whether I would admit her. She was on her yearly holiday with a girl friend, and when I saw her with clothes on I did not immediately recognize her. Finally I invited her in and she bored us for an hour with a very commercial conversation and departed.

I think this must have been the year that the British coal miners went on strike. I was greatly moved by their struggle and when the affair reached the point of becoming a national issue I decided to make a large donation. I cabled my bank in New York to sell the last ten thousand dollars of stock I had left from my grandfather's inheritance. This caused a lot of trouble, because my uncle who gave fur coats to girls disapproved and interfered. He asked the bank if I thought I were the Prince of Wales. I finally managed to get the money but just too late. By the time it reached England the strike was over. Laurence consoled me by saying, "Never mind. There will be just enough for every miner to have a glass of beer."

While I was in Paris Berenice Abbott had asked me to lend her five thousand francs to buy a camera. She said she wanted to start photography on her own. To pay me back she came to Pramousquier and took the most beautiful photographs of Sindbad and Pegeen and me. I certainly was well reimbursed.

About this time Mina Loy and I embarked on a great business venture. With her usual genius she had invented three new forms of lampshade. One was a globe of the world with a light inside it. One was a shade with boats whose sails were in relief. They were fixed on separately and gave the illusion of old schooners sailing in the wind. Her third invention was a double-cellophane shade with paper cut-outs in between, which cast beautiful shadows. I had set her up in a shop on the Rue du Colisée, and she had a workshop next to Laurence's studio on the Avenue du Maine where she employed a lot of girls. I ran the shop and she and Joella, her daughter, ran the workshop. When I went to America I took with me fifty or so of these shades with strict instructions from Mina where not to sell them. I am afraid I disregarded her instructions for I had not paid much attention to them.

For the opening of the shop in the Rue du Colisée we allowed my mother to invite her *lingère* to exhibit some underwear at the same time, as we then thought to make some money; this upset Mina so much that she refused to be present at the *vernissage*. We also sold some hand-painted slippers made by Clotilde, and later we gave Laurence an exhibition of his paintings. They were very decorative, but quite childish. The best one was called *Women and Children*. It portrayed factory women with their children at their breasts and horrible smug factory owners looking on, smirking, with cigars in their mouths. Laurence had not been influenced by the Surrealists who came to Le Lavandou in summer in large bands and wandered in and out of our house in their vague way with their artificial wives. André Masson and Gaston Louis Roux lived very near us and they were good friends of ours.

The lampshade shop was very successful, once I got rid of the underwear. Laurence's uncle was horrified when he heard that I worked there myself. He asked Mrs. Vail if I even accepted money. The Vails were very snobbish and had an awful shock when their cousin, a Rhinelander, married a Negress in New York.

In the summer we took a trip to the Pyrenees and landed in

Font Romeu at midnight. When we drove up to the door of the elegant hotel we surprised the *concierge* by handing out a package that contained a sleeping child, Sindbad. The *concierge* had hardly recovered from his shock when we fished on the floor of the car and handed him a second one, Pegeen. We left the nurse Doris and the children here and drove on to Andorra, the smallest republic in the world. There we found the president raking in hay. It was as democratic a country as it was tiny. From there we went to Barcelona.

We spent hours walking on the Ramblas and hours fighting in our room. Every time we sat in a café a shoe-shine boy appeared and offered his services. The dust underfoot certainly warranted this operation being made every few minutes. The strange thing was that every time my shoes were cleaned they came out a different color; once they were silver, once rose, and once green. Wherever we looked we saw signs that read Gomez Ideales. On the way back we passed the monastery of Montserrat, but the road was so bad we did not dare ascend to its heights.

During the winter Laurence completed his novel, *Murder! Murder!* It was a sort of satire of our life together and, although it was extremely funny, I took offense at several things he said about me. He was so upset that he seized the manuscript and burned it in the stove of his studio. That day Pauline Turkel was coming from Nice to type it. Laurence had to dictate a rough draft of it from memory. This time he was kinder to me.

We had a wonderful life in Pramousquier. We had perpetual sun and therefore needed no heat in the house. We merely burned a big log in the living room in the evening. Laurence swam all the year round. I didn't. All one had to do was jump out of bed, slip on a bathing suit and run down to the beach. I spent hours there reading and sun-bathing. I usually got up at nine or ten, had breakfast on the terrace, then did my daily shopping for bread and ice or went milk hunting, or for whatever else was necessary. The shops delivered the rest of the food from Le Lavandou and Hyères. After that I went down to the beach. About two o'clock we ate lunch on another terrace, which was much cooler in summer as it was sheltered by trees and built on an overhanging cliff that was swept by pleasant breezes. We always drank so much wine, even if it was only the wine of the countryside or Muscadet which came from Clotilde's future family estate, that in summer we took a siesta every afternoon. We lunched out-of-doors all the year round.

In winter we ate on our large terrace overlooking the sea. It was covered with palm trees that blossomed in March, and with orange trees that gave forth the most delicious perfume in the early winter when the orange blossoms flowered. The whole countryside was covered with mimosa which abounded in our garden, and for months everything seemed to have turned yellow. Besides the pine trees the country was covered with olive and cork trees; in fact cork was the great industry of the south. There was a little factory back in the hills at a place called Collobrières. The corks were cut on a machine which one woman manipulated by hand, the process being nearly medieval. At Collobrières there was an inn where we enjoyed wonderful six-course meals for eight francs. Another place we drove to was the Forêt du Dom where wild boars were hunted. Here we had equally good meals of boar, for the same modest prices.

In the afternoon Laurence took us in large groups (consisting mostly of women) for a walk in the country. We had only two directions to walk in. One we named *du côté de chez Swann* and the other *le côté de Guermantes*. There were several variations, however, and we went back into the country and over the hills. Sometimes Laurence went on longer walks right over the top of these hills, called Les Maures after the Moors who had once inhabited this coast. The countryside was covered with towers the Gauls had built to keep a lookout for the greatly feared return of the Moors.

Toward evening we always had our second swim. Sometimes we would vary our life, which was completely directed by Laurence, by going to Le Canadel and having Pernod at Mme Octobon's before lunch or before dinner.

Mme Octobon was a solid Belgian woman. Her husband was a fiery Frenchman who often attacked her with a carving knife, but because of their business they could not separate. They led a sort of Dance of Death. Wherever we went we were accompanied by our four dogs who were most unpopular in the neighborhood. Lola was always my favorite, but Laurence took a great fancy to Lulu, her eldest daughter, who greatly resembled a crocodile. In fact, he insisted on having both these animals share our bed. Lulu grew so enormous there was hardly room for me.

Laurence developed a passion for the game of *boules*. He instituted serious games on the terrace. Joseph the gardener was a great champion. He and Laurence laid out an orchard in front of Laurence's studio. They also raised tomatoes which were delicious when eaten raw and hot. At one period we had a wonderful pig called Chuto, who used to follow Joseph around with the devotion of a dog. It was painful to have to kill and eat Chuto and see his blood turned into black sausages. A specialist came from Le Lavandou to perform this operation in our kitchen. Chuto was so fat after Joseph had wined and dined him for months that we should have had enough ham for years. Unfortunately we had to take all the meat to Paris with us on a trip, and it turned green en route from the cold. We also had a chicken farm, but we spent so much money on grain to induce the birth of a few eggs that in the end we gave it up.

In the winter we suffered from the *mistral*. It lasted for days on end, filling the house with sand, breaking all the windows and obstructing the roads with fallen trees.

After Sindbad was a few years old he accompanied us everywhere, but Pegeen, who was still too young, was left behind with Doris. I think unconsciously she developed the feeling of being not wanted by us and became extremely attached to Doris. Laurence was full of vitality and drove us all over the country, sometimes to Nice and back overnight without our stopping to sleep. Once we went to visit Evelyn Scott at Cassis, arriving at four in the morning. We often went to Toulon to shop for delicacies and to spend a gay evening, or to St. Tropez to dine. Our nearest large town was Hyères but that was so dull and full of English retired civil servants that we went there only to shop. In the evenings if we remained at home we always had guests whom we served the most delicious food and wine. We were rarely alone. Either we had house guests or invited people who lived in the neighborhood. We went to Paris for the rainy season which started in November and lasted two months; and every summer in the middle of August we went to the mountains for three weeks to avoid the terrific heat.

Laurence loved traveling and especially driving. He drove as though the furies were in pursuit of him. Once he took me to Paris in nineteen hours without stopping to sleep. We stopped only now and then to drink enough to keep going. As he drank an awful lot, I was very nervous. I never knew what was going to happen at such moments in the car. He would never let me drive. For years we never set foot in a train. We went everywhere in our Lorraine Dietrich and later in our Hispano. Of course I drove my little Citroën myself.

In the winter of '27 we went again to New York on the *Aquitania,* this time taking with us two babies and two girls. One was Doris, our new English nurse, sent by Hazel to replace Lilly's successor who had gone back to England with boils. Doris was very pretty. She was hospital trained, but she looked more like a Gaiety girl than a nurse. By the time she came to Pramousquier life was quite gay. She soon got herself a beau and Lilly greatly regretted her rash behavior in going back to England when Pramousquier bored her, but then it was too late. The other girl was one of our handsome Italian maids. They both had great success wherever they went, and enjoyed New York immensely.

This time I arrived with fifty lampshades and fifty lamps. Mina had collected Louis Philippe bottles in the flea market, and Laurence had also suggested using the southern glass wine-bottles that we found at Le Lavandou as bases for the wonderful shades. They cost a few cents and I sold them for twenty-five dollars. Mina also used silver, blue and green witch balls for lamps. I became efficient and soon found myself selling everything to all the shops Mina had told me to avoid as well as to all the others. I had to mount the shades myself because I could not find anyone to do it for me. I sold five hundred dollars worth, and sent Mina a check, but she was furious because I had not obeyed her instructions. She was afraid her invention would be cheapened by the department stores. Finally in Paris all her ideas were stolen, and although she had copyrights she had to give up her business. It was impossible for her to conduct it without a businessman and a lot more capital.

When I arrived in New York, Benita told me that she was going to have a baby in August at about the time of my birthday. This was her fifth attempt. She had lost all the others in the early months and greatly desired to have a child, especially for her husband. This time she had great hopes of going through with it for she was already past the dangerous month when she had lost all the others.

Benita looked more beautiful than ever. Her pregnancy did not

in the least unbecome her. Her long slender neck seemed even
more graceful and accentuated as it rose from her rather more
mature form. She had one dress that was black with a pink front.
I used to tease her and tell her the black part was herself and the
pink was the baby. She was shy and embarrassed by this joke. Her
face looked exactly the same as it did when Lenbach painted her
twenty-four years before. Her brown eyes and hair, her tiny nose
and olive skin and her beautiful hands with tapering fingers never
seemed to change. She was calm and happy in her pregnancy and
seemed quite content to drive with me all over New York, while
her Swedish chauffeur helped me to deliver and carry Mina's
bottles and lampshades.

Of course I never wanted to leave her but Laurence insisted on
going up to Connecticut to finish his book *Murder! Murder!* We
stayed in the house where Hart Crane boarded. I don't see now
how Hart endured us with our noisy babies and Doris and the
maid, but he seemed to enjoy having us and was very cordial. He
lived an extremely monastic life up there, seeing nobody for
months on end. In winter he nearly went mad from ennui and
once threw his typewriter out of the window into the snow. He
had a collection of strange records, one of the best being Cuban
music.

Soon I left and went back to Benita for a short while, but
Laurence again tore me away from her. This was much more
tragic as I wanted to be with her for the birth of her child.

Regretfully I allowed Laurence to take me back to Europe. I
promised Benita I would return alone in September after her baby
was born.

When we got to Paris Laurence found a court summons. He
had been tried in his absence and condemned to six months'
imprisonment for throwing the bottles at the four gentlemen in
the restaurant. One of them had not withdrawn his complaint.
This was very serious and had to be dealt with at once. Clotilde's
fiancé produced one of the best lawyers in France, Maître Henri
Robert. He was a *batonnier* and therefore qualified to plead in
court. Laurence was told to take him fifteen thousand francs in
bank notes, as he was not supposed to accept any money for his
services. When he saw Laurence's embarrassment at being unable
to offer the money, he tapped on the table with French practical
sense saying, *"Mettez ça là."* The trial took place in the Palais de

Justice and was very impressive but the result was not satisfactory. The noble name of Lafayette, who was a friend of Laurence's grandfather, was brought up, and a novel of Laurence's, which had been published in America, was produced. Laurence was let off his prison term but given a *sursis,* which meant that if he ever had another offense, six months would be added to his sentence.

Soon after this I met Isadora Duncan who was then living in the Hôtel Lutétia in great straits, but nevertheless she gave us champagne. I am sure she hoped I would help her out of her difficulties, but I am afraid I didn't. She came to visit us at Pramousquier with the little Bugatti car she was so soon to meet her death in. Isadora had bright red hair and a wonderful purple and rose costume. She objected to my being called Mrs. Vail and named me Guggie Peggleheim. She said, "Never use the word wife." She was vital and colorful even at this late stage of her life, although she seemed to be rather demoralized. The news of her death upset me considerably.

In the summer of '27 Mary Butts came to stay with us and brought her daughter Camilla, a charming child but neglected by her mother, who was always up in the clouds. One day she got a sunstroke and was very ill. Doris and I had to look after her. Mary took a whole tube of aspirin in one day when her opium gave out. She believed in black magic and was perpetually trying to initiate Laurence into her mysteries. He loved the atmosphere she produced and she was extremely clever at flattering him.

In the middle of all this one day I opened by mistake a cable that was addressed to Laurence. It told him to break the news to me that Benita had died in childbirth. It was such a shock that I did not realize it. I was like the man who was cut in half by a very sharp sword and who laughed at his murderer. Whereupon the murderer said, "Get up and shake yourself." When he did as he was bid he fell in two. I pretended nothing had happened. I went right on doing some accounts I was in the middle of. When I got up, I felt virtually as though I had been cut in two. I seemed to have lost part of my physical being. My first thought was that I had deserted Benita. I could not forgive myself for having come back to Europe with Laurence. I started to cry and couldn't stop for weeks. All I wanted was flowers. Clotilde and Laurence went to Toulon and brought back all they could find and put them everywhere. Clotilde was very nice and for once she really said the right thing to me; she knew what I felt because of her love for Laurence. I couldn't look at my children for days. I felt I had no right to have any.

Benita's baby was born dead. It was a case of placenta previa, the most dangerous thing in childbirth. It causes a hemorrhage which is usually fatal. The doctors, to cover themselves, pretended it had no connection with her miscarriages, but of course she never should have been allowed to have this child.

Laurence was painfully jealous of my suffering and kept insisting that I still had him in the world. That of course was not what I was thinking about at the time. It so much deranged him that he made dreadful scenes. After that I never felt the same toward him again and I blamed him for having separated me from Benita for all those years.

I received many condolence letters and began writing mad replies. I was slightly off my head. My greatest consolations were listening to the Kreutzer Sonata on the phonograph and the letters that Mary Loeb wrote me. She was Benita's closest friend and was suffering as much as I was. If only we could have been together at this time it would have helped. Peggy suddenly arrived from America with her husband and her daughter who was Pegeen's age. She was actually on the sea at the time of Benita's death and did not know of it. We went to Toulon to meet her and I drank lots of brandy to give myself the courage to break the news to her.

Every summer we had to leave Pramousquier for three weeks to avoid the terrible heat of the Midi which was very bad for the children. This time Laurence drove all of us to a little mountain hut he had found way up in the Alps behind Barcelonnette. He loved the high mountains where he went climbing. We took Peggy and Doris and the three children. Peggy's husband did not come with us. He had gone to Paris on business. I was so miserable I could not eat or sleep. All I did was cry. Doris thought I was going to die. She fed me to prevent my losing any more weight. Laurence kept making scenes all the time. He stopped Peggy from talking to me about Benita by telling her I did not like it. I couldn't understand why she withheld from me my only consolation, and I remained alone in my grief. After weeks we discovered what Laurence had done through his jealousy.

The following year as a result of all this was an unusually

stormy one and finally broke up my marriage. A fortune teller in Paris said to me, "You will meet a man in the south of France who will be your next husband." I laughed at her and replied, "I never see any men in the south of France except our neighbor, an old farmer." But she was right. On the twenty-first of July, 1928, the first anniversary of Benita's death, I met the man who was to give me a new life.

As a result of Benita's death I decided never again to go to America. I inherited a lot of money but I could not bear the thought of spending her money so I gave it all away. Of all the consolations I was offered from everyone the one that impressed me most was from the *chefesse de gare* at Le Canadel. She was a warm, southern type and always helped me out of my difficulties. Living in such an out-of-the-way place, they were numerous. She was supposed to be the whore of the countryside, but she certainly had a very philosophical point of view. When she heard of Benita's death she said, *"Nous ne sommes tous que passagers sur cette terre."* In view of the fact that she lived in a railway station it was most appropriate.

When we returned from the mountains Laurence's friend, Betty Humes, came to visit us, with her friend Dr. Carlozza, a Roman Rosicrucian. He tried to help me in my grief by teaching me his religion. He read my palm and he also predicted another husband for me. This so much enraged Laurence that he made a dreadful scene in Toulon one night. He threw me down on the Boulevard de Strasborg and then he burned a hundred-franc note. He was taken to the police and Peggy and I went to rescue him. When I protested at their interference in what I considered my affair, the police claimed he had a right to knock down his wife if he wanted to, but that he had no right to burn a banknote, as it was an insult to the Banque de France. An hour later he was released in spite of the Banque de France.

In the fall my mother arrived from America. Laurence drove me right across France to Cherbourg to meet her. It was the weekend of the Jours des Morts and of All Saints' Day, and wherever we drove we encountered hundreds of mourners carrying chrysanthemums to their relatives' graves.

The children came up to Paris to see my mother and I placed them in a kindergarten where they immediately got whooping cough. I was worried that we would be put out of the hotel, but the manager pretended not to notice it, and only when we left sent me a bill for disinfection of the rooms.

Laurence went to Mégève, a little mountain resort, at the time quite unknown, to ski with Clotilde. He broke a rib and was laid up for a short while. I remained alone in Paris with the children, still absorbed by my grief. I was glad to be rid of Laurence as he was making terribly jealous scenes over Benita. One night he tore up the photographs I had had enlarged from snapshots taken of her years before. My room was full of them and he hated their being there.

During that winter I met Emma Goldman and Alexander (Sasha) Berkman. They were glamorous revolutionary figures and one expected them to be quite different. They were frightfully human. Emma was very vain and it took me years to see through her. First I worshiped her and when later I was disillusioned she did not like it and she revenged herself by leaving me out of her memoirs.

My mother had given us another car, this time a wonderful Hispano. We bought the chassis and then we ordered a silver-colored open body for it. Laurence always insisted on lots of air. By mistake the body turned out to be sky-blue instead of silver and had to be painted all over. When we finally got it we left for the south, taking Emma Goldman with us. She took to the Hispano as though it were the most natural thing in the world for her to be driving in it.

Unfortunately the Hispano began to limp. It was ridiculous to have such a magnificent car that would barely move at ten miles an hour. It kept stopping all the time. Finally we were forced to remain overnight at Châlons and have the tank cleaned out. Then it flew like a bird. Emma was disgusted with the whole performance.

Very soon after we built the house for Bob and Elsa Coates at Pramousquier Bob decided to go back to America. Elsa remained a year without him and then she followed him. She offered her house to Kitty Cannell and Roger Vitrac. They came to live with us and we had a nice life with them. In the evenings we read Montaigne aloud and had delightful talks. One night we went to a brothel in Marseilles to see a special film. Afterward Kitty, who was unwell, fainted. The whores were very sweet to her and looked after her with great kindness. During this brief moment

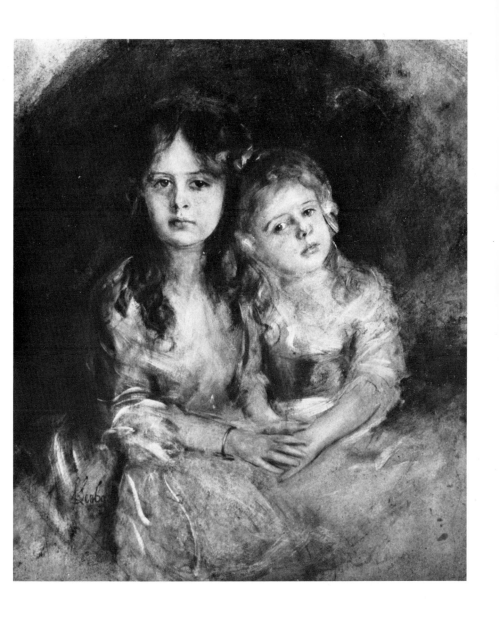

Benita and Peggy Guggenheim as painted by Franz von Lenbach, 1903

Myself in 1908

Peggy, Hazel and Benita Guggenheim
in Lucerne, 1908

My sister Benita looked more
beautiful than ever. Her long
slender neck seemed even more
graceful. Her brown eyes and
hair, her tiny nose and olive skin
and her beautiful hands with
tapering fingers never seemed to
change.

Myself in 1912

Myself in 1913

My Jacoby School graduating class. I
am at the extreme left in the top row.

The King of Bohemia, 1922                         In Egypt, 1923

Laurence Vail

On our honeymoon in Capri, 1922

Myself in my cloth-of-gold evening dress by Poiret, with a headdress by Vera Stravinsky, 1924

Berenice Abbott asked me to lend her five thousand francs to buy a camera. She said she wanted to start photography on her own. To pay me back she took the most beautiful photographs of Sinbad and Pegeen. I certainly was well reimbursed.

Vitrac borrowed a hundred francs from Laurence and rushed upstairs. He got back before Kitty was revived and she was never any the wiser.

But of course we got restless and decided to travel again. Laurence and I put the Hispano on a boat at Marseilles and disembarked at Algiers. This was not the most interesting town of North Africa by any means, it was too Europeanized. I much preferred Tangiers where I had been with Valerie. From there we motored in the desert to Biskra, Bou Saida and right down to Kairouan. At Kairouan we were offered the spectacle of the sword-eaters, but we refused to have this religious ecstasy performed artificially for our benefit.

In the desert we passed a broken-down Ford. An Arab squatted patiently by its side awaiting help, and twenty-four hours later he was in the same position with the same degree of patience. I really believe these people have no sense of time. Once we were arrested for giving a lift to two Arab boys who turned out to be running away from home. When we paid their return fare we were allowed our freedom. We also gave a lift to two English missionary ladies. I am sure they regretted it, because one of them became ill from the fumes of the Hispano and nearly fainted. We had a windscreen that kept out the air so efficiently that no one could bear to be in the back of the car.

Then we went to Constantine and Carthage and ended up at Tunis. Everywhere I bought fantastic earrings to add to my collection. It was all very much like Egypt, except that we had the new experience of driving through the desert.

Early in the following summer I invited Eleanor Fitzgerald, otherwise known as Fitzi, to come to Europe. She was much overworked by her theater activities and needed a holiday. Because of the death of her lover she was extremely unhappy, and as I was still unhappy about Benita, we tried to comfort each other. Fitzi was a great friend of Emma Goldman.

# Chapter 4

# End of My Life with Laurence Vail

In the summer of 1928 Emma Goldman was living at St. Tropez in a charming little house I had given her. She was engaged in writing her memoirs. We had finally convinced her that she must do this, and a fund had been raised to give her the wherewithal to live during this period. I headed it and continued to add to it whenever necessary. She had for a secretary, as she herself couldn't put two words into readable English, a mad American girl called Emily Coleman. Emily, unlike most people who are mad, did not hide it. On the whole it was a pleasant quality because it manifested itself in terrific enthusiasms and beliefs which my cynical entourage would never do more than sneer at. She shared with Blake the persuasion that all things are possible if you have faith. She was passionately interested in people and in literature and life.

Emily looked like a little boy, although she was twenty-nine, and she had a son a few months younger than Sindbad. Even though I liked her at once it never occurred to me what a role she was to assume in my life. Emily insisted that she was a writer herself and was merely helping Emma out in her dilemma. She was, in other words, not Emma Goldman's secretary. Emma adored her and mothered her and spoiled her, and in return, without receiving any salary, Emily lived in Emma's house and knocked her tremendous manuscript into shape.

Poor Emma much preferred anything to writing. She was a woman of action, and was delighted if we motored over to spend an evening with her, when she would give up her work for the day and make us a marvelous meal. She was a Jewish *cordon bleu* and her gefilte fish was her *pièce de résistance*. Laurence thought she ought to write a cookbook instead of her memoirs.

Emily had a nice husband. He was a businessman in the advertising world who had also written a book on psychology. Emily had left him to stay with Emma because she needed this climate for her health. It was the beginning of the end of their marriage, although then she did not know it. At this time she was in love with an Englishman whom she had met at St. Tropez. She was constantly with him and his wife, and produced them in the way she always produced everything she thought she had discovered—with the delight a magician manifests in bringing something out of a hat. And indeed they were miraculous. Their names were John and Dorothy Holms.

When I first met John Holms I was impressed by his elastic quality. Physically, he seemed barely to be knit together. You felt as if he might fall apart anywhere. When you danced with him it was even more apparent, because he could move every muscle of his body without its being noticeable and without the usual jerks one suffers in such cases. He was very tall, over six feet in height. He had a magnificent physique, enormous broad shoulders and small hips and a fine chest. He wore a small red beard and looked very much like Jesus Christ. His hair was wavy, thick and auburn red. His skin was white, but from the southern sun it had turned pink. His eyes were deep brown and he wore glasses; he had a classical straight nose. His mouth was small and sensuous and seemed to be pursed up under his moustache. Like all Englishmen he was proud of his ancestors but hê hated his father, who was Scotch by descent and had been governor-general of the United Provinces of India.

John was born in India and when he was a few years old he was separated from his parents and sent to boarding school with his sister in England. He loved his mother, a beautiful Irishwoman descended from Nicholas Ferrar, the founder of Little Gidding.

He rarely saw his family, who were living in retirement at Cheltenham. He found all contact with them difficult because he belonged to a different world. He knew much too much about theirs, and they knew much too little about his. His father had wanted him to enter the diplomatic service, but when the war broke out he was a student at Sandhurst Military College and joined up at the age of seventeen. At that time, he was as strong as a bull and had killed four Germans by hammering them on the head when he had surprised them breakfasting under a tree. For this, to his great shame, he was given the Military Cross. After six months of war on the Somme in the light infantry, he had been taken prisoner in a night patrol, and had spent the rest of the war (two years) in a German prison camp. In prison he met Hugh Kingsmill, who became a lifelong friend. His other great friend was Edwin Muir.

In the prison, because he was an officer, he had been pretty well treated and was unfortunately allowed to have all the liquor he wanted to buy. This undoubtedly had done him much harm, for his capacity for drink was greater than anyone's I have ever known. He drank about five drinks to other people's one and yet he never seemed to be affected by it until about three in the morning when he looked peculiar, with his eyes half shutting. However, he never behaved badly in any way. Drink made him talk, and he talked like Socrates. All his varied education and knowledge of people and life, which should have been expressed in writing, came out in conversation. He held people spellbound for hours. He seemed to have everything at his fingertips, as though he had been in contact with everything, had seen everything and thought about everything. He was like a very old soul that nothing could surprise. This gave him a detached quality and I was greatly astonished much later when I discovered what passion lurked under this indifferent exterior. I always thought of him as a ghost. He was definitely a frustrated writer, although at one period in his life he had had a great success in London writing criticism, and he still received letters begging him to write articles. He could not get himself to write at all any more. And though he needed money very badly because he received only a meager allowance from his father, he preferred to live in the greatest simplicity at St. Tropez rather than go back to England. He had lived all over Europe since the war, in Ragusa, in Salzburg, in Dresden, in Forte de Marme, in Cagnes, in Zagreb and in Paris. He had been with his wife Dorothy for nine years, and she had traveled nearly everywhere with him. Now, however, they were more like brother and sister, their sexual life being over. They had led a very stormy existence. He had taken her away from a man called Peacock and had gone through months of hell, while she wavered between them. He had carried a pistol constantly, with the idea of killing himself if she did not remain with him. Dorothy at this time was very much absorbed in a book she was writing about Peacock; it was an extraordinary and beautiful book. She adored John and claimed that she was writing it for him. I am sure it was true. She must have been created by him, for no woman could live with him that long and not be entirely reborn.

Dorothy complained all the time about John, even though she loved him. She said she was a governess to a baby and had to do everything for him and could never leave him. She complained because they were so poor. She complained because he would not write. She complained because they did not live in England and because he no longer desired her sexually and she complained because he had never married her. She belonged to a middle-class family and felt inferior because of this. She was attractive and handsome and also, strangely enough, had red hair. But her eyes were not like John's. They were green and cat-like. She had a beautiful white skin and a nice figure, but she was seven years older than John, who was nearly thirty, and that worried her. She was also sad because she had no children. This was also a cause of complaint. They were a strange couple and I was fascinated by them.

The first evening I met John was the anniversary of Benita's death and I did not feel very happy. Laurence insisted on going to St. Tropez to dance in the bistros. In the end I went too. My melancholy turned into a kind of desperation and I remember getting quite wild and dancing on the table. This must have made an impression on John Holms, but all I remember now is that he took me to a tower and kissed me. That certainly made an impression on *me,* and I can attribute everything that followed to that simple little kiss.

Later I asked the Holmses to come to visit us at Pramousquier. They came overnight and we went in bathing at midnight, quite naked. John and I found ourselves alone on the beach and we made love. He talked to me very seriously and asked me what I liked in literature, and for some mad reason all I could think of was May Sinclair. After that I did not see him for a long time, because Laurence and I took the children, Fitzie and Clotilde, Hazel and Milton Waldman to Maloja for a month to avoid the summer heat of the Midi. I did not forget John Holms, and I am certain that I was unconsciously postponing him for my future because the minute I got back, I went to find him.

As I say, the first thing I did when I got back to the Midi was to look for the Holmses. They had left their house, and I did not know where they were. I went to the post office and, when I found out their new residence, I walked in on them. They were surprised and, I think, pleased. John took me for a walk on the hill behind his house. The landscape greatly resembled the English moors. Then he took me swimming at Ramatuelle. I was very happy with him and we got on very well. They had finally decided to go back to England, so that John could make some money writing and live again in the intellectual world from which he had fled. I invited them to come and stay with us at Pramousquier. At first they were reluctant, but when I offered them Elsa Coates's little house next to ours, they said they would think about it. Dorothy wanted peace and quiet to finish her book. In the end John made Dorothy come. She always did everything he wanted her to do. I liked her very much at this time and she liked me. I found her conversation fascinating. Soon she felt uncomfortable in my presence and began gently liquidating me, but that was when she suspected I was becoming a danger to her.

The day before I went to get them I felt a certainty about my future. I was living in the exciting expectancy of one about to enter into a new love affair. I really only acted from a blind force which drove me on and on. I could not live with Laurence any more as our scenes were becoming more horrible. In Maloja we had had another dreadful evening in a café, when he had thrown everything about, and in St. Tropez, after we got back, he had tried one night in a bistro to tear off all my clothes because he was upset by Clotilde's making a spectacle of herself dancing with her skirts up to her thighs, and because he was suspicious of John. Alexander Berkman had to come to my rescue. He stopped Laurence from making me quite nude in public, and then

Laurence slapped me so hard in the face that, although I must have been quite drunk, I became sober.

By this time I had had enough, and I wanted to leave Laurence, but I was afraid to go off on my own. Once Emma Goldman had asked me how I could lead this kind of life. I told her that I could not leave the children and that I did not want to talk about it. But finally I decided things were too bad to continue. A few months before, Laurence had thrown me down the steps of his studio, and then burned up my sweater, and walked on my stomach four times in the same evening. I told Laurence, sort of vaguely and jokingly, that when we separated I would give him Sindbad and I would take Pegeen. I imagine when John Holms kissed me I unconsciously decided I would use him to make my escape.

In the beginning I was not in love with John, but one night when he disappeared for an hour, I got quite frantic. Then, for the first time, I knew I loved him. We used to go out into the country together and make love. Sometimes we went down to the rocks under his house. The minute Laurence went up to his studio and I saw his light lit, I ran over to John's house to fetch him. That was our hour. Soon John began getting difficult about Laurence and asked me to discontinue my matrimonial relations. I found this hard to do. It was all getting too much and I wanted John to take me away, but he couldn't make up his mind. He lived in a perpetual state of paralysis of will, and he hated to give up Dorothy. Dorothy didn't think I was a serious person, but John realized what he could do to me and he was fascinated by the idea of remolding me. He knew I was half trivial and half extremely passionate, and he hoped to be able to eliminate my trivial side.

John and I wanted to be alone, if only for one night. Laurence had asked us all to go to Toulon on a sort of spree. John and I connived very carefully to avoid going on this party. In fact, John was so clever that even up to the last minute I myself did not know if he were remaining with me or not. However, he did. Dorothy went off to Toulon with the others and at last we were free to do whatever we wanted. We went to a real bed for the first time, but got up in the middle of the night, fearing the others would return. We sat in the sitting room for hours awaiting their return, all the time thinking we might have remained in bed. Laurence came home very late. He had left Dorothy in Toulon because she had drunk too much and was sick. The next day we all went back to fetch her. She was hysterical, but still not suspicious of me.

A few weeks of living under this strain was enough for me, and unconsciously I arranged to bring things to a head if John wouldn't. One evening, knowing that Laurence was about and not in his studio, which was the only time we were safe, I went over to John's house and kissed him. Laurence followed me and caught us, which I suppose was what I wanted, but what I had not foreseen took place: a terrible battle from which a death might easily have resulted. John was much stronger than Laurence, but he did not want to hurt him, and when Laurence attacked him, he merely tried to hold Laurence down until I went to get someone to intervene. I lost my head and went to get Dorothy, who was in the bathtub at my house. She took so long to get out, they might have been killed ten times. Finally we got the gardener to come to the rescue, and at the moment he entered the house, John was about to knock out Laurence in desperation because Laurence wanted to hit him with a heavy pewter candlestick. The gardener went to Laurence's rescue as he was his master.

Laurence told Joseph not to interfere, but at least that ended the deadly battle. Both were completely shattered. Laurence went back to our house and I went with him. He told me that he would not stand having the Holmses at Pramousquier any longer and that I was to get rid of them. Dorothy came in during the middle of the conversation and Laurence told her that John and I were lovers. She told Laurence that he was mad, but she looked distraught. Laurence went back to their house and told John that he would kill him on sight if he ever met him again. I was out of my wits, and I immediately arranged to have the Holmses leave by a little back path and take refuge in Mme Octobon's bistro. While escaping, Dorothy injured her leg on the barbed-wire fence. Laurence went to the bistro to look for John, but Mme Octobon hid the Holmses and would not let Laurence see them. Then I knew it was all over, and I planned for everybody's escape. I bribed the gardener to take a note to the Holmses. I sent them some money and told them where to meet me. The Holmses got off to Hyères that night, and I was to join them the following day at Avignon.

It is very strange after living with a man for seven years to know that you are spending your last night with him. In the morning I asked Laurence if he would mind if I went to London for a few weeks to visit Peggy. Of course he thought this peculiar. When he said he would not like it I did not insist. I sent him to Hyères to the bank to cash a check, and when I kissed him goodbye, I wept. I can't imagine why he wasn't suspicious.

We had a very nice, primitive sort of girl staying in the house with us, Clotilde's sister-in-law. She was in love with Laurence and I was always urging him to make love to her, which he did. I hoped that after I left he would marry her, which he didn't. I took her part of the way with me so that she might bring back the car, and I also gave her a talk about Laurence and told her I was leaving him and that I hoped she would look after him. She was shocked and surprised for she had had no idea that was my intention. I kept quiet until the last minute before the train pulled out of St. Raphael, when I left her with a note of farewell for Laurence.

John and Dorothy spent the night in Hyères, and they were still there the next morning when Laurence went to the bank. Dorothy was terrified of Laurence. She thought he was a madman, and when she saw him in the street she made John climb up a water-pipe to hide in their room before Laurence killed him, which she believed Laurence had expressly come to Hyères to do. It was all very humiliating.

# Chapter 5

# My Life with John Holms

When I arrived in Avignon and found John and Dorothy Holms, the first thing I did was to throw away my wedding ring. I was standing on a balcony, and I threw it into the street below.

Though this was a symbolic gesture, I have regretted it ever since. It was such a nice little ring, and I have found myself so often in need of one. Dorothy was very much upset because her leg had become infected escaping over the barbed-wire fence. She still did not know that John was really in love with me, as he had not had the courage to tell her. He always put off everything. We somehow still managed to make love without her suspecting it. But I don't think that would have worried her so much as the fact that we intended to live together.

We wanted to go to London, but Dorothy made me send for my lawyer, who met us in Dijon, which was half-way to Paris. When he saw John and Dorothy he warned me I was jumping from the frying pan into the fire. Unfortunately, he was also Laurence's mother's lawyer, and that caused a lot of trouble as they felt I had stolen a march on them. I only wanted a legal separation, but he talked me into a divorce. I gave him a note for Laurence as the lawyer forbade my writing him. Worst of all he never delivered

this note. He told Laurence of my intentions by phone, for which
Laurence naturally never forgave me. The lawyer sent me home at
once, telling me I had put myself in the worst possible position by
leaving my domicile. After we had been in Dijon for a few days we
left for the South.

The first night we got back we went to fetch Emma Goldman
and Emily Coleman, and we all went to Fréjus for the night to
talk about the divorce. Emma wanted to put in her word with
Laurence so she wrote him a letter that made him furious. She
told him to be big and to give me the children. I was still so afraid
of Laurence that when I went home the lawyer suggested having
me guarded by two thugs, but I declined such protection. When
we broke all this news to Emily, she was rather upset because she
was in love with John herself, and I think that only then did
Dorothy realize what it was all about. Anyhow, I left John and
Dorothy in a hotel in Grimaud and returned home. When I got
there I found Pegeen alone with Doris. Doris told me that
Laurence had gone to Paris with Sindbad and the girl Papi, who
had taken wonderful care of him and had not let him out of her
sight during all those terrible hours when he realized I had run
away.

Laurence and I soon reached a deadlock about the children. I
was willing to let Sindbad live with Laurence and I keep Pegeen,
but I wanted to be guardian of them both. He would not consent
to my being guardian of both of them. In the end he sent down our
mutual friend Peggy, who tried to fix things up. Finally, after
keeping a lawyer waiting for three weeks at St. Tropez, we came
to some agreement, and a document was drawn up to protect
Laurence. His lawyer insisted on it before we filed petition for the
divorce. I wanted very much to live with John Holms, and only if I
renounced him could I have stuck to my point and been guardian
of both children. However, I did not think it fair to take
everything away from Laurence, and also I had no idea how to
bring up a boy. At that time I did not know that John Holms
would be with me for so many years. I also felt compassionate
about Laurence and did not have any idea that he would rearrange
his life as quickly as he did.

The agreement about the children made me guardian of
Pegeen, and Laurence of Sindbad. It was stipulated that I was to
have Sindbad live with me sixty days a year. No condition was

made about Pegeen living with Laurence. The divorce was then filed and asked for on the grounds of desertion of me by Laurence. It had to be brought up in Draguignan, the capital of the Var, the department Pramousquier was in. In three months, we would have to have a *conciliation*. In other words, Laurence and I would have to appear in court together and refuse for the last time to live together again.

Finally, before Christmas, John and I went away together. Dorothy had left for Paris. We motored all over the Bouches-du-Rhône and the Var. It was freezing cold, as only the Midi can be in winter after the sun has set, and I was suffering from sciatica, which I must have contracted in the woods making love with John when we had no other place to go. So the trip was not very successful.

Then we went to London where we did not remain for long. I had to live in Pramousquier, because of the divorce, and I thought I had to hide John, so he spent the winter in the Pardigon Hotel, ten miles away, and I motored over to see him every evening, returning home at four in the morning. Later Laurence told me that Kitty Cannell's sister had reported seeing us together in the hotel, so all my efforts at hiding were useless. In any case this would not have interfered with the divorce once Laurence had agreed to it.

Dorothy had left with the understanding that John and I would try it out for six months. She went to Paris and was unutterably miserable, and secretly hoped that John would come back to her.

In January I had to go to the *conciliation* at Draguignan. The South was covered with snow for the first time in twenty years. Trees were down, and the roads were almost impassable. John, whom I had taught to drive, drove me there. I left him in a café a few miles outside of Draguignan.

It was painful and embarrassing to meet Laurence again. It was the first time I had seen him since I had run away. For his birthday I had knitted him a beautiful sweater and for a divorce present he had sent me a pair of earrings. It was awkward coming face to face with him. He was very bitter, and when we met on the landing of the steps, waiting to be admitted to the judge, Laurence made sarcastic remarks to me.

When we went before the judge I had no idea how to reply to his questions and I kept asking Laurence what to say. I think that prejudiced the judge. He was a Presbyterian schoolmaster and decided that this was only another case of collusion. He could not understand why I was willing to give Sindbad to Laurence. After the *conciliation* Laurence and I had a drink and I wept. Finally I left him and went back to John, who was waiting in the café. He was in a state of anguish because he thought I had decided to return to Laurence.

The divorce actually took another two years to be granted, and then only on the grounds of cruelty. Doris and Peggy and the café-keeper of St. Tropez, all of whom had witnessed the scenes, had to appear in court to prove Laurence's cruelty. For all this I had to pay my lawyer ten thousand dollars (he said he never handled a divorce for less) and two thousand dollars to Laurence's lawyer. It certainly wasn't worth it but I only discovered what it would all come to long after I was in it.

When this was over we were more or less free and were able to start out on our travels. It seems to me that John Holms and I did nothing but travel for two years. We must have gone to at least twenty countries and covered ten million miles of ground. We wanted to go to Vienna. We arrived there on the last train, after all the others were stopped because of the blizzards, and found ourselves the only people in the *wagons-lits*. The Danube was frozen and it was impossible to remain out-of-doors for more than a few minutes at a time. Even then one had to be covered from top to toe. We remained indoors, most of the time in bed. I had never led such a wonderful life before. John opened up a whole new world of the senses to me, a world I had never dreamed of. He loved me because to him I was a real woman. I refused to listen to him talk, and he was delighted that I loved him as a man.

Although in the beginning I refused to listen to him talk and fell asleep at night while he was holding forth to me, little by little I opened my ears, and gradually, during the five years that I lived with him, I began to learn everything I know today. When I first met him I was like a baby in kindergarten, but by degrees he taught me everything and sowed the seeds in me that sprouted after he was no longer there to guide me.

I am sure that during the first two years of our life I was purely interested in making love, but when that lost its intensity I began to concentrate on all the other things that John could give me. I could pick at leisure from this great store of wealth. It never occurred to me that it would suddenly come to an end. He held me in the palm of his hand and from the time I once belonged to him to the day he died he directed my every move, my every thought. He always told me that people never got what they expected from a relationship. I certainly never dreamed of what I was to get from him. In fact, I never knew that anyone like John existed in the world. I don't know what he expected from me, but I don't think he was disappointed. His chief desire was to remold me, and he felt in me the possibilities that he was later to achieve, although he admitted that he got many other things he did not expect.

When I first met John, not only was I ignorant of all human motives, but, worst of all, completely ignorant of myself. I lived in a repressed, unconscious world. In five years he taught me what life was all about. He interpreted my dreams and analyzed me and made me realize that I was good and evil, and made me overcome the evil.

John not only loved women: he understood them. He knew what they felt. He always said, "Poor women," as though he meant they deserved extra pity for being born of the wrong sex. He was so conscious of everybody's thoughts that it was painful for him to be in a room with discordant elements. Therefore he was supremely careful whom he chose to invite together. He had a wonderful gift of bringing out people's best qualities. He spent most of his time reading, and his criticism was of a quality that I had never before encountered. He was a great help to his writer friends, who accepted his opinions and criticisms without reserve. He never took anything for granted. He saw the underlying meanings of everything. He knew why everybody wrote as they did, made the kind of films they made or painted the kind of pictures they painted. To be in his company was equivalent to living in sort of undreamed of fifth dimension. It had never occurred to me that the things he thought about existed. He was the only person I have ever met who could give me a satisfactory reply to any question. He never said, "I don't know." He always did know. Since no one else shared his extraordinary mental capacity, he was exceedingly bored when talking to most people. As a result, he was very lonely. He knew what gifts he had and felt wicked for not using them. Not being able to write, he was unhappy, which caused him to drink more and more. All the time that I was with him I was shocked by his paralysis of will power.

It seemed to grow steadily, and in the end he could hardly force himself to do the simplest things.

When I first met John he dressed badly. He wore his beard much too long, and had a broken front tooth from diving into a rock. After I had succeeded in arousing his vanity he remedied all these things by degrees and began to look quite different. In the beginning I cut his hair for him but later I forced him to go regularly to the barber, which for him was an ordeal. In London he bought some English clothes. He was always at his best in gray flannel trousers with a tweed jacket. He never wore a hat but always had a scarf of some sort which he perpetually left behind in bars when he was tight.

After we had spent six days in deserted Vienna, where all the restaurants were empty and where everyone was dying without coal, we went on to Berlin. Berlin was horrible, like what I imagine Chicago must have been at that time. I walked all over the city and saw nothing to justify my curiosity. We went to the opera and to some night clubs full of gay boys, but it was all very dreary. I was delighted to get home again.

Soon after this we went to Corsica in a new Citroën we had bought, and made a complete tour of the island. John said the scenery reminded him of Donegal in Ireland, where he had spent his childhood. It rained most of the time, but what a beautiful, rugged and savage country it was. The food was not good and the hotels were bad, with the exception of a few English chi-chi places which had been built in the last few years. The land skirting the sea was rather like Italy. It was rarely flat and the roads were very winding where the sea had made deep inlets. We saw Napoleon's birthplace, and the home of the original anise from which Pernod is made.

After we got back John had to pay his yearly visit to his family. Of course he could not take me with him, and although his family thought he was married to Dorothy, she had never been to see them either. Actually, he had always put off legalizing his union with her, and after living with her so long there seemed to be no hurry to go through all the red tape of getting married. Only an extreme crisis could have made him take this step.

When he came back from England I met him in Marseilles, and we went at once on another trip, this time to the island of Porquerolles. It is one of the three islands opposite the mainland of the country we lived in, and could be reached by sailing-boat from Giens. It was tropical and wild, and reminded me of islands in the Pacific, although I had never seen any. There was one little port, and many swimming beaches, and a primitive hotel set in a jungle. We took many walks and, as we were so happy to be together again, it did not matter much where we were.

It wasn't long before Dorothy began to take our love affair seriously. She had spent six months without John in Paris, and of course she hated me. She went about saying the wildest things, and writing John terrible letters against me. I had only seen her once in the interval, and that was entirely by mistake. When on our way back from London we stopped at Paris. John had told her where he was staying on the Quai Voltaire, but did not have the courage to tell her that I was with him. She arrived early one morning and found us in bed. A dreadful scene took place. She beat my feet and told me I was a wicked woman, and she had to be removed by the *valet de chambre*. I was so ashamed afterward that I left the hotel secretly, and allowed John to announce our departure.

Her hostility only egged me on. I must say I was pleased that she was not really John's wife, for that would have put me in a much worse position. But suddenly, in the spring, she decided John had to marry her because she had resolved to return to England. She claimed everyone had believed for years that she was Mrs. Holms and she would be in a false light if people found out she wasn't, especially since she felt like a deserted wife. John said he did not want to marry her. Naturally he would rather marry me if he married anybody, but I was still in the throes of divorce. Finally, she was so unhappy and became so insistent that John went up to Paris and married her.

I was looking after Pegeen at this time for Doris was on her yearly holiday. Pegeen was very much attached to Doris, and became even more so after the divorce, as she felt quite lost and insecure in all the confusion. When she was left alone with me for a month she clung to me like ivy to the oak and would not let me out of her sight. She was the most beautiful thing I have ever seen at this age. Her hair was platinum blond, and her skin was like fresh fruit. She was still under four years of age, and living under these uncertain conditions upset her considerably. She liked John very much, but was surprised to meet him again. It was the first time she had seen him since he had been forced to leave Pramousquier. Pegeen never showed any signs of jealousy toward John; she just never wanted me to be out of her sight, and when once I tried to leave her in Paris for a few days with Peggy and her children, who were Pegeen's friends, she went on strike and I had to take her with me. She felt abandoned and frightened.

Peggy introduced us to Jed Harris in Paris. He wanted to rent our house in Pramousquier, so we went back to put it in order for him. He came down and stayed at Mme Octobon's at Le Canadel and appeared every day making new demands, as he did not think he would be sufficiently comfortable. We put in mosquito-screens for him and painted a room and did various other things to please him. Finally he lost his courage and ran away, sending me a check for five thousand francs indemnity. It was most generous, and later I rented the house to an American princess called Murat, who appreciated my home more than Jed Harris had.

In Paris I saw Sindbad for the first time since the breakup. It was a painful experience and released all the suppressed agony I felt over losing him. Sindbad was then living with his grandmother, but Laurence would not let me see him alone so we all went together to some park. The meeting was unnatural with Laurence present as a spy. Sindbad wore a little white sailor-suit with long trousers and seemed very strange. Although I never actually lost him, I imagine I came pretty near it. Laurence did everything in his power during those first years to separate me from my child. Laurence's behavior was caused partly by revenge and partly through fear that I would take Sindbad back. The divorce had not yet been granted, and the settlement that his lawyer had made was not really valid until it was incorporated in the divorce papers. Though I did not know it at the time, Laurence was living with a woman called Kay Boyle whom he had allowed to take him in hand during his great misery and she was already giving him a child.

Kay and Laurence did everything they could to separate me from Sindbad. Fortunately they never succeeded, because the bond between Sindbad and me was too strong for anyone to break. Laurence was always threatening to take him away, and once he even suggested going to live in Russia. Finally John intervened and made me write the kind of letters to Laurence that would give him confidence in me, and he finally abandoned his suspicions that I was trying to get the child away from him. He more or less came to terms with me. But he never allowed me to have Sindbad for more than sixty days a year to the minute that the letter of the law allowed. The first years of my life with John were completely poisoned, as I was extremely miserable without Sindbad, whom I adored. My only consolation was that Kay was a very good stepmother.

We decided to make an extensive tour of northern Europe in our new Citroën car. There was just room for Pegeen, Doris and my dog Lola. I went south to settle the house, which had been rented for the summer, and to fetch Doris and Pegeen. It was awkward breaking the news to Doris about John. However, if she had any scruples about my living in sin the thought of a trip to Norway and Sweden must have consoled her. We drove up to Paris to pick up John who had been in London for a few days. Then we started on our grand tour.

We motored all through Belgium and Holland, cut through Germany, crossed the Kiel Canal and went to Hamburg. One of my strongest recollections of this part of the trip was my spending a whole day with tears streaming down my cheeks because I had had a terrible dream about my separation from Sindbad; the dream seemed to release all my repressed feelings, and I could no longer control them. By the time we arrived in Sweden, sometime later, I was so upset that I wanted to go back to Laurence. I felt I could no longer endure my life without Sindbad. John said Laurence would not take me back, and that he must have felt great relief (in spite of his first misery) from the fact that the tension which had once existed between us was over.

We went from Germany to Copenhagen, a provincial, dull and Nordic city, and I hated it. I have never been able to get used to the North. It always frightens and chills me. I had felt the same way about Edinburgh years before, although I considered it a beautiful city. Then we went to Oslo, which I liked better than Copenhagen, but I really feel happy only in southern towns, or at least in Latin ones. After Copenhagen we traveled everywhere by boat and took our car with us. It was terrifying to drive it over the two little lopsided planks which were provided for its entrance and exit to boats. Sometimes, the car was picked up in the air by derricks and put on the boat. I once saw a Norwegian pony suffer the same fate, and I felt sorry for it when I saw its legs dangling in midair. Between boats we raced from one ferry to another driving over terrible roads, and perpetually getting out of the car to open and shut gates that enclosed cattle.

It rained every day in Norway and we could barely see the magnificent fjords except for a half-hour a day, between four and four-thirty, when the sun came out like clockwork. We were too late for the midnight sun, but in any case we weren't far enough north to encounter it. We went only as far as Trondheim, which is the most barren town I have ever seen, and certainly as far north as I have ever been.

Lola became pregnant in Trondheim and, since there was barely room for her in the car anyway, her increasing size made life more and more awkward. She and Pegeen shared a sort of bunk, and as Lola got fatter and fatter, Pegeen had to fight for her rights to maintain her place. Twenty minutes before we reached home Lola gave birth to her first puppy in the car, just behind John's neck. We named this offspring Trondjen, which is how we pronounced Trondheim.

We crossed the frontier high up in a part of Sweden that resembled Scotland. It was wild and moorlike, and one could travel hours without seeing a soul. Once we found a lone house with a tree growing out of its roof. We motored for miles through pine forests, with lakes, and as there were no towns anywhere we lost our way in the dark. We finally reached Stockholm at four in the morning. It looked so beautiful in the white night, I was bitterly disappointed when I beheld it in the daylight, all changed. We found the people most amiable and the food wonderful, especially the smorgasbord. Thirty or more dishes spread out for you at every meal! There was plenty of schnapps, but the pubs were open only at certain hours. We had no desire to remain long in this barren country without civilization, so we motored back through Germany just in time to spend a beautiful Indian summer in the Austrian Tyrol in September—what a contrast that was to the gloom of the North; and what a relief to have no more rain. On the way we drove to Weimar and saw Goethe's birthplace, through Thuringia's wonderful forests, and passed several days in Munich. From Munich we went to Bad Reichenhall.

Because of John's chronic mental paralysis, he put off writing to Dorothy all summer, although he carried her manuscript with him everywhere. He was supposed to revise it and return it to her.

I was horrified by what seemed to me to be his callousness, never dreaming how much he himself was suffering from his neglect of her and his inability to do anything about it. Later he told me that he constantly had the feeling that a wolf was tearing at his breast. When we got to Trondheim he finally spent several days on her book and returned it to her. By one of those awful accidents of fate one of the pink feathers from my negligee got into the manuscript while I was reading it. This, when she finally received it, upset Dorothy considerably. She was miserable, for she had hoped that when John married her it meant that he would return to her, but by now she realized this was not the case.

I think one reason John was so attracted to me was because I was just the opposite of Dorothy. I took life rather less seriously and never fussed. I joked about everything and he brought out my unconscious wit; he even enjoyed being a foil for it. I was completely irresponsible and had so much vitality that I am sure I was quite a new experience to him. I was light and Dorothy was heavy. She was always sick and my health was marvelous. Both she and John suffered from insomnia. He would lie awake reading all night while I slept like a baby. Dorothy was dowdy and dressed with no taste. She had piano legs while mine were just the opposite. In fact John named me "Bird Bones." He didn't even mind my strange nose and, in honor of it, called me "Dog Nose." The peculiar thing was that Dorothy and I had the same beautifully shaped cranium and in that one respect we resembled each other.

When we got to Bad Reichenhall in Bavaria, a few miles from the Austrian Tyrol, we decided to remain there for the month of September. John wanted to write an article he had promised to some English paper, but of course he never did it.

The Austrian Tyrol is the country I love most in Europe. I adore the rocky mountains with the trees growing straight up into the air as rigid as telegraph poles. I love the soft-spoken Austrians and the wonderful atmosphere of relaxation they produce. Of course, this was before the Anschluss. Besides the lake that D. H. Lawrence describes in *The Captain's Doll,* there were many others just as beautiful, one with an old monastery in the center. We went to Hitler's future home, Berchtesgaden, without realizing what that name was to mean in a few years, and from there to Salzburg, although we were too late for the music festival. John had lived there at one time and had strange memories of Stefan Zweig whom he had met there.

I think this was one of the happiest times of our life. We had made friends with an Englishman and his Danish wife, and they had a daughter Pegeen's age, so we all had company. Bad Reichenhall itself is a horrid sort of "cure place," where you take baths for your health, but we remained there very little as we were perpetually motoring around the vicinity.

In Munich, we had bought a phonograph and lots of records, and that was the beginning of a real enjoyment of music which John aroused in me. He was horrified by my bad taste. No wonder. In those days I liked Rubinstein's *Melody in F* and Schumann's *Träumerei* better than anything else. Soon he made me appreciate Mozart, Bach, Beethoven, Schubert, Brahms, Haydn, Handel and later Stravinsky and "The Six." After I was once initiated, I sat for hours listening to music, but I always preferred to hear it at home. Occasionally John took me to concerts and to Mozart's operas.

We went back to Pramousquier at the beginning of October, and as I said before, we arrived just twenty minutes too late for Lola, who had already given birth to one puppy in the car. They were very beautiful babies, but the southern climate did not suit them, probably because of their northern heritage, and Trondjen died of distemper.

We soon got restless, and went to Paris to live. At first we had no home other than the Hôtel de Bourgogne et Montana near the Place du Palais Bourbon. I had decided to sell the house at Pramousquier and give Laurence the proceeds, as I really considered it his property, having long since made him a present of the house which was actually in my name. So I sent for all the furniture and divided it with Laurence. My share I placed in storage. I had already given him the Hispano-Suiza, to sell for his divorce expenses.

Laurence was very secretive about his life, but soon I discovered, by chance, that he was a father again. He had had a little daughter and I asked him to let me see her. I felt badly, as I had had an operation performed in a convent by a wonderful Russian doctor called Popoff. The nuns were strict and dirty and had no idea why I was there. However, they tried to take care of me, and on Sunday morning woke me up at six to put a thermometer in my

mouth which they never came back to remove. When I remon-
strated they excused themselves on the grounds of being at prayer.
Dr. Popoff, who was supposed to have been the *accoucheur* of the
Grand Duchesses of Russia, admitted one to this convent for
needing a *curetage,* and then was credited with saying suddenly, in
the middle of the operation: *"Tiens, tiens, cette femme est enceinte."*

When I went south to settle Pramousquier I brought back my
darling dog Lola. She had never lived in a big town before, and the
first morning the maid took her out she got frightened and
escaped. We had wild hopes of recovering her by searching in the
lost dog's home, otherwise known as the *fourière,* and for months
we went there daily. Finally we reduced our visits to two or three
a week. Never have I seen a more heartrending and upsetting
sight. The *fourière* was full of lost creatures who set up the most
horrible howls to attract attention the minute anyone entered.
Every day there were new homeless beasts, but never Lola. The
dogs must have thought we had come to claim them, or rather
they hoped that their masters were about to rescue them. In the
end, we had to give it up. Someone else must have wanted Lola as
much as we did, or they would have brought her back to us
because we placed a touching ad in the *Paris-Midi,* offering a big
reward.

During this period I was slightly more friendly with Laurence,
and he allowed me to see Sindbad every Thursday for the entire
day, but would never let him sleep in my house. Soon after that he
moved to the Marne; I used to meet him half-way, take Sindbad
back to Paris for a short time and bring him back in the evening.
This proved so tiring for the child that I motored down to La
Fierte, where he lived, and tried to find places to go with him. Of
course it didn't work. One day Laurence made a terrible scene
when I brought Sindbad back, so I postponed my visits, expecting
to have the child live with me for part of the summer.

Emily Coleman was in Paris, and we saw her quite often. We
took Sindbad and Johnnie out together on Thursdays, and thus
started a lifelong friendship between the two boys, who were
almost the same age. One night, when we were in a café, I left
Emily and John and went to join Laurence at another table, little
dreaming of the effect it would have on John. It seems he nearly
went off his head, and Emily had to walk him up and down the
street to calm him. The next day she warned me that I was

playing with fire; and for the first time I realized what a passionate person John Holms was underneath his calm exterior.

We had rented a furnished flat with a studio in the Rue Campagne Première and, as it was leased under my married name, John used to be called Vail, which annoyed Laurence considerably. I therefore resumed the name Guggenheim to avoid trouble.

I took John to meet Helen Fleischman and Giorgio Joyce. We saw quite a lot of them and often with his parents, James Joyce and Nora. They lived an intense family life and it surprised John, who was so anti-family, that Giorgio should be so tied up with his parents. Lucia Joyce, Giorgio's sister, was often with them too. She was a sweet girl who was studying dancing. Giorgio had a good bass voice and used to sing for us, frequently with his father, who was a tenor. John enjoyed talking to Joyce but, since he never could have been one of Joyce's sycophants, the relationship was casual. They had both lived in Trieste, and I remember their reminiscing about the Bora wind, Trieste's worst evil. While it blew (and sometimes it lasted for days) ropes were put up in the streets to help people circulate.

Suddenly my mother arrived from America. I hadn't seen her since my separation from Laurence, and although she approved of that, she thought I was mad to give him Sindbad and she never forgave me for it. She had no idea about John, and it was difficult to initiate her. Fortunately, when she arrived Edwin Muir and his wife were in Paris, and when she came to see me she met them at my house. It was a good beginning. She would not believe that I was living with John, and that I wasn't going to marry him. She always called him Mr. Holms and treated him formally. She never liked him; she thought he was a terrible man for having married Dorothy, and because he didn't work. I tried to impress her a little bit by his family. She wrote down in her notebook "Governor of the United Provinces of India." After she had made several inquiries, she came back and told me I was wrong, that his name should have been Lord Reading. However, she had to accept John as she knew I would not see her otherwise. One day when the Muirs were in my house Dorothy came to the door and made a terrible scene saying they had no right to befriend me.

I liked Edwin Muir from the very beginning. He was frail and timid, and so sensitive and pure that you could not do otherwise

than like him. You felt his talents, even though he was shy and
never acclaimed himself. Muir reminded me of a man who has
been asleep in front of a fire too long and could not recover from
his drowsiness. They had had a hard life and had struggled
painfully to keep alive by doing translations. They were almost
better known as the translators of *Jüd Suss* than as anything else.
They had translated Kafka, and thus introduced him to the
English-speaking world. Muir always consulted John before
publishing his own books, and once, when he hadn't, John said
the book was a catastrophe. Muir adored John and after his death,
when I asked him to write something about him, this is what he
sent me. He enlarged on it and used it himself in his own
autobiography, *The Story and the Fable.*

I first met John Holms one Sunday morning in Glasgow in the
summer of 1919. Hugh Kingsmill arrived at my lodgings with him
as I was starting out for a walk in the country: when I opened the
door I heard their English voices echoing up the stairs. Hugh had
to go on to Bridge of Allan, and Holms agreed to come with me. It
was a still, warm day. We wandered about the moorlands to the
south of Glasgow, ate in a little tearoom and returned in the
evening, meeting a two-mile-long line of courting couples as we
approached Glasgow. Holms was in the uniform of a Scottish
regiment, glengarry, khaki tunic and tartan trews. I cannot
remember much about that day except that we had an argument
about Pater, and later discussed the merits of windy and calm
weather: Holms hated bracing winds and I, being then an admirer
of Nietzsche, was in favour of them. As we were returning he
began to quote Donne, whom I did not know at the time, and we
stood leaning against a gate with the scent of hay in our nostrils
while he mildly intoned:

> And while our souls negotiate there,
>     We like sepulchral statues lay,
> All day the same our postures were,
>     And we said nothing, all the day.

Then he recited the opening verse of "The Relic," stopping with
delight at "the last busy day" and the picture of the resurrected
visitor waiting by the lover's grave to make "a little stay." These
lines seemed to be in keeping with the rounded haycocks in the
field and the long line of couples passing like a millennial
procession in the evening light.

The first thing that struck me about Holms was a still watchfulness which set me thinking of the Old Testament, never far from a Scotsman's mind. By the end of the day the watchfulness had turned into a watchful benevolence, which was characteristic of Holms if he liked anyone. The next time we met was in London after my marriage, and I saw a great deal of him later in Dresden, Forte dei Marmi and the south of France, where we both chanced to be living; and afterwards in London.

Holms gave me a greater feeling of genius than any other man I have met, and I think he must have been one of the most remarkable men of his time, or indeed of any time. There was a strange contrast between his instinctive certainty and grace as a physical being, and the painful creaking of his will. In his movements he was like a powerful cat: he loved to climb trees or anything that could be climbed, and he had all sorts of odd accomplishments: he could scuttle on all fours at a great speed without bending his knees: walking bored him. He had the immobility of a cat too, and could sit for a long time without stirring; but then he seemed to be filled with a boundless dejection; it was as if he were a captive imprisoned far within himself, beyond rescue. His body seemed to fit him for every enjoyment, and his will for every suffering. He had constantly the struggle which Wordsworth noted in Coleridge: "the amazing effort which it was to him to will anything was indescribable." The act of writing was itself an enormous obstacle to him, although his one ambition was to be a writer. His knowledge of his weakness, and his fear that in spite of his gifts, which he never doubted, he would not succeed in producing anything, intensified his stationary combat and reduced him to shaking impotence. He was persecuted by dreadful dreams and nightmares.

His mind had a majestic clarity and order, and when turned on anything was like a spell which made objects assume their true shape and appear as they were, in their original relation to one another, as on the day of creation. He once had the idea of writing a poem describing the evolution of the species, pictorially, showing all the various animal forms developing from an archetype by an enormous foreshortening of time; and his talk often gave the same impression. It had no surface brilliance; it was awkward; he often seemed unable to finish a sentence: the same obstacle which kept him from writing kept him from talking as he might have talked. What made his talk unique was its reality, the fact that it was never trite and never secondhand, but always concerned with real things. He could be amusing, and he loved witty conversation, but this was his distinguishing quality. His benevolence came out very strongly in his talk: it was as if were looking at things with a fraternal eye and helping them to find themselves. But he had a keen enjoyment of the second-rate too, I remember him reciting T.E. Brown's poem:

> A garden is a lovesome thing, God wot,

with sardonic gusto, his voice rising with a pained incredulity in the line,

> Not *God*, in GARDENS, when the eve is COOL?

to assume a fine gentlemanly condescension in

> Nay, but I have a *sign*.
> 'Tis very sure He walks in *mine*.

Like Hugh Kingsmill I always had a strong sense of his goodness, although he was not good by his own standards. He gave me more strongly than anyone else I have known, a feeling of the reality of goodness as a simple almost concrete thing. Sometimes he seemed to breathe a goodness so natural and original that one felt the Fall had not happened yet, and the world was still waiting for the coming of evil. These 'good' times always brought with them a feeling of abundance, of fat herds, rich fields, full streams, endless food and drink, and all things gladly following the law of their nature. He had the capacity for simple enjoyment which Yeats says goes with goodness,

> Except by an evil chance,

a line which would have made him smile. He had an equally strong sense of evil, and a profound conviction of sin; but he had no trace of Puritanism, and I think his guilt came finally from his feeling that he was an immortal soul caught in the snares of the world, and both liking and loathing the bondage. His inability to express what was in him may have been partly due to the intensity of this feeling, but that in turn greatly deepened his sense of guilt, which grew with his failure to write.

In the spring, John and I motored all through Brittany with Pegeen and the maid, Doris being on her yearly holiday. It either rained all the time, or seemed to, for the country was covered with mist. We never saw the sun. Brittany had a certain ferocity and wild beauty with its savage cliffs and red earth. There were many pleasant beaches, but without sun they were forbidding. We saw wonderful old Celtic churches and passed on the roadside many early sculptures of Christ. These *calvaires* were unpretentious and astoundingly beautiful.

We wanted to rent a house for the summer but after looking for one in every corner of the peninsula, we gave up the idea. We had not found the ideal spot. John would never make a compromise about where he lived. He would spend months looking for a place that he would only be living in for a short period. We usually wasted half of the summer in search of a residence, but he always ended by finding the perfect place. After Brittany we went all over Normandy and then gave up the idea of living there also. Finally, in desperation, I suggested we go down to the Basque country to St. Jean de Luz where Helen and Giorgio Joyce were spending the summer. As we were leaving, Emily showed up and we took her with us as far as Poitiers. We drove through the Loire country, and visited all the châteaux again. We had exquisite meals and wonderful wine—John was a gourmet and connoisseur of vintages—in all the provincial towns we drove through. We always did ourselves well.

When we arrived in St. Jean de Luz, we again began looking at houses. Helen and Giorgio lived in the center of town and wanted us near them, but of course John rebelled. Finally he found the most beautiful house, a few miles away from St. Jean de Luz out in the country at the foot of the Pyrenees. It was situated high on a hill and was completely isolated. It was called Bettiri Baita and belonged to a painter called Monsieur de Bonnechose, who was the tallest man I have even seen. Even John looked like a dwarf next to him. He himself had built this house out of stone that had been found on the premises. M. de Bonnechose really wanted to sell the house and all the land, but he rented it to us for a minute sum. We spent the most wonderful summer, when we finally got around to it.

At last I was to have Sindbad stay with me for a fortnight. Laurence suggested that he come and live nearby during this visit; I think he was still afraid I was going to run away with Sindbad. In order to allay his fears, I said he could have Pegeen as a hostage, provided Doris went with her. When he consented, we crossed southern France by train to Sainte-Maxime, where we exchanged children. Laurence was then living at Cavalaire near Pramousquier. The exchange was effected and I took Sindbad to

Emma Goldman's house for the day and then home with me.
Laurence had filled him with the most extraordinary stories and
had warned him not to let me run away with him. Sindbad told me
that he had come to visit me because Laurence said that if he
didn't I could send the police after him. Evidently he had also
promised Laurence he would not set foot in Spain (we lived only a
few miles away) for he refused to walk on a bridge which
connected the frontiers. When we visited some underground
grottoes that were partially under Spanish soil, Sindbad insisted
on coming out. We went on a little trip up to Gavarnie and walked
on a glacier and drove around the Pyrenees. Emily was with us
and that made things easier. I sat behind in the rumble seat of the
car with Sindbad and by degrees renewed my acquaintance with
him. I resumed telling him the exciting stories I had always
invented for him. He adored them.

John was a wonderful athlete. When he was drunk he used to
climb chimney stacks and walls of houses with the agility of a cat.
He could dive from terrific heights like a bird and he swam like a
fish. He was also a fine tennis player and because of his height he
was expert at the net. His whole body was so agile and elastic that
he could do anything with it. He climbed rocks like a mountain
goat and used to make the most dangerous trips along the coast. I
was terrified of rock climbing, and Emily went with him instead.
He also took Sindbad, and they became very good friends after
Sindbad thawed out. When the fortnight was over I had to take
him back to Laurence. It was agonizing to be without him again,
especially since I wasn't to see him until Christmas.

After I returned with Pegeen and Doris, John took Emily and
me on a little trip to Spain, high up in the Pyrenees. We lived
practically on the border and the country was filled with
smugglers who brought back fire water and cigars on foot and hid
them in the bushes around our house. We drove to Pamplona, the
city Hemingway had immortalized in *The Sun Also Rises*. I was so
miserable at being separated from Sindbad again that this trip did
not make much of an impression on me. All I remember is seeing
the bulls being driven through the town into the corrals.

Emily and John always spent hours discussing literary matters.
I used to leave them and go to bed early. All day I retired into my
shell and read Dreiser's *An American Tragedy*. Once I had a dream
that I walked into the bathroom and found Emily and John in the

bathtub reading poetry. I both loved and hated having Emily with us. She had so much life that, in spite of my jealousy, I always sent for her when I got bored. She was determined to squeeze every drop of knowledge she could from John and was at him all the time. Once, when she was angry with him, she burst out in a fury, saying, "I wish I would never see you again." I was sitting calmly writing to Sindbad and I replied nonchalantly, "It could be arranged," but of course it never was, and our lives got more and more tied up. Emily was always staying with us or going on trips with us. She was like our child. She was passionately interested in writing and she used to send John pages and pages of her poems when she was not with us. Sometimes he groaned and moaned in despair; sometimes he thought they were good.

During this summer my divorce was finally granted, after two years.

In the fall we went back to Paris and lived in the Royal Condé Hôtel, near the Odéon. We began hunting madly for a house, and John as usual refused to live in anything we found. At the last minute, while I was trying to bully him into a very nice apartment that he didn't want, he found the ideal house. It might have been built for us, it was so perfect in every respect. Georges Braque, the painter, had built it for himself. It was like a little skyscraper with one or two rooms on each of its five floors. It was in a working class quarter, way out of the center of Paris, on the Avenue Reille, almost at the Porte d'Orléans; but opposite us was the reservoir and behind us was a garden. Our neighbors were artists. On one side Amédée Ozefant had his school of painting. The view from the top floor was miraculous for Paris. In front of us stretched a whole field of grass which grew on the reservoir. In summer, the haycocks were neatly piled, we thought we were living away from the city. On the roof we had a terrace and a little pool, which we did not discover until years later when we lent Gabrielle Picabia the house and she unearthed it. We slept on the top floor, and it was like a nest in the tree-tops. John had a study here too. It was cold and uncomfortable and certainly the last place he would ever have worked in, even if he had been able to write, as it overlooked the reservoir. On the next floor below we had one room the whole depth of the house, which served as library, living room, dining room and guest room when necessary; also as a music room, where we played the phonograph all day. In the second year we bought an English handmade gramophone with an enormous papier maché horn. This room was like a large studio. It had windows front and back that reached to the ceiling. Underneath, Pegeen and Doris had a floor to themselves with two rooms, and below that was the kitchen and cook's room, and on the street floor was the garage, where we kept our Peugeot.

We lived in this house three years, but of course we always went on trips and never seemed to be stuck there. Before we had rented it we had signed a lease for three small apartments in an enormous building not far from the Avenue d'Orléans. It was built for artists, and each flat had a studio. The whole place was cheaply constructed and consequently the walls were thin. John, who could not bear any noise, insisted on having cork walls put into his apartments. This building was owned by a company that went broke, and it took years before they completed it. By that time we were living in our skyscraper house. We tried to recover all the money we had put into that place, but the French are good at holding on to anything they actually have in hand. Our lawyer was unsuccessful in recovering any part of the two thousand dollars we had invested in advance for rent, alterations, etc. But little did I dream what service I was rendering a future husband. When years later I met the tenant who eventually occupied the flat he told me that a mad American woman had much improved his studio by inserting cork walls like those which Proust had. (That tenant was Max Ernst.)

John drove me to Antwerp to visit Emily, in a new Delage we had just bought. These were the last six months she was to spend with her husband, who was manager of an advertising agency. It was the worst possible time of the year to go north, and the whole trip was made through fog. We did not remain long, and the best thing we did was to hear Mozart's opera, *Don Giovanni*, sung in Flemish. It was heavenly. On the way back I stuffed the car with Belgian-made Player cigarettes, for they were so much cheaper than in France. At the frontier the car was searched and the cigarettes dragged out from all their hiding places. Every time the customs official asked if there were others I insisted that he had found them all. It became more and more embarrassing as he kept finding new ones. At last he found all and fined us heavily, saying that he could confiscate the car, but would not go to such limits.

He took every cent we had and all the cigarettes, and we had to drive home penniless.

During this winter we saw quite a lot of Harold Loeb, my cousin, formerly editor of *Broom* magazine. Both he and John were very fond of Jean Gorman whose husband, Herbert Gorman, was writing a book on James Joyce. Gorman used to bring out of his pocket the most insulting replies from people he had written letters to about Joyce. But Gorman was so delighted with the letters that he did not seem to realize how insulting they were to him.

John never wanted to go to bed. He liked to sit up conversing and drinking very late. Evidently Jean Gorman, whom we saw nearly every day, complained to James Joyce because she brought us this little poem he had written for her about us:

> To Mrs. Herbert Gorman who complains that her visitors kept late hours:
>
> Go ca'canny with the cognac and of the wine fight shy
> Keep a watch upon the hourglass but leave the beaker dry
> Guest friendliness to callers is your surest thief of time
> They're so much at Holms when with you, they can't dream of
>     Guggenheim.

I was quite jealous of Jean Gorman; John liked her so much. I liked her too; she was a vital, proud little thing. She looked like a lizard. She was unhappy with her husband, and although she was breaking up with him, she had the pride and character to maintain a deep silence about her affairs, even when drinking. Finally she left for America, got her divorce and married Carl Van Doren.

At this time Pegeen was in Marie Jolas' bilingual day school in Neuilly and was very happy. Doris drove her there every morning in a new little Peugeot car I had bought to run around Paris in, and either Doris or John and I went to fetch her every evening. That was about the only hour I saw her for she was already in school by the time we woke up.

John got up late as he slept so badly. He read most of the day and went out every night to night clubs in Montmartre or to cafés in Montparnasse or to friends' houses, or we had people at home.

John always liked society after six in the evening, so when Pegeen went down to have her supper and go to bed, we usually went out in search of people. Sometimes we brought home for dinner lots of unexpected guests for whom there always seemed to be enough food. We had a marvelous cook. If John stayed out very late, which he often did, I got so bored I went home without him. I hardly ever drank in those days and I could not keep up with him. Sometimes he spent the whole day in bed with a hangover and got up only for the evening. This used to make me extremely angry because I felt cheated of his company. He never wanted me to leave him, and was just as unhappy without me as I was without him. He was extremely dependent on me and never wanted me out of his sight.

In May we took Mary Reynolds with us and went to Italy, first to Florence and then to Assisi where Emily was spending a few months for her health. John wanted to go to the Abruzzi, a part of Italy I had never visited. We drove down the Adriatic coast which was different from the other coast of Italy that I knew so well. John drove the Delage as if it were an airplane. I always felt we were in the air, not on the earth.

Going over a high mountain pass to Aquila we struck a blizzard, though it was in May, and the wires of the car froze. We had stopped on a very slippery road covered with snow to see the scenery a few feet before the peak. On our right was a drop of thousands of feet. John insisted before we died of the cold we turn the car around and go back. We could start it by rolling downhill, but the danger of pushing it over the cliff while we turned it around was terrifying. We had to calculate it to an inch, and it was almost impossible because the car kept slipping on the ice. I really don't know how we ever did it; it must have been the fear of dying in the cold that egged us on.

Emily, who was with us, refused to help in any way; she disliked the blizzard, and she just sat in the Delage while Mary and John and I, by sheer force of will, managed to get it turned around without its going over the side. John put his scarf under the front wheel to stop it from skidding and then we rocked the car back and forth, fearing any moment it might fall over the precipice. Even this did not make Emily budge. We pushed and pulled and made tracks in the snow for the wheels to be free. Finally we got to an inn at Norcia in the valley below where we

were treated regally. It was the most primitive place I had ever
been in. A whole baby goat was brought on the table for us and
gallons of Abruzzi wine. Our beds were warmed with copper
warming pans. The innkeepers were so sweet to us that we were
happy we had not perished in the blizzard. We were thrilled to be
in the country of D. H. Lawrence's *Lost Girl.* John and I were
great admirers of Lawrence's books.

We left Emily in Assisi and went to Venice. For the first time
since I had been with John he let me down—he did not share my
passion for this miracle city. I got up early and walked miles alone
every· morning before he awoke. He complained about it all
afternoon and made me so unhappy that finally I decided to leave.
I think it is the feeling of death that permeates Venice which
upset him. I can't explain in any other way his taking a dislike to a
place that has so much beauty to offer in every form and from so
many ages. We drove down the Brenta and saw the strange
summer palaces of the Venetian nobles, so varying in type but all
built within a hundred years of each other.

In June we began again to travel all over France to find a house
for the summer. My relations with Laurence had reached a more
friendly state, and Sindbad came to me regularly Christmas and
Easter and for one month in the summer. Pegeen went to
Laurence for an equal length of time. This made things easier.
We took a beautiful trip through the part of France that lies
between Marseilles and the Spanish frontier. It resembled the
country of the Var, but was even wilder and covered with
grapevines. The few small towns, Port-Vendres, Banyuls, Cer-
bère, were filled with artists, and the life there must have been
much like that of St. Tropez. After that we paid a visit to our
friends, the Neagoes, at Mirmande, in the Drôme near Valence.
They had bought three old houses in the one-street village and
lived a peaceful life, he writing and she painting, in this strange
medieval town perched high up on a hill with its ancient
crumbling structures. John did not want to leave but I egged him
on as I was anxious to find a home for Sindbad, whose visit I was
so much looking forward to. We went next to the Haute-Savoie
and looked all around the Lac d'Annecy, but ended up in Paris,
where fortunately we were able to contact M. de Bonnechose and
rented his house again.

This year the Joyces, Helen and Giorgio, were not at St. Jean de Luz. They had been married in the spring and had gone off with his parents, James and Nora Joyce, to the north for the summer. We missed them and our wonderful tennis parties. Emily joined us for part of the summer bringing with her an unpleasant little Italian who had followed us each separately around the streets of Assisi, even into the church, while we gazed at Giotto's masterpieces. He was so unbelievably unattractive and uninteresting in every way that John was horrified and began to work on Emily to disillusion her. It took many months. I said that at least I might as well benefit by his presence and use the occasion to refresh my Italian, since he could not speak French or English. That saved John a lot of unnecessary conversation. He could not speak Italian.

During this visit of Sindbad's he and Pegeen began fighting like cat and dog. I think there was a terrible jealousy between them because of the divorce. The first few days of Sindbad's stay were always rather a strain because he came from Laurence and Kay full of hatred for John. Sindbad used to say we led such easy rich lives while Laurence and Kay had to work hard. Kay was a second-rate novelist, but not quite bad enough in those days to make the large sums of money she did later, when she frankly became a pot-boiler writer. They did translations. I gave Laurence and Kay a large income, which they kept secret, and Sindbad could not believe it when finally, after years of my being taunted, Djuna came to my rescue and told him the facts. Sindbad really was fond of John, who was marvelous with children and fed them spiritually and mentally, as well as taking them rock climbing, swimming and playing rough-house games with them.

One day John drove Emily, her Italian and me to Spain for the weekend. We were so excited by the country we remained ten days with no other clothes except what we were wearing. For the first time in my life I went to bullfights and became more and more fascinated. We saw every type of bullfight, from little intimate country ones to Madrid's best. After I was satisfied that I had witnessed every variety, my curiosity died out and I never saw another one until fourteen years later, in Portugal. My most vivid memory of this trip was the desert we drove through from Burgos to Madrid, for every time the road curved we found ourselves in a different scene. The variety was unending, and the road was

excellent. It had been built by King Alphonso for his personal
benefit. In Madrid we met Jay Allen, an old friend of Emily's.
They had worked together on the Chicago *Tribune* in Paris.

Once when the car broke down, John tried to explain, in a few
broken words of Spanish, to a mechanic what was wrong with it.
The mechanic politely told John not to exert himself so much,
because the engine spoke much better Castilian than John did. At
Avila, where we arrived at four in the morning, we found sheep
grazing on the cathedral lawns, and at Toledo we spent the whole
day searching for El Greco's painting of that city, not knowing it
was in the Metropolitan Museum in New York.

We had to put up with Emily's Italian friend all winter, and
finally one day she sent for John and told him that it was all over. I
was greatly relieved and could now come out with a few of the
things I had been repressing. In fact, I was so nasty about him
that she finally gave me a black eye, and had even worse
intentions, but John saved me by removing her. She was in a
dangerous state. Of course my mother thought that John had
given me the black eye. I did not see Emily again for many months
as I really was annoyed with her.

At Easter time I had arranged to fetch Sindbad and take him
somewhere in the south for ten days. Laurence and Kay were then
living in Nice and were on the verge of getting married. For some
morbid reason Laurence decided he would like to have John and
me attend this ceremony and the wedding party that was to follow.
He therefore forced our hand by choosing for the great event the
week we arrived in Nice. We did not want to go to the wedding,
but we had to, so as not to offend the children. Emily and her son
were with us and we all drove from Le Rayol, where we were
staying, to Nice. It gave the impression to the outside world that
we were all excessively friendly.

Peter Neagoe, who always called me "Lady Peggy," had come
down especially for the wedding, and he asked us to drive him
back to Paris with us. We were delighted, except for the lack of
space. We had Sindbad, Pegeen and Johnnie Coleman as well as
Emily and innumerable suitcases. I don't know how we all got
crammed into the Delage. Only John was comfortable—he was in
the driver's seat. To make matters worse, Peter said we had to go
to Mirmande to fetch some mysterious packages that he had to

take to his wife. After Mirmande one of these packages suddenly flew out of the car. We were forced to stop and retrieve what turned out to be his wife's corsets.

After we got back to Paris we went to London for a few days, and suddenly John got the idea that it would be nice to remain in England all summer. He hadn't lived there for years, and he felt it would be the ideal place to find a country house to live in for several months. We rented a car and drove all through Dorset, Devonshire and Cornwall. We were tempted by Dorset, but of course John would not make up his mind about any of the houses we had seen. Only after we got back to Paris did he consent to write to the owner of a magnificent place we had found on the edge of Dartmoor. We took this house for two months.

The children were with Laurence in Austria. I flew to Zurich, which was half-way, to meet them, and brought them back to Paris. Of all the trips I had ever made in a plane, this was by far the most beautiful. We flew over the eastern part of France which is dotted with farmlands of every color, and then over the Jura.

After I had collected the children, we started out for England in both our cars with Djuna Barnes, our cook, the maid and Doris, who drove the Peugeot. We took a night boat from Le Havre and in the morning landed at Southampton. From there we drove down to Devonshire.

# Chapter 6

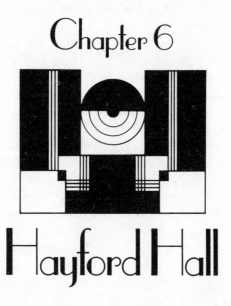

# Hayford Hall

The house we had rented was called Hayford Hall. It was a spacious, simply built, graystone structure about a hundred years old. The rooms centered around a large hall with a fireplace. This hall was well proportioned, but its paneling was of an ugly new-looking wood and its furniture, though comfortable, was not attractive. The walls were covered with the usual ancestral portraits, shipbuilders from the Clyde. At the end of this room was a big cathedral-like window. All one could see through it were vast trees that kept out the sun. Apart from the eleven bedrooms, we never used any of the other rooms, except a very dreary dining room, in which we ate our meals, adjourning immediately after to the hall. I am sure so much conversation was never made in this hall before or since.

The children had their own wing which consisted of several bedrooms and a large schoolroom downstairs where Doris reigned supreme. This was an ideal arrangement, but I was torn between the brilliant conversation in the hall and my children's company. They ate lunch with us and they rode with us and swam with us and played tennis with us, but they were not admitted to the hall except on rare occasions. The bedrooms were simple and adequate, except for the beds which were as hard as army cots. One bedroom, however, was rather dressed up in rococo style, and it looked so much like Djuna that we gave it to her. It was in this room, in bed, that she wrote most of *Nightwood*. Later she did not agree, and said we gave her this room because nobody wanted it.

We never used the respectable-looking sitting room armed with chintz-covered furniture, or the little writing room supplied with a library of the world's worst books, a fox's brush and an elephant's foot waste-paper basket. The house, one may gather, was not the main attraction. It was the situation and the surroundings that were beautiful beyond belief. Hayford Hall's back door gave out on to Dartmoor. Its front entrance was approached by a driveway of monkey-puzzle trees. In the early morning we were awakened by rooks, who inhabited a tree outside our window.

Although situated on the edge of Dartmoor, Hayford Hall had its own vast gardens which were half cultivated and half wild. There was one garden, a quarter of a mile long, with herbaceous borders. There were beautiful lawns, a well kept grass tennis-court and two ponds covered with lilies where we swam, but on the whole one had the impression nature had not been tampered with, and that this place was still part of the moor. At nightfall thousands of rabbits scurried over the grounds in all directions. We also had some woodland with a stream going through it; and another stream ran by the house.

The moor is hard to describe; it was so varied and so vast. It was hundreds of miles square and completely uninhabited except by wild ponies. The ground was strewn with bones and skeletons. The only plants that grew were bracken and heather. In the parts that were swamps, as if to warn one, there grew a little feathery white flower. The moor was covered with streams and enormous boulders. It was hilly but there were magnificent stretches for riding. Far on the other side was Dartmoor prison, but it was so far away that it meant a whole day's riding to get there and back. The wild ponies were rounded up once a year and tamed. We rented them for rides and though they were ridiculously inadequate, the children learned to ride them in a paddock. After a few weeks we took them on the moors. We had one real horse. When the ponies bolted after throwing the children, this horse, generally ridden by John, went in chase of the ponies.

The ponies belonged to a one-armed epileptic, who was sweet and patient with the children. He never tired or complained, and brought us as many as eight ponies at a time. Their bridles and saddles were forever slipping off or breaking, and it was impossible to get one's stirrups even. I remember one saddle whose girths would not hold, and I ended up by slipping more and more forward until I found myself on my pony's neck. The first year we had no serious accident. The second year was fatal, but that will come later.

Of course Emily spent the summer with us and she was always trying to get the best horse (there was really only one good one). It was called Katie and was a hunter. The other pathetic creatures were called Starlight, Mollie, Trixie, Polly, Ronie, etc.

One day Sindbad was thrown by Starlight, the children's favorite. He stood in the middle of the paddock crying, "Starlight, Starlight, come back!" But Starlight ran away and had to be chased for hours before he was caught. The great danger was the swamps, and we were generally guided by our one-armed groom who knew all the tracks over the moors. But often we left him with the children and went off with John, sometimes galloping for miles, getting lost, and escaping bogs by the skin of our teeth. Once John rode into a bog. Emily and I screamed at him to get off his horse, and he did so, just in time to pull the animal out.

Our life at Hayford Hall was completely cut off from the world. Apart from the visitors who came we saw nobody. Djuna and Emily and Emily's son were with us all the time, and we asked other friends down for the week-ends.

Emily's father, a puritanical gentleman from New England, came the first summer. Of course, he thought I was married to John and called me Mrs. Holms, as did the two maids who were left in the house to guard it, in case we turned out to be barbarians. Emily's father was fascinated by our life and especially by John. He told Emily that he thought John was a superman who lived in another world. Emily's father was terrified by Djuna. She called him Papa, which he didn't like.

Emily's father was shocked by his daughter's behavior, as she was greedy at table, and made scenes if she were not allowed to ride Katie, which was really John's horse. Emily said one day, after her father had scolded her about her table manners, "I don't want to be a pig." I replied, "What are you going to do instead?"

Djuna was annoyed because Emily tried to monopolize John and wanted to talk to him by the hour. They used to sit up until the early hours of the morning, John drinking but not Emily. She seldom drank. She did not have to; in fact she was overstimulated all the time. Djuna once told her she would be marvelous company slightly stunned.

Milton Waldman came down for a few days. He was having a nervous breakdown and, although he was greatly impressed by Hayford Hall, I doubt that he enjoyed it. My mother came but would never stay in my house, because I was not married to John. She was surprised when she saw in what style we were living, as she considered me a wild Bohemian on the edge of the gutter. William Gerhardi came with Vera Boyse. Antonia White and her husband, Tom Hopkinson. All these people made life amusing, but we really had a better time when we were alone with our little foursome, even if we fought and it all got intense. We somehow spurred each other on. We liked to insult each other. Once John asked Sindbad to fetch a pair of scissors. Sindbad was busy and refused. John was indignant. He said, "That boy is ten years old and can't even fetch a pair of scissors." I replied, "You are thirty-five and you can't fetch anything." When I was complaining that John never wrote, he said to Emily, "Peggy would like to be the wife of Stravinsky." I replied, "Which one?" Once Djuna said to John, "Why, I wouldn't touch you with a ten-foot pole." I replied for him that he could easily touch *her* with one, a gentle compliment meant for John, not Djuna. One night Djuna appeared looking quite different. She had just washed her hair. I called her "cutie redcock." Later I fell asleep, as was my habit when fatigued by Emily's conversations with John, and when I woke up, John was playing with Djuna's soft fluffy hair. I looked at them and said to John, "If you rise, the dollar will fall." Djuna said to John, "You smug little red melon of a Shakespeare. Busy old fool, unruly son."

Djuna was writing *Nightwood*. She stayed indoors all day, except for ten minutes when she went for a daily walk in the rose garden and brought me back a rose. Emily had threatened to burn *Nightwood* if Djuna repeated something Emily had confided to her by mistake. As a result Djuna was afraid to leave the house. She felt it necessary to guard her manuscript. She had no suitable clothes for the country, but in the evening she wore one of two very beautiful French gowns. Emily always wore a dirty sweater. She even rode in it. I usually wore riding pants and so did John. He looked handsome in them.

All our food came from Buckfastleigh, a little town miles below, where an abbey was being built. Doris drove down to shop every day with Marie, our French cook. On Thursdays she took Marie and Madeleine, the maid, to the coast for their day off. We were about twenty miles from Torquay, a gay seaside resort. On Thursdays we ate steak and kidney pie and cottage pie cooked by the English maid, who had been left there to oversee us.

John often drove us down to the sea and discovered wild coves where we could bathe in peace and quiet. We also went to local horse races, where our ponies were entered, so you can imagine what kind of racing was involved. It was all very crooked anyhow. We soon learned that the winners were controlled by the local butcher.

At the end of the summer Djuna took Sindbad back to Paris, where he met Laurence. She wrote me they met in a clinching embrace. We let Pegeen and Doris go to visit Peggy and her children, and we went to Bath and Glastonbury cathedral and through Somerset with Emily and her father. After they left us, we went to Cheltenham where John was to visit his family. Of course I could not meet them as we were not married, but his sister came to the hotel to see me. She must have been shocked by the whole affair because she had heard such wild tales from Dorothy about me. John tried to impress her with our domestic life, led with the children at Hayford Hall, so that she would realize how different it all was from what she imagined. When she said goodbye she told me to look after John. I was surprised because he always looked after me. I never dreamed of looking after him, as future events will show.

In January we went up to Austria to Gargellen to ski with the children. While we were away, Laurence and Kay lived in our house in Paris. Sindbad was a good skier and even Pegeen by now had had some practice with Laurence and could stand up. Emily came with us and asked her friend, Samuel Hoare, to join us. He was a dark little Scotsman, a frustrated writer, who in desperation had buried himself in the Foreign Office. Emily had been on his trail for four years already. He loved her, but he would not marry her, and only someone with her intense belief in performing miracles could have persevered so long. She had given it up temporarily, when she had gone away to Italy, but had gone back to it again. John liked Hoare because he was so intelligent and he could talk to him. I liked him too, but at first he was very shocked by my frankness. I tried for years to restrain myself in front of him, so as not to horrify him. I succeeded so well that I finally gained his confidence and friendship. Hoare was a very good skier and took Johnnie, Emily's son, and Sindbad on long trips. We could not have chosen a worse place for skiing, as Gargellen was on the wrong side of the valley. All the time we were there we were waiting for snow that never came. I don't know how John stood the strain of trying to ski for the first time in his life on these slippery frozen slopes. I never skied, of course, but went on a sled. At the end Johnnie got the chicken-pox, but we did not realize it and went on skiing. Afterward Pegeen and Sindbad came down with it.

During this winter Sindbad, who had been madly in love with Marlene Dietrich for over a year, wrote her a very touching letter. He told her he liked beer and skiing and added, "I hate Greta Garbo. Don't you?" He asked her to send him a signed photograph. After several months he received a letter from one of her secretaries saying he could have one for a dollar.

In the middle of March we went to London. Dorothy seemed to want to end her hostilities against me. Astrology was her new hobby and she cast my horoscope—some fifty pages. We took her on a motor trip through the Cotswolds and Wye valley. We made our headquarters in a place called Morton-in-the-Marsh, where John and I slept in a feather bed. Emily was living on a farm somewhere nearby, and we motored all over the place together, ending up in Wales. It was very pleasant except for one evening when Dorothy made a dreadful scene. I think it was when she discovered that Emily had been at Hayford Hall. Dorothy was no longer jealous of me; she had transferred all her feeling of hatred to Emily.

John wanted to help Djuna publish her novel, *Ryder,* in England, as it had been published only in New York. He wrote a note to an old friend of his, Douglas Garman, who was a publisher in an avant-garde publishing house. He met us in the Chandos pub. Some immediate combustion must have occurred. Garman took a great fancy to me and leaped into the rumble seat of the car, where I had installed myself after we left the pub. He asked if he could lend me five pounds. This was because a moratorium had been declared in England and all American banks were closed. My mother had had the bright idea at this moment to wire me not to sell my capital. I could not even get a penny out of the bank. Garman never published *Ryder*. I believe he did not like it, but he asked us if he could come to stay with us in Paris at Easter time. When he came, I fell in love with him. I did not tell John. I was very surprised and perturbed by the whole thing. I imagine I felt Garman was a real man and John was more like Christ or a ghost. I needed someone human to make me feel like a woman again. John was indifferent to the worldly aspects of life and did not care how I looked or what I wore. Garman, on the contrary, noticed everything and commented on my clothes, which I found very pleasant. One day he discovered me with a broom in my hand. The maid was sick and I was trying to clean the house. He took the broom and insisted on cleaning for me because he said I was doing it so badly. We soon found that we had the same recurring dream of encountering in the middle of the Atlantic an unknown island with three smokestacks. John got jealous, and after a dinner-party I had to be put to bed drunk. Garman came up and tried to look after me and this caused more trouble. He went back to England and we did not see him again for several months. But I had a strange premonition that in one year I would be his mistress.

In the spring Milton Waldman offered us a house in London he had borrowed, so we went to live in Trevor Square. We gave lots of parties and got quite settled and felt we should remain in England. We sent for Pegeen and Doris and the cook as we had decided to go back to Hayford Hall. Pegeen arrived at Folkestone with her hair so wild and fluffy that John named her Flossy, which name she kept for many years.

Garman was separated from his wife. He had a daughter, Debbie, about Flossy's age. We invited them to tea one day. They looked so much alike it was unbelievable. They both had a sort of stolid quality and resembled two oxen in harness. Garman was exceedingly handsome. He was taller than John and had brown hair and eyes, one of which was damaged, and a beautiful nose, slightly tilted. He was pale. He was another frustrated poet. Garman had produced a book of poems and John was embarrassed because Garman wanted to discuss them with him. However, John found one line he liked and, with his usual tact and hypocrisy, coped with the situation. He did not much relish Garman's conversation.

In Paris that spring we had met Eugene Jolas, the editor of *transition*. John liked him very much and they used to sit up very late drinking and reciting Hölderlin's poetry, which Jolas knew by heart. Jolas's wife, Maria, used to sing duets with Giorgio Joyce. She had a lovely voice, too.

In July we went back to Hayford Hall. It seemed all the more wonderful the second year, for nothing had changed, and we felt we owned it. The only difference was that we were trusted, and the formidable housekeeper-maid and her assistant were not there to guard us. To replace them we brought two more servants of our own who had been working for us in Trevor Square: Albert, a miraculous cockney who played at being butler, and his wife, a sad Belgian called Louise. We still had Marie, our cook, but Madeleine, our maid, had remained in France. Albert now took over the catering and went with Doris every morning to shop for food. He took everything in hand and saw to it that we were well supplied with liquor, which seemed to be his weakness. He also saw that other people were supplied at the back door. I told him to sell all the empty bottles but he said no one would buy them. However, one morning at six, he disturbed us by wheeling this fantastic assemblage past our windows and thus got caught red-handed. He made great friends with the butcher and did a lot of dirty deals with him at the pony races. I don't doubt that he sold or gave him all the empties. On Thursdays, when Doris took the servants for their outing, she had great trouble in bringing Albert back, he got so tight. He also served as a witness against Mrs. Boyse whose husband divorced her soon after her visit to Hayford Hall.

The second summer we seemed to have many more guests than the first. Of course Emily, who behaved worse than ever, and Johnnie and Djuna were with us, and Samuel Hoare came several times. My new friend Wyn Henderson, who was later to become so closely associated with me, dropped in on her way to Cornwall. My mother came again and at the same time Djuna's friends, the American-French painter Louis Bouché and his wife and daughter. He was an enormous man of some six feet or more with the width of a giant. His wife was a little dainty creature with a very young face and white hair. He had a beautiful daughter Sindbad's age and Sindbad fell in love with her. The Bouchés drank as much as John did, or even more, and had to go to bed after a few days, they were so sick.

In late August the children flew to Munich with Doris. Laurence was to meet them there. I accompanied them to London, where we spent the night with my mother. I had written Garman that I should like to see him. He had tried to come to Hayford Hall and had phoned us somewhere on his route to Cornwall but never found us. When I wrote to him my intentions were very clear to me, but not in the least so to him. He was in Cornwall when he got the letter and never suspected why I was writing to him. He thought that I was alone in London and wanted to be friendly.

Soon after I returned to Hayford Hall, John met with the accident that was to cause his death five months later. It was due to a series of mishaps, all completely unnecessary.

One afternoon in late August we went horseback riding in a typical Dartmoor rain. The rain wasn't bad enough to be uncomfortable but it was enough to cloud over John's glasses. Half-blinded, he allowed Katie, his horse, to stumble into a rabbit hole and throw him. His wrist was entirely dislocated. For some strange reason I felt a kind of pleasure when I saw he was helpless, but I soon recovered. John walked home leading Katie, and Emily galloped back to get a doctor. Our local doctor came up from Totnes, a few miles away. I helped him to administer chloroform and he set the wrist very badly. John was in terrible pain and I was quite insistent that we get some morphine for him. The next day he was still in agony and we drove him over rough roads to the hospital where he was X-rayed. It was necessary to have his wrist in a plaster cast for six weeks, during which time I had to dress and undress him like a baby.

Finally, at the end of the summer, I decided Emily had gone too far. When she was about to leave in a few days she said to me, "I had such a happy summer." I replied, "You're the only one who has." She was so insulted she rushed upstairs and began to pack her bags. She intended to leave at once. Everyone hoped that I would ask her to remain. I didn't and not even at the station did I relent. John begged me to change my mind, but I would not; I was adamant.

As soon as we got to Paris I took John to the American Hospital, where he was examined and again X-rayed. They said he had a little piece chipped out of his wrist and recommended hot salt baths and a masseur. The masseur was blind. He was supposed to break down the extra muscle tissue which had grown in the wrist and was preventing its being used freely. The agony John went through every time this blind man treated him was terrible to witness. Sweat streamed down his face and all over his body. Finally the masseur dismissed John saying he could do no more for him.

We had decided by this time to live in London. John had written only one poem in all the years he had been with me. I had done nothing but complain about his indolent life, never dreaming how unhappy he was about it. He thought that maybe in London, surrounded by stimulating people who spoke his own language, he might be able to start writing again. He spoke French so badly that he never could have intellectual conversations with the French.

When he drank a lot he always complained saying, "I'm so bored, so bored," as though this cry came from his very depths and caused him great pain.

We sublet our house in the Avenue Reille and put Pegeen in a *pension* with Doris, near Mrs. Jolas' school, with the idea of their joining us as soon as we were settled in London. By this time John's wrist allowed him to drive, but he still could not use it freely.

# Chapter 7

# Death of John Holms

We were invited by Milton Waldman and Peggy to stay with them at Orchard Poyle until we had found a house. We motored into London every day where we saw every kind of unsuitable house and motored back to Buckinghamshire at night. Once when we went out on our tour Emily was with us and suddenly I got confidential and told her secretly about my attempt on Garman. She was horrified and told me that I was completely irresponsible and mad and that I risked losing John. She frightened me so much that I then and there decided never to see Garman again and lived up to my resolution until after John was dead.

We finally found a house through Wyn Henderson. It was in Woburn Square and, though very English eighteenth-century, it was really quite nice by the time we made it a little less formal. John was to live here only six weeks as he died in this house. Of course he never got around to writing, but he did have many people to talk to in London, including Hugh Kingsmill, who came back into his life a short time before his death, and Edwin Muir whom he loved, and Gerhardi who amused him frightfully, and Hoare and other people.

Shortly after we were living in the house I got drunk one night

and became very bitchy and taunted John about Garman. I told
him of my letter and my desire for Garman. John nearly killed me.
He made me stand for ages naked in front of the open window (in
December) and threw whiskey into my eyes. He said, "I would
like to beat your face so that no man will ever look at it again." I
was so frightened that I made Emily stay all night to protect me.

John had always sent Dorothy all the money that he received
from his father. It was very little, only two hundred pounds a
year. On one of his visits to England he succeeded in getting an
extra forty pounds a year. This was still not sufficient for Dorothy
to live on and she wanted some assurance of security. She would
have preferred a settlement but, since all my money was in trust,
all I could do was to sign a legal document engaging myself to give
her, for the rest of her life—even if I died first—the sum of three
hundred and sixty pounds a year. Shortly after this John's father
gave him outright five thousand pounds, in order to avoid death
duties. He invested it in some safe government stock. I made him
make out a will in my favor. Dorothy, having forced the marriage,
was his legal heir, and I felt that in all fairness as she was now
protected, I should be the heir. The strange thing was that I
thought so much about death and seemed to have a premonition
that John would die. I was always worrying that because I was not
his wife, I would have no right to bury him if he died and would
have to get Dorothy's permission or his family's. Of course I
wanted to marry him but the thought of going through a divorce
from Dorothy was too much for John and I was too proud to insist.
He was practically paralyzed by this time in his will power and
could not even write a note. Finally, when we were settled in
Woburn Square, he decided he would get a divorce and intended
to speak to Dorothy about it, but of course it was never to be.

At Christmas, Sindbad came to London. Pegeen was with us
and I had a hectic time trying to amuse them. They got so spoiled
that they did not want to go any place except to cinemas, circuses
and pantomimes.

All the time we were in Buckinghamshire John had been taking
more massages from a person recommended by Milton Waldman.
This came to an end when the masseur dismissed the case,
claiming he could do no more. He said that if John wanted to be
completely cured, he would have to undergo an operation. This
was confirmed by a Harley Street doctor. It was a matter of taking

an anesthetic and having the extra growth in his wrist broken. It would take three minutes. John decided to have this done. The operation was arranged for, but had to be called off at the last minute as John had the flu.

At the end of the Christmas holidays, I myself took Sindbad all the way to Zurich to meet Laurence who was then living in Austria. The parting was extremely painful. When he left, Sindbad cried as he did not want me to spend the whole day alone in the station waiting for a return train, which I was forced to do. I too started crying and couldn't stop. I cried the whole way back to Paris where I went to see Mary Reynolds. She begged me to stay with her, but some strange thing was pulling me back to John and I left by the next train. When I got back to Victoria Station I thought of Sindbad and mentally blamed John for all the years of agony that my separation from Sindbad had caused me. I swore a terrible oath that I never wanted to see John again. In less than thirty-six hours he was dead.

He met me at the station and took me home. Our house was full of people. He suddenly announced that, during my absence, Emily had arranged for him to have the operation and it was to take place the next morning. All his friends were worried. They seemed to have a premonition that it was bad. Gerhardi, who was writing a book about the Astral, warned John that he would surely leave his body under the anesthetic. John replied, "What if I never come back?" He stayed up drinking very late and the next morning woke up with a hangover. If I had had any sense of responsibility I would not have allowed the operation to take place. I can't imagine now why I was ashamed to tell the doctors, who had already postponed the operation once because John had the flu, that it would have to be called off again. Anyhow I allowed the doctors to come. John wanted me to remain with him, and there was no reason why I shouldn't. I held his hand until he was asleep, but then the doctors firmly and politely waved me out of the room and I went downstairs to wait. The whole thing should not have lasted more than half an hour. When that time elapsed I got nervous and went upstairs to listen outside the bedroom door. There was no sound, so I went below again. Shortly afterward one of the doctors went to get a little bag from the front hall. This made me feel that something had gone wrong and I was terrified, but I did not know what to do. After what seemed hours they came down all together—our doctor, who was a general practitioner, the surgeon, and the anesthetist, who was anesthetist to the king. The minute they came into the room I knew what had happened. John's heart had given out under the anesthetic.

After the operation all three had gone over to the other side of the room and had left him to his fate. Suddenly the physician noticed that John was failing, and then they had tried, too late, to revive him. They had cut open his chest and injected adrenalin into his heart and massaged it, but to no avail. They had killed him and they knew it. They were frightened. Everything they said made them seem more horrible to me. They had the insolence to apologize for the embarrassment of having this occur in my house. Then they told me stories of people dropping dead on the street from heart failure. They were worried because they knew there would be an inquest and they wanted to save themselves. Our physician, who was Milton's doctor, phoned to Buckinghamshire and asked him and Peggy to come and look after me. Knowing that it would be hours before they could arrive, the doctors departed and left me completely alone. I went up and looked at John. He was so far away it was hopeless. I knew that I would never be happy again.

The strange thing was that I had, for a second, felt a sense of relief when the doctors told me he was dead. It was as though I were suddenly released from a prison. I had been John's slave for years and I imagined for a moment I wanted to be free, but I didn't at all. I did not have the slightest idea how to live or what to do. I was absolutely bankrupt. Peggy and Milton arrived. None of us acted in the least solemnly or artificially. I was calm and there was no fuss. They sent for Emily. Peggy, who was practical, asked Emily to live with me as she herself had to go back to her children in a few days.

For years I had told Emily that if John were to die, I would never see her again. Now I was only too happy to allow her to give up her own life and stay with me. She slept in our room and we talked about John for nearly two months and that saved me. I can't think of anything else that would have been better. All my feelings of jealousy vanished when we wept together and shared our grief. I said to her, "Now that John is dead, we are running into eternal danger." We were.

In the afternoon the undertaker came to take away John's body.

I asked to have his watch and his dressing gown removed and I put them on at once and felt nearer to him and slightly safer. But as his body was being taken down the stairs, I suddenly remembered the oath I had made at Victoria Station wishing never to see him again, and I let out a terrible scream, because I felt I had killed him.

I wanted to have John cremated and we sent for his sister Beatrix and Dorothy. John died on January 19, 1934, at the age of thirty-seven. The next day was Dorothy's birthday, and he was cremated on Emily's birthday, January 21st. There had to be an autopsy and an inquest. Edwin Muir insisted that I have a lawyer present at the inquest in case any trouble arose. I was questioned by the coroner, and gave a report of the history of John's accident and of its consequences. The coroner was very polite and human. To my great surprise, he said to me more as a statement than as a question, "And you lived with him." And I replied, "Yes, for five years." Then a report was read on the autopsy. It seemed that all of John's organs were very much affected by alcohol and he was in rather bad shape. The doctors were exonerated.

After that we had the cremation. I didn't have the courage to go. Muir and Hugh Kingsmill and Dorothy and John's sister and Emily and Milton were present. I would not allow anyone else to be there. I went, during this hour, to a Catholic church in Soho with Peggy and we lit a candle. After that I came home and sat on the floor in our bedroom, where John had died, and listened to Beethoven's Tenth Quartet on the phonograph. While I sitting there in my extreme agony, John's sister came up to say goodbye to me. She had caught me completely unaware and for the first time she realized what John had meant to me. She said, "Whatever your life is to be, I hope it will be happy." It seemed strange at that moment to think of the future.

Emily spent a lot of time with Dorothy and tried to look after Pegeen. We didn't want to tell her that John was dead. She loved him very much. One day, when we were in a bookshop, she asked me when he would come back from the nursing home where she believed he was staying. I said, "Never. He is in heaven with the angels." A few days later she came home early from her school in Bloomsbury and refused ever to go back. Emily and I tried to find a new one in Bloomsbury. In the middle of my misery I endeavored to talk to the principal about Pegeen. The strange

thing was that the principal of the school, whom I met again years
later, told me that the day in which I had come to her was the
worst day of her life. It certainly was one of mine. Doris had just
been married and, although she was willing to come back, I was so
jealous of her that I used her marriage as an excuse to look after
Pegeen myself. But, in my awful state of misery, I wasn't very
good at the task. Pegeen got the flu and was in bed for weeks
because the doctor thought she had a higher temperature than she
really had, as I did not take it by mouth. I finally found a good
school for her in Hampstead where she was happy.

By the time Dorothy left we had come to some new agreement
about her future. I gave her all of John's money and books and
promised to give her another one hundred and sixty pounds a year.
This time she trusted me and tore up our legal contract.

After John died I was in perpetual terror of losing my soul.
Every day I looked in the mirror and watched my mouth sag more
and more. That was a symbol of what I feared was happening to
me. I did lose my soul and I knew it. If I found it again, how could
I cope with it without John to guard it? I believe that in the future
life some day I will find John again and my soul will be safe.

Edwin Muir and Hugh Kingsmill came often to my house. They
felt that by sitting there they could in some way be closer to John.
We were all most unhappy. I felt perpetually like seizing
someone's hand and begging them to say something emotional.
William Gerhardi was offended that I had not allowed him to go to
the cremation, and had even wept about it, but we soon had a
reconciliation. I received many letters of condolence. They were
comforting. All John's friends saw him in a different light.

One day I received a letter in Garman's handwriting. I nearly
fainted, for I had completely forgotten him. He wanted to know if
he could do anything for me. He wanted to help with the usual
things, thinking I was a foreigner in England. But it was too late,
as they had all been attended to. As for the rest, it was too soon.
But I began to think about him again, and by degrees I realized
that I would use him to save me from my misery.

In February the lease of our house in the Avenue Reille
expired, and I was forced to go to Paris to see the landlord and
come to some terms with him, as we had made several alterations
on the ground floor.

We had sublet the house to a sweet little couple, Charlotte and Ronnie Morris. I had taken a liking to her at once because she so much resembled my friend Peggy. They could not afford the house but we let them have it at their price. When I went to Paris it was at the time of the Stavisky scandal and I had just received a cable from my mother saying, "Avoid Paris dangerous." It certainly was. A maid had been shot on a balcony at the Crillon Hôtel and there had been a sort of revolution and lots of street fighting. It was over when I arrived. When I went to the Avenue Reille to remove my furniture I found a little bunch of roses Charlotte Morris had placed for me on the table of our living room. I was touched at what I assumed to be her understanding of how I felt about returning to this house where I had been so happy with John. I hated the thought of their having lived in it, but I was glad at least that they were such nice people. I had all the furniture removed and put into storage. When the house was empty I felt better—nothing remained there of my life with John for other people to be connected with.

# Chapter 8

# My Life with Garman

Besides John's friends, who came to our house as though to be nearer him, I saw very few people. Wyn Henderson was our neighbor in Woburn Square, and she kept sending her son Ion to see me. I allowed him to sit and play our E.M.G. gramophone but I barely noticed his presence in my house. I began to think more and more about Garman. It became an obsession, and I finally realized nothing else would save me from my misery. I told Emily that I wanted him, and then said I didn't mean it. Soon I made her write to him and meet him in order to see how he felt about me. They had a drink in the Café Royal. When she came back she told me that he had spoken nicely about me and that at least he was free, being separated from his wife. I invited him to dinner, and Emily invited Hoare. I must have made my intentions very clear this time because Garman took me home with him. He thought I was a wonderfully brave woman, prepared to start a new life. I had fooled him completely, and when I burst out crying he realized his error and wrote this poem for me which he produced the following day.

> Doubting I lay, but you too brought
> Tears from a world I had not shared,

> Till in accord our bodies stirred
> And broke the tyranny of thought
> Finding again what treasure lies
> In secret hushed between your thighs.
> And stillness in the blood confirms
> The age-old act we thus rehearse
> An uncontracted universe
> Swing in the circuit of our arms,
> For the wild gift between your thighs'
> Drove out the terror from my eyes.

Garman fell very much in love with me and thought I was like Cleopatra, and quoted Shakespeare to me. "I found you as a morsel, cold upon dead Caesar's trencher." I imagine he thought of himself as Antony and of John as Caesar. He also said that I reminded him of the following very flattering lines, "Age cannot wither her, nor custom stale her infinite variety /Other women cloy the appetites they feed; but she makes hungry where most she satisfies/ For vilest things become themselves in her; that the holy priests bless her, when she is riggish." However, it was all very painful because of my unhappiness about John. I had been completely dependent on him; I was incapable of thinking for myself. He had always decided everything and as he was so brilliant it was much simpler to accept his judgments than make my own. He had told me that when I tried to think I looked like a puzzled monkey. No wonder I avoided it whenever I could! Apart from this I had a bad conscience about being untrue to him only seven weeks after his death. I tried therefore to hide Garman. I did not want anyone to know about the affair, and I always managed to get home before dawn.

Soon after John's death Mary Reynolds came to London on some business and she stayed with me in Woburn Square. I gave a big party for her and in the middle of it I retired to my room and wept. I was not prepared to face the world.

Wherever Garman took me I had memories of John and often burst out crying in public. Poor Garman always hoped that I would get over my grief and that we would eventually be happy together. He told me much later that I cried on his shoulder every day for a year and a half. Garman deserved a better fate, especially since he had been unhappy with his wife for a long time and had ended up with a nervous breakdown. He had been married for nine years, but had not lived with his wife all that time. They were uncongenial. They had been to Russia together after the revolution and Garman, who was a revolutionist at heart, had fallen in love with a Bolshevik woman. He remained with her for six months after his wife had returned to England, only to have to return home himself in the end as his passport expired. After that Garman went to Brazil to his brother's ranch to recover his lost health. He had been sick for years.

Garman was the son of a family doctor who had had a large practice outside Birmingham. There he had lived in a big house with a garden, completely removed from the world, with his one brother and seven sisters. His father died while Garman was still at Cambridge, and Garman felt his loss very much and his early responsibilities of being head of the family. His mother was a gentle English lady living in retirement and great modesty. She was supposed to be the illegitimate daughter of Earl Grey, and indeed she looked aristocratic. She was so feminine and so ladylike she had always done exactly what her husband had wanted, and now, although she rarely saw Garman, she adored him and treated him in the same way. He had just bought a little house for her in Sussex near the downs and he intended to go down there for weekends.

Garman was working in an avant-garde publishing house that belonged to one of his brothers-in-law, a millionaire who wanted to spend some of his money usefully.

Soon after I was with Garman I had to leave him to go and spend Easter with Sindbad. I had promised Sindbad in the station at Zurich, when he had cried so much, that I would. I did not want to go at all because I considered Laurence John's worst enemy, and it would be unpleasant for me to be with him and Kay at this time. In the end I decided I could bear it, because Nina, an Irish friend of Kay and Laurence and strangely enough also of John, was there, and I knew she would make things easier for me.

I took Pegeen with me and we spent about ten days in Kitzbühl. It was extremely painful to go back to the Austrian Tyrol where I had been so happy with John. But I was glad to be with Sindbad, and Laurence was very kind and made a great effort to get closer to me again. I suddenly realized that all my troubles with him about Sindbad were over. A few years before, a fortune-teller had

told me, "You will get your child back through someone's death."
It had never occurred to me it would be through John Holms's
death. I had thought of everybody else's.

Laurence came up to my room and put me to bed every night.
He wasn't satisfied until he made me cry. He forced me to talk
about John. I didn't want to. I finally accused him of being very
happy about John's death, but obvious as it was, I never got him to
admit it. He said I should have another man. Of course I did not
tell him about Garman, but he suspected I had somebody when I
returned to London so soon. I went home leaving Pegeen with
Laurence as it was her Easter holiday.

When I got back to London Garman met me and told me that he
had been very sick during my absence, and that we had to go away
to the country at once. We drove down to Surrey and stayed a few
days at an inn. I had a new Delage by now, because after John's
death I could not bear to see the old one any more or drive in it
without him. My mother had made me a present of another car. I
got rid of the Peugeot also and bought one that I could drive
myself.

Garman drove me to Sussex to show me the house he had
bought for his mother. It was in a little English village called
South Harting, just under the downs. The village was absolutely
dead, like all such places in England, but it was in the midst of
the most lovely country. Naturally, it had a fine pub. Garman also
took me to see his sister Lorna and his brother-in-law, the
publisher Ernest Wishart, whom he called Wish. They had a
lovely home. Garman and Wish seemed to be the very best of
friends, having been to Cambridge together. Wish's wife Lorna
was the most beautiful creature I had ever seen. She had
enormous blue eyes, long lashes and auburn hair. She was very
young, still in her early twenties, having been married at the age
of sixteen. Out of seven sisters, she was Garman's favorite. They
were all extraordinary girls. One of them was married to a
fisherman in Martigues, and another one had three children by a
world-famous sculptor. Another lived in Herefordshire with her
illegitimate child, while a fourth spent half the year as a
maidservant in order to be able to live in peace the other six
months in a cottage she had bought on Thomas Hardy's favorite
heath. Later she adopted a little boy and was reported to have had
a love affair with Lawrence of Arabia, whom she met on the

heath, but when I knew her she was most virginal. Another one was married to the famous South African poet Roy Campbell. They were Catholic and later became Fascist and lived in Spain. One very normal one married a garage owner and led a happy life with two children. In his youth Garman must have been overwhelmed by so many women, and preferred not to see most of them any more. However, I was fascinated by them and eventually managed to meet them all. Garman had a younger brother whom he liked. He had returned from Brazil and was now farming in Hampshire.

Garman was a straightforward, honest person with a wonderful sense of humor, and a fine mimic. He was simple, and disapproved of all snobbishness and chi-chi. He was a puritan and a frustrated poet. He was a revolutionary at heart, but all his habits and tastes belonged to the class in which he was born. He spoke beautiful English as well as excellent Russian, French and Italian. He was well educated. His tempo was quite different from mine. I moved about ten times faster than he did, and almost went mad waiting for him to finish sentences. He was five years younger than I which made me self-conscious. He found me very sloppy and would have liked me to dress much better than I did. He did not like me to have any gray hair.

After six months the lease of my house in Woburn Square expired and I moved to Hampstead with the greatest of delight. I could not bear to have Garman come to the house where John had died. It was a relief to be in a place where Garman could visit me freely, and even stay at night. Of course I continued to hide him.

Pegeen's school was near this house which was why I rented it. For the first time since Doris left she was very happy.

In summer Garman helped me find a house in the country for the children. I fussed nearly as much as if I had been John Holms, and Garman got very annoyed with me and made me rent a lovely place that was a few miles away from his mother's, in South Harting. He was editing a book and wanted to live at home, where he could work easily and yet be able to come and visit me.

The house I rented was called Warblington Castle. It was a pretty farm house with nice gardens and a tennis court, and was supposed to be an historic sight, since it could boast of a twelfth-century tower, still standing on its grounds and forming part of a wall with a moat. It was a public monument and open to the public who visited it on occasions.

Emily and Johnnie Coleman came down with us and Sindbad, who for the first time had traveled all alone across Europe. I invited Garman's daughter Debbie, who lived with his mother, as well as one of his nieces, to stay with Pegeen. Emily's friend Phyllis Jones adored our children and I persuaded her to come and look after them. Pegeen learned to ride a bicycle and I was in fits and trembling all summer over this fact. I have never been able to do this simple little thing myself.

We could not swim very much at Warblington as it was on a muddy inlet. We had to motor over to Hayling Island, ten miles away, in order to reach the sea.

Warblington Castle was very large, so we could invite quite a few guests. Garman came and went, and when he was with me I hid him in the tower bedroom I had chosen, away from everyone else. One day when Antonia White came into my room there was a pair of Garman's gray flannels on my bed. In order to keep my secret I wore the trousers myself, although they were several sizes too big for me. At breakfast Garman and I would arrive separately and greet each other politely. Even Sindbad did not suspect, but finally had to be told, because he resented Garman's correcting him. We managed to get horses and went for wonderful rides. The whole time I was bemoaning Dartmoor but Warblington Castle was a perfect place for the children.

Once when Garman was away working on his book we sent for Samuel Hoare, telling him to come and join the women and children. Emily was always begging me to invite Hoare, because she had so much trouble making him do what he really wanted to do. He resisted her with all his strength. He adored the life she gave him, but he made her fight for every gram that she forced on him, knowing all the time he would die without it. Of course he came to Warblington.

When Antonia White visited us she was rather worried by my vagueness, and Emily told me that I should behave more like the sort of hostess that Antonia expected. I rushed out and bought her a croquet set and various other things which I thought might please her. Emily said, "You mustn't overdo it," and I replied, "Oh, but I must."

Milton Waldman had given us a sweet little Sealyham dog. He wasn't quite a thoroughbred but he was nice-looking in his funny way. When John had died the dog was unhappy for he felt he had no master anymore. Our butler Blisset took charge of him and brought him everywhere. He even took him to the cinema where Robin, as the dog was called, barked wildly at his counterpart on the screen.

During the summer I bought a wife for Robin. She was a thoroughbred Sealyham, and Sindbad, with his great passion for tennis stars, named her Borotra. When I got her home, I discovered she had one bad eye and realized then why she had been sold to me so cheaply.

We had various guests, among them were Milton and Peggy, and Mary and Willard Loeb who arrived from New York with two daughters. Willard was one of my favorite cousins. He was a great music lover and owned ten thousand phonograph records. He played tennis like a champion. Mary had been Benita's best friend and this was the first time I had seen her since Benita died. John's death seemed to have wiped out the agony of Benita's, but I was happy to be able to talk about her to Mary. As usual I hid my relations with Garman from all these people, or thought I did. After five weeks our lease was up and the children had to go to Kitzbühl to stay with Laurence. Garman and I drove them down to Dover and put them on a boat. They went alone together, right across Europe. Sindbad was eleven years old and Pegeen was nine. They were a wonderful little pair. Sindbad wore Tyrolian pants with a dagger thrust in his belt.

After they had left, Garman took me to live in his house at South Harting. His mother was away on her summer holiday with one of her daughters and allowed me to stay there. Garman was finishing his book and I had very little to do all day. I lay in bed late reading *The Possessed* by Dostoevsky. It is the only one of his novels I have never grasped, even after reading it twice. It is so confusing, none of the characters stand out. The only part I like is the scene of the childbirth, which takes place in an adjoining room while all the political drama is going on next door.

When Garman finished editing his book we drove to Wales. Lorna and Wish had been to Pembrokeshire and had sung its praises, so we went there too. It is the only place in the British

Isles that looks anything like the Continent. The houses were all painted bright colors, as in Italy. There were beaches miles long with enormous boulders and there were no people to be seen anywhere. The coast was rocky and wild.

We took long walks over fields and moors covered in heather, and visited manor houses. The Welsh gentry had had an eighteenth-century social life like that of the Irish.

We lived in a little boarding-house on a river which was owned by a half-mad ex-sea-captain and his wife, who had formerly been the Duchess of Manchester's maid. She gave us a bedroom and a sitting room and wonderful five-course meals, with three choices for each, all for the modest sum of fifteen shillings a week per person. (Fifteen shillings was equivalent to three dollars and seventy-five cents.) It was unbelievable. Her husband, the captain, had built this house to resemble a boat, and it was surrounded by his derelict fleet in which he had once sailed up and down the coast. He had been an important shipping agent in former days. Now he was as finished as his boats, and although he always talked of mending them we knew he never would.

Opposite this house, on the other side of the river, lived a mad family. It seems they had two daughters whom they had kept under the table sewn up in bags for years and never allowed out until the authorities intervened.

I was still very unhappy about John all the time I was in Wales.

On the way back Garman took me to the Black Country where he was born and raised. He took me to see his family home which had been sold, and in return I took him to Warwick Castle where one of my uncles had lived with a mistress. I don't think Garman believed me until the guide, who was taking us over the Castle, mentioned their names.

When we got back to South Harting I tried to rent a house near Mrs. Garman so that Pegeen could go to day school with Debbie, Garman's daughter, and his niece Kitty. There were no houses to be rented, but there was one little Elizabethan cottage for sale and Garman made me buy it. Soon after I took this step I decided to commit suicide, I was still so unhappy about John. I therefore put the house in Garman's name as I intended to die. Of course I didn't and I went to live in the house instead.

It took some time to get my furniture over from Paris and settle the house. In the meantime Pegeen came back from Kitzbühl and lived with Mrs. Garman. Mrs. Garman had about thirteen grandchildren. She lived entirely for them and for her own children, but she immediately accepted Pegeen and was very kind to us both.

# Chapter 9

# Yew Tree Cottage

Yew Tree Cottage was my new home. It was named from a tree which must have been over five hundred years old, and which grew in front of the house, towering over its roof. It was a beautiful cottage because of its exposed rafters and beams. In the sitting room was an enormous fireplace, so spacious people could have sat in it. The windows of the house were small and from the sitting room you could see cows grazing in meadows a few feet away. It was a small house with two living rooms and four bedrooms, one bathroom, a kitchen and larder. The great attraction was the grounds. There was about an acre of land belonging to this property, but the whole countryside seemed to be a part of it. It was at the foot of the downs, but we were actually in a valley and we had a stream running through our garden, which was all sloping.

The real reason I wanted this house was because it was on the bus line between Harting and Petersfield, where Pegeen wanted to attend school with Garman's daughter Debbie and his niece Kitty. It was one hundred yards from a little road that was not a main road, but which I always insisted on calling so, as a result of summers spent on the moors. I felt upset by the thought of the world being at my gate, but I later appreciated the convenience of the bus and the deliveries it made for us from the shops.

Garman immediately engaged a gardener for me and began laying out the most lovely lawns and flower beds. He was a very good gardener himself and did a lot of the work. He had what is called a "green thumb."

Pegeen and I lived alone in this cottage with a darling little Italian maid we had had since London in Woburn Square. Garman came to visit me but he would not live with me, and I was unhappy every time he left.

At Christmas I was to visit Sindbad again in Kitzbühl. I wanted Garman to accompany me but he thought he wouldn't. However, at the last minute he decided to come. I had Pegeen with me and I got an extra berth for Garman in another stateroom. He happened to share this stateroom with Ira Morris, whom none of us knew at that time, but who had contributed years before to *The Calendar of Modern Letters,* a review edited by Edgell Rickword with Garman's assistance. He was traveling with his beautiful Swedish wife, Edita, and their child, Ivan. Ira was my Aunt Irene's nephew and though I had heard a lot about him I had not met him. His father I knew quite well. He was the eccentric millionaire meat packer who had been American Minister to Sweden. Both Edita and Ira were very ambitious writers.

Garman, who had never skied before, was much too venturesome and had a bad accident the first day. He broke several fingers and had to have his hand put into a horrid apparatus that pulled his fingers back into shape. This apparatus was about one foot long and as it stuck out in front of him it preceded Garman wherever he went. Every day he had to go to the doctor to have a heat treatment. This whole business upset me for it reminded me of all the agonies John had been through just before he died. I am afraid I was not nearly as sympathetic to Garman as I should have been.

I spent many hours reading to Sindbad, who had just recovered from pleurisy and was still in bed. Kay acted the efficient nurse, and made me feel *de trop* as much as she could. Garman was badly neglected and besides he felt quite out of our family life. He liked Edita very much and got on quite well with Kay, who had had her first story published in his review—he no longer liked her books, as she wrote worse and worse novels.

Myself with Sindbad and Pegeen, 1934

Pegeen, 1937

Emma Goldman was very
vain and it took me years to
see through her. She was a
Jewish *cordon bleu* and her
gefilte fish was her *pièce de
résistance*.

She had for her secretary a
mad American girl called
Emily Coleman who shared
with Blake the persuasion
that all things are possible if
you have faith. In the
summer of 1928 she was in
love with John Holms, an
Englishman whom she had
met in St. Tropez.

John Holms was very tall and had a magnificent physique. He wore a small red beard and looked very much like Jesus Christ. In World War I he had killed four Germans for which, to his great shame, he was given the Military Cross. Drink made him talk and he talked like Socrates. He held people spellbound for hours.

John Holms and myself, 1931

Douglas Garman was a straightforward, honest person with a wonderful sense of humor, and a fine mimic. He was a revolutionary at heart, but all his habits and tastes belonged to the class in which he was born.

Myself with my mother, 1938

Myself with Yves Tanguy, 1938

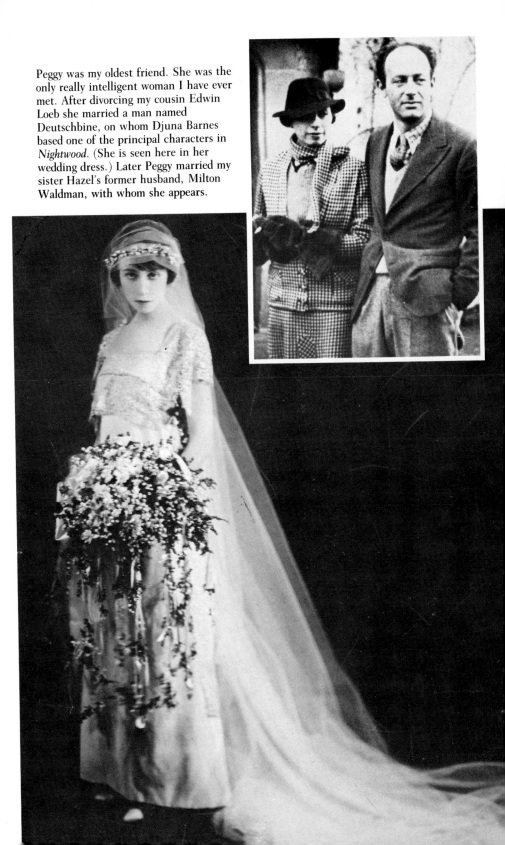

Peggy was my oldest friend. She was the only really intelligent woman I have ever met. After divorcing my cousin Edwin Loeb she married a man named Deutschbine, on whom Djuna Barnes based one of the principal characters in *Nightwood.* (She is seen here in her wedding dress.) Later Peggy married my sister Hazel's former husband, Milton Waldman, with whom she appears.

John Tunnard looked a little like
Groucho Marx and was as animated as a
jazz-band leader, which he turned out to
be. His gouaches were as musical as
Kandinsky's, as delicate as Klee's, and as
gay as Miró's.

Humphrey Jennings was dynamic and
always bursting with a new idea; but, as
he had too many, he never got much
accomplished. He was a sort of genius,
and he looked like Donald Duck.

E. L. T. Mesens (*left*), the Surrealist poet and art dealer, was a gay little
Flamand, quite vulgar, but really very nice and warm. Henry Moore (*right*) was a
very direct simple man from Yorkshire whose wonderful Surrealist drawings I
liked better than his sculpture.

Samuel Beckett (whom I called Oblomov) and his friend Geer van Velde at Petersfield, where they visited me one weekend in 1938

Herbert Read looked like a prime minister and was reserved, dignified and quiet. He became a sort of father in my life and behind his back I called him Papa. He treated me the way Disraeli treated Queen Victoria. I suppose I was rather in love with him, spiritually.

Constantin Brancusi, Marcel Duchamp and Mary Reynolds in 1929. Mary was tall and elegant and had soft eyes. One night she lost her key and she went home with Duchamp. That started what one might designate as the Hundred Years' War. Mary was much too beautiful for him, but in the end she managed to get him anyhow. It took years, but that probably made it more exciting. Brancusi was half astute peasant and half real god. He made you very happy to be with him. Unfortunately he got too possessive, and wanted all of my time. He loved me very much, but I never could get anything out of him.

Jacqueline, André Breton's blonde, Surrealist-looking wife, had been an underwater dancer but came from a bourgeois family. She is seen here, in 1940, with Victor Brauner, who had lost an eye in 1938, after which he made great progress in painting, as though he had been freed from some impending evil.

Against his better judgment Garman decided, because of my insistence, to come and live with me in Yew Tree Cottage and bring his daughter Debbie with him. When we told this to Kay she had the impudence to ask me how I could take the responsibility of looking after Debbie. It was rather strange considering she had brought up Sindbad for over five years. I told her Debbie was so responsible she would look after all of us. Kay basked in the idea of my being an incompetent mother in order to prove her superiority.

When we got home Garman and Debbie moved into Yew Tree Cottage, and I found myself once again the mother of two children. I loved Debbie. She was just the opposite of any child I had ever known. She was so mature, calm, sensible, self contained and well behaved, and so little trouble. She was intellectual like her father and loved to read and to be read to. She had a wonderful influence over Pegeen, and Pegeen over her. She became less priggish in our home. They got on marvelously and were soon like sisters. They used to dress up in a strange collection of old clothes and costumes we kept in a chest, and gave charades, plays and all sorts of performances. Kitty, Garman's niece, was the third actress. Their only audience was Garman's mother, her lady companion and myself, and occasionally Garman, when he could be torn away from his intense intellectual life. In the evening I read to Debbie and Pegeen while they ate their supper.

Garman was wonderful to the children. They adored him. But one day Debbie said to him, "Pa, you look so monotonous." When we asked her what she meant, she replied, "You know, sort of going on and on." Garman wanted to instruct the children in the facts of life and procreation. He drew all kinds of diagrams for them, which meant nothing to Pegeen. Finally we reminded her of the times when she had seen dogs mating. She was so horrified that she turned to me and said, "Mama, you mean to say that you did that?" and then as an afterthought she added, to put everything right, "Of course, only twice to make me and Sindbad."

Soon after Garman moved into Yew Tree Cottage I made him give up his job as director of his brother-in-law's publishing firm. At the end of our garden he built himself a little one-room house in which to write. His health was bad and he needed a quiet life in the country with exercise and little drinking. He wrote a lot and became interested in a new review which he helped to edit. He soon began to read Karl Marx's *Das Kapital* and was immersed in it for months.

During this time I read Proust. I sat in bed under the Tudor rose which adorned my wall wearing fur gloves and shivering from cold. Dreadful drafts circulated from the holes in the ceiling where the beams were located. My room was so big it was impossible to heat it. I had a few little oil burners which I carried around with me when I got up and dressed and retired into the bathroom. Garman disapproved of my reading Proust. He wanted me to read Karl Marx.

Downstairs the sitting room with the enormous fireplace was filled with smoke. Garman did everything he could to alter this catastrophic state of affairs. Finally two local builders called Peacock and Waller, who had built Garman's little house, overcame the smoke problem by raising our chimney a few feet and cutting some branches off the yew tree. After that Garman, who loved building and remodeling houses, completely did over the second sitting room. Here he had already installed a stove that burned day and night. At least we had one warm room to come down to in the morning, which was a great blessing. By tearing down walls and closing up the formal ugly entrance door he made a really beautiful room. He had wonderful taste and chose perfect furniture and glazed chintz hangings. Then he had lovely bookshelves made for my records. The room gave out onto the garden, and in summer the sweet smell of tobacco plants wafted in through the windows.

Garman had foreseen everything except one thing. In rebuilding the house he had accidentally imprisoned my old Venetian oak chest and we realized it could never come out of the house again. In fact it is still there, though the house is sold, and I shall have to go back and tear down a wall if I want to get it back again.

Besides making such a beautiful home for me, Garman had a gravel tennis court built, and a little swimming pool and a cricket pitch for Sindbad. He sowed grass seeds to make lawns. He completely transformed the grounds and made the most lovely gardens by collecting every variety of plant he could find.

We had an amiable gardener called Jack, who played on the local cricket team in Petersfield. He worked very hard as he had to keep two engines going to feed us light and water. About a quarter of a mile from the house, down by a lake which belonged to our neighbor, we had a little house with a gasoline engine to pump water up to us. Our tank was small and the water problem was a daily affair. The engine was perpetually out of order but Jack knew how to cope with it. When he went on his yearly holiday I was very nervous, and once we had to carry buckets of water for three days.

The engine that generated electricity was in the garage just in front of our house. It made a terrible chuck-chuck noise and gave us feeble light. Only after I had lived in the house for four years was I able to connect up with the main electric line and thus end all our troubles.

The first winter we lived in Yew Tree, Garman and I rented a flat in London in the Adelphi quarter with Phyllis Jones, She had just returned from America where I had sent her for a little trip as she badly needed a change of thought.

However, I rarely went to London with Garman, for I still felt ashamed of my faithlessness to John's memory and preferred to hide in Yew Tree Cottage. In any case, I was very busy trying to retype all of John's manuscripts that I had fallen heir to. I wanted to have them published. Hugh Kingsmill had a whole collection of letters he had conserved and Dorothy had the replies that Hugh Kingsmill had written to John. We decided to do a book of these. I did not want Garman to know how much I was still preoccupied with John, and I tried to work without his knowing it.

Garman and I were really not at all congenial and the situation got more and more obvious and painful. We did not like the same people and we did not like the same things. He hated me to drink and for some perverse reason I now found it necessary to do so, though when I had lived with Laurence and John, who drank so much, I had indulged very seldom. I was all the time comparing Garman with John and even went as far as to tell Garman that he had bored John and that John had only gone to find him in London because he wanted to publish Djuna's book.

Garman's writing did not go very well and he was unhappy. He began to spend more and more time on Karl Marx.

In the spring Sindbad came to stay with us for two months. Laurence decided to put him in an English school and in order to be with him the first year, he also decided to stay in England, though he disliked it heartily. Garman taught Sindbad Latin and I taught him English grammar.

When Laurence and Kay came they left all their many little daughters in the pub at South Harting and went down to Devon to find a house. Sindbad had to live in a warm climate because of the touch of pleurisy he had recently recovered from. So they settled at Seaton and spent a year there, frankly hating it.

Sindbad became great friends with Jack, the gardener, and went with him to watch him play cricket. This must have started his great passion for that exceedingly dull game, because Sindbad thought of nothing else for years to come. He soon knew the scores and the names of all the famous players and became a great authority on the subject. He also played on his school team. I could not share this enthusiasm, and in fact have never even understood the game. Sindbad was a good tennis player and swimmer, and Yew Tree Cottage was an ideal home for him with the court and the little pool and the cricket pitch.

After I had been with Garman about a year and a half I began to get the idea of running away from him. I tried it on various occasions, but he always got me back. I didn't want to live with him and I didn't want to live without him. He still loved me very much, though I did everything to destroy it. I don't see how he could have endured me so long. Once I was so awful to him that he slapped me hard in the face and then was so ashamed of himself that he burst into tears.

In the summer we went back to the same place in Wales and the following Christmas we flew to Paris and went to Martigues to visit Garman's sister who had married the fisherman. I took to her at once. She was beautiful, like all Garman's sisters, but she was not at all happy. She seemed to have got herself into an awful jam. I think she wanted to leave her husband. He was a big, rough, handsome, Swedish-looking fisherman who had an inferiority complex as a result of marrying into another class. Helen, his wife, couldn't leave him because of their child. They both adored it. They lived a very simple life and she had to work hard at some job because his fishing did not bring in enough for them to live on.

We stopped in Paris on the way back. Garman wanted to see Dorothy Dudley who was translating a book about Mussolini for his firm, of which he was still adviser. We also met Gala Dali for the first time. She was a friend of Mary's and, though she was handsome, she was too artificial to be sympathetic. Garman was very much impressed by Mary's wonderful taste and found her new house in Montsouris exquisite. I had taken it for granted, but of course he was perfectly right.

My life in Yew Tree Cottage was so domestic I seemed to do nothing but look after Pegeen and Debbie. They were always having colds and flu. No wonder, as our house was so cold, and the temperature of the rooms so uneven. I seemed to spend weeks administering inhalations and medicines, taking temperatures and reading to sick children. All this made me desire to have a child by Garman. After his long illness he seemed incapable of giving me one, and I wanted to find out if it was really his fault or mine. It was, I discovered, his.

My mother adored her grandchildren with such fervor that Pegeen could not do otherwise than be touched by her affection and reciprocate it. Sindbad was not grateful. Once when my mother arrived from America, after a long absence due to her bad health and several operations, Pegeen said to her, "Oh, grandma, how striped you look." My poor mother certainly had grown older.

When she arrived at Yew Tree Cottage she met Emily. My mother had traveled on the *Ile de France* and asked Emily, who had just come on a ten-day boat, if she had ever been on the *Ile de France*, adding, "The vibration is terrible, terrible, terrible." Once when I told my mother how frightened Laurence was of Kay and how she kept him in order, my mother replied, "Too bad he wasn't frightened of you, frightened of you, frightened of you."

The third summer Garman took me on a sailing trip on the Norfolk broads. We invited Edgell Rickword and his wife Jackie to accompany us. Rickword was Garman's oldest friend. They had been co-editors of *The Calendar* and both had been directors of Wish's publishing house. Rickword was a good poet and critic. He was painfully introverted and very shy unless he was drunk. Jackie I had known for years. She was a good-natured, lively girl who helped make Rickword more comfortable in the world by being natural, if not hearty. I don't know how she ever got into the Bohemian world, but once there she stuck fast.

They were very agreeable on this trip and we had a good time, except that I hate sailing more than anything I can think of. It

makes me restless, nervous and unpleasant. I probably ruined
everyone else's fun. In fact, I think Jackie and I finally left the
men to sail alone and walked down the shore.

We all went to Woodbridge, a miraculous eighteenth-century
town, famous for its sheepskin industry, with at least a hundred
pubs and an old market place with a beautiful building. All the
houses were over two hundred years old. I bought a pair of
beautiful gloves and soon after this Yew Tree Cottage was filled
with natural sheepskin rugs that I kept ordering by mail.

Not long after our Woodbridge trip. Garman's wife wanted to
marry again. For years she had been in love with a young actor
and finally decided she wanted a divorce. Garman said I would
have to be co-respondent. I protested violently because Mrs.
Garman had left Garman long before I met him, and I considered
this most unfair. But Garman said I was living with him, and
there was no other way to do it, since he would not divorce his
wife. The whole thing was very silly. We had to be found in a
room together, Garman in a dressing gown and I in bed. A
detective came down from London early in the morning, so that
the children would not know about it. After that he wanted to
come again, but Garman said he would not go through it a second
time, it must suffice. The divorce was granted on the "humble
petition of Mrs. Saddie Garman." It read that Garman and I had
sinned not once, but many times. I often wondered how they
knew. The only place this fact was ever recorded was in my diary,
where I had written, "fighting all day, f——all night."

We had very few guests at Yew Tree Cottage and I led an
extremely lonely life, getting more and more depressed. I was
almost melancholic. The long winters with nothing to do but
remain indoors, or take walks in the mud, or play tennis and
freeze kept me inactive most of the time. My only joy was reading.
I reread *Anna Karenina,* my favorite book, *War and Peace,*
*Wuthering Heights,* Henry James's novels, all the novels of Defoe,
given to me by Garman, *Pepys' Diary,* and the Countess Tolstoy's
life of her husband. I started to ape her fiendishness and found
myself behaving more and more like her. In the evenings I read
*Robinson Crusoe* and *The Last Days of Pompeii* aloud to the
children. But I wasted a lot of time buying our food myself and, as
I always forgot something, I used to drive into town several times

a day. Emily came down on a few occasions, but she never felt that Garman liked to have her there, though he said to her, "Emily, you make me feel like a welcome guest."

Emily, who passionately disliked playing tennis, one day when I asked her to have a set broke out into a fury and threatened to smash every racquet in the house if I ever invited her to play again. As I had several tennis racquets on approval from a shop in Petersfield I became terrified and immediately rushed them back. But Emily loved the children and they adored her. She seemed to fit in with people of every age.

Jackie and Rickword came several times, When Laurence and Kay first came to England they paid us a visit, but then Garman decided he was not going to see them any more, since he disbelieved in all this false friendship. Kay and I really hated each other. Djuna came down once, and Dorothy Holms several times. The Morrises came, but they were not in England often. Once we had a visit from the Muirs with their strange child, who was an infant prodigy and at the age of eight played the piano like a virtuoso. Mary came once, Phyllis came once, caught the flu and didn't come for ages. On the whole I lived alone, except for Garman's family whom we saw quite a bit of. I liked Lorna and her husband and also Garman's brother, the farmer. Garman had one friend called Wilson Plant, who was in the British Colonial Service and was stationed on the west coast of Africa in the bush. Out there he read Joyce and Djuna Barnes's books and seemed to be *au courant* of everything. He came to see us whenever he was home on leave.

Whatever else I found inferior to my former life, I certainly could not include the downs. They were just as fine as the moors and much safer to walk on. One was in less danger of getting lost or drowned in a bog. They extended for miles and although the scenery was not so varied as Dartmoor, it was equally beautiful and its vegetation and wild flowers far surpassed what grew in Devon. We constantly took walks on the downs and at a certain time we rode there. One could drive right up to the top and then park the car and walk for hours.

Bertrand Russell had a house up there. I think he lived with a new wife and a young baby. One night he gave a lecture in Petersfield about the horrors of the next war and everything he foretold was not far from the actual truth as most of it occurred. It was a good prophecy but in no way helped to save the world from its doom.

The whole countryside abounded in pheasants which were shot down during the season in the woods that belonged to our neighbor, a general. He was an unpleasant bowlegged man who owned the biggest estate in the vicinity with a false Elizabethan house. We used to take long walks and we had a right of way through his estate. One day when I was with Debbie and Pegeen, Robin, the Sealyham, began chasing pheasants and the general, meeting us in his fields, screamed and swore at me because Robin was not on a lead. He was so extremely rude that Garman wanted to write him demanding an apology, but we were handicapped by Garman's not being able to think of the correct title for me. Debbie suggested that Garman should refer to me as his darling Peggy. In the end we had to give it up.

As we were not married the gentry did not call on us, thank God, and we did not frequent our neighbors.

At the edge of our property were beautiful woods. In the early spring they were filled with wild garlic and later with bluebells, campion and irises, and a strange flower that resembled an orchid. This was in contrast to all the flower beds and rock gardens that Garman had planted. The children loved to find bird nests and we had the heavenly cry of the cuckoo and at night there were nightingales. What the children loved most was wandering around in our garden without clothes and swimming in our little pool.

Our food was very bad since Jack, the gardener, had introduced into the household as cook his fiancée Kitty. She really knew only how to make Yorkshire pudding and roast pheasant. I decided to have her taught cooking and I invited Wahab, John's old friend and a schoolmate of Dorothy's, to teach Kitty. Wahab consented to give her a course. We had a real fiesta. It lasted over a week and we cooked about four dishes a day. I learned them all as well, to spur Kitty on, and that was how I began to cook. Never before had I tried to do anything except scramble eggs.

We made the most marvelous meals and tried them all on Garman. He loved them but he said he didn't care who made them. At the end of the ten days, I turned out to be a real cook instead of Kitty. I finally succeeded in getting her to put salt and pepper in our food which I felt was a great feat. After that we had the most delicious *paellas* and *boeuf en daubes* and Spanish omelettes, onion soups, *coq au vin* and chicken in sherry. I used to collect recipes for Kitty on the rare occasions when I went anywhere.

Soon after that, Kitty and Jack were married in the Petersfield church. It was an impressive affair, with Debbie and Pegeen as bridesmaids. Poor Kitty was terrified as she did not quite know what to expect, and Jack even more so, since he did know. They went off on a honeymoon and when they came back they talked as though they had done everything except what had worried them so much before. They were a happy couple and they created a lovely atmosphere in the cottage. Garman soon built them a new wing onto the kitchen. Fortunately they had no children till long after.

During the winter that Laurence lived in Devonshire he lost his uncle, his father and Clotilde. She died in the American Hospital at Neuilly, where John had been. She died, strangely enough, under the same circumstances as John. She had an operation and passed out under the anesthetic. Laurence was terribly upset, and when I saw him shortly after, he was bitterly armed against my sympathy, for he knew how much I had hated Clotilde.

Laurence had come up to Petersfield to see Pegeen act in a school performance of *The Pied Piper of Hamelin*. She had the leading rôle and I had made the most marvelous costume for her, half yellow and half red. Pegeen attended a little dame school in Petersfield with Debbie and her cousin Kitty who still lived with Mrs. Garman. I felt guilty about separating Debbie and Kitty when Debbie came to live with us, but Mrs. Garman said it was natural for Debbie to live with her father, and indeed it seemed to do her a lot of good.

Pegeen was embarrassed by the fact that I did not have the same name that she had. She wanted me to use hers, Vail, but I thought I ought to use Garman's. He sent me to the principal of the school, a very respectable old maid, and told me to ask her what to do. We walked up and down the garden for ages before I had the courage to approach this delicate subject. Finally when I did, she asked me if I were going to marry Garman. When I said no, she told me that I should keep my own name, since it was really mine. That ended the problem, but I never forgave Garman for making me have this idiotic interview.

In the spring of 1936 the French Surrealists gave a huge

exhibition at Burlington House. It was their first showing in London and it had a great success. Garman was excited about it and tried to get Djuna and me to go. We were both blasé and refused, saying Surrealism was over long ago, and that we had had enough of it in the twenties. In view of future events this was a most strange coincidence.

# Chapter 10

# Communism

By degrees Garman got more and more interested in Karl Marx and fell more and more under his spell. He began applying Marx's theories to everything. He gave a course of lectures to prove that all the great writers were revolutionary. He lost all sense of proportion and criticism and saw everything in one light. I went to these lectures and asked questions to embarrass and confuse him. After John's brilliant mind and detachment, all this was too silly for me to endure.

Garman got more and more involved and finally joined the Communist Party. All the money I gave him, which formerly went to paying for the building he had done on the house and on other things, now went to the Communist Party. I had no objection to that at all. I merely got bored listening to the latest orders from Moscow, which I was supposed to obey. Garman wanted me to join the Communist Party but he said that they would not accept me unless I did a job for them. I wrote a letter to Harry Pollitt, the head of the Party, and said that I wanted to join, but that I could not take a job as I lived in the country, took care of two little girls and had no free time. Of course I was accepted. Which was what I wanted to prove.

Garman went around the country in a second-hand car he had bought for the purpose, giving lectures and trying to recruit new members. I saw him less and less as he was so busy. I was more and more alone, and became more and more unhappy. It was during the period of the Spanish War and he was very excited about it. I was afraid he was going to join the International Brigade, but his health would not permit.

The only people he now wanted to invite to Yew Tree Cottage were Communists, and it didn't matter what other qualifications they had: if they were Communists they were welcome. I found myself entertaining the strangest guests. Any person from the working class became a sort of god to Garman. As I got more and more bored I fought more and more with Garman. Not that I was against Communism as a principle. I just found it difficult suddenly to have my whole life directed by Garman's new religion, for it had certainly become that. He was like Sir Galahad after he had seen the Holy Grail. During the time of the Moscow purges I was upset because I thought Stalin had gone rather far, but Garman explained it all away. He had a marvelous way of convincing me that everything the Communists did was right. I must say they are pretty clever.

At Yew Tree Cottage, Robin, our dog, became quite ferocious and suddenly turned into a wonderful watchdog, barking at everyone who passed on the road and biting everyone who wore a uniform. The postman delivered the mail in fear and trembling. Finally Garman had to tie up Robin in a barrel. He beat him so badly that I was horrified, but he did manage to cure him and we were able to let Robin loose once more. Robin finally married his fiancée Borotra and gave her a lot of puppies. After which he became so bored with Borotra and her offspring that we had to give her away. In the winter the house was filthy as a result of all the mud the dogs brought in from their long walks over the downs. It really was intolerable. Robin got sadder and sadder as he got older, but later he consoled himself by playing with cats.

Garman bought a Siamese cat which went around the house crying like a baby all day. One day we found it poisoned in the garden behind Garman's little house. We suspected the General.

Garman liked to ride and he bought himself a horse, but when his Communist activities became all-engrossing he gave the animal to his brother, so that he himself would be free and have more time to devote to the cause. He gave up everything for Communism and enjoyed his asceticism. Of course I found life worse and worse under these conditions.

If Garman didn't succeed in getting me to "go Communist," he was successful with his brother-in-law Wish, who soon drove Lorna crazy with the *Daily Worker* doctrines. Eventually Wish turned his publishing house into an organ for Moscow. Rickword became a staunch Communist and Jackie, being the ideal wife, swallowed Communism whole to ensure having a peaceful life. I made an honest attempt to be dishonest and I just couldn't make the grade. I became like a bull when it sees red. Only in my case I saw red every time I heard Communism mentioned. If Garman were angry with me, instead of calling me a whore, he would call me a Trotskyite.

When Garman's oldest sister and her husband, the South African poet, Roy Campbell, fled from Spain during the revolution we went to see them. They were living at Wish's house and behaving like refugees. They were so outrageously Fascist that Garman would never see them again.

Once when Garman was away on a Communist job, William Gerhardi came down to visit me at Yew Tree Cottage. He made me promise that he would not see Garman as they were so far apart intellectually and politically. Suddenly Garman returned without warning me and a most awkward situation arose. They got into terrible arguments and Gerhardi never would believe that I had not arranged it all on purpose.

We often had invasions of rats and, since there was no Pied Piper in the region, Garman had to take upon himself the job of exterminating them. He lured them all into hay piles to which he set fire, and as they ran out he killed them by knocking them with a big stick. To enable himself to do this horrid business he pretended the rats were Fascists and called them ugly names each time he hit one. The rats got into the house and died from a poison we left for them. They died in the most awkward places: under floor boards which had then to be taken up, and one rat even got into our water tank. This caused a fearful commotion, as its dead body stopped the flow of water and the whole tank had to be cleaned out.

In the summer of 1936 I went alone to Venice for ten days. I had to take Sindbad back to Laurence, who was once more on the

Continent, so I stayed over and met Mary in Italy. The first few days I was with Sindbad and Mary, but after they left, when I was all alone, how happy I was. It had never occurred to me before that I could enjoy being alone, without talking to anyone except casual people for days on end. I kept the most peculiar hours and did anything that I felt like. I was unhampered by any influence or criticism and could enjoy Venice to my entire delight.

I walked miles all over the city at any time of the day or night and ate anywhere I happened to find myself. I revisited all my favorite churches and museums, and felt the same delight I always had in Carpaccio. I had only one temptation during these ten days, but I fled from it as though it were from the devil. It was a good-looking young man whom I kept meeting everywhere, but I was still in love with Garman.

On the way back I stopped over in Paris with my mother and bought some clothes. That always made her very happy. She had been down to Yew Tree Cottage a few times for the day and was very surprised by my new life and more disapproving than ever. She wanted to give me her pearl necklace but Garman told me if I took it I would have to sell it and give the money to the Communist Party. Of course my mother kept it.

When I returned to London Garman had found a three-room flat he wanted to take opposite the Foundling Estate. It was high up in the tree-tops and very small, but quite cozy. We had long since abandoned the place in the Adelphi, as it was too small for Garman amd Phyllis. Garman furnished this place with his usual good taste. I did not live in it very much for I stayed down in Petersfield.

Sindbad was now a boarder at Bedales boarding school. It was the first established co-educational school in England and was supposed to be progressive. Sindbad adored it because he played cricket on the school team and thought of nothing else. I was delighted Laurence had placed him in school so near me. It was only about six miles from Yew Tree. I fetched him every Sunday for the day, when he played tennis and swam and ate Kitty's *paellas* and English truffles.

Debbie had graduated from the dame school and was now in a progressive boarding school at Wimbledon. Pegeen wanted to be with her, so she went too. In the beginning both Pegeen and

Sindbad hated being in boarding school but they soon got to love it. Pegeen came home every weekend with Debbie.

In December 1936 the news of Mrs. Simpson and the King's intended marriage began leaking through to all the readers of American papers. No English people knew of it. *Time* magazine was censored and cut before it was sold, but Kay had given me a subscription which arrived straight from America; so I was one of the few people who knew about the affair. I told Garman and we made a bet that if it were true and the King married Mrs. Simpson, he would marry me.

One night when Emily and I were in Yew Tree, Garman sent me a telegram announcing "the great American victory" and congratulating me. Naturally I told him he had to keep his bet and marry me. But he knew it was too late and since we were getting on so badly about Communism there was no point in tying ourselves up. He had just made his last attempt on me by trying to recruit Emily, but he had failed.

I was so furious when he refused to marry me that I went out into the garden and tore up his best flower bed. It contained many rare plants and I took every one of these and hurled them over the fence into the field next door. It happened to be the coldest night of the year. The next day I was so ashamed that I collected all the plants and got Jack to assist me. He acted as though nothing unusual had occurred and helped me to place them in a wheelbarrow. We replanted them all with the exception of the few which had died of the frost overnight. This incident did not help to further my matrimonial aspirations. But I named the flower bed Mrs. Simpson's Bed.

During the week of the abdication we lived in the greatest state of excitement. Everything in England came to a standstill except the sale of extras. All the shops were empty, people just couldn't think of anything else. Finally we heard the King's abdication speech over the radio and even Garman cried.

Sindbad was staying with me during this exciting period as he was recovering from scarlet fever. He even forgot about cricket for a week in favor of the latest abdication bulletins.

Suddenly everything was over with Garman. He could endure no more. He said he had done all he could for me during the past three years and it was of no use, it wasn't what I wanted. I had killed his feelings for me and he was through. He really meant it. I don't see how he had stood it so long. The trouble was that I was still in love with him. He hated this because he said that I had never loved him, that I was only in love with him. It was true.

We had to separate, so Garman kept the flat in London and I retained the cottage. Garman asked if he could come down for weekends. He wanted to see Debbie and he loved Yew Tree, which was really his own creation. Of course, I said yes, he could come, for which I suffered greatly.

I lived alone all week for the children were in school and on weekends I looked forward to Garman's visits. When he came he insisted on sleeping with me. This caused great confusion. One weekend, when Phyllis Jones was with me, Garman and I had a row about Communism and I got so bitchy that he hit me. I slipped and fell. There was blood everywhere. Phyllis tried to stop me from sleeping with Garman but we always started again somehow.

At Eastertime I went to Paris and tried to forget Garman. I didn't. When I came back he told he was in love with a young Communist woman called Paddy, who used to work in a publishing house that amalgamated with his but who was now doing a Party job. She was very attractive and I had been the first one to remark on it. She looked rather American, with a tip-tilted nose and a smart little figure. I met her at Garman's flat one evening when she and Garman had been working late.

Garman had another staunch follower, Greta. She was in love with him and when I finally had to tell her about Paddy in order to clarify the situation, she became even more political and attended a summer school for Communism. She did this, however, only to get some life. The poor woman lived alone with three daughters on a hill the other side of Petersfield. Greta loved to have men around and thought of the summer school as a last resort to recruit them. She was right, because she found wounded soldiers from the International Brigade and invited them to her house to recuperate. Greta was a strange woman from the upper middle class, and she had led a peculiar life and was completely *déclassée*. When I first met her I thought she was a D. H. Lawrence heroine. But she became a good friend of mine and when Garman neglected her I consoled her by my friendship. Finally her eldest daughter married a truck driver and she didn't seem to mind, for she thought it was a sign of the times.

Garman was very upset about his new love affair because Paddy had a husband. They seemed to belong to the Communist Party to the extent of having no say about their private lives. Garman did not want to interfere and break up their marriage, and anyway Paddy wasn't quite ready to leave her husband, who was much older than she was, and whom she rarely saw. Also they had a child. They both belonged to the working class. Suddenly they were sent abroad on a mission together and Garman was very unhappy.

Garman and I took six months to really end our mutual life. As he came down to the cottage and insisted on sleeping with me the whole thing became very painful. I found myself being dragged into my life with him again and again instead of making a clean break. Once we even tried to live together in London. If I were in town, I stayed with Phyllis. But then Garman suddenly invited me. Of course it didn't work. We were too incompatible to live together anymore.

The one thing we had in common was the children. He adored them and that was what had kept us together. They loved him too.

In the summer Garman went down to Swanage to attend a Communist summer school. He wanted me to come too, with the children. I couldn't make up my mind but in the end I joined him. It would have been a wonderful holiday if only we hadn't been so at loggerheads. I loved Dorset ever since I had been there with John. Garman took us to beautiful places and we walked and swam and enjoyed the three children's company.

Garman was upset about Paddy and worried about what Harry Pollitt thought of this affair. I teased him unmercifully by telling him that Pollitt had sent for me to come and talk to him, and Garman believed me. The strange thing was that a year later Pollitt did send for me; so I lied only in so far as I set the date too soon.

My mother arrived in Europe that summer very ill and, although I knew she had had several operations. I got a fearful shock when her maid told me that she had only six months more to live. I stayed with her in London and later in the summer I joined her in Paris.

All the strength the poor woman had left she expended on the International Exposition that was held in Paris in the summer of 1937. She loved it and we spent hours there.

At this time I said to Emily, "I think my life is over." Emily replied, "If you feel that way, perhaps it is."

# Chapter 11

# Guggenheim Jeune

When the fact dawned on me that my life with Garman was over I was rather at a loss for an occupation, since I had never been anything but a wife for the last fifteen years. The problem was solved by my friend Peggy Waldman, who suggested that I start a publishing house or open an art gallery in London. I immediately renounced the idea of a publishing house, because I decided it would be too expensive. Little did I dream of the thousands of dollars I was about to sink into art.

The obvious person to help me was Emily's friend, Humphrey Jennings. He was a young Surrealist painter of thirty. He was also a photographer, a poet and a producer of films. He was dynamic and always bursting with a new idea; but, as he had too many, he never got much accomplished. He was a sort of genius, and he looked like Donald Duck. We began our collaboration by searching for a place for the gallery. Everything was vague on my part. My mother was dying, and I knew that I would never settle down to anything before she died. I expected to go to New York to spend Christmas with her, the last one of her life; and I was really only playing with the idea of a gallery.

Humphrey came down to Petersfield for the weekend. Emily

was there, and as she was finished with him, she offered him to me as though he were a sort of object she no longer required, and I went in his room and took him in the same spirit. He had strange ideas about pleasures in life, and one was to spend the weekend in a millionaire yacht club. He never achieved this ambition with me, since it was so far removed from my normal taste. But he did follow me to Paris where I was staying with my mother in the Hôtel Crillon. When Humphrey came I took a room in a small hotel on the Rive Gauche. It was filled with Napoleonic furniture and looked very formal.

Humphrey was very pleased with his ugly, emaciated body. He kept jumping all over the bed saying, "Look at me! Don't you like me? Don't you think I'm beautiful?" I had no desire to spend the weekend in bed. I insisted on going to the Paris Exposition every time I could manage to get him out of the hotel. He wanted to meet Marcel Duchamp, so I took him to see him, and in return he took me to meet André Breton in his little art gallery, Gradiva. Breton looked like a lion pacing up and down in a cage.

Humphrey came a second weekend, but then I refused to leave the Hôtel Crillon, and he had to take a room alone. I had Debbie with me, and used her as an excuse not to live with him. I really could not endure the thought of another weekend in bed with Humphrey. We went to see Yves Tanguy to ask him if we could exhibit his work in London. Humphrey had wild ideas about the way of presenting Tanguy's paintings. None of us understood these ideas, but Tanguy politely agreed. He must have been surprised by the strange trio we made.

Finally, I had to tell Humphrey that our affair was over, and that we could only be friends in the future. I put the blame on Garman, and said I was still in love with him. We were standing on one of the bridges of the Seine, and I remember how Humphrey wept. I think he had hopes of some kind of a wonderful life with me, surrounded by luxury, gaiety and Surrealism. After this was settled we had a good time at the Exposition, where I was able for the first time to study modern art.

After Humphrey left, Garman came to talk over our separation which really had to be settled. It was complicated because of the children, the house and the flat. We did not make much progress over these matters, since, to Garman's great surprise, I took a double room and we spent all our time making love and visiting the Exposition. He was very happy in Paris because of the *Front Populaire*, which was at its height.

Garman had come to talk over our separation, but I begged him not to leave me until I was settled in the gallery. He was adamant, however, and insisted on ending our life upon his return to London. I remember spending a whole day at the Exposition with tears streaming down my cheeks. But it did not alter things in any way. Garman expected soon to live with Paddy, but when he got back to London he wrote me of his great disappointment—she would not leave her husband. That did not alter his decision in any way about me.

My children came up from Mégève and we all lived at the Hôtel Crillon with my mother. Those were the last days we spent with her; she died in November in New York before I could reach her.

When I took the children back to England, Garman and I finally arranged our separation on a practical basis. He moved to Hampstead and I kept the flat. I gave him the furniture and rented Yew Tree Cottage from him. He now had a job with the Communist Party and this extra rent money came in very handy. He asked me to continue having Debbie for weekends with Pegeen. I was only too pleased, but her mother made a lot of trouble and the situation became almost as complicated as my divorce from Laurence. In the end it was decided that Debbie would come every third weekend.

After a while things petered out with Humphrey. He had so many other occupations that we gave up our collaboration. I finally rented a beautiful second floor in a building on Cork Street and engaged my friend Wyn Henderson as secretary. She was extremely clever and had the whole place decorated for me while I went off to Paris to try to arrange a Brancusi show. She named my gallery Guggenheim Jeune.

When I got to Paris, Brancusi was not there. But Marcel Duchamp and Mary introduced me to Cocteau and we decided to give him the opening exhibition.

At that time I couldn't distinguish one thing in art from another. Marcel tried to educate me. I don't know what I would have done without him. To begin with, he taught me the difference between Abstract and Surrealist art. Then he introduced me to all the artists. They all adored him, and I was well received wherever I went. He planned shows for me and gave me lots of advice. I have him to thank for my introduction to the modern art world.

Marcel first presented me to Jean Arp, the sculptor, who was an excellent poet and a most amusing man. He took me to Meudon to see the modern house he had built for himself and his wife Sophie. They each had a whole studio floor, and there was a garden full of Arp's work. Sophie was an abstract painter and a sculptress. His work was more Surrealist, but he managed to remain on both sides of the fence and exhibited with both groups. Sophie, a Swiss ex-school teacher, edited an interesting magazine called *Plastique*. Arp was always trying to further Sophie's career and, since her work was dull, it often became painful to be so bothered about nothing. They had done one good sculpture together called *Sculpture Conjugale*. Sophie was a wonderful wife. She did everything possible for Arp besides doing her own work and running the magazine. The first thing I bought for my collection was an Arp bronze. He took me to the foundry where it had been cast and I fell so in love with it that I asked to have it in my hands. The instant I felt it I wanted to own it.

I must have gone to Paris expecting something to occur but I never dreamed for an instant what was in store for me. In spite of the fact that I took every consolation which crossed my path, I was entirely obsessed for over a year by the strange creature, Samuel Beckett. He came into my life the day after Christmas, 1937. I had known him slightly. He had been to our house on the Avenue Reille. I knew that he was a friend of James Joyce, that he had been engaged to his daughter and had caused her great unhappiness. Beckett was not Joyce's secretary, as everyone has since claimed, though he was perpetually doing errands for him. Joyce had a Russian Jewish intellectual for secretary, called Paul Léon, who was later killed by the Germans.

Beckett was a tall, lanky Irishman of about thirty with enormous green eyes that never looked at you. He wore spectacles, and always seemed to be far away solving some intellectual problem; he spoke very seldom and never said anything stupid. He was excessively polite, but rather awkward. He dressed badly in tight-fitting French clothes and had no vanity about his appearance. Beckett accepted life fatalistically, as he never seemed to think he could alter anything. He was a frustrated writer, a pure intellectual. I met him again at Helen Joyce's.

That evening we dined at Fouquet's, where James Joyce gave us an excellent dinner. Joyce inquired a lot about my gallery in London, and as usual was charming and very attractive. He wore a beautiful Irish waistcoat which had belonged to his grandfather.

After dinner we went back to Helen's and then Beckett asked if he could take me home. I was surprised when he took my arm and walked me all the way to the Rue de Lille, where I was living in a borrowed apartment. He did not make his intentions clear but in an awkward way asked me to lie down on the sofa next to him. We soon found ourselves in bed, where we remained until the next evening at dinner time. We might be there still, but I had to go to dine with Arp, who unfortunately had no telephone. I don't know why, but I mentioned champagne, and Beckett rushed out and bought several bottles which we drank in bed. When Beckett left, he said very simply and fatalistically, as though we were never going to meet again, "Thank you. It was nice while it lasted." During his short disappearance Joyce, to whom he was a sort of slave, got very worried. Helen guessed he must be with me, so our secret was public. After that I moved to Mary Reynolds's house as she was in the hospital and I did not see Beckett for some time. One night I met him on a traffic island in the Boulevard Montparnasse. I must have been looking for him without realizing it, as I was not at all surprised when I found him. It was as though we had both come to a rendezvous.

We went home to Mary's house where we lived for twelve days. We were destined to be happy together only for this short period. Out of all the thirteen months I was in love with him, I remember this time with great emotion. To begin with he was in love with me as well, and we were both excited intellectually. Since John's death I had not talked my own, or rather his, language. And now I suddenly was free again to say what I thought and felt.

In spite of the fact that I was opening a modern art gallery in London I much preferred old masters. Beckett told me one had to accept the art of our day as it was a living thing. He had two passions besides James Joyce. One was Jack Yeats and the other a Dutch painter, Geer van Velde, a man of nearly forty, who seemed to be completely dominated by Picasso, and he wanted me to give them both exhibitions. I could not refuse him anything, so it was agreed. Jack Yeats luckily realized that his painting was not at all in line with my gallery and let me off. But I agreed and gave the Van Velde show. In fact, I bought some of the pictures which were rather like Picasso's, secretly under various names in order to please Beckett, but even after this Van Velde, not knowing I had done so, asked me for five hundred dollars, which I could not refuse him.

Beckett was a writer and brought me his works to read. I thought his poems were bad. They were so childish. But one of his books, *Murphy*, which had just been published, was rather extraordinary, and his previous study on Proust was excellent. I suppose he was much influenced by Joyce, but he did have certain strange and morbid ideas which were quite original and a wonderfully sardonic sense of humor.

The thing I liked best about our life together was that I never knew at what hour of the night or day he might return to me. His comings and goings were completely unpredictable, and I found that exciting. He was drunk all of the time and seemed to wander around in a dream. I had a lot of work to do because of my gallery and often I had to get up in the afternoon to see Cocteau, who was to have the opening show. Beckett objected to this; he wanted me to remain in bed with him.

It seemed ironic that I should create a new existence for myself because I had no personal life, and now that I had a personal life, it had to be sacrificed. On the tenth day of our amours Beckett was untrue to me. He allowed a friend of his from Dublin to creep into his bed. I don't know how I found it out, but he admitted it saying that he simply had not put her out when she came to him, and that making love without being in love was like taking coffee without brandy. From this I inferred I was the brandy in his life, but nevertheless I was furious, and said that I was finished with him. The next night he phoned me, but I was so angry that I refused to speak to him. A few minutes later he was stabbed in the ribs by an unknown maniac on the Avenue d'Orléans and taken to a hospital. I had no idea of this and as I was leaving for London I wanted to say goodbye to him. When I called his hotel the proprieter told me what had happened. I nearly went mad. I rushed to all the hospitals in Paris but could not find him. Finally I phoned Nora Joyce, who told me where he was. I went to him at once, and left some flowers and a note telling him how much I loved him and that I forgave him everything. The next day James Joyce went to see Beckett in the hospital and I went with him. As he was semi-blind, it took Joyce a long time to be conducted by his secretary to the right ward. But by a sort of instinct I rushed in and without any help found Beckett. He was surprised to see me, as he thought I had left for London. He was very happy. I said goodbye to him. I knew he was in good hands because Joyce was looking after him, and that he would be laid up for a long time. I had to go back to London to open my gallery, but I meant to return to Paris as soon as I could.

The arrangements for the Cocteau show were rather difficult. To speak to Cocteau one had to go to his hotel in the rue de Cambon and try to talk to him while he lay in bed, smoking opium. The odor was extremely pleasant, though this seemed a rather odd way of doing our business. One night he decided to invite me to dinner. He sat opposite a mirror, which was behind me, and so fascinated was he by himself that he could not keep his eyes off it. He was so beautiful, with his long oriental face and his exquisite hands and tapering fingers, that I do not blame him for the delight he took in his image.

His conversation was as fascinating as his face and hands, and I longed for him to come to London for the show, but he was not well enough. However, he wrote the introduction for his catalogue and Beckett translated it.

My life in London was hectic. There was so much work to be done, I don't know how I survived. To begin with I had to refurnish my flat, since I had given Garman all the furniture. Then I had to open the gallery, and obtain the names of hundreds of people to invite to the opening, and have a catalogue and invitations printed and sent out. Luckily Mary Reynolds and Marcel Duchamp flew over for the opening and Marcel hung the show and made it look beautiful.

Cocteau sent me about thirty original drawings he had made for the décor of his play *Les Chevaliers de la Table Ronde*. I had also borrowed the furniture which he had designed for it, and he especially made some dinner plates which were in the same spirit. He also made some drawings in ink in the same spirit as the

others, and two on linen bed sheets that were especially done for
the show. One was an allegorical subject called *La Peur donnant
ailes au Courage,* which included a portrait of the actor Jean
Marais. He and two very decadent looking figures appeared with
pubic hairs. Cocteau had pinned leaves over these, but the
drawing caused a great scandal with the British Customs, who
held it up at Croydon. Marcel and I rushed down to release it. I
asked why they objected to the nude in art, and they replied it was
not the nude but the pubic hairs which worried them. On
promising not to exhibit this sheet to the general public, but only
to a few friends in my private office, I was permitted to take it. In
fact, I liked it so much that in the end I bought it.

Jean Cocteau, *La Peur donnant ailes au Courage*

This was before I was thinking of collecting. But gradually I
bought one work of art from every show I gave, so as not to
disappoint the artists if I were unsuccessful in selling anything.
In those days, as I had no idea how to sell and had never bought
pictures, this seemed to be the best solution and the least I could
do to please the artists.

The opening of Guggenheim Jeune in January 1938 was a great
success, but what pleased me most was receiving a wire of *auguri*
signed "Oblomov."

I called Beckett Oblomov from the book by Goncharov that
Djuna Barnes had given me to read so long before. When I met

him I was surprised to find a living Oblomov. I made him read the book and of course he immediately saw the resemblance between himself and the strange inactive hero who finally did not even have the will power to get out of bed.

Conversation with Beckett was difficult. He was never very animated, and it took hours and lots of drink to warm him up before he finally unraveled himself. If he ever said anything to me which made me think he loved me, as soon as I taxed him with it he took it back by saying he had been drunk at the time. When I asked him what he was going to do about our life he invariably replied, "Nothing."

As soon as we could leave London, Mary, Marcel Duchamp and I went back to Paris. Beckett was now out of the hospital and was convalescing in his hotel. I took a room there but I don't think that pleased him at all. My sister Hazel had a wonderful flat on the Ile Saint-Louis which I was able to borrow. It had no furniture, only a big bed and lots of her own paintings (she was a good primitive painter). I tried to take Beckett to live with me on the island, but he refused to remain there all the time. He came and went and always brought champagne to bed.

Beckett had a friend called Brian Coffey. He was a little dark man, a sort of dried-up intellectual and a Thomist. He tried hard to attach himself to me, and I used to tease Beckett about him with great tactlessness. I often said I wanted to sleep with him. Beckett had an inferiority complex, and as I had talked to him so passionately about John Holms, and also made fun of Humphrey Jennings to him, he conceived the idea that he really was not at all the man I wanted. One day he announced that he was never going to sleep with me again and told me to have Brian, for then at least I might be satisfied. I was so infuriated by this proposition (though I now realize it was entirely my stupidity that made Beckett suggest it) that I went and slept with Brian. Beckett looked dignified and sad as he walked away from us, knowing what was going to happen. The next day Beckett asked me if I liked Brian, but I must have said "No," because Beckett came back to me. We were very happy together for twenty-four hours, and then everything was ruined. We met Brian for lunch and he asked Beckett if he were interfering in his life, as he had only just realized that I really belonged to Beckett. To my great surprise

Beckett gave me to Brian. I was so horrified I rushed out of the
café and walked all over Paris in despair. I went to Beckett's hotel
and made a terrible scene, but it did no good. He said he was no
longer in love with me.

Even if our sex life was over nothing else was. Our relationship
continued unchanged in every other respect. We were perpetually
together, and I felt the same ecstasy in his society as I had
previously. At night he walked me home over the bridge behind
Notre Dame. When we reached my front door Beckett went
through the most terrible agonies trying to decide what to do. But
he always ended up by pulling himself together and running away.
This caused me incalculable misery and I spent nights lying
awake, longing for his return.

Beckett had little vitality and always believed in following the
path of least resistance. However, he was prepared to do anything
for Joyce, and he was always leaving me to see his great idol. I was
very jealous of Joyce. I think Joyce loved Beckett as a son.

In February 1938 Joyce had his fifty-sixth birthday. Maria Jolas
gave him a dinner party at Helen Joyce's. Beckett was in a state of
great excitement about suitable presents. He went with me and
made me buy a blackthorn stick. God knows why. As for his own
gift he very much wanted to find some Swiss wine, Joyce's favorite
beverage. I remembered that John Holms and I once years before
had dined in a Swiss restaurant with Joyce, and I went back to the
Rue Ste. Anne, found the place and asked them if they would sell
some wine. Of course they consented when I told them whom it
was for. Beckett went to get it and was very happy. At the dinner
party Joyce offered a hundred francs to anyone who could guess
the title of his new book (*Finnegans Wake*), which was just about
to be published. Beckett I am sure won the bet. At the party were
present only Joyce's sycophants. I met again Herbert Gorman,
whom I had not seen for years. The table was decorated with a
plaster model of Dublin through which ran a green ribbon
representing Joyce's beloved Liffey. Joyce got very tight and did a
little jig by himself in the middle of the room.

Marcel sent me to see Kandinsky. He was a wonderful old man
of seventy, so jolly and charming, with a horrid wife some thirty
years younger called Nina. Everybody adored him and detested
her. I asked him if he wanted to have an exhibition in London,

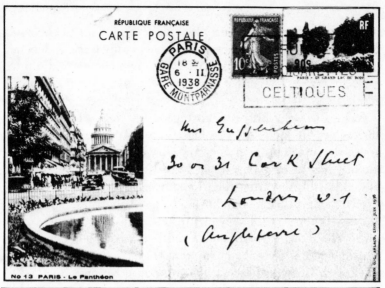

Postcard from James Joyce thanking me for my gift of a blackthorn stick

and as he had never shown there he was delighted. He had a friend in England who owned a lot of his pictures, Sir Michael Sadleir.

Kandinsky, who was upset by my uncle Solomon Guggenheim's supplanting him by Rudolf Bauer, his third-rate imitator, claimed that though he had encouraged my uncle to buy Bauer's paintings now that Bauer had taken his place he never told my uncle to buy Kandinsky's paintings. He wanted me to get my uncle to buy one of his early works. It seems that it was one my uncle had wanted for a long time. I promised to do my best, never dreaming of the result.

Kandinsky and his wife arranged the whole London show themselves. It included paintings from 1910 to 1937. I merely sent them a plan of the gallery and they even decided where each picture was to be hung. They were very businesslike. No one looked less like an artist than Kandinsky, who resembled a Wall Street broker. Mrs. Kandinsky behaved horribly and I am surprised they ever sold any pictures: she was so grasping. At the end of the show, I bought one of the 1937 period and none of the marvelous early ones. Later in New York I bought many others, but I wish I now had several that were in my show.

One day, during the exhibition, an art teacher from a public school in the north of England came to the gallery and begged me to allow him to show ten Kandinskys to his pupils at the school. I was delighted with the idea and wrote to Kandinsky for his permission. He wrote back that he was very much pleased but with his usual businesslike attitude added that the pictures should be insured. When the show was over my schoolmaster came and strapped ten canvases on to his car and drove away with them. I am certain Kandinsky had never been so informally treated before. When the schoolmaster brought back the paintings he told me how much they had meant to the school.

As I had promised Kandinsky, I wrote to my uncle asking him if he still wanted to buy the painting that he had so long desired. I received a friendly answer saying that he had turned the letter over to the Baroness Rebay, the curator of his museum, and that she would reply herself. In due time I received this extraordinary document:

Dear Mrs. Guggenheim "jeune"

Your request to sell us a Kandinsky picture was given to me, to answer.

First of all we do not ever buy from any dealer, as long as great artists offer their work for sale themselves & secondly will be your gallery the last one for our foundation to use, if ever the need to get a historically important picture, should force us to use a sales gallery.

It is extremely distasteful at this moment, when the name of Guggenheim stands for an ideal in art, to see it used for commerce so as to give the wrong impression, as if this great philanthropic work was intended to be a useful boost to some small shop. Non-objective art, you will soon find out, does not come by the dozen, to make a shop of this art profitable. Commerce with real art cannot exist for that reason. You will soon find you are propagating mediocrity; if not thrash. If you are interested in non-objective art you can well afford to buy it and start a collection. This way you can get into useful contact with artists, and you can leave a fine collection to your country if you know how to chose. If you don't you will soon find yourself in trouble also in commerce.

Due to the foresight of an important man since many years collecting and protecting real art, through my work and experience, the name of Guggenheim became known for great art and it is very poor taste indeed to make use of it, of our work and fame, to cheapen it to a profit.

Yours very truly,

H. R.

P.S. Now, our newest publication will not be sent to England for some time to come.

During the Kandinsky show Brian came to visit me in London. We did nothing but talk about Beckett, whom we both adored. I think Brian wanted to marry me, but I had no such desire. It was a great relief when he returned to Paris after a week.

Cedric Morris, one of my oldest friends, was a painter of flowers who had an iris farm and a school of painting in Suffolk. He wanted to have a show in my gallery, but he did not want to exhibit his beautiful flower pictures for which he was famous. Instead he wished to exhibit some fifty portraits he had done of London celebrities. The portraits were in most cases nearly caricatures, all of them on the unpleasant side. There was no reason for showing them in any Surrealist and Abstract gallery, but Wyn and I loved Cedric so much that we could not refuse. He covered the walls three rows deep. I think he must have hung nearly one hundred of them. One evening during the exhibition we gave a party to stir up a little trade. The result was most unexpected. All we stirred up was a terrible row. One of the guests, an architect I shall call Mr. Silvertoe, so much disliked the portraits that in order to show his disapproval he started burning the catalogues. Cedric Morris, naturally infuriated, hit

Mr. Silvertoe and a bloody battle took place. The walls of the
gallery were spattered with blood. The next day Cedric phoned to
apologize and offered to remove his paintings. Of course we did
not let him.

A few months later Arp came to visit me. Marcel Duchamp had
helped me arrange a show of contemporary sculpture, and Arp
who was one of the exhibitors came over to further it himself. Arp
was very domestic about the house. He got up early and waited
impatiently for me to wake up. He served me breakfast every
mornng and washed all the dishes. We had so much fun together
and were so gay that it really was a delightful week. We went to
Petersfield. Arp was enthusiastic about the English countryside
and loved the little Sussex churches. He went back to Paris with a
porkpie hat and a bread box under his arm. He knew only one
word of English, "candlesticks." His vocabulary did not increase
during his stay.

During Arp's visit I was invited by Jacob Epstein to go and see
his work. Of course I took Arp with me. This greatly enraged
Epstein who barely wished to admit Arp until we protested that he
was a great admirer. Epstein hated the Surrealists and thought
Arp should not be interested in his work. But on the contrary Arp
was fascinated by the strange things we saw, among them the
enormous figure of Christ lying entombed. Epstein's portraits are
miraculous. They certainly are as good as anything done in the
Italian Renaissance; but I hate his other concoctions.

I soon got into trouble again with the British Customs. Marcel
Duchamp had sent me from Paris a sculpture show, consisting of
works by Brancusi, Raymond Duchamp-Villon, Antoine Pevsner,
Arp, his wife, Henri Laurens and Alexander Calder. Henry
Moore was to represent England. But the Customs would not
admit the show into England as an art exhibition. J. B. Manson,
the director of the Tate Gallery, had not passed on it, and
therefore it could enter the country only if the exhibits were
admitted as separate pieces of bronze, marble, wood, etc. This
would have meant my having to pay heavy duty on them, which I
would have done had it come to the worst. This was because of a
stupid old law which existed to protect English stonecutters from
foreign competition. It rested with the director of the Tate Gallery
to decide in such cases what was art and what wasn't. Mr.
Manson, the director, abused his privilege and refused to pass my

**GUGGENHEIM**

# EXHIBITION
# OF CONTEMPORARY
# SCULPTURE

Brancusi

Laurens

Hans Arp

Duchamp-Villon

Henry Moore

Pevsner

Calder

Tauber-Arp

*April 11 — May 2*

**30 CORK STREET (BOND STREET) W.1**

**JEUNE**

Printed at The Curwen Press Ltd. for the Proprietors, The London Gallery Ltd.

show, which he declared was not art. This was really so scandalous that Wyn Henderson got all the art critics to sign a protest against this verdict. As a result, my case was brought up in the House of Commons and we won it. Mr. Manson not only lost his case, but pretty soon his job as well. I thus rendered a great service to foreign artists and to England.

All the papers immediately took up the story and the exhibition became famous. Brancusi's Sculpture for the Blind was reproduced in Tom Driberg's column in the *Daily Express*.

At this moment what I had told Garman a year before to tease him actually came true. Harry Pollitt, having read so much about my success in my battle against Mr. Manson, decided that I was much too important a person to have lost. He sent for me, telling me that he was certain he could fix up all my difficulties about Communism in ten minutes. I wrote back and said I was much too busy to go to him but that he "should come up and see me some time." He never did. By this time Garman was living with Paddy. Later he married her.

One day Edgell Rickword invited me for dinner and asked me if I would render a great service to the Communist Party. They wanted to borrow my flat for Louis Aragon and a whole convention of Communist writers who were coming to London. They needed a very chic apartment, as when the English writers had been invited to Paris they had been royally received at a hotel on the Avenue de l'Opéra. I protested, saying my flat was not nearly grand enough as it was on the third floor without a lift and was a modest little affair in Bloomsbury without servants. The Communists had to look elsewhere.

Wyn Henderson was a most remarkable woman. I don't know what I would have done without her. She made everything go like clockwork in the gallery, though she had had no previous experience of this kind. She was a typographer by profession and had run several modern presses. Therefore, we had the most beautiful invitations and catalogues printed. She had a lot of common sense, extraordinary tact and social grace, remembering the faces of all the people who came to the gallery whom I never recognized. She had a great zest for life. One day I made her count up her love affairs. When she came to a hundred she stopped. At this period she was very fat, although she must have resembled a Venetian beauty in her former years. To her great sorrow she now had much less success with men than before, but she was never jealous of anyone else's happiness. In fact she was always egging me on to enjoy myself. Years before she had pushed her favorite son Ion in my way, and now she tried it with Nigel, the younger one. He was a darling but I really only regarded him as a sweet baby, but I loved his soul and felt we were made of the same clay. When this did not work and she discovered that I was still in love with Beckett, Wyn sent me back to Paris. Beckett was flattered by my visit and by my constancy. He was in a strange state, and told me that our life would be all right one day. Ever since his birth he had retained a terrible memory of life in his mother's womb. He was constantly suffering from this and had awful crises, when he felt he was suffocating. He never seemed to be able to make up his mind whether or not he was going to have me, but he did not want to give me up. (To replace our sex life, we used to drink wildly and then walk all over Paris until the early morning.)

My passion for Beckett was inspired by the fact that I really believed he was capable of great intensity, and that I could bring it out. He, on the other hand, always denied it, saying he was dead and had no feelings that were human and that was why he had not been able to fall in love with Joyce's daughter. *

I asked Helen Joyce what to do about Beckett and she suggested that I rape him. So one night, when he was very indecisive and seemed to be yearning toward me and floating into me in spite of himself, I went home with him thinking how much less I should really like him if I ever had him. In fact, as he took my arm, I had the illusion of everything being settled and I thought, "How boring." Nevertheless I went home with him and insisted on remaining all night. He suddenly became terrified and rushed away and left me in his apartment alone. I was so upset that I got up at four in the morning and wrote a poem which I left on his desk, and then went back to England.

* A poem written by Beckett: They come
                         Different and the same
                         With each it is different and the same
                         With each the absence of love is different
                         With each the absence of life is the same

A woman storming at my gate—
Is this inevitable fate?
From far away the hammer fell:
Was that my life or death's last knell?

To my void she came much wanting
Shall I chance this fear unending?
Shall I face the pain of rupture?
Shall I execute the future?

Every step I take she battles,
Every inch the death-knell rattles.
Shall I kill her Holy passion?
Destroying life, not taking action.

So once again I had to renounce Beckett. I was, however, destined to see him soon in London, where he came for the opening of his dearly beloved Van Velde's show. When the paintings were hung in my gallery, they looked more Picasso than ever. All the critics seemed to think so and they gave Van Velde little publicity. However, Van Velde was very happy, as I kept buying all his paintings under different names, or as gifts for my friends. This was all because I loved Beckett so much and he loved Van Velde.

I took the Van Veldes down to Petersfield for the weekend and filled the house with Van Velde gouaches. Beckett followed us after much deliberation. We had quite a nice house party, since the George Reaveys came too. When I had gone to bed in the dining room, having given my bedroom to the Reaveys, Beckett came and talked to me. He told me he had a mistress and asked me if I minded. Of course I said no. She sounded to me more like a mother than a mistress. She had found him a flat and made him curtains and looked after him generally. He was not in love with her and she did not make scenes, as I did. I had met her once in his room before she was his mistress, when I was, and I could not be jealous of her; she was not attractive enough. She was about my age, and we were both older than Beckett. After he told me all this, I was even more keen than I had been to get off with Mesens.

E. L. T. Mesens was a Surrealist poet and the director of the London Gallery, my neighbor in Cork Street. We had a united

# GUGGENHEIM JEUNE
## 30 CORK STREET, LONDON W.1

---

## GEER VAN VELDE
### CATALOGUE

1. Promenade des Anglais
2. L'anniversaire
3. Minuit 36-37
4. Femme
5. Paysage
6. Nature Morte
7. Rencontre dans la ville
8. Femme
9. Nature Morte
10. A la fenêtre
11. Fête foraine
12. Dans le midi
13. Aventure
14. Diseuse de bonne aventure
15. Couple
16. Mme. L. de la S.
17. Femme
18. Composition
19. Corbeille de fleurs
20. Eclairs à l'horizon
21. L'imprévu
    *collection S.B.*
22. Le Musicien
23. Hiob
24. Nature Morte, meridionale
25. La Dame au Balcon
26. La Silencieuse
    *collection B.C.*
27. Composition
28. Composition
29. Etrange visite
30. Masse
31. Des fleurs au clair de la Lune
32. Composition figurale
33. Concentration feminine
34. Jazz Band
35. Silence
36. L'Invitation
37. La Ville Lumière
38. Kermesse
39. l'Hiver
40. Portrait de Mr. M. H.
41. Portrait de Mr. E. K.
42. Coup de vent
43. Chartres
44. Méditation
45. Aprés le diner

### GEER VAN VELDE

Born the third of four April 5th 1898 at Lisse near Leyden. Tulips and Rembrandt. 1911 apprenticed to a house-painter. Wanderings in Holland and Brabant, rubbing colours in order to buy them. Since 1925 in Paris. 1927 South of France. 1931 Britanny. Exhibitions; 1925 at the Hague, 1926-30 in Paris with Independants. 1933 with his brother Bram Van Velde at the Hague, 1937 at the Hague, Pictures in Amsterdam in the Stedelijk and the Regnault collection, at the Hague in the Stedelijk and the Kramers collection, in private collections in Brabant, France, Germany, U.S.A. and even England.

Believes painting should mind its own business, *i.e.* colour. *I.e.* no more say Picasso than Fabritius, Vermeer. Or inversely.

Samuel BECKETT

15

front and we were very careful not to interfere with each other's exhibitions. I bought paintings from Mesens. He was a gay little Flamand, quite vulgar, but really very nice and warm. He now wanted me as his mistress, so we were to have dinner together. Before Beckett went back to Paris I went off with Mesens and took a diabolical pleasure in doing so.

The affair with Mesens did not last long. I told him how much I loved Beckett, and then I ran away and went to Paris again to see him. Mesens was the editor of the *London Bulletin*, a Surrealist paper which was rather good, but, like Mesens himself, a little too commercial. The paper advertised everything Mesens sold in his gallery, and he produced my catalogues free of charge in exchange for an advertisement that I paid for. I wanted to get control of this paper and improve it, but Mesens was jealous and would have no other collaborator besides Humphrey Jennings. This time I went to Paris and took my car with me for Beckett. I wired him I was coming, but he did not meet me at Calais as I had hoped. He merely waited for me listlessly in his apartment and seemed bored with me.

One afternoon at his flat, when the Van Veldes were there, Beckett and Van Velde began to exchange clothes. It was a rather homosexual performance, disguised, of course, by the most normal gestures. I accused Beckett of being in love with Van Velde. After that we went to a dancing place and an awful scene followed; Beckett went away leaving me with the Van Veldes.

Beckett and I did not get on well after this and I did not see much of him. I was living in Mary's house and one day I said to her, "There's no point in my being here, as a I never see Beckett." I decided to go back to London. Before leaving I wrote him a letter telling him I would like to say goodbye. This seemed to bring him back to life, as we then arranged to drive the Van Veldes to the Midi where they were going to live.

It was difficult to leave because Beckett always spent the weekends with his mistress and he could not suddenly change his habits. He managed to get off at two o'clock on Sunday, and we all departed in my Delage. Beckett drove us to Marseilles and then we went to Cassis for the day. The Van Veldes were surprised by all this, as they never could make head or tail of our relationship. They had seen Beckett and me fight so often that they never dreamt we could always begin all over again where we left off.

We deposited them in Marseilles and started off for the north. I had wasted so much time waiting around Paris for Beckett that now I really was in a hurry to get back, as I had to drive Yves Tanguy to London in time for his exhibition. On the way back we stopped at Dijon. I had many memories of this sad town; I did not think I would ever add any more. Beckett's behavior was so strange that I can never forget what happened this time. By mistake we had a dreary dinner in a depressing restaurant, which was stupid, considering Dijon is famous for its excellent food. Beckett had no flair for the right places, and his Protestant upbringing made him automatically shun the pleasant things in life. When we went to a hotel he took a double room. This I thought strange, but then all his behavior was most peculiar. We got into separate beds. I soon crept into his, and Beckett jumped out and got into the other bed saying I had cheated. When I asked him why he had taken a double room he said it was thirty francs cheaper than two singles.

The next morning we walked all over Dijon. I was happy to be with Beckett, who really was an ideal companion as he loved to see beautiful things. It was a pleasure to visit the museums with him. We really got on marvelously well, and I told him how much nicer he now was than he had been. He said I was much easier to get on with, since I no longer made scenes. This trip ended all too soon because of Tanguy. We parted with sorrow, Beckett as usual regretting he relinquished me.

Early the next morning I left for England. For some unknown reason the car would not start, and I wasted an hour before I could get off. This made me late for Tanguy and his wife. Our whole trip consequently was a mad rush to Boulogne and we nearly missed the boat. The Tanguys had never been to England and this was an exciting adventure for them. They were unspoiled and so different from all the blasé people I knew that it was a pleasure to be with them. When we arrived in London I turned them over to Peter Dawson, an English Surrealist who had invited them to live with him. He was frantic with joy about their being in London and felt he owned them, although he barely knew them, having met them only once in Paris.

I had to go down to Petersfield to see Pegeen, whom I had abandoned for five weeks. Peter and Tanguy were to hang the show over the weekend. Hazel was living in my house and Pegeen spent weekends with her. We unpacked an enormous trunk containing my mother's silver, which had arrived from America. Hazel and I divided it up while a friend took the rôle of referee. Neither of us really wanted any of it, it was ugly and Victorian. There was the enormous tea set I have already referred to. We both refused to accept it and decided to sell it. Later, when Djuna saw it, she said we should give it to Nora Joyce: it was just her style. Too bad I did not follow her advice, because I left it to be sold in a jeweler's shop in Petersfield and have no idea what has happened to it even today. After the weekend I went up to town leaving Pegeen at her school in Wimbledon.

The Tanguy exhibition was beautifully hung and looked wonderful. It was a retrospective show, and some of the earlier paintings were entirely different in feeling from the later ones. There were two of this early period I wanted very much. One called *Palais Promontoire* belonged to Mrs. Tanguy and she would not sell it. It had almost no color, which made the drawing show to greater advantage. The other one was a yellow canvas that Peter Dawson owned. Instead, I acquired *Toilette de l'Air,* which was full of color, and produced a strange rainbow effect when you looked at it upside down. Mesens insisted on giving me a small painting as a present for bargaining with Tanguy, which annoyed us all. There was also a wonderful painting called *Le Soleil dans son écrin.* This picture frightened me for a long time, but I knew it was the best one in the show, and I finally got over my fear and now I own it.

We had lots of parties all the time; Mesens gave a wild one in Roland Penrose's home where he lived. Penrose, the owner of the gallery Mesens ran, had a lovely house in Hampstead. He was not in London at this time. He was rich and was always traveling. Everybody was tight at this party and the next day the neighbors complained about the goings-on in the garden. Peter Dawson had a girl who kept appearing in a different costume every hour with the most silly excuses.

Finally Tanguy and I decided to leave together and go to my flat. We must have warned Wyn, for she facilitated our departure, but a man called Charles Ratton, who had come to London specially for the show, insisted on following us. He suddenly remembered, when we were in the cab, that he had forgotten his braces and wanted to go back. We wouldn't hear of it and we got

Yves Tanguy, *Palais Promontoire (Promontory Palace)*

rid of him as soon as we could and went to my flat where we spent
the night. After that it was difficult to see Tanguy alone because
of his wife. Wyn came to our rescue and invited Mrs. Tanguy to
lunch and kept her occupied all one afternoon.

The Tanguys soon got bored with the Dawson ménage and
came to live with me. Tanguy had a bad ulcer, and he suddenly
had a severe attack. I ran all over London trying to find him a
medicine called Tulane. When I obtained it he revived, and we
went to Petersfield for the weekend. Tanguy got on very well with
Hazel, whom he named *La Noisette*. The house was full of so
many people, including Hazel's friends, that no one knew where

to sleep. Finally Hazel left, or rather I packed up her things and sent them to London where she had gone for a few days. Hazel didn't at all mind this barbarity.

The Tanguys and I remained alone with Pegeen and Debbie. We left the gallery to Wyn. The Tanguys adored the children— Mrs. Tanguy particularly, as she had never had any of her own. The girls really were like creatures in a fairy tale. They dressed in wonderful clothes and had long flowing manes, Debbie very dark and Pegeen very blond. They painted in Garman's little house. Tanguy and Pegeen exchanged paintings.

Mrs. Tanguy was not very happy, as she was jealous of my being with Tanguy all the time. One day she disappeared, and we got a phone call from the pub in South Harting asking us if we knew her, and should they lend her money to come home in the bus. They thought she was the children's governess, as she was French. She must have been exceedingly tight for a governess.

Our enormous fireplace had a very strange effect on me; for years I wanted to jump into it. I had to hold myself together not to do so. One night when Tanguy was with me I nearly achieved my purpose, but this time by mistake. We were having a heated argument and in my animation I slipped and was rescued by Tanguy just in time or I would have been where I had wanted to be for so long, among the flames.

Before we left London Wyn conceived the marvelous idea of renting a motorboat and giving a party on the Thames. We took lots of people and drinks with us, and at midnight found ourselves at Greenwich. The party was wild and drunk, and many scenes occurred from various jealousies. This was supposed to replace the publicity parties we usually gave in the gallery in the evenings, but it certainly did not result in selling any pictures.

Suddenly Tanguy found himself rich for the first time in his life. As Surrealism was just becoming known in London his show had been a great success. He was a simple man from Brittany, who had been in the *Marine Marchande* for years. His father had once had a position in one of the *Ministères,* and Tanguy said he was born in a building on the Place de la Concorde. This did not make him pompous. On the contrary, he was completely unpretentious. He had come to André Breton in 1926 and joined the Surrealists, painting in their style. Yves had been mad at one time, and of course was exempted from the French army. He had a lovely personality, modest and shy and as adorable as a child. He had little hair (what he had stood straight up from his head when he was drunk, which was quite often) and beautiful little feet of which he was very proud. Tanguy was about thirty-nine years old. He adored Breton the way Beckett adored Joyce, and seemed to think his whole life depended on his being a Surrealist. It was worse than having a religion, and it governed all his actions, like Garman's Communism. He left a Manx cat in Paris with a friend and every few days sent him a pound note in a letter. The pound was really destined for the maintenance of the friend, Victor Brauner, a Romanian painter, more than for the cat. After a few weeks I drove the Tanguys down to Newhaven and they went back to France. I was sad and Mrs. Tanguy cried, but I knew I would be seeing Tanguy again before long.

Soon after, Pegeen had to go to Mégève to spend her summer holidays with Laurence. Sindbad was staying with me for his vacation. My mother's maid had just arrived in Paris with my mother's string of pearls, which she was bringing to me. This was a small part of my inheritance.

I wanted to see Tanguy. I had to maneuver quickly and cleverly. I sent Sindbad to Garman's for the weekend, took Pegeen in my car down to Newhaven where we caught the afternoon boat, and wired Laurence's mother to meet us. She was delighted to take Pegeen in charge and keep her till the train left for Mégève. I then went to see my mother's maid and got the pearls. She was in an awful state about them and was delighted to get rid of them. They were the least of my concerns. I was to meet Tanguy in a café at six.

While we sat plotting our elopement so many people saw us together that we had to move to a less known café, and even then we decided it would be safer to leave Paris at once. Tanguy had no baggage of any kind. I had only a little bag. We took a train for Rouen, where we arrived at three in the morning. It was almost impossible to get a room and we went to at least ten hotels before we found one. The next day we wandered around Rouen and took a train for Dieppe, where it was pouring rain. We had missed the last boat so we spent the night at Dieppe in a chic hotel on the port. So far no one had seen us except Nancy Cunard, who tactfully pretended she had not. We were worried for fear Mrs. Tanguy would discover our whereabouts. When we arrived in

Newhaven and got into the car, we felt safe and drove home in
great style.

Sindbad liked Tanguy very much but had no idea why he was
there without his wife and kept asking for her. While Tanguy was
with us he did a lot of drawings in green ink, which was the color
he always used. There was one drawing that looked so much like
me I made him give it to me. It had a little feather in place of a
tail, and eyes that looked like the china eyes of a doll when its
head is broken and you can see inside. Tanguy read Proust, which
I think must have bored him, and we took long walks and went to
a cricket match and were very happy. But he got restless and
wanted to go back to Paris to do things for Breton who was soon
returning from Mexico. Sindbad and I motored him down to
Newhaven and then we went to visit Hazel in Kent. We went up
to London for a few days as Sindbad wanted to go to a cricket
match.

Suddenly Beckett appeared. He was on his way to Ireland. I put
him up in my flat. When Beckett saw a photo of me and Tanguy
on the mantelpiece looking happy together, he became curious and
could not help showing it. I was leaving the next day for Paris and
offered him my flat in London. He wanted me to remain with him
until the next day, when he was going to Dublin. I refused. I
suppose he wanted me because he knew that I had somebody else.
I told him I was forced to have all my other lovers in order to keep
him as a friend, and I blamed him for my double life. He offered
me his apartment in Paris. It was on the Rue des Favorites, which
made everyone laugh when I gave them the address. It was in a
workmen's building, but it had a nice studio, bedroom and kitchen
and bath. There was no telephone and it was far away, in the
fifteenth *arrondisement,* but I accepted it as I knew Mrs. Tanguy
would never find me there.

I drove Sindbad to Paris and put him on the train, which we
made by one minute. It was a mad race through Paris. I don't
know how we ever did it. Little did Sindbad suspect Tanguy was
waiting for me in the station when I said goodbye. Tanguy and I
spent the first night in Beckett's apartment and then he disappeared for forty-eight hours. As neither of us had a phone I was
rather worried and thought all sorts of awful things had occurred.
Finally he came back and told me what had happened. There had
been a row at a Surrealist party, and it had ended up with poor

**Yves Tanguy,**
*Portrait of Peggy Guggenheim*

Brauner, the painter, losing an eye. He had had nothing to do with the row, in fact he was an innocent onlooker. Dominguez, a Surrealist painter, an awful brute, had seized a bottle and hurled it at someone else, and it had broken and rebounded in Brauner's eye, which fell out. Tanguy had taken him to the hospital, where an operation was performed to remove the pieces of glass and replace his eye. Tanguy promised Breton he would go to see Brauner every day. As Brauner was a Surrealist, Breton felt responsible for him. Tanguy and I now had to give up our project of going on our holiday to Brittany and I remained in hiding from Mrs. Tanguy in Paris. I was careful what cafés I frequented so as not to meet her.

One day, when I was having lunch with Mary Reynolds, Tanguy and Mrs. Tanguy came into our restaurant. I was very embarrassed and didn't know what to do. Mary told me to go and say *bonjour* to her. Her reception was not cordial, but it was definite. She didn't utter a word. She just picked up her knife and fork and hurled three pieces of fish at me. Tanguy took her home soon after, but the owners of the restaurant were not very pleased. It happened to be the restaurant where I always went with Beckett. The owners were old friends of ours. They had once allowed us to go up into their private apartment to hear Giorgio Joyce sing on the radio. We had been making a futile search for a radio and at the last minute they had come to our rescue.

Now that Mrs. Tanguy knew I was in Paris, life became more difficult. Tanguy was afraid she would follow him or find us together. Of course she did not know where I lived, but she was a woman with a mystic sense and often knew things for no obvious reason. I really liked her and did not want to make her unhappy. I never meant to take her husband away from her, and he had had many other affairs. Tanguy told me that she stayed home and wept. I must say this upset me. One day when he was in the hospital with Brauner, where he told me not to come for fear of meeting his wife, I waited for him next door in a café. We were supposed to go and see a doctor for Tanguy's ulcer. Mrs. Tanguy followed him to the café and made an awful scene. He had to take her away in a taxi. This was most unfortunate, as it meant giving up the doctor. Tanguy was sick and neglected his health badly, and Mrs. Tanguy was incapable of looking after him. She was just like a child. They both drank too much and had fearful rows, but in some way were very much attached to each other. Sometimes when they had rows she disappeared for days.

Every morning Tanguy came to my house to fetch me. We spent the whole day together, then he went home to his wife. I was living in Beckett's apartment. He had gone to Brittany with his mistress in my car. I was still terribly in love with him. Tanguy once said to me, "You don't come to Paris to see me, you come to see Beckett."

We were all upset by Brauner's accident. The poor thing had to have a second operation on his eye, as the doctor had not removed all of the glass. After that we bought him a glass eye. He had enormous pride and courage and began to paint very well once he was readjusted to life. I went to see him with Tanguy and bought one of his paintings. He showed me the painting he had done of himself the year before with one eye falling out of its socket. He seemed to have prophesied this catastrophe, and after it occurred his paintings made great progress, as though he had been freed from some impending evil.

Victor Brauner, *Self-Portrait*

If Mrs. Tanguy and Brauner had a mystic sense, I don't think I fell far behind them. One day Tanguy took me to a bookshop to find a volume called *Huon de Bordeaux* by Gaston Paris and illustrated by Orazi. This was a book Tanguy had received as a prize in his schooldays. I paid little attention to what he was doing, in fact I didn't even know what he was searching for. I went next door to look at a Larousse Encyclopedia which I wanted to buy for Tanguy. When I came back I walked absent-mindedly up to the bookshelves and the first book I pulled out was the one Tanguy had been seeking for half an hour. I think this pleased him more than anything I ever did for him. Tanguy really loved me, and if he had been less of a baby I would have married him though the subject was never mentioned. He always told me reproachfully that I could have had anything I wanted from him. Laurence and my children were all for the marriage, but I needed a father and not another son.

I went back to London just in time for the Munich crisis. I must admit I have never been so scared in my life. I completely lost my head. When the war came a year later I felt no personal fear of any kind; but this time I was panicky. I began by having all the paintings from the gallery moved to Petersfield. They did not belong to me and I felt a great responsibility about leaving them in London. As for myself and the children I thought we ought to get away. I was going to Ireland with them and Djuna. She sat at the bottom of my bed wrapped in my marabou cover and said, "We'll be bombed in feathers." Sindbad refused to leave his school, and Laurence phoned from Mégève and said that if I went to Ireland he would never be able to see us again, so we decided to remain. I was also worried about Tanguy and wired him to leave Paris. I had a fixed idea that London and Paris would be bombed the first day of the war. The evening Chamberlain came back from Munich I spent with Ira and Edita Morris. They took me to Edward O'Brien's house, where we heard Chamberlain on the radio. Then we realized it was over. "Peace in our time," or one year.

When Breton came back from Mexico he brought with him a collection of extraordinary nineteenth-century portraits and all sorts of popular peasant art. I wanted to exhibit this collection, but as most of it was very fragile it turned out to be impossible to transport to England without paying a high insurance rate for breakage. It was shown in Paris, however. Breton had a studio

apartment in Montmartre full of paintings and objects he had
been collecting for years. The best things he never wanted to sell,
but when he needed money he was willing to part with a minor
object. As this was now the case, Tanguy took me there and I
bought a beautiful pair of plaster hand-painted Mexican can-
delabra. They were so delicate they were perpetually breaking and
finally had to be abandoned.

Breton was a marvelous talker, he seemed more like an actor or
a preacher than a poet. He sat in a café surrounded by his
disciples. Sometimes there were as many as forty. When the war
was declared it was funny to see him appear in the uniform of a
medical officer. In the last war he had served in the Army as a
psychiatrist and this time they made him a doctor, though he had
forgotten everything he ever knew about medicine. He went
around with medical books in his pockets. Breton was a handsome
man of about forty, with a head like a lion and a big shock of hair.
He had a kingly appearance, but his manners were so formal and
so perfect that it was difficult to get used to being treated so
courteously. He was pompous, and I always felt he had no sense of
humor. He had a blonde, artificial, Surrealist-looking wife called
Jacqueline. She had been an underwater dancer but came from a
bourgeois family. They had a child called Aube. Both Jacqueline
and Aube followed Breton everywhere and the child was a pest in
cafés. Tanguy adored the whole Breton family.

At this time there was a terrible feud among the Surrealists and
they were split into two camps. Paul Eluard had taken away half
or more of Breton's followers. They were both too strong to be
leaders of the same party, and as one or the other had to give in,
and as neither of them would, the party broke in two. Breton must
have given orders to his disciples not to speak to any of the rebels,
because Tanguy would not permit himself to remain in the room
with any of the other group. The whole thing was ridiculous. All
this complicated my life even more, because, while I could never
go anywhere with Tanguy, fearing I might meet Mrs. Tanguy, he
could never go anywhere with me where he might meet the rebels.

After bringing back all the paintings from Petersfield to the
London gallery, we opened the season with an exhibition of
children's paintings. I had been to Pegeen's school to speak to the
art master there. He was an ideal teacher and gave the children

complete freedom. As a result they did the most beautiful work. I borrowed a lot of his star pupils' work, and Laurence sent me some his children had done. I also received a batch from Paris from Maria Jolas' school. Dora Russell sent me some from her school as did the schoolmaster who was the admirer of Kandinsky. Peter Dawson who taught art sent me a lot done by his pupils, but everyone said he did them himself. At the last minute Freud's daughter-in-law brought in some paintings done by Freud's grandchild, Lucien. One was of three naked men running upstairs. I think it was a portrait of Freud. We sold a lot of these paintings. All of Pegeen's were sold, and my dentist ordered a duplicate of one. Roy Campbell's daughter had made a very pretty little watercolor. One of her grandmothers brought it in and her other grandmother who bought it took it back to South Africa. Mesens bought a gouache that he thought was very Surrealist, done by one of Laurence's children, and Roland Penrose purchased another.

One day a marvelous man in a highly elaborate tweed coat walked into the gallery. He looked a little like Groucho Marx. He was as animated as a jazz-band leader, which he turned out to be. He showed us his gouaches, which were as musical as Kandinsky's, as delicate as Klee's, and as gay as Miró's. His color was exquisite and his construction magnificent. His name was John Tunnard. He asked me very modestly if I thought I could give him a show, and then and there I fixed a date. (Later he told me he couldn't believe it, he was so used to being turned down.) During his exhibition, which was a great success from every point of view, a woman came into the gallery and said, "Who is this John Tunnard?" Turning three somersaults, he landed at her feet saying, "I am John Tunnard." At the end of the show I bought one of his best paintings, one with the extraordinary title *PSI* in green letters. Alfred Barr, director of the Museum of Modern Art in New York, admired it so much when he saw it years later that he wanted to buy it for the Museum, but I would not part with it, and he had to find another one instead. I was happy to think that I had discovered a genius.

Another day Piet Mondrian, the famous Dutch abstract painter, walked into Guggenheim Jeune and instead of talking about art asked me if I could recommend night clubs where he could dance. As he was sixty-six years old I was rather astonished, but when I danced with him I realized how he could still enjoy himself so much. He was a very fine dancer with his military bearing and full of life and spirits, although it was impossible to talk to him in any language. Possibly his own, Dutch, would have been more satisfactory than his very odd French and English, but I somehow doubted that he even spoke his own native tongue.

I still had many paintings by Tanguy in London and I kept selling them all the time. There was one I wanted Roland Penrose to buy as he had the best collection of Surrealist painting in England. When he came to the gallery to see this Tanguy, he immediately appreciated it and bought it though he already owned several other Tanguys. It was in this way, in trying to render him a service, that I rendered Tanguy a great disservice, because I got friendly with Penrose at the same time. Penrose had a pretty little house in Hampstead and gave wonderful parties and entertained a lot. If he had no passion, he replaced it by charm and good taste. He certainly was capable of love. All his walls were covered with Surrealist paintings. He was the great promoter of Surrealism in England, and had arranged and brought over the big Surrealist show in 1936 which had been such a success. Penrose was extremely attractive, quite good-looking, had great success with women and was always having affairs. He had one eccentricity: when he slept with women he tied up their wrists with anything that was handy. Once he used my belt, but another time in his house he brought out a pair of ivory bracelets from the Sudan. They were attached with a chain and Penrose had a key to lock them. It was extremely uncomfortable to spend the night this way, but if you spent it with Penrose it was the only way. In his house he had beautiful paintings by the romantic Belgian Surrealist Paul Delvaux whom Mesens had discovered and was furthering. Once we slept under my favorite Delvaux painting, *The Call of Night*. I was so thrilled; I felt as though I were one of the women. I own one of these paintings which I bought from Mesens. It represents four women growing out of trees. Their legs are replaced by the bark of the trees. They are always the same women, as Delvaux's model was his wife, whom he adored. It is strange how different she can appear from different sides. In the paintings she is very handsome but her breasts are too big.

After a few months Tanguy finally got to London, where he had been meaning to visit me for ages. I met him at the station and the minute he saw me he knew something was wrong. I did not admit it for days, but in the end I told him I was caught in a trap and had to extricate myself, and that I was unhappy. I knew Penrose was in love with an American girl in Egypt. I did not tell Tanguy who it was that was causing me all this trouble, but Penrose gave a party and, as we sat holding hands all evening, Tanguy must have guessed. He was sad all the time he was in London, even though we went about a lot and lived together quite happily. We went to a cocktail party where the host asked if I were Mrs. Tanguy. We decided that I would be Mme Tanguy de Londres.

Tanguy felt rich as he was selling so many pictures. He had already spent, given or thrown away all the money he had made from the show. When he returned to Paris he used to take pound notes, roll them into a ball and throw them to people in cafés. I think he even burnt them. How I wished I had kept the money for him. He told me I should not have given it to him all at once. Now he bought us all presents. He gave me an orchid every day, and he gave me a painting. He gave Sindbad a wonderful stopwatch full of gadgets, Pegeen a miniature paintbox, and bought himself some English clothes. He soon went back to Paris as he was unhappy about Penrose. On the way back he made friends with the captain and was allowed to steer the boat into the harbor.

Henry Moore was a very direct simple man from Yorkshire, about forty years old, and he taught art to earn a living. He was having great success selling his things in London and exhibited in all the galleries. He did wonderful Surrealist drawings also. I liked them better than his sculpture. He lent us a very large wooden reclining figure, which looked beautiful in the center of the gallery. I would have liked to have bought it, but it was much too large for my home. While Tanguy was in London we were invited with Penrose to Moore's for dinner. Moore's wife, a Russian, cooked us a wonderful meal. Afterward Moore showed us his new sculptures. They were minute. I think I had given him the idea of making smaller things by writing him, at the time of my sculpture show, how much I admired his work, but how sorry I was that I had no room in my house for any of it. Now I could easily have one. One day, months later, he arrived at the gallery like a traveling salesman, carrying a little handbag. From this he brought out two elegant reclining figures, one in bronze and one

in lead, and asked me to choose one. I infinitely preferred the
bronze, which I acquired.

During this period I gave a collage show. Half of it was sent
from Paris by Arp, who had gone to great pains to collect it. The
rest I found in London. I borrowed some from Penrose and other
people, and I got all the artists to make amusing new ones. As
there was no limitation to the material used, we received every
kind of object. Benno made one with a kitchen grater on it.
Penrose hung the show for me. We put the old Picassos, Braques,
Arps, and Massons in one room and all the less restrained works
together in another room. Laurence sent some very obscene
collages which we had to hide. Penrose lent me a few by Max
Ernst, who was certainly the master of collages. As he was not
mentioned by the critics in the reviews, Penrose was disgusted by
their ignorance. After the opening I gave a large party at the Café
Royal, as was my habit. I remember suddenly, in the middle of
dinner, urging Penrose to go to Egypt to get his ladylove. He was
surprised and asked me why I took such an interest in his affairs.
I said, "Because I like you so much I want you to be happy, and if
you don't go and storm her gates she will never come." He was
touched by my interest in his affairs and followed my advice and
brought back the lady he had been pining for so long.

In January 1939 I went to Paris and finally got over my passion
for Beckett. I remember saying to him one day, "Oh, dear, I forgot
that I was no longer in love with you." I think it was as a result of
consulting a fortune teller. She seemed to think it was the
moment to marry him or give him up. She said he was an awful
autocrat. When I told this to Beckett he said, "Have you decided
not to marry me?" I was relieved to say "Yes." After thirteen
months of frustration it was about time it was over.

I was still friendly with Tanguy and saw him constantly. He
painted a little pair of earrings for me. I was so excited I couldn't
wait for them to dry and ruined one by wearing it too soon. I then
made him paint me a second one. The first two were pink, but I
thought it would be more fun if they were different colors, so he
now made one blue. They were beautiful little miniature paintings and Herbert Read said they were the best Tanguys he had
ever seen. Tanguy also designed a little phallic drawing for my
cigarette lighter which he had Dunhill engrave. It was the

smallest Tanguy drawing in the world, but unfortunately I left it later on in a taxi.

The earrings that Tanguy made for me

I came back to London giving up the idea of both Beckett and Tanguy. But I soon was in worse trouble. I got involved with an English artist called Llewellyn. The affair was very vague, but the consequences were disastrous. The pleasure gained from it was hardly worth the trouble it cost me. It all started because he was at rather loose ends, his wife being sick, and I took him home with me one night, which caused him great remorse, because of his wife. He had to be discreet and could see me only secretly or on business. We worked hard together on a Spanish Relief Committee which he organized. He collected paintings donated by all our artists from Paris and London. He wanted to borrow my gallery in order to hold an auction sale of these pictures, but in the end he found a house in Regent's Park that was more suitable. We held three auction sales on three successive nights, and sold the pictures for ridiculously low prices; most of the people, taking advantage of the artists' generosity, came for bargains. The whole thing was run in a state of great confusion and the auctioneers were ignorant of art. We had a nice drawing of Joyce done by Augustus John and a handsome 1937 Picasso, which raised good prices. I bought my first Ernst and a Llewellyn for normal prices, but most of the things were underbid, and we had to put a minimum on them. We raised a few hundred pounds, but we should have done much better considering the quality of the work and the cause involved.

Llewellyn had a wonderful house where he and his wife both worked and gave parties to which it was considered quite an honor to be invited. They were snobbish and both belonged to old English families.

All my troubles arose from the fact that John Davenport invited us to France for a weekend, I mean Llewellyn and me and another couple. No one knew of my connection with Llewellyn; in fact he sketched most of the day with John's wife and I spent all my time talking to John, who was a delightful companion. He took us to marvelous restaurants, and we had a most enjoyable two days, and then the others went on to Paris and I returned to Sindbad, who was spending his Easter holiday with me. When I departed Llewellyn brought me a little bottle of brandy to the boat, and I am sure he was delighted I left before we were found out. After that I spent three months in a state of great uncertainty, not knowing whether or not I was pregnant.

Every time I thought I was, I decided I wasn't, and vice versa. I had a stupid female doctor who spoke to me over the telephone and refused to see me. She was convinced I had had a miscarriage. I seemed to have had three. As time went on I got more and more ill and remained in bed for days. John Davenport invited me for the weekend to his beautiful home in the Cotswolds. I spent a whole afternoon weeding the gardens and pushing a heavy wheelbarrow, hoping it would have some effect, but it didn't alter matters.

One afternoon Llewellyn asked me out to his house to see his wife's work. The minute I entered the room and saw her I knew we were both pregnant. Shortly after this she had a miscarriage. She was taken to a hospital in the middle of the night in a dangerous condition. The irony of the situation was that they wanted a child. I offered mine to Llewellyn, but he refused it on the grounds that he could make a lot more.

After weeks of uncertainty I went down to Petersfield and consulted my local physician. I took an awful chance, but I must say he stood the shock very well. He had a test made on a mouse in Edinburgh, and after several days told me that it had proved positive. I then asked him to help me out of my troubles, but he said he could not take the risk. I protested on the grounds of being so ill, but he said that would doubtless pass in a few weeks time. I then went up to London and finally consulted a German refugee doctor. He said a blind man could see that I was pregnant and that I was much too old to have a child especially after not having had one for fourteen years. I was greatly relieved to find someone to end my troubles.

While I was in the nursing home John Davenport came to see me, bringing armfuls of flowers. He had no idea what ailed me, and little did he suspect the dangers I had incurred in France. Another visitor to the nursing home was Herbert Read. He looked so paternal. I am sure all the nurses thought he was the father of my child. He was even less suspicious than Davenport of my illness. He came to talk about our museum project, which by this time was well under way.

In March 1939 I had had the idea of opening a modern museum in London. It seemed stupid to go on with the gallery, which was suffering a loss of about six hundred pounds a year although it appeared to be a successful commercial venture. I felt that if I was losing that money I might as well lose a lot more and do something worthwhile. I approached Herbert Read, who was trying very hard to promote modern art in England. I liked him immensely and felt we could work well together. I made him give up his position as editor of the stuffy *Burlington Magazine,* and in exchange gave him a five-year contract as director of the new museum which we were to open in the fall. Wyn Henderson chose the title of "registrar" for herself. God knows what my position was to be. Herbert Read offered to help me for six months without accepting any money until we started; but he borrowed one year's salary in advance as he wanted to become a partner in Routledge's publishing house and buy some shares in it.

We spent weeks trying to find a suitable place for the museum but did not succeed until summer. I tried to think of ways to cut down my own personal expenses, in order to have sufficient money for the project. In fact, I had decided to live a monastic life in order to be able to produce the necessary funds. Actually I did not have nearly enough money for this venture as I had commitments of about ten thousand dollars a year to various old friends and artists whom I had been supporting for years. I could not suddenly let them down for the museum, much as I wanted to. I intended to buy no more clothes, sold my Delage car and bought a cheap little Talbot. Every penny that I could raise was to be used for the museum. As we had no money to buy paintings, we decided to borrow them or try to get people to give them to us. I went to my aunt, Irene Guggenheim, asking her if she thought I could get my uncle Solomon to give me something, but all she said was that the Baroness Rebay would have to be consulted and then maybe I would get a Bauer. I thanked her very much and left. Mr. Read did better—he got promises from lots of people. We had a marvelous press. Mr. Read's photo appeared in all the papers. The *Evening Standard* came out with a hideous photo of me with Pegeen. I really looked horrible, although I am generally photogenic. Djuna Barnes's comment was wonderful. She said, "The only chance you had, you muffed."

One day a young woman came into the gallery. She looked very masculine and said she had been sent by Marcel Duchamp, so we treated her well. She wanted to photograph Read and me in color. She had a large collection of celebrities she had already photographed, and was doing more in London, where she had succeeded in making everyone in the intellectual world pose for her. I thought it would be amusing to give her a chance to show her slides in my gallery. I combined this with a farewell party. Hundreds of people came, mostly gate crashers. Gisèle Freund showed her slides. Everybody was delighted to see celebrities in color, even more so than in black and white. We also had an enormous bar, so the party was a success. I was so ill at the last minute that I nearly did not appear. Llewellyn's wife, who had just recovered from her miscarriage and had no idea I was pregnant, told Llewellyn to throw me over his shoulder and take me to the next party. When I said I could not stand up, she asked me what ailed me and I said I had a sprained ankle.

After that Miss Freund photographed Mr. Read and me in my little flat. We couldn't get the camera far enough away, so I sat at Read's feet, while he showed me a book of Duchamp's. Behind us was a painting by Tanguy. We had to choose whether to cut this or ourselves in half. We decided to favor ourselves. Later Miss Freund gave me two photographs of Read's head. She had done a wonderful job. You could even see his closely shaven beard getting ready to grow again.

Mr. Read was a distinguished-looking man. He looked like a

prime minister, and seemed to be very well bred, though he boasted of being the son of a Yorkshire farmer. He had gray hair and blue eyes, and was reserved, dignified and quiet. He was learned and had written innumerable books, which I made him autograph as I had copies of all of them. He soon became a sort of father in my life and behind his back I called him Papa. He treated me the way Disraeli treated Queen Victoria. I suppose I was rather in love with him, spiritually. We had many meals together and we got very friendly; we talked a lot about John Holms and I made Mr. Read promise he would finally have the book of John's letters published for me. He told me how much he thought of John's criticism. I found an old article of John's about Read which was only moderately flattering, so I did not show it to him. It had appeared years before in *The Calendar*, the quarterly journal of modern letters that Garman had edited. Mr. Read and I had planned a wonderful future for ourselves. We were going to New York after the opening of the museum to raise money and to study the workings of the Museum of Modern Art. I blush now to think of our innocence.

Djuna was very much against the whole project and was extremely nasty about it all. She told me that I would soon find myself in the rôle of signing checks for Mr. Read, who would be running the whole show. Mr. Read had been rather nervous about staking his future with me. He wanted some kind of a reference, and as I could not give him one he went to T. S. Eliot, his best friend, and asked him what to do. Mr. Eliot, whom I had never met, reassured Mr. Read by saying, "I have never heard Mrs. Guggenheim spoken of in any but the highest terms." That settled it, I guess, for Mr. Read.

Mr. Read could hardly believe his good fortune. He must have thought I had tumbled from heaven. He had been curator of several museums, and could easily have been one again, and was eventually knighted; but all his life he had dreamt of making an ideal modern museum, and he showed me an article he had written on the subject. His first idea was to have an opening show in which we would exhibit borrowed paintings of the whole field of art we were to cover. Most of these were to be brought from Paris. This list, which was later revised by Marcel Duchamp, Nellie van Doesburg and myself because it contained so many mistakes, became the basis of my present collection. He wanted to start with the first Abstract and Cubist paintings from 1910, but every now and then he would relapse into Cézanne, Matisse or Rousseau and other painters whom I thought we ought to omit.

When Mr. Read came to visit me in the nursing home he brought a specific proposition from Mesens and Penrose, who wanted to be in on the project. It seems that they had been offered free a whole floor in a building of a famous dressmaker's in Berkeley Square. If we accepted this gift and Mesens with it on a small salary, Penrose promised to lend several of his best Picassos. All this seemed unnecessary to me, as Mesens and Penrose were my avowed enemies by then. We had had a terrible fight about an Abstract show which I had given in my gallery. You can therefore imagine my surprise when Mr. Read brought me this offer. I categorically refused it, but I think Mr. Read wanted to accept it.

Phyllis Jones came and took me out of the nursing home and brought me to Petersfield to recover from the operation. I was in a state of collapse and spent most of my time in bed rereading Proust and making budgets to find enough money for Mr. Read.

One day Mr. Read phoned me to say that he had been offered the ideal spot for the museum. It was Sir Kenneth Clark's house in Portland Place. I made a great effort and came up to town to look at it. I was still very feeble. In fact I did not recover for another three months—in all, six months of my life were ruined by this illness.

Lady Clark showed me all over her beautiful house. It really was the perfect place for the museum, even though it was Regency and not modern. Lady Clark, who had been a gym teacher, was particularly pleased with an air-raid shelter she had made in the basement. She told me she was going to live in the country to please her children. I was so silly I did not realize that she was preparing for the fast approaching war, and I thought I was very lucky to acquire her house. The only trouble with it was that it was too large, so I conceived the idea of living on one of the upper floors. But to my dismay Mrs. Read conceived the idea of living on another. We soon began arguing about which floor we would occupy.

We actually took the house, but as our lawyers were away on a holiday I never signed the lease, and when war was declared, I had no legal obligation toward Sir Kenneth Clark. He, however, thought that I had a moral one, and told Mr. Read he expected an indemnity as he could have let the house to someone else. He suggested that I give the indemnity to a committee he had formed for artists in distress, to which he had by then sacrificed his house. Mr. Read considered Sir Kenneth Clark was richer than I. Therefore I concentrated on Mr. Read to whom I felt not only legally but morally obligated.

After all this I began to think about a summer holiday. I needed a good rest and I wanted to go abroad before the museum opened. I was also to meet Mr. Read in Paris in the fall and have all the pictures lined up for him by then. For months I had been trying to get down to Chemaillere in the Ain, where Gordon Onslow Ford had a château for entertaining the Surrealists. I hoped he would give us some paintings out of his collection for our museum. Tanguy expected me to come there, but because of my health I had put it off. I wrote to Tanguy, but his replies got more and more vague, and I finally realized that I could not join him and that he must have a new girl friend.

I then accepted the invitation of Nellie van Doesburg to go to the Midi. Nellie was my newest friend and I did not know her very well at this period. About a year before she had walked into my gallery and given me a long lecture on who her husband had been and who she was. I was not in the least impressed and thought she was funny. I allowed her little by little to force her way into my life. I don't like women very much, and usually prefer to be with homosexuals if not with men. Women are so boring. Anyhow I asked Nellie to live in my flat, or most likely she asked herself, and as I had a guest room I let her come.

Nellie was a well-groomed woman of my age with a neat little figure, blue eyes, and red hair which was sparse and dyed. She dressed carefully, looked very attractive but made up too much. Because of her excessive vitality even I envied her. Her passion for abstract art was fanatical, which was why she had come to me. For ten years she had been the widow of Theo van Doesburg, the co-editor, with Mondrian, of the magazine *De Stijl*. He was also a painter, architect and theoretician. He was a sort of twentieth-century da Vinci, and Nellie worshippped his memory, which fact touched me very much.

One night in Paris Carl Nierendorf took us out to dinner, and we all got tight, Nellie and I weeping on his shoulder about our dead husbands. He never got over it. As a sentimental German he thought it was wonderful, which it was. When Nellie came to London I always put her up in my flat, and when I was in Paris she did her best to make me stay with her in her home in Meudon that her husband had built before his death. I always refused to live in Meudon because of Tanguy, but I never told her why. I once brought Nellie down to Petersfield and she made great friends with my children. She was so young and vital that they loved her.

In August I started out for France in my little Talbot car, never dreaming I was saying goodbye to Yew Tree Cottage forever. I let Sindbad drive through Normandy. It was also the last time I saw Normandy. Now I can't bear to think of the devastation and ruin that war brought to that beautiful country.

When I arrived in Paris I got Sindbad a sleeper to Mégève and then collapsed. My health was still fragile. As soon as we could Nellie and I started out for the Midi. We decided to go to Mégève and stop on the way, if possible, to see Onslow Ford. For some reason we never got there, but we did get to Mégève. The children had been begging me to come to visit their new home for years. Laurence had bought a house there in 1936. With Nellie as an excuse I could easily live in the hotel and leave in a few days. So we spent a week in this little skiing village, which by now was quite fashionable in winter. I did not like the place and never have, but the children adored it. Laurence and Kay were very hospitable; they had a beautiful home and the children were happy to have us there.

After that we motored to Grasse where we were to be the guests of Mr. Sides, Nellie's friend. He was a cordial businessman of Armenian extraction, a sort of adventurer who couldn't bear to feel money near him without getting at it somehow or other. He suggested every possible combine to me in order to attach some of my money, but as he was not nearly crooked or clever enough, none of his propositions came to a head. His latest interest was modern art, about which he knew nothing, but for which he was prepared to do anything. He was even ready to replace Mr. Read though he had no qualifications to do so.

Sides and Nellie had just put on three exhibitions of Abstract art in Paris. The artists told me they were awful, but artists are never satisfied, and I did not believe it was as bad as they made out. Nellie really knew her job. She had wonderful judgment, and I never saw her make a mistake.

Mr. Sides had rented a house and Nellie and I shared it with him. There were two floors; he lived downstairs, and Nellie and I lived upstairs. There was one bathroom for us all. It could be reached only through our bedrooms, which it connected, so I named it the Polish Corridor.

Mr. Sides saw to it that we had wonderful meals and lots of drinks. We really had a nice life in this funny little house lost up in the hills of Grasse. Sides had great vitality and although he was still going around on two canes, as a result of a train accident which had nearly cost him his life, he rushed around the country in my car and bought a chapel in La Tourelle which he started to transform into a house. He was very ambitious and was a *chevalier de la légion d'honneur*. Nellie and I saw him as the future mayor of La Tourelle. He was over fifty-five.

Every day Nellie and I drove down to the sea. We were always trying to get away from Mr. Sides and go on trips. We managed to escape to Le Canadel to Mme Octobon, where we spent a few days with this old friend, the innkeeper. I wanted to see my home at Pramousquier. It had been sold to bourgeois people and was completely transformed into a conventional Midi home. I hated to see it like that.

While we were at Le Canadel we went to see the Kandinskys. They were living in the stuffiest hotel of the whole coast, the Kensington at La Croix. I am sure Kandinsky's wife chose it. We drove them around, and when we showed them where we lived in Mme Octobon's café they nearly fainted. It was so unchic. I think they thought we were joking. During our visit a general mobilization was declared, and we rushed back to Mr. Sides.

Mr. Sides was the most optimistic man I have ever known. Of course he didn't believe there was going to be a war. When it was declared, he thought it would be over in a few weeks. The more he listened to the radio, the more encouraged he felt. God knows why. I certainly was rather worried and had no idea what to do next. Mr. Sides said, *"Elle cherche les enfers."* He thought I was looking for trouble.

At the beginning of the war I was a pacifist and was afraid Sindbad would join up. Nothing could have been further from his

thoughts at that time. He was only sixteen. I did not know what to
do about the future, but Laurence kept very calm and decided
everything for me. He wrote me reassuring letters and I took no
steps for the time being.

In Grasse we were surrounded by the army. Soldiers seemed to
be everywhere. They were billeted all around our house and
looked completely unprepared for war, which they turned out to
be. Whole regiments passed by our house at night, and even in the
daytime. We never knew where they were going. The mobilization went on for days and there seemed to be no equipment or
organization. It all looked hopeless. There was a lot of time to be
gained while Poland was being taken, but no one went to her
rescue.

One day when I was down in Cannes waiting in line to send
one of my many wires to Laurence or to Kitty to move everything
from London to Petersfield, a strange incident occurred. We were
all terribly tense, as people are in the first stages of a war, and no
one felt like joking, especially in that rather fatiguing business of
getting off long wires. A homosexual who was a few steps ahead of
me suddenly came out with the wonderful remark, "Dear me, the
way everyone is acting one would think France was at war!" If we
hadn't been so upset I think we would have all burst out laughing,
but I am afraid he missed his shot. One day we were told that
Cannes would be bombed in two hours. It didn't seem to make
much impression on anyone.

We had great trouble in getting gasoline, but always managed
somehow. Sides did not want us to use what we had, but I was so
excited about being in my beloved Midi again that I couldn't bear
to stay still; I perpetually wanted to drive and revisit all the places
that had meant so much to me during the four years I had lived in
that region. I was in a state of excitement every minute and had to
show Nellie all the places where things had happened to me in
that very emotional period of my life.

I soon gave up the idea of going back to England, as Laurence
decided the children should remain in France. We could not all be
scattered about in different places, and the war would soon make
travel impossible. I therefore had to relinquish the museum,
which would have been impossible anyhow, since we could not
have borrowed paintings and exposed them to the bombings of
London.

I conceived a wonderful scheme of forming an artists' colony for the duration of the war, and inviting all the artists who wanted to join us to be my guests, and to receive a small allowance. In return they would give me paintings for the future museum. Nellie and I began looking all over the south of France for suitable accommodations for our colony. We looked at hotels, châteaux, houses. This gave me a good excuse for traveling, and as I really believed in the project it became a sort of mission. At one moment we thought Les Baux would be the ideal place, but it was not available, as the French Government was going to requisition it.

Had I known more about artists at that time I never would have dreamt of anything so mad as trying to live with them in any kind of harmony or peace. Nellie really should have known better. As soon as I got back to Paris and met a few of the people we had thought of inviting, I realized what a hell life would have been. They not only could not have lived together, but did not even want to come to dinner with each other. There were so many little feuds and jealousies, it was unbelievable.

While we were in the south we went to visit Albert Gleizes and his wife. They had several homes, one at Calvaire, and one at St. Rémy, and another across the Rhone. The first was a comparatively simple house near the sea, but at St. Rémy they had an enormous estate which they had been trying unsuccessfully to farm for years. At the outbreak of the war Mrs. Gleizes had been lent a donkey by the *commune,* and with it and a couple of Spaniards she had serious intentions of raising enough food to help save France from starvation. She wanted me to join her in her efforts, but vague as my project was, I felt hers was even more so. They had had a beautiful house built in the real Provençal style, and received us in a delightful manner. They were vegeterians, but produced exquisite meals which they served at the most peculiar hours, having no sense of time. Gleizes was an intellectual and was as much a writer as he was a painter. They were very charming people, and like most married couples provided great mirth for the public in their personal relations. Mrs. Gleizes interrupted him every time he tried to speak, which was really a pity as he was a very interesting man.

When we finally got back to Paris I went to live with Nellie in her home at Meudon. Her house was so constructed that in order

Antoine Pevsner was a timid little man who reminded me of Al Jolson's joke, "Are you man or mouse?" He conceived a great passion for me, but as he was mouse, not man, I did not in the least reciprocate this feeling. He behaved like a schoolboy in the spring, and we became great friends.

Arp had been born in Alsace, but he was now a Frenchman with the name of Jean instead of Hans. He was madly anti-German and would not let us listen to any German music. He served my breakfast every morning and washed all the dishes. He went back to Paris with a porkpie hat and a bread box under his arm. He knew only one word of English, "candlesticks."

Max Ernst had a terrific reputation for his beauty, charm, and success with women. He had white hair and big blue eyes and a handsome beak-like nose resembling a bird's. He was exquisitely made.

Jimmy Ernst looked so sweet with his wonderful, big blue eyes. He longed to be friends with Max but Max felt uncomfortable in his presence and did not know how to talk to him. I immediately took Jimmy to my heart and became a sort of stepmother to him.

Leonora Carrington was a young pupil of Max Ernst and not well known but very good and full of imagination in the best Surrealist manner. Her skin was like alabaster and her hair was rich in its black waviness. She had enormous, mad, dark eyes with thick black brows and a tip-tilted nose.

Djuna Barnes was handsome with her white skin, magnificent red hair and beautiful body. She wrote most of *Nightwood* in a rococo-style bedroom in Hayford Hall that looked so much like Djuna that we gave it to her.

One evening I went to Piet Mondrian's studio to see his new paintings and hear his boogie-woogie records. He kissed me and I was surprised to discover how young he still was at seventy-two.

Marcel Duchamp was a handsome Norman and looked like a crusader. Every woman in Paris wanted to sleep with him. He hadn't painted since 1911. Now he only played chess. I have him to thank for my introduction to the modern art world.

Yves Tanguy was a simple man from Brittany. He had a lovely personality, modest and shy and as adorable as a child. His hair stood straight up from his head when he was drunk, which was quite often.

Myself at Art of This
Century seated before a
picture by my daughter
Pegeen

Frederick Kiesler was a man
about five feet tall with a
Napoleon complex. He told
me that I would not be
known to posterity for my
collection of paintings, but
for the way he presented
them to the world in his
revolutionary setting.

Art of This Century's Surrealist Gallery had curved walls made of gum wood. The unframed paintings, mounted on baseball bats, protruded about a foot from the walls. Each one had its own spotlight. The lights went on and off every three seconds, to everybody's dismay.

In the Abstract and Cubist Gallery the paintings were clustered in triangles, hanging on strings as if they were floating in space. At the right is Kandinsky's *White Cross*.

Kenneth McPherson came into my life when I most needed him and when he most needed me. He immediately gave me a sense of peace, and when I sat with his arm around me I was perfectly happy, happier than I had been for years.

I can't say I like the music of John Cage, but I went to every concert of his in Japan. He was not interested in sightseeing and would not let us out of his sight. Everything we saw we had to do by stealing away from him.

to make a new room all you had to do was to move a rolling door. It was very convenient.

I found Tanguy again. He was living alone in a beautiful apartment owned by Kay Sage, an American princess. I had once sent him to see this lady, as I hoped she would buy a picture. The description he had given me of her the next day would never have made me suppose she would be his future wife. She had just left for America, and he was to follow her if he could get his papers. She had done everything she could to help him, and then went ahead trusting he would follow. If not, he was to join my colony.

I ran around Paris with Tanguy while he got his final papers and then he suddenly disappeared. He was spending the last days with his wife. A touching thought. She and I now became good friends again, as I was no longer her enemy. She sold me the painting I had wanted for so many months, *Palais Promontoire,* and I promised Tanguy I would pay her monthly installments for it. So in a way I inherited her after Tanguy's departure.

I put Djuna on the same boat that Tanguy sailed on. She was in a complete state of collapse, and I told Tanguy to look after her. Of course he didn't. I saw them off at the Gare d'Austerlitz late one night. It was very dramatic, and really gave one a feeling that we were at war. There was a terrible tension in the air, and the station was almost in darkness. I did not have the slightest desire to leave, and was not in the least afraid.

Laurence wrote me he was thinking of putting Sindbad in an English school near Pau. I decided to go to see the school and look for houses for my colony, as I had not yet found the ideal place. We drove from Mégève right across France in two cars, which seemed ridiculous. Sindbad and I drove the little Talbot, and Kay and Laurence had their Renault. As we were to part company at Pau we found it necessary to have both autos. The trip was beautiful through Dordogne and the Massif Central with the late autumn reds and browns. We visited wonderful old churches and ate magnificent meals in the old French tradition. Pau is a very dull town but the war seemed to have livened it up. The school was a silly little place compared with Bedales, and Sindbad frankly hated it. He was very unhappy to renounce cricket and not be allowed to return to Petersfield.

I stayed on a few days after Kay and Laurence left, hoping

Sindbad would get settled. In the meantime I began looking around for a château again. I got hold of an agent and went all over the countryside with her. By this time my project had assumed an official character, as I found myself using the name of M. de Monzie, the Minister of Education, who the agent thought had sent me to find a château. It was a complete error, but I let it go at that as I thought it sounded better. In France such things are useful. I had some vague connection with M. de Monzie, whom I had never met. As a result of this I was royally received everywhere, and was shown the most beautiful châteaux, which of course I never took.

In my absence Nellie, who was by now the secretary of the new scheme, went around to see all the artists to find out if they were interested in our project. There was little enthusiasm shown except by certain artists who were on the rocks. To everybody's relief we finally gave up the idea.

I then had to face a settlement with Mr. Read. I tried to get a visa to England, as I wanted to go and talk to him. This was refused me, but I was told that I could apply for one for the duration of the war, if I were prepared to go back with my children, and remain there. As this was out of the question I gave up the idea. It was a good excuse to give Mr. Read, as I really did not want to go on with the thing. Mrs. Read's resolution to live in the museum rather terrified me. Some time later my friend Hoare, in the Foreign Office, said he could get me a visa. By then I had arranged everything by correspondence. Our lawyers broke our contract, and Mr. Read accepted half of five years' salary, minus what he had already received. He bore me no ill will, but he was very much disappointed, as he thought London would have been the ideal place for the museum during the war. I felt I had rendered him a great service in freeing him from his dull job on the *Burlington Magazine,* and as he was two thousand five hundred pounds the richer for our brief association, and as a result of this, a partner in Routledge, I had no qualms. He soon decided to write a book about his life and dedicate it to me. He wrote the book, but his wife may have objected to the dedication, as he omitted it. When all this was over he decided to call me Peggy, and thereafter we remained the best of friends and continued to correspond.

# Chapter 12

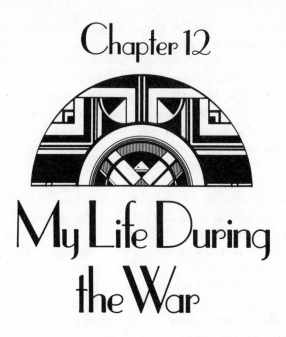

# My Life During the War

Giorgio Joyce was in great trouble. His wife Helen had gone mad and was rushing around Paris with two blue Persian kittens which she took everywhere in order to attract attention. She was having an affair with a house painter in the country, and also tried to seduce every man she met. Giorgio had retired to Paris and was living with our friend Ponisovsky. He came to get me hoping I would console him and give him some advice. He was very worried about his child, and wanted to get it away from his wife. One night, when we were in a restaurant his wife came in with the nurse who was supposed to guard her. She made an awful scene and I left at once. The whole thing was painful and Ponisovsky and I were terrified that Giorgio was going to have her locked up. We did not realize how ill she was and we tried to prevail upon Giorgio to leave her in freedom. She was going about incurring debts with all the dressmakers, as she had the *folie de grandeur*. She went to the police and denounced as spies her friends Elsa Schiaparelli, James Joyce and some other people. She really was getting dangerous, but I hated the thought of her being locked up. This she finally brought on herself by becoming violent. Giorgio had removed the child, and this was too much for her. The police finally took her to a horrible *maison d'aliénés,* but Giorgio had her moved to a sanatorium where she was supposed to be looked after, but of course wasn't. We cabled her brother Robert Kastor to come to take her back to America, and he arrived by Clipper. He was not surprised, as she had already been in a sanatorium for over a year in Switzerland. Giorgio had remained with her there, and had looked after her, but now he felt he had come to his end. Her brother could not remove Helen, as she was too ill, but he arranged to have her go as soon as she was calmer. He wanted Giorgio to take her to New York, but Giorgio refused. He said he could not leave as he was subject to induction into the French Army. In the middle of all this I had a bad accident.

One night after dining with Brancusi I came home and received a visit from Beckett and Giorgio. I was living in Mary's house, which she had lent me as she had gone to Arcachon with Marcel and the Dalis. She did not want to leave Paris, but Marcel was so afraid of being bombed that he could not remain, and she followed him unwillingly. Beckett got very tight, and Giorgio and I put him to bed. We sat up drinking. The next morning Beckett was still in the house, so I decided to take him with me to meet Kandinsky, to whom I was going for tea. I had always wanted him to see Kandinsky's studio out in Neuilly-sur-Seine, in a modern apartment house. Beckett had translated the preface to the catalogue for Kandinsky's exhibition, and, as he was an authority on German art, I thought he ought to see Kandinsky's paintings.

We were not destined to see Kandinsky that day. When we went down the marble steps to the door we passed Fanny, Mary's maid. I caught her eye, and it occurred to me that she recognized Beckett, to whom she had served breakfast in bed when we lived in Mary's other house. (She had moved again to a bigger one next door.) The memory of all this was so upsetting that I missed my footing and fell down the stairs. I landed on my right knee and completely put it out of its socket. Fortunately Nellie was with us as Beckett stood by quite helplessly in his usual paralyzed state. Nellie made him carry me to a sofa, and sent for her doctor. He put the knee back into position, but I already had water on it. The next day, Nellie took me to the American Hospital in an ambulance where I was X-rayed and sent home, nothing being broken. I had to remain in bed, as I couldn't move, so I got used to lying quietly and peacefully during air-raid warnings. We never were bombed at this time, so I did not mind the sirens.

In a few weeks after a great deal of massage I was able to walk again. I had to find a place to live because Mary and Marcel were returning to Paris since it seemed so safe. Giorgio wanted me to take a room in the hotel where he was living with his family. I certainly did not want to get so much involved with him, so I went to another hotel.

At Christmastime I returned to Mégève to see the children, but the slippery winter weather made it almost impossible for me to get about with my bad leg, and I did not enjoy it. On my way home I went down to the Lac d'Annecy to see a new school that Sindbad was entering. Pau had not proved a success.

When I got back to Paris I started very seriously to buy paintings and sculptures. I had all the museum funds at my disposal, now that the problem of Mr. Read was settled, and lots of free time and energy on my hands. My motto was "Buy a picture a day" and I lived up to it.

I rented Kay Sage's apartment which I had found Tanguy living in. It was the most beautiful place I had ever seen. It was on the Ile St. Louis behind Notre-Dame on the Quai d'Orléans, on the seventh floor, having been retrieved from the attic, and under the eaves. It had a terrace, where you arrived in the lift, and across which you walked in order to enter the flat. There was a big studio with three exposures and a little silver-papered bedroom and dressing room and an elegant bathroom. The Seine played the most lovely reflections on the ceiling of my bedroom; I always lay in bed Sundays watching this. I was happy as all my life I had wanted to live by a river.

Here I gave a lot of dinner parties. I cooked the dinners myself with the help of Fanny, Mary's maid, who came to me daily. Nellie hated my home; she said there was no place to hang pictures. Nevertheless I managed to place all the smaller ones. The big ones had to remain in storage, where I could see them whenever I wanted.

Giorgio's wife stayed all winter in that dreadful nursing home, and they would never have relinquished her, and all the money she brought them, if I had not again insisted that her brother send for her. Finally, with the help of two nurses, a doctor and lots of drugs, she was put on a train for Genoa and caught a boat to New York. I went with Giorgio to a storage house and packed all her clothes. I then inherited her two Persian cats, who were no longer the darling little kittens they had been. One so much resembled Giorgio that I named it after him, and the other one I called *Sans Lendemain.*

Before Tanguy had left, he had taken me to see Brauner. Brauner had by now quite recovered from his accident and was painting very well. (He was living with a Jewish girl, who worked in one of the *Ministères,* to support him.) Nellie and I went to see him and I bought another of his paintings. It was so much admired by my doctor that I gave it to him to settle part of my bill. Brauner's paintings always had a great success. I remember giving another one in England to a schoolteacher who could not afford to buy it.

All winter I went to artists' studios and to art dealers to see what I could buy. Everyone knew that I was in the market for anything that I could lay my hands on. They chased after me, and came to my house with pictures. They even brought them to me in bed, in the morning before I was up.

For years I had wanted to buy a Brancusi bronze, but had not been able to afford one. Now the moment seemed to have arrived for this great acquisition. I spent months becoming more and more involved with Brancusi before this sale was actually consummated. I had known him for sixteen years, but never dreamed I was to get into such complications with him. It was very difficult to talk prices to Brancusi, and if you ever had the courage to do so, you had to expect him to ask you some monstrous sum. I was aware of this and hoped my excessive friendship with him would make things easier. But in spite of all this we ended up in a terrible row, when he asked four thousand dollars for the *Bird in Space.*

Brancusi's studio was in a *cul de sac.* It was a huge workshop filled with his enormous sculptures, and looked like a cemetery except that the sculptures were much too big to be on graves. Next to this big room was a little room where he actually worked. The walls were covered with every conceivable instrument necessary for his work. In the center was a furnace in which he heated instruments and melted bronze. In this furnace he cooked his delicious meals, burning them on purpose only to pretend that it had been an error. He ate at a counter and served lovely drinks made very carefully. Between this little room and the big room, which was so cold it was quite unusable in winter, there was a little recess, where Brancusi played Oriental music on a phonograph he had made himself. Upstairs was his bedroom, a very modest affair. The whole place was covered in white dust from the sculptures.

Brancusi was a marvelous little man with a beard and piercing dark eyes. He was half astute peasant and half real god. He made you very happy to be with him. It was a privilege to know him; unfortunately he got too possessive, and wanted all of my time. He called me Pegitza.

Brancusi told me he liked going on long trips. He had been to India with the Maharajah of Indore in whose garden he had placed three *Birds in Space*. One was white marble, one black, and the third one bronze. He also liked to go to very elegant hotels in France and arrive dressed like a peasant, and then order the most expensive things possible. Formerly he had taken beautiful young girls traveling with him. He now wanted to take me, but I would not go. He had been back to Romania, his own country, where the government had asked him to build public monuments. He was very proud of this. Most of his life had been very austere and devoted entirely to his work. He had sacrificed everything to this, and had given up women for the most part to the point of anguish. In his old age he felt it very much and was very lonely. Brancusi used to dress up and take me out to dinner when he did not cook for me. He had a persecution complex and always thought people were spying on him. He loved me very much, but I never could get anything out of him. (I wanted him to give Giorgio Joyce a portrait in crayon which he had done of his father, James Joyce, but I could not make him do so.) Laurence suggested jokingly that I should marry Brancusi in order to inherit all his sculptures. I investigated the possibilities, but soon suspected that he had other ideas, and did not desire to have me as an heir. He would have preferred to sell me everything and then hide all the money in his wooden shoes.

After the row, I vanished from Brancusi's life for several months, during which time I bought for one thousand dollars a much earlier work of his, *Maiastra*, from Paul Poiret's sister. It was the very first bird he did in 1912. It was a beautiful bird with an enormous stomach, but I still hankered after the *Bird in Space*. So Nellie (whom he called Nellitska) went to see Brancusi and tried to patch up the row. I finally went back to his studio and we began all over again to discuss the sale. This time we fixed the price in francs, and by buying them in New York I saved a thousand dollars on the exchange. Brancusi felt cheated but he accepted the money.

One day I was having lunch with him in his studio workshop and he was telling me about his adventures in the last war. He said he would never leave Paris this time. In the last war he had gone away and as a result he had broken his leg. Of course he did not wish to leave his studio and all his enormous sculptures. They could not possibly be removed. At this point of our conversation a terrific bombardment of the outer boulevards of Paris took place. He knew at once that it was the real thing, but I did not believe it, as we had had so many false air-raid warnings. We were only a few blocks from the Porte de Vaugirard, where some bombs were falling, and the noise was infernal. He made me move from under the glass roof into the other room, but I paid no attention at all and kept going back to fetch wine and food from our lunch table. Afterward we emerged into Paris, where the news was confirmed. All the factories of the outer boulevards had been bombed, and a lot of school children killed.

Brancusi polished all his sculptures by hand. I think that is the main reason they are so beautiful. This *Bird in Space* was to give him several weeks' work. By the time he had finished the Germans were near Paris, and I went to fetch it in my little car to have it packed and shipped away. Tears were streaming down Brancusi's face, and I was genuinely touched. I never knew why he was so upset, but assumed it was because he was parting with his favorite bird.

I wanted to buy a painting by Jean Hélion, and heard that he was in the Army, stationed near Paris. Nellie wrote to him and he came in on a flying trip to sell me one. As he had been in the Army and deprived of the company of women he was delighted to be with Nellie and me. We appeared very feminine and brilliant to him with all our make-up, and he said we were the first paintings he had seen for a long time. We rushed all over Paris to find his works that were stored in various places and I bought an enormous canvas that we found in the attic of a friend's house. I

Constantin Brancusi,
*Bird in Space*

214 OUT OF THIS CENTURY

gave Hélion Herbert Read's anthology, *The Knapsack*, especially compiled for soldiers, and I felt at the time that I would never see him again. Little did I imagine that he would one day by my son-in-law. (Later, when he escaped from the German prison camp where he had been interned for nearly two years, he found the money for his painting still available in a French bank and it saved his life.) We had a wonderful dinner opposite the Gare Montparnasse and he rushed back to join his regiment.

One day I found a funny little picture at a dealer called Poissonnière, who claimed it was a Dali. It was extremely fascinating and very cheap, but it was most unlike Dali. I said I would buy it if he would get it signed by Dali. So poor M. Poissonnière, who was waiting to be transferred from Paris any minute, being in the Army, rushed down to Arcachon with the painting. He brought it back duly signed.

After that I still wanted a real Dali, by that I mean one that would be recognized by the public, and one of his best period, 1930 or thereabouts. A handsome little one was brought to me in bed early in the morning and I bought it at once, from a lady dealer. But it was very small and I still wanted to buy a big important one. Much as I objected to Dali and his goings-on, I still thought it necessary to represent him in my collection, which was supposed to be historical and unprejudiced. Mary was a great friend of the Dalis, so the first time Gala came to Paris she invited us to dinner together. We got into terrible arguments about my life, of which Gala did not approve. She thought I was mad to sacrifice it to art, and that I should marry one artist and concentrate on him as she did. The next day she dragged me all around Paris to find a Dali painting. We went to a storage house and to their mad apartment which was empty while they lived in Arcachon. I found a good painting, which she thought more appropriate than the first over-sexual one I had chosen quite innocently, not noticing what it represented. The one she chose certainly is sexual enough. It is called *The Birth of Liquid Desires* and is horribly Dali.

I also wanted to buy a sculpture by Giacometti, whose studio was in a tiny street off the Avenue du Maine and was so small I don't see how he could have worked in it. He looked like an imprisoned lion, with his lionesque head and an enormous shock of hair. His conversation and behavior were extremely Surrealist and whimsical, like a divertimento of Mozart. One day I found a badly damaged plaster of his in an art gallery. I went to see Giacometti and asked him if he would mend it for me if I bought it, as I wanted to have it cast in bronze. He told me he had a much better one in his studio. As it proved to be just as good I bought this one, and he promised to see to the casting of it.

This took several weeks, and one day, after he had the bronze cast, he arrived on my terrace with what resembled a strange medieval animal. He looked exactly like a painting by Carpaccio I had seen in Venice of St. George leading in the captive dragon. Giacometti was extremely excited, which surprised me because I thought he had lost interest in these early abstractions, which he had long since renounced in order to carve little Greek heads, which he carried in his pocket. He had refused to exhibit in my modern sculpture show because I would not exhibit one of these. He said all art was alike, but I did not agree. I saw no reason for his little Greek heads and much preferred my bronze, which certainly was far from classic. It was called *Woman with a Cut Throat* and was the first of Giacometti's works ever to be cast, and when, years later, I returned to Europe after the war, to my great horror I seemed to see it everywhere, though I suppose the number of casts must have been limited to about six.

May I here introduce Howard Putzel. He was nearly my twin in age, a man of great force of character. Since I got to know him I did everything he wanted, or resisted him with all my strength. The latter weakened me so much that I had no energy left for more important matters. He first became known to me in the winter of 1938, when he wrote me from Hollywood to wish me good luck on the opening of my gallery and to announce the closing of his. At the time, he sent me some Tanguy paintings that he had exhibited out there and that were to be included in my forthcoming show. I met him a few months later at Mary's in Paris and was surprised to discover he was the opposite, phys-ically, of what I had imagined he was going to be. I had expected to meet a little black hunchback. Instead of this he turned out to be a big, fat blond. At first he was nearly incoherent, but little by little I realized the great passion for modern art that lurked behind his incomprehensible conversation and behavior. He immediately took me in hand and escorted me, or rather forced me to accompany him, to all the artists' studios in Paris. He also made me buy innumerable things that I didn't want; but he found me many paintings I did need, and that balanced our account. He used to arrive in the morning with several things under his arm for my approval and was hurt when I did not buy them. If I found and bought paintings "behind his back," as he must surely have considered any independent action on my part, he was even more offended. He and Nellie disliked each other only as rivals of extreme passions can.

In the winter of '38–'39 Putzel decided he would take me to meet Max Ernst. I resisted futilely as usual. I knew Ernst's work well, and really wanted to buy a painting. He had had an exhibition in London in Mesens' gallery and Penrose owned a great number of his best works. Ernst knew who I was and I suppose he assumed I came to buy a painting. Ernst had a terrific reputation for his beauty, his charm, and his success with women, besïdes being so well known for his paintings and his collages. He certainly was still very good looking in spite of his age. He was nearly fifty. He had white hair and big blue eyes and a handsome beak-like nose resembling a bird's. He was exquisitely made. He talked very little, so I was forced to carry on a continuous chatter about Mesens and their gallery and mine. At the feet of Ernst sat Leonora Carrington, his ladylove. I had seen them around Paris and thought how intriguing they appeared together. She was so much younger than Ernst; they looked exactly like Nell and her grandfather in The Old Curiosity Shop. I tried to buy a painting of Ernst's, but the one I wanted belonged to Leonora, and another I liked was declared by Putzel, for some unknown reason, to be too cheap. I ended up instead by buying one of Leonora's. She was a young pupil of Ernst and not well known but very good and full of imagination in the best Surrealist manner and always painted animals and birds. This canvas, which was called The Horses of Lord Candlestick, portrayed four horses of four different colors in a tree. Everyone was delighted by this purchase and I never thought about Ernst again until the winter of the war, when I found some marvelous paintings of his at a dealer's and bought three at once. At this time he was in a concentration camp.

Nellie took me to meet Antoine Pevsner, the Russian Constructivist. I had known his work in London, and knew his brother Naum Gabo quite well. Pevsner was a timid little man who reminded me of Al Jolson's joke, "Are you man or mouse?" I think he was mouse. His constructions were beautiful, and I bought one which must have been inspired by a mathematical object. Pevsner was an old friend of Marcel Duchamp, but had never met Mary Reynolds. We took her to Pevsner's for dinner, and when she told him she had been Marcel's mistress for over twenty years he just could not believe it. He did not even know of her existence, and he had seen Marcel every week of his life for as many years. Pevsner conceived a great passion for me, but as he was mouse, not man, I did not in the least reciprocate this feeling. He behaved like a schoolboy in the spring. We became great friends. When he could not get his wife to leave Paris during the German occupation, I sent him money, and looked after him all during the war.

At Eastertime I went down to Mégève to fetch Sindbad and Pegeen and took them to the Col da Voza to ski. I brought with me Jacqueline Ventadour, a friend of theirs. We drove in my little Talbot singing old southern ballads, which she taught me on the way. We all enjoyed the holiday very much except Pegeen, who was unhappy to leave Mégève. Sindbad and Jacqueline had a fine time and so did I, as I became enamored of a little Italian in the hotel. He was perfectly horrible, an impossible creature, but very handsome in a flashy way. This occupied most of my thoughts as I was left alone all day, not being a skier. On the way home I drove Sindbad back to Mégève with my new acquaintance. After the Italian had left by train I stayed the night with Kay and Laurence. The next morning, just as I was leaving, I slipped on the stair and sprained my ankle and cut open my elbow. Kay and I, as usual, were not getting on well, so I insisted on leaving after I had had two clips put in my arm. I don't know how I ever got back alone in my car to Paris in this state, as I couldn't walk and couldn't use my right arm.

During the winter I spent much time with Virgil Thomson. He and Putzel and I used to eat a lot of our meals together. Virgil was going to help me arrange concerts in my museum if I ever had one. He gave charming Friday evening parties at which he kept open house. He did a musical portrait of me which was not in the least resembling, but for which I posed quietly for several hours, reading his book, *The State of Music,* which is very smart. I thought it would be nice to marry Virgil to have a musical background, but I never got far with the project.

One night at Mary's there was an awful row about my saving my paintings. Mary said it was indecent to think of anything except the refugees. She intimated that if we managed to get a *camion* we would run down the refugees with the paintings. Virgil was very sweet to me and I remember weeping in his arms in my little car afterward while he tried to console me for what I considered my oldest friend's unnecessary tongue-lashing.

Virgil left Paris before I did, and when I got to America he was one of the first people I looked up. By then he was the most famous music critic in New York, and was so well known he told me he no longer did anything he didn't enjoy. He was quite independent. When I told him I had brought Max Ernst to America and was living with him he made a prize remark. He said, "Lots of ladies seem to have enjoyed that before." But I am getting way ahead of events.

The day Hitler walked into Norway, I walked into Léger's studio and bought a wonderful 1919 painting from him for one thousand dollars. He never got over the fact that I should be buying paintings on such a day. Léger was a terrifically vital man, who looked like a butcher. During his stay in New York, where he finally got after the German occupation of France, he became a sort of guide and took us all to foreign restaurants in every quarter of the city. He seemed to know every inch of New York, which he had discovered on foot.

The next day I bought from Man Ray one of his early works, a 1916 painting and several Rayograms.

I tried to rent a suitable place to show my paintings, but the Germans were advancing so quickly that I finally had to rescue my collection and ship it out of Paris. I had actually rented a beautiful apartment in the Place Vendôme. This apartment was not only the place where Chopin had died but also had been the establishment of O'Rossin the tailor. The first day I saw it was the fatal day Hitler marched on Norway. The owner of the building did everything in his power to discourage me, but when I insisted, he said, "Think it over and come back tomorrow." I went back and told him I had not changed my mind, so he had to give in. I gave him my lawyer's name, who turned out to be an old friend of his, and this greatly facilitated matters. I then got the architect Georges Vantongerloo to draw up plans for the remodeling of this spacious place so that I might live in it as well as make a museum there. It was much overdecorated in the *fin de siècle* style, and I insisted on having all the angels removed from the ceiling and scraped off the walls before we started painting it. At this point, however, it was so obviously impossible to continue with the scheme that I finally realized the only thing to do was to ship the pictures out of Paris before it was too late. At the last minute I made an attempt to use the cellars for the museum. However this was not allowed as they were being reserved for air-raid shelters. The extraordinary thing was that I neither signed a lease nor paid a cent deposit on this apartment, and in spite of that the owner removed all the *fin de siècle* décor without any guarantees from me. After I left Paris, I had a bad conscience and sent him twenty thousand francs indemnity. I have never known such a landlord.

The only thing to do with the paintings was to pack them and get them out of Paris before it was too late or store them in an underground vault. Léger told me he thought the Musée du Louvre would give me one cubic meter of space somewhere secret in the country where their pictures were being sent, so I had my pictures taken off their stretchers and packed when, to my dismay, the Louvre decided the pictures were too modern and not worth saving. What they considered not worth saving were a Kandinsky, several Klees and Picabias, a Cubist Braque, a Gris, a Léger, a Gleizes, a Marcoussis, a Delaunay, two Futurists, a Severini, a Balla, a Van Doesburg, and a "De Stijl" Mondrian. Among the Surrealist paintings were those of Miró, Max Ernst, Chirico, Tanguy, Dali, Magritte and Brauner. The sculpture they had not even considered, though it comprised works by Brancusi, Lipchitz, Laurens, Pevsner, Giacometti, Moore, and Arp. Finally my friend Maria Jolas, who had rented a château at St-Gerand-le-puy near Vichy to evacuate her bilingual school of children, said she would keep my collection in her barn. So I sent them there.

This was a most fortunate choice, as things turned out, since the Germans were there for only a short period and were quite unaware of the presence of my cases in the barn.

After that I really should have left Paris myself. The Germans were advancing so quickly, but I could not tear myself away from my new friend Bill. For two months I had been with him every afternoon. We used to sit in cafés and drink champagne. It is really incomprehensible now to think of our idiotic life, when there was so much misery surrounding us. Trains kept pouring into Paris with refugees in the direst misery and with bodies that had been machine-gunned en route. I can't imagine why I didn't go to the aid of all these unfortunate people. But I just didn't; instead I drank champagne with Bill. At the last minute my traveling permit expired, and when I tried to renew it I was refused a new one. I had a dream that I was trapped in Paris. When I found that I could not leave, I remembered my dream and was very scared. The Germans were getting nearer every minute. All my friends had left. Bill decided to stay, as his wife was too ill to be moved.

Finally I fled with Nellie and my two Persian cats three days before the Germans entered Paris. I took the Talbot, as I had plenty of gasoline. I had been saving it up for weeks in *bidons* which I kept on my terrace. We left for Mégève just as the Italians declared war. By then I did not need any papers, as there was a general exodus of about two million people. It was terrific. The main road to Fontainebleau was jammed with cars four abreast, all creeping along in first gear. They were laden down with every conceivable household object and advanced at the rate of one mile an hour. Everything was enveloped in a cloud of black smoke let loose by the Germans or by the French, I never found out which or why. We were covered with soot. I managed to get off the main roads finally and followed little side-paths. But after the first few hours it was much easier to advance, as nobody was going east. Everyone was trying to get to Bordeaux. Several times I was warned not to go east or I would meet the Italian army. In fact I was afraid I would be sent back by the police if I insisted. But we were allowed to continue and, needless to say, did not meet the Italian army, which never got far into France. On the way we learned the dreadful news of the fall of Paris and a few days later came the tragic armistice terms. There wasn't much left of France, but what there was we clung to desperately.

I found Laurence and the children resolved not to move. He did not want to add to the miseries of the road. As the Germans advanced everyone went on the road hoping to escape them. The confusion and misery and hunger and bombings that they suffered were unbelievable. After the armistice no one seemed to realize what had happened to France. The people all seemed to be in a daze as though they had been hit on the head with a hammer. It was very sad to see France like this. We still had plenty of food, but we realized how much was being sent to Germany. We were quite cut off from occupied France and had great difficulty in getting letters across the border. We soon discovered that for five francs letters were carried at many points, so we did not lose touch with our friends.

My children were happy to see me, and I decided to take a house for them for the summer at Le Veyrier on the Lac d'Annecy. Pegeen and Sindbad, at the tender ages of fifteen and seventeen, were terribly in love with a brother and sister called Edgar and Yvonne Kuhn. My son especially was suffering all the pangs of a first love affair which was unfortunately one-sided. In order to please them I took a house practically next door to their friends, and as a result I never saw them. They spent all their time with this strange half-American, half-French family. They played tennis and they swam and they went on picnics and they went to Annecy on motorbikes. They returned reluctantly for meals, and then went down to the Kuhns again. This was all quite natural, as they were so in love, and I had neither a tennis court nor a lake to offer them. Sometimes I joined them, but on the whole I preferred to keep away from this mad family, as they later proved themselves to be.

For company I had Arp and his wife and Nellie, who lived with me. They were worried about the future, as they could not go back to Meudon in occupied France. They were Hitler's avowed enemies, besides which they had left all their possessions in Meudon. Arp wanted to go to America and start a new sort of Bauhaus. He was very nervous about the war as all his predictions had come true and he foresaw the future in very gloomy terms. He was madly anti-German and would not let us listen to any German music. If Mozart or Beethoven came over the air he immediately turned off the radio. Arp had been born in Alsace, but was now a Frenchman with the name of Jean instead of Hans, which he had dropped.

During the summer I got rather bored and started having my hair dyed a different color every few weeks to amuse muself. First it was chestnut, which certainly was the nearest to nature, but then I got the wild idea of having it bleached bright orange, which made me look like Dorothy Holms. When I came home from the hairdresser's Sindbad laughed, but Pegeen burst into tears and made me have it changed to black, which way it remained thereafter. As a result of all the time I spent in the beauty parlor I conceived a sort of weakness for the little hairdresser who worked so hard on my beauty. From re-reading D. H. Lawrence I also got a romantic idea that I should have a man who belonged to a lower class. Therefore, on the coiffeur's free days I used to fetch him in my car and we drove off into the country together. He took me to a marvelous bistro where we danced. Later I took Laurence there and we gave a birthday party, but we did not invite the coiffeur. In fact, I was ashamed of him and kept him hidden. I spent hours sitting with Pegeen in the beauty salon, as my own hair didn't take up enough time. She never suspected anything, but she considered him a bad hairdresser and regretted that I had made her get a permanent wave from him.

Soon this got boring and I needed a change. There was not much choice. The only other man about was an old fisherman, who looked like Brancusi and took a great fancy to me. He let Nellie and me swim off his raft, which was a great privilege. It was very nice because in that way we could avoid the Kuhns. There was also a very amusing pansy who lived on the top of our hill. One day, seeing "G B" on the back of my car, he left a note in it, inviting us to his house as he claimed to be a friend of the English. He proved to be a good neighbor and gave us wonderful meals and sold us delicious wine which he made from his vineyard.

There was no one else except Mr. Kuhn or his brother-in-law, who suddenly came home as an escaped prisoner. It was a touching scene to witness, as the whole family got hysterical, especially Mrs. Kuhn, who nearly went off her head with joy. Laurence was down from Mégève visiting us at the time, and we retired discreetly in the middle of the family emotions. One night I went down to the Kuhns, where I was always welcome, with the idea of finding the brother-in-law, or *l'oncle,* as Nellie and I called him. I brought him back to our house for dinner. The next night, just when he was leaving, in came Mrs. Kuhn, his sister. She asked for her brother. I was rather surprised and realizing I must be careful said he had gone home long ago. At this moment he heard her loud voice claiming him, and he jumped out of the window into the garden before she could find him. She then searched the whole house saying she could not sleep unless he came home. She made a terrible noise, and not only the Arps, but the children and the cook were awakened. The next day, when we were swimming off the fisherman's raft *l'oncle* came and told me that he could never see me again. I insisted on getting in his boat and trying to talk to him but he looked nervous and soon brought me back. I never saw him again, though Sindbad did everything to bring him to me. Instead I had a visit from Mrs. Kuhn, who came, she said, to warn me that her brother was a *maquereau* and that she would not allow me to be imposed on by him. I said I was old enough to look after myself, and later I heard from Mr. Kuhn that she had done the same thing before on a similar occasion.

Mr. and Mrs. Kuhn hated each other and lived together separately. She was his housekeeper and they both adored their children. Mr. Kuhn had an old mother of eighty, who made great friends with me. The old lady supported them all. Not knowing about the *histoire* I had had with *l'oncle,* she told me that her daughter-in-law had suddenly become very ill and nearly died. I gathered this was a way of recapturing her brother when she thought she had lost him. She must have extracted a promise from him never to see me again. Mr. Kuhn was quite amusing and Laurence and Arp made friends with him. He was very entertaining. He thought I should go to Africa with him and try to wipe out syphilis among the natives. I never took this proposition seriously. When Nellie's twenty-five-year-old African friend arrived to visit her, the whole Kuhn family was horrified. Mr. Kuhn came up for dinner to meet him, and the young man spent the evening trying to inform Mr. Kuhn about the Negroes' position in Europe and Africa. He was an intellectual and talked very well. Later he became president of Dahomey.

By the end of the summer I got my pictures sent from the château by Giorgio Joyce who was living nearby. They were at the Gare d'Annecy for weeks before we realized it, and then when we found out, we had no idea where to put them. Every day Nellie and I went to see if they were safe. We covered the cases with tarpaulins and tried to keep the rain off them by moving them away from the part of the ceiling that was leaking. They remained on the *quai de petite vitesse* for months.

Being Jewish, I could not go back to Paris, but I wanted to

exhibit the pictures somewhere. Nellie was a friend of M. André Farcy, the director of the Musée de Grenoble. He liked modern art, so I sent her to see him and ask him to help us. She came back with no definite promise but with an invitation to me to send my pictures to the Musée, where he would at least shelter them. That was better than the *quai de petite vitesse.* We immediately dispatched them and followed them ourselves.

M. Farcy was in a very bad jam himself at this time and nearly lost his museum directorship and finally ended up in prison. Because of the Vichy government he couldn't do much for me. He did want to give an exhibition of my paintings, but he was so scared that he kept putting it off. The museum's collection of modern art he hid carefully in the cellar, as he was expecting Pétain's visit to Grenoble. He gave me perfect freedom in the museum, where I unpacked my paintings and had them photographed. I could bring my friends to see them; in fact I could do anything except hang them. I had a room to myself where they were all stacked against the wall. M. Farcy would never fix a date for the show, claiming that he must pave the way with Vichy first. He did not want me to remove the paintings, but after six months I lost my patience and told him that I was going to America. He begged me to leave the paintings with him. I hadn't the slightest intention of leaving them with him and I also had no idea how I could send them to America, but I knew that I would never go without them.

M. Farcy was a funny fat little man in his fifties. He liked to get away from home and from his adoring wife. Whenever we invited them for dinner he came alone, giving some excuse about his wife's inability to accompany him. Later I discovered he never conveyed my invitation to her. He was very gay when he was with Nellie and me, and told us wonderful stories. In his youth he had been a cyclist and had done the *tour de France.* You could hardly believe it from his present appearance. One evening after six, when we were sitting in the museum, he took my hand and began caressing my palm. Then, in a low voice, he asked me if I did not feel anything. I insisted that I did not feel the slightest tremor, as it suddenly occurred to me that his great weakness for ladies probably led him to make love to them in the museum after closing hours. He was forever running all over France giving lectures, and as he often stayed away a longer time than his wife expected we wondered what he was up to. He loved modern art, but he didn't know one thing from another. He often asked me who painted my paintings, and invariably when we came round to Marcoussis he said, "What, Brancusi?" I had one painting by Vieira da Sylva he liked, because he thought it was a Klee. When I left Grenoble, I offered him this painting or a Tanguy as a present. But when he asked me for the hundredth time if it were a Klee and I said "No," he chose the Tanguy. In spite of this he had managed to collect quite a nice number of modern paintings for the museum without any funds to back him. That probably was why he was not very well in with the Vichy government, which nearly dismissed him.

Through Nellie I had met Robert Delaunay and his wife Sonia. He had been an important and good painter about thirty years before. I wanted to buy one of his paintings of that period, as his contemporary ones were horrible. But he was foolish enough to ask me eighty thousand francs for it, so of course the deal did not come off. Putzel had found one at Leonce Rosenberg's of the same year for ten thousand. When I was in Grenoble the Delaunays were exiled from their home, which was in occupied territory, and they were living in the south of France. They had rescued a few paintings, and they began again to try to sell me one. They wrote and phoned Nellie every minute to make her get me to take the painting which I had not bought in Paris. Finally I got so bored that I offered to buy it for forty thousand francs.

Delaunay came up to Grenoble and he really was charming. I think most artists are better without their wives. He brought his painting with him. He very kindly restored for me a Gleizes I had bought in Paris, from the widow of Raymond Duchamp-Villon, Marcel's brother who had died in World War I. When Delaunay left, I gave him my darling cat Anthony as I could no longer endure living in one room with these two foul-smelling creatures. Delaunay loved cats, and this one took to him at once. Soon after this Delaunay got very sick and wrote me many letters about his own illness and about the cat. I had no idea Delaunay was dying and I was sad when I got the news.

Laurence had decided it would be safer for us to go to America in the spring, as we were being perpetually threatened with

German occupation of all of France, and we knew that the United States would be involved in the war sooner or later. The American consul had been urging us to leave for over a year and a half, and we had difficulty in renewing our passports. We had the children to consider and the possibility of being cut off from America with no money. Worse still was the prospect of being put in a concentration camp. I was determined to go to Vichy to see our ambassador and try to get him to help me with the shipment of the paintings. But we were more or less snowbound all winter and could not travel. Just at this time, as though he had fallen from heaven, René Lefèvre Foinet arrived in Grenoble.

When René came to Grenoble I had been having terrible rows with Nellie, and I more or less insisted that she should go to live in Lyons. Her African friend was working there in the university. After we were separated we got on much better. In fact there was no reason for our fights, but I was happier working alone on the catalogue of my collection. I typed for hours every day, but my room was so cold that I had to retire to a little office which the manager of the hotel lent me. Arp had written a preface for the catalogue and I was trying to get Breton to do one as well. Laurence could not make head or tail of these quarrels, which I explained to him passionately ,every time he came down to Grenoble. He called it all the Battle of Grenoble and we let it go at that.

René was one of the partners of the firm in Paris which had handled for me all shipping of paintings from Paris to London, when I had the gallery there. I told him my troubles, and to my great surprise he said nothing could be easier than to ship my collection from Grenoble to America as household objects, provided I could send some personal belongings too. He suggested sending my little car which I had left in a garage six months before, as I was not permitted to drive it because of gas shortage. The trouble was I forgot which garage I had left it in. So we wandered around to all the garages of Grenoble and finally came across it. M. Farcy had to give us his authority to remove the paintings, and then René and I set to work and together we packed them up in five cases with my linens and blankets. This, of course, was a great favor René conferred on me, but by this time we were having an affair, so he was very happy to render me any service. All this lasted for two months and it was very enjoyable. So there was really no hurry about getting the cases packed.

At the end of two months I ran away from René and went to Marseilles. This was my second trip there that winter. I will explain the other one first.

During my stay in Grenoble I received a cable from Tanguy's new wife Kay Sage asking me to help rescue and finance the passage to America of five distinguished European artists. When I cabled to inquire who they might be I received the reply, "André Breton, Jacqueline Breton, his wife, and his daughter Aube, Max Ernst and Dr. Mabille, the doctor of the Surrealists." I must say I protested that Dr. Mabille was not a distinguished artist, nor were Jacqueline and Aube, but nevertheless I did accept the charge of the entire Breton family and of Max Ernst. I was also trying to rescue Victor Brauner who had written me to ask if I could save him. He was hiding in the mountains near Marseilles living as a shepherd, and since he was a Jew I felt he might eventually get in great trouble. Breton was in Marseilles. I now combined my efforts and went down to Marseilles to see the Emergency Rescue Committee.

Varian Fry, the head of the committee, raised and distributed a lot of money among stranded refugees, many of whom were in hiding from the Gestapo. He worked underground to get them into Spain and Portugal or Africa and from there to America or Cuba. He also helped to repatriate the British soldiers who were still in France after Dunkerque and who wanted to join de Gaulle. Fry's right hand man was Daniel Bénedité, who had previously worked in the office of the prefect of police in Paris. They were assisted by Bénedité's English wife, Theo, and various other efficient people. With them was a handsome American girl, Mary Jayne Gold, who gave them vast sums of money for their noble work, in which she also took a hand. They all lived in an enormous dilapidated château called Belle Air outside of Marseilles. At the moment, Breton and his family were their guests. Here Breton held court and surrounded himself with Surrealists. Before I arrived Breton and Fry and Mary Jayne Gold and Bénedité had been arrested and held incommunicado on a boat for days during Pétain's visit to Marseilles. They had finally managed to get a secret note through to the American consul who rescued them.

Fry asked me to come and work with the committee. He wanted me to take his place while he returned to the States for a brief visit. I was so frightened by the fact that they had been arrested and by the general black-market atmosphere of Marseilles and all the strange goings-on that I went to the American consul for advice. I wanted to know what the committee really represented. The consul warned me to keep out of it. He did not tell me why, and at the time I had no idea what a dangerous job Fry was doing. The American government was perpetually trying to get him to go back to America to avoid difficulties with the Vichy government. However, he stuck it out to the bitter end. Living in Grenoble and thinking only about art I was completely unconscious of the underground and had no idea what all this was about.

The whole atmosphere of Marseilles was dominated by the black market and everyone was engaged in some illegal deal to get a visa, a passport, or some food or money. Later I got used to it, but in the beginning I was terrified. I went back to Grenoble after giving Breton and Fry some money.

After I had promised to pay Ernst's passage to America, Laurence and René suggested that I ask him to give me a painting in exchange. I wrote to him and he wrote back and said he would be delighted and sent me the photograph of one he considered suitable. It was a lovely painting, but from the photo did not appear to be very much, so I wrote back and said I thought it was a nice little picture, but perhaps I would prefer another one.

In the meantime Ernst had written asking me to send him six thousand francs and a letter for a lawyer, testifying that I had seen the sculptures in his house, and that they were worth at least a hundred and seventy-five thousand francs. It seems Leonora Carrington had gone mad and made over their house to a Frenchman in order to save it from the Germans, not knowing he would take advantage of the situation and seize the property. When Ernst emerged from the concentration camp and discovered what had happened, he thought he might at least try to recover the sculptures with which he had decorated his house. He was able to get his paintings out at night. I had seen his sculptures reproduced in *Cahiers d'Art,* and was glad to do this for him. Max Ernst had a reputation of liking very young girls, and one day

René said to me, "What would you do if Ernst ran away with your daughter?" I said, "I would rather run away with him myself." Ernst had also written to tell me how Leonora had disappeared and that he thought she was in Spain and had gone mad. It all sounded very coldblooded. Later I was to discover how passionately he still felt about her.

# Chapter 13

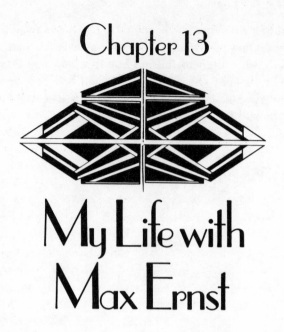

# My Life with Max Ernst

When I arrived in Marseilles the second time the whole atmosphere of the château had changed. It was no longer dominated by Breton, who had finally managed to get all his papers, and had gone to America with his family. The Surrealist court had disappeared, but Max Ernst was living there, hoping to get away soon. Brauner met me at the station.

The very first night we met Ernst in a café and made a date with him for the next day to see his paintings at the château. This was the first time I had seen Ernst since I had been to his studio with Putzel two years before, and he certainly appeared much older after all his experience in concentration camps. He looked very romantic wrapped in a black cape. He seemed happy to see me and delighted at the prospect of showing me his new paintings. The next day Brauner and I went out to the château, and Ernst made a mervelous display of all his new works. I think that he was upset because I was so much more excited about the old ones, and tried to buy them all, instead of the new ones which I frankly did not yet like. I didn't manage to conceal my feelings. We soon came to some agreement, by which I was to give Ernst two thousand dollars minus the money he already owed me, in return for which

I was to get innumerable paintings. Brauner kept rushing around finding collages of historic interest, and Ernst said that I could have all these too. He was very generous. In the end we celebrated with a bottle of wine that Ernst had brought from his vineyard in St. Martin d'Ardèche. As the next day was his fiftieth birthday, we decided to have a party.

In the morning I met René on the Canebière and asked him to come and see Ernst. I then tried to persuade him to go and rescue some of Ernst's paintings that were left behind in his village, but René balked at this. Ernst invited us all to celebrate his birthday by eating seafood with him in the *vieux port*. Afterward we went to a black-market restaurant with Fry and had a wonderful dinner. René, who was with us, was supposed to return to Grenoble. But I took compassion on him as he had stood up in the train all the night before, and I said that he could spend the night with me and should leave next morning.

By this time I was very attracted to Ernst, and when he asked, "When, where, and why shall I meet you?" I replied, "Tomorrow at four in the Café de la Paix and you know why." As Brauner followed me everywhere (he was always with us) I had to slip my key to Ernst, and pretend to say goodnight to him, in order to fool Brauner.

When I began my affair with Max Ernst it was not serious but soon I discovered that I was in love with him. After ten days I had to leave him, because I had told Laurence that I would come and spend Easter with him and the children at Mégève.

At this time Laurence was having a sort of crisis in his affairs with Kay. They had been breaking up for a year, and he was unhappy. When Max put me on the train he cried, and he promised he would follow me to Mégève. So I felt pretty sure this was not the end of my life with him. He had given me all his books in Marseilles and even one that he had previously inscribed to Leonora in no uncertain terms. "To Leonora real, beautiful, and naked." He also gave me her books, which he had illustrated. I read them on the train, and wrote him from Valence how much I liked them; then from habit I wired René to meet me at Grenoble where I had to spend the night on my way to Mégève. I tried to explain to René that I was in love with Max. The next day I left for Mégève.

I didn't hear a word from Ernst and was very unhappy. Finally

Laurence and I went down to Lyons to obtain visas for Spain and
Portugal, as we hoped to be able to leave for America in about a
month with all six children and Kay. We were to meet Marcel
Duchamp in Lyons and I had planned to go back to Marseilles
with him to try to find Max again. The minute we arrived in the
hotel in Lyons Max phoned that he was in Mégève. Of course I
decided to go back. Marcel was surprised and annoyed at my
sudden change of plans. As soon as we had obtained the visas,
which we did with great ease since we were Americans, Laurence
and I returned to Mégève.

Max had arrived at Mégève wearing his black cape, and the
children thought he was a very romantic figure. Pegeen knew his
books, so she welcomed him warmly. It seems he spent the whole
evening telling them tales about himself and Leonora, about her
departure and his troubles. They were most sympathetic, and he
held them spellbound for hours.

After a week Max and I went back to Marseilles. We sat up all
night in the train and it shocked me to see how old he looked when
he was asleep and snoring. We had great difficulty in getting a
room in Marseilles as the population had tripled since the fall of
France. He took me to the château. Afterward I got a room in my
old hotel and Max stayed with me at night.

We were all busy trying to get to America. Kay had reserved ten
places on a Clipper for us, hoping to include her new friend whom
she was rescuing from a concentration camp. But Laurence,
though he behaved like an angel to her all through this period,
refused to travel with this gentleman. I must say I didn't blame
him. That left us one extra seat on the Clipper, and of course
Max hoped to get it. Brauner also wanted this seat, but his papers
were not yet in order and in the end the poor man was denied a
visa as the Romanian quota was filled for two years. We had a
third candidate, Jacqueline Ventadour, the friend of Pegeen and
Sindbad. She had a very insistent mother who succeeded in
forcing us to take her daughter with us. She did pay the girl's
passage, however, which was a great relief, as I had to pay all the
others.

Kay finally bought her friend a place on the *Winnipeg*, a boat
which sailed from Marseilles. When he was out of danger, that is,
out of France, she began to concentrate on our departure, which
until then was more or less of secondary importance to her. She

was living in Cassis at this time with her friend and some of her babies, who were ill, and came down to Marseilles to see the children, whom he adored.

Our papers were not exactly what one might call in order. I had forged a false date on my traveling permit in order to prolong it, and Laurence didn't have one at all. Max's visa to America had expired and we spent days getting it renewed. All the foreigners had to queue up in the streets outside the American Consulate, but Americans showing their passports were admitted at once. I used to accompany Max and wave my passport at the officials, so he never had to wait in the street. He had not only been in three concentration camps, but he was Hitler's avowed enemy and he was therefore to travel on an emergency visa. In order to leave the station at Marseilles, you had to show your traveling permit to the police, but we knew an exit through the *buffet de la gare* where there were no police. When Laurence arrived we took him out that way. Kay came into Marseilles to meet him, and though we frankly detested each other she tried to be friendly, as I was taking her and her whole family to America.

I had dinner with Max and Kay, Laurence and Marcel, and René who turned up in Marseilles again, this time with a whore from Grenoble. During dinner Kay, who was always dramatic, told me that the boat on which I had shipped all my paintings to America had been sunk. She loved to imagine things like this. Then she and Laurence got into a terrible row, because she refused to go to Mégève to pack before she had dispatched her friend to America. Laurence began throwing things around the café. Max was rather surprised, but Marcel and I were used to this. René quieted him down and then Kay wept; I offered Kay and Laurence my room for the night although they were no longer living together, and went to the château with Max.

Max had many friends from concentration camps. He was perpetually meeting these people. They seemed more like ghosts than anything else, but to him they must have been real and brought back many memories. To me they represented a new, strange society. He always mentioned the name of the camp where he had met them, as casually as if he were referring to St. Moritz or Deauville or Kitzbühl or some other equally well-known resort.

At this time all Jews were being combed out of the hotels in Marseilles and were being sent to live in special places. Max told

me not to admit that I was Jewish if the police came to question
me, but that I should insist I was an American. It was a good
thing he had warned me, because early one morning after he had
left and the breakfast cups were still on the table, one of the police
arrived in plain clothes. I was absolutely terrified, but I insisted
that I was an American and said I was leaving soon for America.
He examined my papers and saw that I had changed the date on
my traveling permit. I swore the officials of Grenoble had done
this. Then he complained because I had not registered in
Marseilles. I was frightened not only for myself, but for Max and
Laurence. The former had no right to sleep in Marseilles and the
latter was traveling without a permit. I also had a large sum of
money on me from the black market, for which I wouldn't be able
to account if I were searched. When the detective asked me to
whom Laurence's valise and beret belonged I said they were my
husband's, who was in Cassis. That made him all the more
certain I was Jewish, as that was the spot where the Jews were
segregated. He asked me if my name were not Jewish and I said
my grandfather was a Swiss, from St. Gallen. He had never heard
of it. Then he began looking around the room and under the bed
to see if I were concealing any Jews. Finally he asked me what
was in the cupboard. I told him to look and that he would find no
Jews in there. In the end he said, "Come with me to the police.
Your papers are not in order." I refused to get dressed in front of
him, and I did not want to let him take my papers away with him,
so I told him to wait outside the door. He took my papers and went
outside. I followed him as soon as I could. I was worried that I
might disappear and that Laurence and Max would not be able to
find me. I wanted to leave a note for them and hide all my money,
but I did not know how to do either. When I came out of my room
the detective was not in the hall. He was with his chief in the
lobby. When his chief saw me he apologized and told his
underling to leave me alone. At this time Americans were popular
in France, as we had just sent the French a big shipload of food. I
was then politely asked to go and register with the police in
Marseilles, where I actually intended to go that day in any case,
and the chief told me how to get there. He seemed happy to be
able to direct me. Later on when I complained to the hotel
manageress about this visit, she said. "Oh, that is nothing,
madam. They were just rounding up the Jews."

Leonor Fini was a great pet of Max's. She came to see us in Marseilles and arrived just after I had got rid of the police. I always accused Max of having two Sophies instead of one, like Arp. He had Leonora Carrington and Leonor Fini, and was perpetually trying to further their careers. Fini was a very handsome girl with a free manner. She came from Monte Carlo, where she was refuged and was painting portraits in order to live. She wanted to see Max's new paintings and brought me a little one of hers which I had previously bought after having seen a photograph of it. Laurence, Marcel and I did not like her spoiled vedette manner. Max adored her and wanted me to. He always seemed to require my approval of everything. He introduced me to Fini as a patron of the arts, not as his mistress. I am certain that he wanted to hide this fact. The painting Fini brought with her was a charming little affair that looked like a picture postcard. Later, in New York, Breton very much objected to its being in my collection, but because of Max he couldn't do anything about it. Max thought it was wonderful because Fini painted it, but then he liked the work of any beautiful young girl who admired him. With male painters he was not so indulgent.

Soon after this, Max got all his papers in order and wanted to leave for Spain. He needed fifty dollars in bills in order to travel through Spain and arrive in Lisbon with some money. It was forbidden to export any francs. In order to obtain this money he should have applied to the Banque de France for a permit, but he did not have time. The only other way was the black market which was then not available. Fry had told me that the painter Chagall had the large sum of eight thousand dollars he wanted to transfer to America before he sailed. He made Fry ask me if I would not take this money from him and give it to the committee for their relief work and reimburse Chagall in New York. Naturally I could not afford to do this, but I did take one thousand dollars, which I gave Fry for his fine work. Knowing how much Chagall had, Max and I went to him and asked him to lend us fifty dollars. When we asked Chagall for the money, Chagall hemmed and hawed and said he knew nothing about money, but added that his daughter arranged all his affairs for him. He said we could come back and talk to her in the afternoon, but when we came back she was not there. By this time we were quite desperate. We happened to meet Fry in the street and told him our troubles. He immediately took sixty dollars out of his pocket and handed it to Max.

The next day Max left with all his canvases rolled up in a suitcase. I had to remain in Marseilles in order to arrange to withdraw from the Banque de France the five hundred and fifty dollars each that we were entitled to for our Clipper passages. Application had to be made to the Banque de France and the money registered on our various passports. All this took about three weeks, much longer than I had expected. I had bad bronchitis and retired to bed reading Rousseau's *Confessions*.

One day, when I was walking to a restaurant, I met my old friend Jacques Schiffrin. He was surprised to see me, and happy too, if anything could have made him so at this stage of his collapse. I have never seen anyone so demoralized and frightened of the Nazis. Of course, he was right to realize what his fate would be if he remained in Europe: concentration camps, torture and death. But he hardly had the strength left to get out of France. I think all his papers had expired one by one while he was waiting for a boat. I did everything I could for him, but it was difficult to get him passage. Finally at the last minute, Fry managed to find room for him on a boat and he got off, only to be seized en route and taken to Lisbon, where at least he was safe; eventually he reached New York.

Nellie came down to Marseilles to stay with me until I left. We were reconciled, and I tried to do everything I could to get papers for her to come to New York. Unfortunately it all had to be done from the other side, and I left her behind, with only faint hope of her following me. The Banque de France business took so long that I grew impatient, as I wanted to join Max. I had had one letter from him from the frontier and also a note asking me to save the tenth place on the Clipper for him. All the time I was trying to get Brauner to America, but his case soon became hopeless. At the last minute I had to wait for Jacqueline, who was to go with me. Laurence and all the children got off before I did, to my great joy, as I did not want to travel with so many babies and suitcases.

Jacqueline and I had a lovely trip by ourselves. It was strange getting out of France, and at the frontier I was searched from head to foot, naked. It was wonderful to be free of the Gestapo and to enjoy life again. We had marvelous meals in Spain. The markets overflowed with food. It seemed almost wicked after France, where I had lost about ten pounds from under-nourishment. I am sure there was terrible poverty in Spain: the people looked miserable, as though they were still close to all they had been through.

When I arrived at the station in Lisbon I was met by Laurence, Pegeen, Sindbad and Max. Max looked strange and, taking me by the arm, he said, "I have something awful to tell you." He walked me down the platform and surprised me by saying, "I have found Leonora. She is in Lisbon." I felt a dagger go through my heart, but I pulled myself together and said, "I am very happy for you." By this time I knew how much he loved her. Max was overcome by my reply. My children were very much upset by this, and my son thought I was getting a dirty deal.

We all went to the hotel and tried to be natural, and had a drink out of a bottle I had brought. Max took me for a walk all over Lisbon and told me the whole story of how he had managed to discover Leonora's whereabouts. I felt as though I had been stunned and wandered around in an agonized daze. Finally he took me to meet Leonora at the home of an English girl. There was a lot of talk about a Mexican, whom Leonora was about to marry in order to get a passport to go to America. She said he was very sensitive, and she did not want him to know that we knew about it. They asked me to join them for dinner, but I refused. Before she left she kissed Max goodbye and pinned a carnation on him.

I went back to the hotel and sat through a painful meal, consisting of some ten courses, with Laurence, Kay and the children. The next day we all moved to different hotels. Jacqueline, Sindbad and I went to the Frankfort-Rocio Hotel, and Laurence, Kay and all their children moved into a *pension* where Max was living. Pegeen soon left them and joined us. We remained here for two weeks.

I was so unhappy I wanted to go back to England and get a war job, and I began trying for a British visa. This, of course, was practically impossible, so I got the idea of marrying an Englishman whom we had met on the train and with whom we had become very friendly. In this way I could have re-entered England. Fortunately, my Englishman disappeared, but anyhow Laurence told me I had no right to abandon my children and that it was my duty to take them to America. I therefore gave up this mad project.

I saw very little of Max at this time and tried to put him out of my mind, but I soon had a definite feeling that my life with him was not yet over. He seemed to spend all his days with Leonora and at night was alone and used to wander around Lisbon with Laurence. This I found painful, as they rarely took me with them. I couldn't make head or tail out of all the complications with the Mexican. I did not realize Leonora was living with him. (Max carefully hid this fact from me.) One night we all had a crazy party together, Leonora, Max, Laurence, Kay and the Mexican. He turned out to be very nice but possessive about Leonora and took her home and locked her up in their apartment. This made me realize that she was living with him. It was a mad evening, full of terrible scenes. Kay left early and the rest of us went and danced in a night club where Sindbad hoped to lose his virginity. He was ashamed to arrive in America with it. We all tried to dissuade him from losing it in a country that was so rampant with venereal disease as Portugal.

After this party I told Max it was a *charmante soirée,* and from then on we called such wild, fighting parties *charmantes soirées.* There was a wonderful café called the Leão d'Ouro where we all went to eat seafood. Sometimes we met Max and Leonora there. She was not very friendly toward me, so I was rather astonished one day when she brought Max to my room and seemed in some strange way to be giving him to me.

Soon after this, Leonora went to a hospital to have an operation on her breast. Max spent the whole day with her and only left her in the evening, when the Mexican, who was by then her husband, came to see her. I went to visit her and realized more than ever how much Max loved her. They spent the whole day reading and doing drawings together and seemed to be in perfect harmony. He was completely happy when he was with her, and miserable the rest of the time. She had become great friends with Kay, who was in the same nursing-home for sinus. Leonora could not make up her mind whether to go back to Max or remain with her husband. She never knew what she wanted in life, and seemed to be perpetually waiting for someone to hypnotize her in order to make her decide. She was a pure medium and could be easily influenced. In the end it was Kay who persuaded her to remain with the Mexican. As he had originally been a friend of Max, Max felt bitter about this and thought it was a dirty trick. He despised the Mexican and always made fun of him, calling him an *homme inférieur*. The three of them were often together and must have had an unpleasant time. I don't think Leonora really wanted either of them. There was a moment when she preferred a certain toreador she had met to both of them. She felt that her life with Max was over because she could no longer be his slave, and that was the only way she could live with him. Leonora was beautiful; I realized it more than ever in the hospital when I saw her in bed. Her skin was like alabaster and her hair was rich in its black waviness; it swept all over her shoulders. She had enormous, mad, dark eyes with thick black brows and a tip-tilted nose. Her figure was lovely but she always dressed very badly, on purpose. It was connected with her madness. She had just come out of an asylum, where she had been confined for months, long after she was well. She had written about all her adventures and they were really terrifying. God knows how she ever got out of the place, but after she did she met the Mexican in Lisbon, and he looked after her. He was like a father to her. Max was always like a baby and couldn't be anyone's father. I think she felt she needed a father more than anything else, so as to give her some stability and prevent her from going mad again.

When Leonora left the hospital Max begged her not to go back to live with the Mexican, but she said she must remain with him until she left for America. Max had reserved another place for her on the Clipper and when she told Max this, he was so upset that he decided to leave Lisbon and go out to Monte Estoril with Laurence where he had taken rooms for himself and the children. Of course I went along too. As we were waiting for the Clipper, we had no idea how much longer we would have to stay in Portugal. The seaside was a much better place for the children than Lisbon.

On the first night at Monte Estoril my life with Max began all over again. I was looking for Laurence to say good night to him when I met Max in the hall. I asked him the number of Laurence's room. He told me the number was twenty-six, which was actually his own. Of course I never said good night to Laurence.

This only started a new round of trouble. Max was constantly waiting for Leonora to phone him. She often came and spent the day with him and I felt so let down that I wouldn't speak to him for days. But as we were at Monte Estoril for five weeks there were plenty of variations.

One night when I went to Lisbon with Laurence for dinner I met Leonora at the Leão d'Ouro. We had a terrible scene and I told her either to go back to Max, as he wanted nothing more than that, or to leave him in peace with me. She said that she saw him only out of pity and had no idea he was with me, and that she certainly would leave him alone. In the train on the way back I begged Laurence to save me from Max, but he said Kay had told him not to interfere, that I would only hold it against him afterward if he did. I was so upset that I rushed into another compartment of the train and got off at the next station and went back to Lisbon where I took a room at the Frankfort-Rocio. The next day I phoned Laurence to tell him where I was. He was greatly relieved.

Laurence had dragged Max out of bed when he discovered I was not on the train, and made him come down to the station and wait with him for the last train. He said to Max, "This is your business. You wait for the train." When I told Max about my scene with Leonora he was so upset that I wrote her a letter asking her please not to end her visits. But she never came again. I think her husband preferred it that way.

All the time we were in Portugal Laurence behaved like an angel to Kay. When she was sick in the hospital she was perpetually making him send telegrams to her friend. These cost hundreds of *escudos,* and not only did he send them, but paid for them even when all our funds were getting low. Kay was worried that her friend would not get into the States. He had several adventures en route, his boat being captured and, in the end, would not have been admitted to the United States without a five hundred dollar bail. Kay asked Laurence if I would lend the money, and when I said I couldn't, she made him cable his mother for it. Not knowing anything about their separation, Mrs. Vail lent them a part of the money. I was so enraged to see Laurence behave so angelically to Kay, when she had made him act so fiendishly to me in our divorce, that I quarreled with him. Max, who hated the Mexican with a ferocious hatred, disapproved of

Laurence's superhuman behavior, and lectured him on the sweetness of revenge.

Our life in the hotel was rather strange. The children were looked after by Laurence, by Pegeen and by Kay's oldest daughter, as Kay remained in Lisbon and came for the day only on Sundays. We had a long table in the middle of the hotel dining-room. I sat at the head between Laurence and Max. On either side of them were long rows of children consisting of Sindbad aged eighteen, Pegeen aged sixteen, Jacqueline aged sixteen, Bobby (otherwise known as Sharon) aged fourteen, Apple aged eleven, Kathe aged seven and Clover aged two. No one knew whose wife I was or what connection Kay and Leonora had with us. We were always being asked the most embarrassing questions. There was a porter in the hotel whom Laurence named Edward the Seventh, because of his resemblance to the King. His tact was so great that on one occasion, when I phoned from Lisbon to say what train I was arriving by, he guessed my dilemma and, not knowing to whom I wanted the message delivered, went to the dining room and facing both Laurence and Max, said impersonally, "Madam arrives on the nine o'clock train."

The children were also leading a terrific life of their own. They too had many problems. Jacqueline was in love with Sindbad and Sindbad was in love with Miss Kuhn. He was also very worried about his virginity. One evening when Laurence was in Lisbon, Max and the children and I got into a terrific argument about who was the greatest genius in the world, living or dead. Sindbad claimed it was Napoleon, and Max and I claimed Max was a much greater person than Napoleon. No one could prove his case, and I am sure the children thought I had gone mad from being so much in love.

Portugal's chief source of income undoubtedly comes from its fishing industry. Next to Monte Estoril was a little fishing village called Cascais, which was a quarter of an hour's walk from our hotel. For a change we sometimes went there to swim, as we spent most of the day on our own beach. But it was after dinner that we liked best to stroll there. The fishing boats came in at night, and we went down to the beach to watch them unload. Millions of silver creatures were carried in baskets on the heads of the peasant women to the market a few hundred yards away, and at midnight the fish were all sold. One could buy marvelous lobsters for almost nothing. Apart from these women and a few whores, no other women appeared in Cascais. When the men danced in the streets or did running-jumps over bonfires, it was without female companions. The people had a great dignity but looked sad. Cascais appeared to be more like an African village than a European one. There was something rather mysterious about it and you never knew what was going on inside the houses. They seemed to be hermetically sealed, their walls closing up the lives of all the women, who were not allowed on the streets.

One night, when Max and I were wandering around, we saw two beautiful girls in a window combing their hair. They beckoned us to come into the house. We did so with much difficulty, forcing our way through closed doors and a courtyard; and when we finally reached the first floor, our beautiful girls had entirely disappeared and in their place was a Trappist monk lying on a bed praying.

There were many little wine shops which offered indifferent Portuguese wine for a few *milreis*. You could sit on wooden benches and talk or make signs to the fishermen. They were friendly and were always asking us to go fishing with them. They never went far out to sea. In fact, they usually clustered together in the port within swimming distance. One day I swam out to them and when I got close they wanted me to come on board their boats, but I was frightened and swam back.

One evening at Cascais I went swimming naked. It was pretty dark, but Max was terrified. The Portuguese are Catholic and we were always being taken up by the police for wearing what they considered indecent bathing-suits. As they could not speak French or English they used to measure the outstanding parts of our bodies, make scenes, and then proceed to fine us. We protested violently and went back to the shops which had sold us the suits. They exchanged them for others, but the police were never satisfied. Men were not allowed to wear trunks alone and women were supposed to wear skirts. It was a great pity because Max had such a beautiful body. The evening I swam naked Max was also terrified that I would drown. He kept wailing from the beach, "What will become of me if you drown?" I think he was afraid he would never get to America without me, because when he arrived in Lisbon he could not get the passage which presumably the Museum of Modern Art had reserved for him and had even paid a deposit on. After this wonderful midnight bath I dried myself with my chemise and we made love on the rocks. We soon discovered our error, as it turned out to be the town's chief latrine. Fortunately we were lying on a raincoat which we had borrowed and we had to scrub it for hours before returning it. On the way home we stopped in the bar of the chi-chi hotel next door, and I hung my chemise on the bar railing to dry. Max loved my unconventionalities.

One night I sprained my ankle when we were walking home. Again I fell into some *merde*. It seemed to be my fate. For days I could not walk, and Max carried me around on his back. It gave him an occupation and took his mind off his troubles. He seemed to enjoy looking after me. One night when we were sitting in a café in Cascais the fireman from the fire-station opposite came to get us and insisted on showing us all his wonderful fire engines. He saw that I could not walk and offered, in spite of Max's presence, to take me home in one of the vehicles. Naturally I declined.

There was a riding stable very near our hotel and Laurence made the children ride every day. Max had bought a lot of riding tickets and rode with Leonora in the country for hours. Her husband joined them on occasions. But when she no longer came to see Max he took me instead. The country was wonderful in its tropical luxuriousness. The further inland we went the richer it became.

One night, when we were all out for a stroll, Laurence picked up a strange-looking girl in a salmon satin dress. She had a dark face and a little black mustache. We could not talk to her, but we took her along with us to our café in Estoril and gave her some ice cream. After that she became so devoted to us that we were never rid of her. We had great difficulty in finding out what she did. She said that she sewed, but when we asked her to to make some dresses for the children she took us to a friend in Cascais who was a real dressmaker. Laurence's girl, who wrote her name on the sand as Jesus Concepção, became devoted to me. She insisted on drying me when I came out of the sea and when I sprained my ankle carried me on her back, to Max's great annoyance. She had a sister, and between them they owned two dresses and one bathing-suit. This caused great complications when they came to the beach together. We took Concepção everywhere with us. But she was not welcome in the English Bar or in our hotel, where Edward the Seventh frowned on her, and practically refused her admittance. By degrees we gathered what her real occupation must have been. But to us she was just a friend, and Laurence swore he never gave her a penny, even when he was alone with her on the beach at night. She taught us to speak Portuguese. Every morning we found her waiting for us on the beach. The same in the afternoon when we came out after our siesta. She was our only native friend.

We often went to Cintra, a wonderful palace built high up on a hill and surrounded by incredible boulders, which looked as if they had been brought there on purpose. The gardens had tropical flowers and trees of every description. The castle itself was more like a dream than a reality. It had a Surrealist quality, as it was all covered with fantastic sculptures. Apart from this it had terraces and ramparts like Elsinore. Hamlet's ghost might well have walked there and felt quite at home. The interior was not so exciting: there were a great many Victorian bedrooms and an enormous reception room with many sofas and chairs arranged in little groups. When Max saw this he said it would be an ideal place for a *charmante soirée*. The Portuguese royal family had lived here fifty years ago. I think the sculptured walls reminded Max of the work he had done in his home at St. Martin d'Ardèche and made him very miserable. But it also must have stimulated him, for I am sure they had an influence on his future painting.

Max had a very strange gift of foreseeing the future, or rather of "forepainting" it. He always painted countries before he got to them. He painted the Far East long before he ever saw it, and he did the same thing with America. Everyone thought he painted the Petrified Forest while in the west, but he painted it while he was in the concentration camps of France.

All the time we were in Portugal Max was very miserable about Leonora, and Laurence was very miserable about Kay. We used to sit for hours in the little English café that overlooked the sea wondering if we would ever leave. The extreme unhappiness of these two men saddened me and I was pretty wretched myself. It all seemed so silly that we could not help each other out of our miseries.

One day, in broad daylight, the spirit of John Holms appeared to me and burning two holes in my neck warned me to give up Max, saying that I would never be happy with him. This was like a vision or stigmata. If only I had accepted his warning! But it is my fate to go through with the impossible. Whatever form I find it in, it fascinates me, while I flee from all the easy things in life.

Max could not get a visa for Trinidad, and the Pan-American Airways could not sell him a ticket until he obtained one. I sent many cables to England and Herbert Read saw to it that he got the visa at once.

Finally on the thirteenth of July, 1941, the Pan-American Airways sent us all off together on the American Clipper. We were eleven people: one husband, two ex-wives, one future husband and seven children.

The Clipper trip was very dull except for one hour spent in the Azores, where I bought a gigantic hat, in which the reporters insisted on photographing me upon my arrival in New York. The worst part of the whole trip was half a broiling day spent in the Bermudas. Here our luggage was gone through and all our books and letters read by the censors. We were examined separately by the British Intelligence about conditions in France. We all told them completely different things, which must have left them confused. The children were air-sick and kept vomiting into paper bags and losing the braces which they were wearing for the purpose of straightening their teeth. Max had a terrible fight with Pegeen while our beds were being made, because he thought he was being cheated out of one. To settle the matter I took Pegeen in with me, and she gave him hers. Early in the morning there was a magnificent sky that looked like a Tanguy painting. For the rest of the trip we saw nothing but sea. At one moment we passed over the American boat that was carrying Leonora and her husband to New York. During the voyage we sat in comfortable chairs and walked in and out of the Clipper's three rooms and drank whiskey.

Before we landed, Max asked me to leave the family and take a room with him. Laurence's mother had reserved a large suite at the Great Northern Hotel, and we were all invited there as her guests. As soon as we arrived she reimbursed me for the Clipper passages of Laurence, Kay and their children.

The first sight we had of America was Jones Beach. It looked very beautiful from that height. There were about forty people on the Clipper when it started out, but thirty more came on at the

Bermudas. We seemed to be the only ones the press seized upon. We were all photographed over and over and asked a million stupid questions. Lots of our friends met us, including Jimmy, Max's son, who had been in America for four years, and of course Putzel. He told me that my collection had arrived safely. Jimmy had enormous blue eyes like Max and was so delicately made that he looked like a miniature. Just as Max was about to greet Jimmy he was seized by the officials, and not allowed to talk to him. This made a marvelous photograph for the Press and appeared in the papers. It seems the Pan-American Airways could not accept the responsibility of admitting a German into the United States without a hearing. I offered bail, but to no avail. Poor Max was whisked away. I gathered from the officials that the last boat had left for Ellis Island, so Max would have to spend the night in a hotel as a guest of the Pan-American Airways, guarded by a detective. He was not supposed to talk to anyone, but they said they would let me know where he was being taken, and the rest was up to me.

I followed Max to the Belmont-Plaza and took a room there. Then I began phoning him every half-hour. About the third time he told me the detective gave him permission to meet me in the hotel bar, otherwise known as the Glass Hat. I went there with Putzel and we met Max and had a drink. Then the detective, who called me Max's sister, suggested we all have dinner in Max's room. We said we preferred to go out, and he gave his consent. He followed us through the streets at a respectful distance and refused to join us at dinner, but remained alone at the bar of the little restaurant.

It was very strange to arrive in New York on the fourteenth of July after an absence of fourteen years and have to be followed by a detective. The first person we saw in the restaurant was Katherine Yarrow, a girlfriend of Leonora's who had been instrumental in helping her to escape from France. In fact, she had taken her to Portugal. Max was so upset by this that he refused to shake hands with this girl, and we almost had a dreadful scene. After dinner the detective said he wanted to take us to Chinatown, but we preferred Pierre's bar. He told us we were wasting our money and tried to prevent us from going there. Suddenly he chucked me under the chin and said, "Peggy is a marvelous girl." When we went back to the Belmont-Plaza he

asked Max if he didn't want his sister to sleep with him, saying it
was perfectly safe, as he would be sitting outside the door all night
with a gun in his pocket, guarding not only Max but a G-man in a
room opposite. I declined his offer, as I was scared, and the next
morning he phoned me early to say it was time to go to Ellis
Island. He apologized for not having known who I was the night
before, but I never understood what he meant by this. He so
much admired a five-cent straw hat and walking-stick that Max
had bought in the Azores that he accepted them as a parting gift.
At the ferry he handed us over to an official of the Pan-American
Airways.

We were accompanied by Julien Levy, Max's dealer in America,
who was prepared to testify at the hearing if necessary. The
minute we landed Max was whisked away and imprisoned. I spent
the next three days from nine until five on the Island waiting to be
called as a witness in Max's hearing. I was almost out of my head,
fearing he would be sent back to Europe. I could not speak to him
on the phone, because I was at Ellis Island, but he was free to
phone me if he wanted to. I went to all the relief societies working
there and sent him reassuring little notes. Julien tried to get his
uncle, a borough president of New York City, to help, but there
really was nothing to do except to wait patiently. Unfortunately a
Spanish boat had docked half an hour before the Clipper and there
were fifty people on that boat, who had to pass before Max.
Luckily Julien came out the first two days and helped me while
away the dreary hours. I had not seen him for years and he had
very much changed during that time. He was quite fascinating
and wonderful company. He had greatly improved since the days
when, as a young man in Paris, he had married Mina Loy's oldest
daughter. From him I found out all about America. On the third
day his business prevented him from coming, so I was forced to be
alone. Julien wanted to know if he should find a girl for Max.
This was almost prophetic as things turned out, but at the time I
said it was too late. He did not seem to know I was in love with
Max, or maybe he was trying to find out what our relationship
was.

Luckily Jimmy turned up on the island on the third day. He had
been sent by the Museum of Modern Art with letters of
recommendation. He looked so sweet with his wonderful, big blue
eyes. I knew Max was saved when Jimmy was called as a witness.

Suddenly a guard said, "Your case has been heard. Your friends are waiting for you outside." I nearly fainted. Max was free.

Jimmy had a job with the Museum of Modern Art at fifteen dollars a week. I don't know how he managed to live on it. His health had suffered greatly from it, and he used to have attacks of nervous cramps. I think they came from his being underfed for so long, but they were also brought on by any emotional strain. Our arrival in America and all the excitement that it entailed gave Jimmy cause for quite a few of these attacks. The minute Max got out of Ellis Island Jimmy asked him if he could leave the Museum. His job was not only very badly paid but it was also of a menial order; so of course Max said, "Yes." He promised to give Jimmy double what he had received at the Museum.

Jimmy longed to be friends with Max but Max felt uncomfortable in his presence and did not know how to talk to him. I immediately took Jimmy to my heart and became a sort of stepmother to him. In a way I always felt like Max's mother too. It seemed to me he was a baby deposited on my doorstep and that I had to look after him. That was why I was so frantic every time he was in trouble. I always felt that when I would no longer be useful to Max he would have no further use for me. This spurred me on to doing the most difficult things for him. I not only tried to obtain everything he needed, but also everything he wanted. It was the first time in my life that I had felt maternal toward a man. When I told Max that he was a baby deposited on my doorstep, he said, "You are a lost girl." I knew he was right and was surprised that he realized it.

Max, like all other babies, always wanted to be the center of attention. He tried to bring all conversations around to himself, no matter what they were about. He loved beautiful clothes and was jealous when I bought new dresses, because he would have loved to wear them himself instead of drab, male garments. In his paintings he portrayed himself and other men in marvelous Renaissance costumes. Once in Marseilles, when I bought myself a little sheepskin coat, Max was with me and he was so envious that I ordered him one too. No man had ever bought anything in this shop before, and the shopkeeper was rather surprised. However, the coat was made to order for Max, and when he wore it he looked like a Slavic prince.

We decided not to go back to the Belmont-Plaza and chose the

Shelton instead. Jimmy said we should take separate rooms. They were adjoining but not connecting. Then a very strange life began, and I suddenly felt married again. I had lived alone for four years.

Now I acquired a stepson. I felt much more at home with Jimmy than with Max. He was awfully happy to have a step-mother and we got on wonderfully well. Everything I didn't do with Max I did with Jimmy. I took him to shops, while I replenished my wardrobe (I had given away all my clothes in France). But if I took Jimmy to buy clothes with me, Max couldn't go shopping without me. He made me choose everything he ordered. I encouraged him to buy a trousseau. He looked so beautiful in American clothes, for he had a perfect figure and was extremely elegant by nature. I gave him the diamond and platinum lorgnon with the watch that had belonged to my mother, and he used it instead of glasses. It suited him perfectly, making him look English and aristocratic.

While Max was on Ellis Island I went to see Breton. He was installed in an apartment Kay Sage had rented for him for six months in the Village. It was very comfortable, but looked unlike his usual surroundings. He seemed worried about his future, yet in spite of this he was determined not to learn a word of English. He wanted to hear all about Max and our life in Lisbon and what had occurred between Leonora and Max. The report had gone around New York that Max would not leave Leonora in Lisbon, and that that was why we had remained there so long. Breton did not gather that I was in love with Max. We talked a lot about Leonora and Max, and Breton confirmed my opinion that she was the only woman Max had ever loved.

This was the first opportunity I had to thank Breton for his poem *Fata Morgana,* which he had sent me before leaving France. The Vichy government refused to allow its publication, but in America he soon found a publisher and it was translated into English. Breton had had many adventures on his way to America and had spent weeks in Cuba waiting for a boat. I think he was depressed and did not know what to do next.

As soon as Max was free he went to see Breton and asked him to dinner. Breton was anxious to get Max back into his group again. After all, Max was his biggest star and Breton had lost him during the Eluard crisis. The Surrealists were always playing at cat and mouse, and it was comparatively easy for Max to be seduced again. As soon as I arrived at the Brevoort Hotel, where I joined them for dinner, Max rushed up to me and kissed me, so that Breton would know what our relationship was. I think he was terribly surprised.

At the request of Kay Sage I soon put Breton's mind at rest and promised to give him two hundred dollars a month for a year. That would give him time to find out what he would do in New York, without worrying.

The first thing we did was to go down to Long Island for a weekend with Louis and Marian Bouché. They came to see me and said that they would be glad to have us visit them some time near Oyster Bay. I asked them to take us at once out of the terrible heat of New York. Bouché, though he was not an Abstract or Surrealist painter, had long been an admirer of Max's work and seemed to know all about it. They were very sweet to us and gave us a lovely weekend. The last time I had seen them was at Yew Tree Cottage in 1938.

When we arrived in New York the Museum of Modern Art was having a Picasso show. Penrose had sent all his paintings to New York for the duration, and some of the ones I knew best were in this exhibition. The Museum owned a lot of Max's paintings and collages, since Alfred Barr had bought fourteen. Most of them were in the cellar, however, as was the custom of the Museum of Modern Art. I remember going down into the depths there and finding Brancusi's sculpture *The Miracle*. It was a miracle to find it there. Upstairs they did show a *Bird in Space* very much like mine but made twenty years earlier. The collection of the Museum was pretty fine. They had wonderful Picassos, Braques, Légers, Dalis, Rousseaus, Arps, Tanguys and Calders, but not one Kandinsky. In the garden they showed sculpture. The atmosphere of the whole place was that of a girl's college. Yet at the same time it looked rather like a millionaire yacht club. I am sure Humphrey Jennings would have adored it.

We went to see my uncle's museum. It really was a joke. There were about a hundred paintings by Bauer in enormous silver frames which overshadowed the twenty Kandinskys. There was one marvelous Léger of 1919, a Juan Gris, a lot of Domelas, a John Ferren, a Calder, a Delaunay and a few other less interesting painters, whose names I can't remember. From the walls boomed forth music by Bach—a rather weird contrast. The museum was a beautiful little building completely wasted in this atrocious manner. Max called it the Bauer House; the Museum of Modern Art he called the Barr House; and Gallatin's collection in the New York University building was the Bore House. It really was boring because, although Mr. Gallatin had some nice abstract paintings, the surroundings were so dull that one had no pleasure in looking at them. Max was annoyed because Mr. Gallatin, no longer considering his painting sufficiently abstract, had removed it. This collection is now in a museum in Philadelphia.

What Max liked best in New York was the Museum of Natural History. He was delighted by the mathematical objects, which he claimed were much better than Pevsner's constructions. Another museum Max adored was the Museum of the American Indian, the Heye Foundation, where Breton took us. It had the best collection of British Columbian, Alaskan, Pre-Columbian, South Sea, Indian and Mayan art.

In contrast to the Bauer House there existed in the Plaza Hotel a really fine collection of modern paintings owned by my uncle, Solomon Guggenheim, but accessible to the public only by special invitation. Aunt Irene lived there with my uncle surrounded by the most beautiful Picassos, Seurats, Braques, Klees, Kandinskys, Gleizeses, Delaunays, Chagalls and a Lissitzky. I took Max there and Aunt Irene was delighted to meet him, but being rather confused, she thought he had replaced Herbert Read in my life. I told my Aunt Irene to burn all the Bauers and move these paintings to the Museum. She said, "Shush! Don't let your uncle hear that. He has invested a fortune in Bauer." Next time I saw her was when she came to my house, and, meeting Laurence whom she hadn't seen for seventeen years, she mistook him for Max. When I put her right she said, "I thought something was wrong because Ernst looks so much older." As a matter of fact they were born the same year, but Max certainly looked ten years older than he was. Max and Laurence were often mistaken for each other. One day when Laurence invited us all to lunch to meet Bob Coates, Bob first met Max and asked him if he were Laurence, whom he had not seen for fourteen years. Max took him along and presented him to his long-lost friend.

One night Jimmy met Leonora in a drugstore in Columbus Circle, and was in a terrific state of excitement about it. He

hadn't seen her for years. He had been alternately in love with her
and jealous of her because of his abnormal attachment to Max.
Max couldn't wait until he saw Leonora. She had brought all his
paintings with her. When he got them, he hung them up in Julien
Levy's gallery and invited Breton, Putzel, Laurence and a few
other people to see them. They were greatly admired. Max saw a
lot of Leonora and, just when I told Jimmy I couldn't stand it any
longer and I was going to leave Max, we were all invited to
California by my sister Hazel.

Max was delighted to be invited anywhere, and I was pleased to
see my sister again and to get out of the heat of New York. I also
wanted to see Arenberg's famous collection of paintings in
Hollywood. Sindbad, to whom I had just given my little Talbot
automobile, went up to Rhode Island with Laurence and all his
children. Pegeen and Jimmy came with us. Just when we were
leaving by airplane, Hazel wired that she was getting a new nose
and could we postpone our visit for a few days? It was too late to
change our plans, so we went to San Francisco. From then on we
called Hazel *le nouveau nez*.

The trip over America was incredibly beautiful. Max and I
were thrilled every minute, but Jimmy and Pegeen were very sick.
We flew so high poor Pegeen nearly died, and had to be given
oxygen. At Reno I took her out, thinking the air would help her
but she nearly collapsed in the ladies' room. She therefore missed
all the marvelous scenery over Salt Lake, miles and miles of land
covered with salt, where the sea had receded, and then stretches
of blue and purple water. It was better than any painting, the
colors were so delicate and the expanse so vast.

At San Francisco is was very exciting to see the Bay and all the
bridges from above. It is a beautiful city and from the air the
approach is ten times better. We enjoyed the Chinese restaurants
and theatres and the modern art museums. We went to the
Courvoisier Gallery and bought two paintings by Charles Howard.
It was so nice to come into contact with his work again after all
this time and he had made great progress since I had given him a
show in London in 1939. It was very pleasant seeing him again.
He was working in a shipyard and I think was rather sad.

We went to Dr. Grace McCann Morley's fine San Francisco
Museum. I asked if I could see her but her secretary said she was
too busy. I was very much offended. However, I was not

prevented from meeting her, as Sidney Janis, the art dealer, was in the Museum, where he was showing a large exhibition of his primitives. When he told Dr. Morley that Max was there she took us out to a wonderful fish dinner, in what seemed to be America's Marseilles, and drove us all over the countryside showing us the sights. She was hospitable and charming and full of life. I asked her if I could send her exhibitions when I got my museum going, and she replied she would like it very much. She told me she gave a hundred and twenty exhibitions a year.

Max thought the primitive paintings quite remarkable. There happened to be a reporter in the Museum at the time, who interviewed him, and quoted his enthusiasm for this show. A scandal ensued as *The Art Digest* refused to take Max seriously, and said he was making fun of the American public. I had to write a letter to *The Art Digest* telling them that he really meant it, and admired this painting more than any other produced by Americans.

Before we left San Francisco we got into awful rows with Pegeen about Kay. Max hated Kay because she had induced Leonora to go off with the Mexican, and I too had always found Kay objectionable. Poor Pegeen had lived with Kay for two years because of the war, and was fond of her. She tried hard, but with no success, to justify Kay's behavior to Laurence. The fight became so fierce that Pegeen refused to come with us to Los Angeles. We nearly missed the plane, but at the last minute she gave in, and came along, because she was afraid to remain alone and penniless in San Francisco.

When we arrived in Los Angeles we found Hazel with a beautiful young husband. He seemed such a contrast to Max who looked so old. He was studying to be a pilot, as he wanted to be in the air force (in which he was to lose his life) as soon as America joined the war. They seemed very happy together, in fact it was the only time I ever found Hazel happily married. She painted a lot and one day asked Max if he could teach her to paint a jungle. He was amused and gave her a lesson, but afterward he claimed she had not paid much attention to what he had told her.

Max and I had no idea where to live, or where to establish the museum. We began to look at houses all over California. The place we came nearest to buying was a fifty-room castle at Malibu, built high on a hill. An American woman had conceived the idea of this extraordinary establishment but her funds had given out, and she had been forced to abandon the place  There were thousands of tiles, made by Spanish workmen, who were brought to America especially for that purpose. The tiles had never been incorporated in the castle, however, and were stacked on the floor. We thought the whole place in its unfinished state was like a Surrealist dream. In Marseilles I had invited Breton to live in my museum in America and hold his Surrealist court there, and this place seemed to be the ideal spot for all these activities. Of course no one ever would have come out here. The distance made it impracticable. Another disadvantage was that the road to the castle disappeared in the rainy season.

There was one other house that tempted us very much, but it was situated on a steep incline overlooking the sea. The drawback was that the land was gradually slipping away at the cliff end of the garden. One tree was already lost and we did not know how long the house could remain, since it was so perilously near the edge.

Pegeen's one idea at this time was to meet or at least see movie stars. Hazel took her to a cocktail party where she met Charlie Chaplin. On her sixteenth birthday I gave her a dinner party at Ciro's, the restaurant most frequented by the movie people. Unfortunately it was the worst night of the week and there wasn't one star present. Pegeen burst into tears in the car going home. But to compensate for this I sent her to a Red Cross ball given by the Royal Air Force, where she could be sure to have her heart's desire and see all the movie people. She went quite alone, dressed in a long white evening dress and little white fur cape, looking like Cinderella dressed for the ball. She swept in majestically and had a most wonderful evening. Only long afterward did she admit she had not recognized the stars.

Hazel had a secretary, Albert Bush, who was a poet. He conducted a poet's hour on the radio. He wanted Max to give a little talk about France and what was happening there and why he had been forced to leave, and what his impressions of America were. I interviewed Max and translated what he said, and taught him to pronounce and read it in English which he couldn't speak at all. Jimmy and I sat in our newly acquired Buick listening to Max's interview on the radio. He did very well and made only one funny error in pronunciation. That was when he came to the word "hospitable," which he spat out with the accent on "pit." Jimmy had a pronounced father complex and adored Max as much as I did. We were always trying to do everything we could to make Max feel important in America. Jimmy was very good at publicity and Max was happy when he appeared in the public eye. He didn't seem to exist unless people noticed him. However, he was always very dignified and never made a fool of himself.

In Hazel's house we had a bedroom, a sleeping porch and a nursery at our disposal. I was supposed to share the nursery with Pegeen, but I slept with Max in his room, or we slept on the sleeping porch. Sometimes I changed my room three times a night to fool the maids. Over our bed was a family motto in Latin saying, "Never too much." It was Hazel's husband's room.

Max painted on the sleeping porch, and I was particularly thrilled when I woke up there to find opposite me, on his easel, his latest paintings. It was like being present at their birth.

I think my brother-in-law must have found it very trying to have us all descend upon him in this way, especially as Max didn't speak English and he couldn't speak French or German.

At one of Hazel's parties we met George Biddle, who considered himself America's greatest painter. He made a great effort to be nice to Max and talked about Surrealism, which I am sure he must have hated. Not knowing who he was, I naively said to him, "Do you paint too, Mr. Biddle?"

On my birthday Max and I cooked dinner for fourteen people. He made a wonderful fish soup, from fish which he had caught himself early that morning, and I made a *paella*. At this party we met Hazel's friends, the Gonzaleses, both painters, who lived in New Orleans. He was Spanish and she was a charming American girl. Albert Bush drank to my health saying, "Only Peggy knows 'The Importance of Being Ernst.'" In Hollywood we found Man Ray (with a new young wife) and Bob McAlmon and Caresse Crosby. It was nice to see old friends from France again. Bob tried to help me find a college for Pegeen, but all she wanted was to go to dramatic school and become a star in the movies, so I finally decided to leave this demoralizing atmosphere.

One reason I had come west was to visit Arensberg's collection of modern art. It was probably one of the finest in the world. Every room of his funny old Victorian house was crammed with magnificent paintings. Even the corridors and the bathrooms were like the best rooms of a museum. Apart from owning practically all the works of Marcel Duchamp, he had many fine Brancusis, a wonderful Rousseau, a Chirico, Kandinskys, Klees, Mirós, lots of Picassos, a few Ernsts, Tanguys, Dalis, Gleizeses, Delaunays. His Cubist collection made me very jealous, but his later things were not nearly up to mine. In fact where he left off, I began. Lately he had been collecting mostly Pre-Columbian sculpture. He was a sad man, who by now had a much greater interest in proving Bacon wrote Shakespeare than in anything else. In spite of this, he had a great passion for Duchamp. In his house I met the painter John Ferren and his wife Inez. Ferren had lived in Paris for years and wore a red beard. Later I bought two of his paintings in New York and his wife brought out my catalogue (to say nothing of typing the manuscript of this book).

After we had been with Hazel for three weeks, we motored to the Grand Canyon where I was to meet Emily Coleman. She was now married to a cowboy and living on a ranch. At this time Max was showing some pictures in San Francisco where Julien Levy had rented a gallery and I told Max to go there if he wanted to, and join me later, but I think he was afraid of losing me so he came along. When we got to the Grand Canyon I left Max with Jimmy and went to Holbrook with Pegeen to fetch Emily. When I kissed Max goodbye he said very pathetically, like a baby, "Are you ever coming back?" For two days he wandered around alone, as he never could speak to Jimmy, and found a shop with wonderful Indian masks, totem poles and Kachina dolls. He wanted to buy them all. He was like a child, and having found himself suddenly in the position of being rich he wanted to buy everything he fell in love with. I put him off as much as I could, but in the end he always got what he wanted.

Emily and Max got along very well. She told me how much I showed my insecurity with him, and that pained me. I had hoped to hide it. After a few days we took Emily back to her sordid home on the ranch. I could not understand how she could live in such unspeakable squalor. I never saw her husband.

From there we drove on to Sante Fe. We passed Albuquerque and Gallup, where there were beautiful shows of Indian art. We were supposed to go to the Indian reservation to see the Hopi dances. That was one of the reasons Max had come west. But Jimmy told us we had passed the road miles after we were beyond it, and we were so furious we never went back. When you have to drive hundreds of miles a day, you do not want to add to the number. Max did all the driving, which made me angry, but I let him and made terrible scenes afterward. We spent several days in Santa Fe and played with the idea of living there, but much as we loved the scenery, we knew life there would be deadly.

While we were motoring through the Texas desert, Pegeen developed a bad sore throat and a high fever. We were forced to remain four days in the most extraordinary place I have ever been in. Wichita Falls was like an oasis, an oasis for cockroaches. They came in from the desert at night, attracted by the lights of the town. When you walked in the streets, you felt them scrunch under your feet four layers deep. They climbed up the walls of the houses and managed to get in, despite the screens. At the movies they got into my low-necked dress and into my hair. When we came home we found Pegeen and a bellboy on all fours searching under the bed for one of these creatures. Pegeen could never endure any bugs, and these were too much for her. In the daytime they all vanished. Apart from this, Wichita Falls was a very dull place. The heat was unbelievable. You just couldn't go out until after sunset and then there was no place to go. If you drove half a mile in any direction you were in the desert. You had to buy your drinks in a drugstore and carry them with you to the hotel restaurant. That was a Texas law. We had stolen from some hotel a book telling us about the state liquor laws. As they varied so much, it was just as well to be prepared beforehand.

I was also much interested in the state marriage laws, because I wanted to marry Max. Every time we came to a new state, I sent Jimmy to find out what were our chances of marrying at once. Pegeen, however, soon put an end to all this by making Max admit that marriage was too bourgeois for him to go through with. She was jealous of my feeling for him and was clever at putting in her oar.

Our next stop was New Orleans, where the heat was terrific, although it was September. When we asked for a mint julep we were told that summer was over and there was no more mint. The same thing happened when we wanted bananas. Hazel's friends, the Gonzaleses, were charming to us and showed us everything, including plantation houses and swamps. They introduced us to all their friends. Dr. Marion Suchon showed us his paintings in

his office, where he painted between patients' visits. We had
wonderful meals in the French quarter and felt more at home
there than anywhere in America.

Max had a long interview with a local paper and was
photographed in our bedroom with one of his paintings that the
Museum of Modern Art later acquired. The next day the social
editor came to interview me and took my picture with Pegeen and
Jacqueline, who lived in New Orleans. I hid everything that
belonged to Max that was in our room, thinking it more proper.
But to my dismay in walked the same photographer who had been
there for Max the day before. Max was jealous that we were
having publicity and Jacqueline's grandmother, a Southern lady of
the old school, had the evening edition of the paper omit our
photograph.

After New Orleans we motored back to New York. Of all the
states we went through, I liked Tennessee the best. It had the
most wonderful scenery and red earth. But we were destined to
live in New York.

When we arrived in New York we went to the Great Northern
Hotel. The first thing to do was to put Pegeen in school. I chose
the Lenox High School, a preparatory to Finch Junior College.
She boarded at Finch and came home weekends. Nothing could
have been less appropriate than this stuffy school. She managed to
survive it for two years, when she was graduated. Snobbish Finch
Boarding School was too much for her to endure even during the
week, and as soon as we had a house she insisted on living with
us.

I started to look for a place for my museum. Laurence, who was
living in Connecticut, tried to get us to be his neighbors. There
were two houses we almost bought, one of which particularly
fascinated Max because thirteen suicides had taken place there.
The other house was sold ten minutes before we saw it.

In New York we looked everywhere. Finally we found a dream
of a house on Beekman Place overlooking the river. We thought it
would be the ideal place for the museum, except that it was too far
away from the center of town. But we couldn't resist it. We
intended to sleep in the servants' rooms when we were there, and
to live in the country. However, we were not allowed to open a
museum in this section. We had to take the house for ourselves,
to live in instead. It was the most beautiful house in New York. It

was a remodeled brownstone mansion called Hale House on the East River and Fifty-first Street. It had a big living room or chapel with an old fireplace that might well have been a baronial hall in Hungary. The chapel was two stories high and the whole front of the room gave on to the river, where we had a terrace. There was a balcony above with five little windows overlooking the chapel. Here five choirboys might well have sung Gregorian chants. On the third floor we had our bedroom in the back of the house, and in the front Max had a beautiful studio with another terrace. Pegeen had the second floor to herself. Out of the servants' rooms we made a guest suite. We had a big kitchen and, since we both cooked a lot, we ate many meals in there. Max was a marvelous cook and made especially fine curries.

It had been the Museum of Modern Art, at the request of Jimmy, which had started the machinery in motion to bring Max to America. When we arrived we expected a warm reception from the Museum, which we did not get. Alfred Barr was in Vermont and sent Max a telegram of welcome. He made a little show in the Museum of Max's and other people's collages, but we did not see him until the fall. Collage was undoubtedly Max's greatest contribution to art.

I had heard a great deal about Barr from Nellie van Doesburg and other people. His books on modern art had been my Bible for years, so I was naturally longing to meet him. We went to see him one day, and I was surprised to find someone who looked like Abraham Lincoln. His conversation was serious and learned. He was shy but very charming, and I liked him at once. Later, when I knew him better, I hated his cagey quality, and never knew what he was driving at; but he was one of the people whom I respected in the world who had done a pioneering job and done it well. When we were in the Great Northern Hotel he came to see Max's paintings. He was crazy about them, but he never could get the Museum to buy what he wanted. He always had to fuss and fuss and bargain, and drove me crazy with his indecision. Just before he arrived a sparrow flew in at the window. Barr was delighted to find Max, the King of Birds, harboring this little creature. Finally Barr gave me a Malevich, of which he had thirteen in the cellar, for an Ernst. Everyone was delighted, and Barr was impressed by my genuine passion for art. I gave Max the money that was not involved in this exchange.

When we moved into our house we gave a huge house-warming party. Leonora came, looking most ravishing, for once marvelously dressed in a sort of impromptu costume with a white mantilla. There was a terrible fight between enormous Nicolas Calas and little Charles Henri Ford, and in the middle of it Jimmy rushed to take down the Kandinskys from the walls before they were splattered with blood. Barr thought that was real devotion on Jimmy's part, to rescue my paintings before Max's. Jimmy was already my secretary. He was efficient and bright and knew everything, and I loved him and we got on marvelously. The house was entirely warmed by the blood of these two intellectuals. Maybe that started us off badly because we never had a moment's peace in that wonderful place. Peace was the one thing that Max needed in order to paint, and love was one thing I needed in order to live. As neither of us gave the other what he most desired, our union was doomed to failure.

When I finally got my paintings out of storage and hung in the house, I asked Alfred Barr to come to see them. I was in a state of great excitement to know what he would think of them. We invited him and his wife to dinner. I had already been to their house for cocktails, when Daisy Barr had embarrassed me terribly by asking what had occurred between Max and Leonora in Lisbon. I began by hating her, but the more I saw of her the better I liked her. She was a very attractive woman and delightfully un-American. Daisy Barr seemed Irish, but she was half Italian. They came for dinner and brought Jim Soby and his wife. At this time Soby was being broken-in to take Alfred Barr's place in the Museum of Modern Art, but I did not then realize all the machinations of that institution and never will. They were much interested in my collection and thought I had some very fine things. Soby bought a painting of Max's, a sort of portrait of Leonora sitting on a rock. It was called *Arizona*. He had painted it in Europe and finished it in California.

After Julien Levy came back from California he took a small gallery on Fifty-seventh Street. He had not been very successful in the west. We were annoyed with him because he had sold one of Max's paintings much too cheaply. Max did not want to exhibit in his gallery in New York as it was too small, so he decided to show with Dudensing's instead. This was my idea; I had talked Max into accepting Dudensing's offer.

When I first lived with Max I had no idea how famous he was, but little by little I realized it. People were always coming up to him and treating him with reverence and respect, like a great master. He took his adulation very well. He was perpetually being photographed for the press. He loved this, and he hated to have me included. Once, however, he had to succumb and we appeared in *Vogue* with our little dog Kachina, a Tibetan Lhasa terrier, who was all overgrown with white hair and looked like Max. Max bought an enormous chair about ten feet high. It was a Victorian theatrical prop. He sat in it as though it were his throne, and no one else ever dared use it, except Pegeen. He was always photographed in this chair.

The paintings Max had done in France between periods in concentration camps, or while he was actually in them, started a completely new phase of his work. The backgrounds of these paintings greatly resembled the desert land of Arizona and the swamps of Louisiana which he was soon to visit. It is unbelievable that he had this foresight. It seems to have been his special gift to forepaint the future. As his painting was completely unconscious and came from some deep hidden source, nothing he ever did surprised me. At one time, when he was alone in France after Leonora had left, he painted her portrait over and over in all the landscapes that he was so soon to discover in America. I was jealous that he never painted me. In fact it was a cause of great unhappiness to me and proof that he did not love me.

One day when I went into his studio I had a great shock. There on his easel was a little painting I had never seen before. In it was portrayed a strange figure with the head of a horse, which was Max's own head, and the body of a man dressed in shining armor. Facing this strange creature, and with her hand between his legs, was a portrait of me. Not of me as Max had ever known me, but of me as my face appeared as a child of eight. I have photographs of myself at this age and the likeness is unquestionable. I burst into tears the minute I recognized it and rushed to tell Max that he had at last painted my portrait. He was rather surprised as he had never seen the photos. Because my hand was placed where it was and because it was between two spears, I named the picture *The Mystic Marriage*. I asked for it as a present, telling Max that now he need never marry me, as this sufficed. I have still to describe the rest of the painting, as this was only one-third of it. In the center was a figure which Max admitted to be Pegeen's back, and on the left hand side was a terrifying sort of monster. It portrayed a woman in a red dress with her stomach exposed. This was undoubtedly my stomach, but the figure had two heads which resembled nobody. They were animal heads and one looked like a skeleton. Sidney Janis claimed I was this monster, which he considered very strong, but that was later, when Max took this for a theme and made an enormous canvas of it. In this new painting my beautiful girl's head disappeared completely and gave way to a portrait of a strange unknown person accompanied by Pegeen. The original Pegeen in this painting gave way to a totem pole with a head made of a substance resembling brains. Much later I showed these photos to Alfred Barr because I wanted him to corroborate my theory, and he was much impressed by the resemblance.

I don't think Emily really liked Max's paintings but she did appreciate his collages. She gave him long lectures about them which he did not in the least understand. However, to hide his ignorance and show his appreciation he always replied, *"Oui, oui, oui."* I once said to Emily, "There are three reasons why I love Max: because he is so beautiful, because he is such a good painter and because he is so famous."

At this time I was still trying to complete my collection and buy all the pictures that Mr. Read and I had meant to exhibit in London, in our opening show, as a survey of modern art from 1910 to 1939. There were many paintings that I had not been able to obtain in France because of the war. These I now bought in America. Breton and Max helped me a great deal in my choice. I was finishing the catalogue, and every time I bought another painting I rushed a new photograph and biography over to Mrs. Ferren, the publisher. Max did a beautiful cover for the catalogue. I was rather worried about the book, however, and decided it was very dull. I asked Breton to save it. He was always telling me it was *catastrophique*. It probably would have been if it had not been for him. He spent hours of research and found statements made by each artist; we included these and photographs of their eyes. Breton's preface was excellent, containing a whole history of Surrealism. I got Mondrian to do another preface for me, which Charmian Wiegand put into English, and I included the one Arp had done for me in Europe. Besides that,

Breton told me to add the manifestos of the different movements in art of the last thirty years, and then we included statements by Picasso, Max, Chirico and others. In the end the book turned out exceedingly well, being an anthology of modern art rather than a catalogue. We called it *Art of This Century*.

As Max sold more and more paintings he bought more and more Indian, Pre-Columbian, Alaskan and New Guinea art. We had practically no furniture and all these things made the house look very beautiful. Max got hold of a little man called Carlebach, or rather Carlebach got hold of Max. He let him have his collection on credit and Max paid him whenever he sold a painting. I was very much annoyed that Max refused to contribute to the household expenses. I think he based his refusal on the grounds that I still supported Laurence. Finally, Max reached the point where he would not even put aside money to pay his income tax. Carlebach used to phone Max almost every day to come around to his shop on Third Avenue to see some new things that he had found for him. He was perpetually scurrying around and finding things with which to tempt Max. There was no end to his ingeniousness and his activities. He even made deals with museums and got them to cede things to Max. Once he found out that I collected earrings and immediately got together a large quantity and began to work on me. But I did not succumb. Of course Max did, and bought me a beautiful pair with Spanish baroque pearls. But I resisted any further efforts on Mr. Carlebach's part, as I considered him sufficiently dangerous with his totem poles and masks. One day Max bought a beautiful, wooden painted animal that looked like a burial object. He said he had bought a little table, but it certainly was more like a cradle. At one time Max had had a passion for wooden horses and the house was full of these. He also bought a British Columbian totem pole twenty feet high. It was a terrifying object and I hated to have it in the house.

After Pearl Harbor the question of marriage came up again. I did not like the idea of living in sin with an enemy alien, and I insisted that we legalize our situation. In order to avoid publicity and the taking of a blood test, we decided to go down to Washington to visit my cousin Harold Loeb, and get the thing done quickly in Maryland. The night before we left we had an awful row, and when Pegeen came home Max was still looking unhappy. Pegeen, who was against my marrying, said, "Mama, how can you force the poor thing to marry you? Look how miserable he is." Max and I both said he looked this way because of our row, but Pegeen would not believe it, and convinced me she was right. I was so upset the next morning that I ran to Putzel and told him all my troubles. He said that I should get married if I wanted. I phoned Max and asked him how he felt. He said he wished to go to Washington, so we drove down there.

In Maryland they refused to marry us. We only had divorce papers in foreign languages which they could not translate. Besides, Max could not prove his first divorce, and they would not accept his second as proof of his first. They told us to go to Virginia. In Virginia you had to be a resident, over eighteen years of age and have a blood test taken. We did not have much difficulty in proving that we were of age; the Loebs gave us the residence. As to the blood test we managed to survive it. Compared with being a blood donor, it was nothing. When we got our marriage license we were asked when we wanted to marry. We said, "At once." They telephoned a judge who lived around the corner and he said we could come immediately. However, he did not admit us for some time but kept us waiting on his doorstep. We were accompanied by Harold's wife, who was doing everything to help us. When the judge finally admitted us, we found he had a girl with him. He said, "This poor little thing's husband, a doctor in the Navy, has just gone to sea and I am consoling her." We understood why he had kept us waiting so long. Max could not speak English and when he was asked to *wed* me, he understood *wet,* which he repeated. The ceremony was very simple and I did not have to promise to obey. When it was over we did not know how much to give the judge. Vera Loeb thought five dollars, but Max only had ten which he offered. The judge and his girl friend were so delighted that she tickled the palm of Max's hand. I think that partially consoled him for being no longer free. Afterward we went back to Washington and Max invited my cousins to a wonderful dinner to celebrate.

The marriage gave me a feeling of safety, but did not stop our rows, as I had hoped. They were awful and often lasted forty-eight hours, during which time we would not speak to each other. The fights were about nothing of importance. We fought if Max took my scissors without asking my permission. This annoyed me because they were the scissors John Holms had used to cut his beard. We fought if Max would not let me drive the car because he preferred to drive himself. We fought when he got bored because I had the flu and took too long to convalesce. We fought about the layout of my catalogue, after we had both worked peacefully on it together for hours. We fought most of all about his buying too many totem poles. It was all ridiculous and childish. The quarrels upset him terribly. He could not work and wandered around New York for days. I was also very unhappy and was always the first one to make up. He was too proud to do so himself. The worst of it all was that we fought in public. We fought anywhere we happened to be.

During the winter we made great friends with Amédée Ozenfant, a most fascinating man. For three years he had been my neighbor in the Avenue Reille, where I lived in Paris with John Holms, During all that period I had not known him. Now he lived on Twentieth Street, and we often went there to delicious dinners cooked by Marthe, his wife. I wanted to buy one of Ozenfant's Purist paintings, as I considered it of historic interest. All my advisers were against it, but I bought it all the same. I am very glad, because the Museum of Modern Art neglected him badly and bought a Jeanneret instead. There was no reason to consider Jeanneret superior to Ozenfant. They worked together in 1920 and it was unfair not to realize their equal value.

I was very busy all winter working on my catalogue, and postponed renting a place for the museum until this was finished. People came to the house to see the paintings and ended up on the top floor in Max's studio. Putzel brought customers and Max sold a lot of paintings and bought more and more totem poles and Kachina dolls and masks. It took me all winter to get my catalogue ready, as Breton took so long to do his article, which turned out to be about sixteen pages, and then Laurence had to translate it. By then the spring had come and the art season was over.

One of the things from which I suffered most was the fact that Max was never intimate with me. He considered me a sort of lady whom he was slightly afraid of, and never addressed me as *tu;* because of this I never felt he really loved me. Once, when I asked him to write something in the books he had given me, he merely wrote, "For Peggy Guggenheim from Max Ernst." This was upsetting, as I remembered what he had written for Leonora. He always made me feel that he would have liked me much better if I had been young and vulgar. He admitted that he liked stupid, vulgar girls.

Leonora used to phone Max to come and take her to lunch. Sometimes he would spend the whole day with her and they would wander around New York, something he never did with me. It made me wildly jealous and I suffered agonies. In the morning he always worked after we had breakfast, so he never bothered to wear street clothes. If I found he was dressed to go out my heart sank, because I knew he was going to dedicate the day to Leonora. On these occasions I used to lunch with other people. Sometimes with Alfred Barr, but more often with Jimmy Stern, whom I invited to our house. He was a fascinating Irishman, a friend of Beckett and Laurence. I had quite a *béguin* for him, but as our conversation was restricted to intellectual matters and to long talks about John Holms, whom he had never met, he did not suspect my feelings. He is a very good writer and surprisingly little known for one so talented.

Max was so insane about Leonora that he really could not hide it. Once I made him bring her back to lunch and asked Djuna Barnes to come and meet her. Djuna said it was the only time that Max seemed human or showed any emotion. Normally he was as cold as a snake. He always protested and said he was no longer in love with Leonora, and that I was the person he wanted to live with and sleep with. But I was never reassured and I was very happy when she went to Mexico.

We went to lots of parties at various houses, but the best ones were given by Mrs. Bernard Reis. She was a wonderful hostess and served marvelous meals. She loved to fill her home with Surrealists and then give them a free hand to do what they liked. Of course Breton took advantage of this to make us all play his favorite game, *Le jeu de la vérité*. We sat around in a circle while Breton lorded it over us in a true schoolmasterly spirit. The object of the game was to dig out people's most intimate sexual feelings and expose them. It was like a form of psychoanalysis done in public. The worse the things that we exposed, the happier everyone was. I remember once, when it was my turn, asking Max if he had preferred making love at the age of twenty, thirty, forty or fifty. Other people asked you what you would do about sex if your husband went to war or how long you could go without it, or what your favorite occupation was. It was ridiculous and childish, but the funniest part was the seriousness with which Breton took it. He got mortally offended if anyone spoke a word out of turn; part of the game was to inflict punishment on those who did so. You had to pay a forfeit. Breton ruled us with an iron hand, screaming *"Gage!"* at every moment. In the end the forfeits were redeemed in the most fantastic manner. You were punished by being brought blindfolded into a room on all fours and forced to guess who kissed you or something equally foolish.

In the spring Max had his exhibition at Dudensing's. I gave a big party for him after the opening. It was one of the best parties I have ever given. It went right off from the start with no effort.

The show had a great *succès d'estime,* but the pictures were not sold as they were priced too high and Dudensing had the wrong clientele for them. The same week the Hartford Atheneum bought one that was not in the show. After that Putzel and I sold the paintings, all to different people who came to the house. I loved being a painter's wife and by this time was insane about the new paintings. Charles Henri Ford devoted a whole number of his magazine *View* to Max. It was an amusing issue and good for Ford as well as for Max. Max appeared in it photographed on his throne by Berenice Abbott, and on our terrace with his Kachina dolls photographed by James Soby. Breton, Calas, Sidney Janis, Henry Miller, Julien Levy and Leonora wrote articles about him for this issue, and he wrote his own biography. A lot of paintings were reproduced with the catalogue of the exhibition.

After that Max went to Chicago where he was to have a show. I did not want to accompany him. My catalogue was finally coming out and I was extremely excited. He had a good time while all I thought about was my book. Several bookshops made window displays for me and it was thrilling to see my first production so well received. It began to sell at once, thanks to Jimmy's foresight in advance publicity.

I could not sleep all winter until Clifford Odets left for California. He occupied the two top floors of our house and his study was over our bedroom. Every night he rehearsed his plays until four in the morning. I have never heard such noise. One night his bath ran over and began leaking through my ceiling, and dripping on to my dressing-table. To make amends he gave his friend, J. B. Neumann, two seats to take me to see *Clash by Night.*

I much preferred it to *Waiting for Lefty,* which Garman had taken me to see in London in a Communist theatre which had benches without backs.

Shortly after Max came back he became infatuated with a very wild and crazy girl, who was either pereptually drunk or under the effects of benzedrine. She was very funny, quite pretty and full of life; but she was terribly American, and at the time seemed to be nearly off her head. One could always tell if Max were excited about a woman: his eyes would nearly pop out of his head with desire, like Harpo Marx's. Nothing much occurred with this girl, however, and we left New York to spend the summer on the Cape. As soon as we were gone, Jimmy fell madly in love with her. Because of unforeseen circumstances we were only away a fortnight, but when we came back Jimmy had clinched the affair. He did not want Max to know anything about it, and I suspected the whole thing was caused by his father complex.

Our summer was curtailed because Max had trouble with the FBI. It was my fault. I was forced to go down to Washington for a hearing on Nellie van Doesburg's case. I had been trying to get her to America, but it was not easy. When I finally got the affidavit through, the State Department refused it; but with the help of Summer Welles, who was a friend of Helen Joyce's brother, I obtained a hearing in Washington and the visa was granted. It was too late, however. I could no longer get Nellie out of France.

I sent Pegeen up to Wellfleet, Massachusetts, with Max in the car to Matta's, where they stayed for a week to look for a house. When I arrived they thought they had found one. It was a horrid little affair in the wilderness with a kerosene stove and a gasoline pump. This reminded me of our Yew Tree Cottage pump and of all our efforts to keep it going when the gardener was on holiday. I decided not to take it and we looked for others all over the vicinity. We ended up by taking a dreary affair belonging to a lady painter in Provincetown. She lived below us. There was a studio and some living rooms and lots of bedrooms. Max got the studio and as usual wanted everything else too. Pegeen had to fight for her rights to get a place where she could paint.

I then made Max leave Matta's, in spite of the fact that he told me he ought to get permission from the Board of Enemy Alien

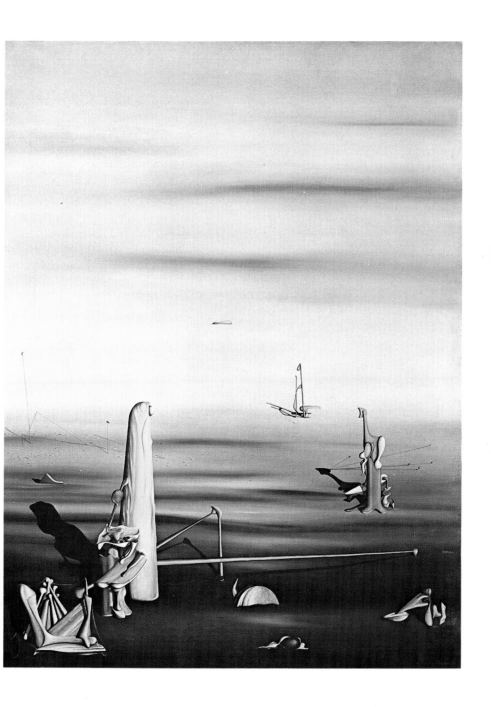

Yves Tanguy, *Le Soleil dans son écrin* (*The Sun in its Casket*), 1937

John Tunnard, *PSI*, 1938

Jean Hélion, *Large Volumes*, 1935

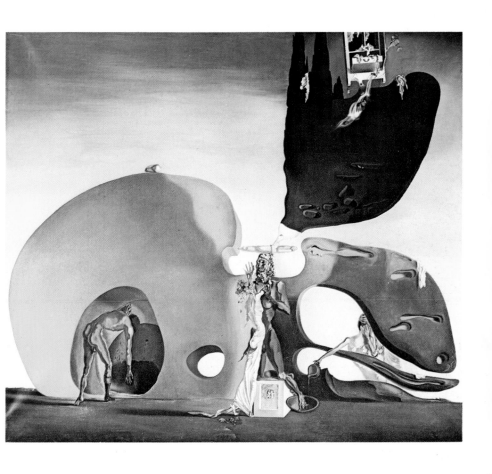

Salvador Dali, *The Birth of Liquid Desires*, 1932

Max Ernst, *The Anti-Pope*
(2 versions), 1941-42

Morris Hirshfield, *Two Women in Front of a Mirror*, 1943

Paul Delvaux, *The Break of Day*, 1937

Jackson Pollock, Mural, 1943

Pegeen, one of a series of oils and pastels

Myself on my marble chair

Registration. It seemed silly to bother, when we moved only fifteen miles away.

The first day we were in Provincetown the FBI drove up alongside us as we were walking in the street and seized Max by the wrist. They said they wanted to see him. We told them to come at two o'clock. When they arrived they searched the whole house, asked us where we all slept, looked in our suitcases, and went off with Max and a box of matches with a Free French sign on it. They said, "We are taking your husband for a ride." I was terrified and did not know what to expect. They kept him for hours and he returned in an awful state. It seems they had tried to terrorize him into denouncing Matta as a spy. They wanted to know how many *ladders* Matta had on his roof. Max misunderstood them to say *letters* in his name, and answered five. They had already been to Matta's house before I arrived in Welfleet and had questioned Max.

They complained because the radio was too loud and, when Max turned it off, they said he had no right to touch it as it was a short-wave set. They now used that against him and made a report which they sent to Boston. They told him that if he didn't tell everything he knew about Matta they would hold him until his gray hair was much grayer than it already was. From then on, every time we sat down to a meal, they walked in and bothered us some more. Finally they came one day and took Max off to sign the report they had made, warning us that it was no longer in their hands to judge the case. We waited in fear and then one day, at lunchtime, they came and said Max would have to go to Boston to have a hearing with the district attorney. I insisted on going too, and as I was his wife they could not refuse. At last I could prove to Pegeen that marriage was useful. We left her with some friends and told her we had no idea when we would be back.

It took hours to get to Boston in their car and, when we arrived, it was almost too late for a hearing. The district attorney was very nice and allowed us to explain who Max was and who I was. He had once had some job with the Guggenheims. Unfortunately he could not discharge Max without first submitting him to a hearing before the jury, and that meant he would have to keep him in custody overnight. In order to spare Max this unpleasantness, he decided to phone the New York Bureau of Enemy Aliens and see

what they had to say. Luckily for us they accepted full responsibility, claiming Max was their case, and asking to have him sent
back. We got a pass to travel and were given seventy-two hours in
which to return, which was better than having Max imprisoned in
Boston. So we went back to Provincetown.

The next day we met Varian Fry, who happened to be in
Provincetown, and having lots of connections there he tried to
arrange matters for us. But it was no use. We had to go back to
New York. Once we were home again we phoned our friend,
Bernard Reis, who knew about everything and always helped
everyone in difficulties. He made contact with someone in the
Bureau of Enemy Aliens and explained the case. When we went
down there we were well received and Max was set free at once.
He was allowed to go back to Provincetown, but was advised to
keep away from the coast.

We remained all summer in New York in our lovely house on
the East River. This was very bad luck for three people. One was
Marcel Duchamp, to whom we had lent the house; the second was
Jimmy, who was having his holiday and liked to bring his new love
to breakfast on our terrace; and the third was Sindbad, who had a
key to the house and often brought his girl-friend there, having no
other suitable place to take her. Marcel Duchamp remained with
us and moved into the little guest suite, but our sons were out of
luck.

Meanwhile I had been trying to get my museum started, and
finally I found a top story at 30 West Fifty-seventh Street, but I
didn't know how to decorate it. Putzel said to me one day, "Why
don't you get Kiesler to give you a few ideas about decorating your
gallery?" Frederick Kiesler was the most advanced architect of the
century, so I thought this was a good suggestion, never dreaming
that the few ideas would little by little end up in my spending
seven thousand dollars for the construction of the gallery. He was
a little man about five feet tall with a Napoleon complex. He was
an unrecognized genius, and I gave him a chance, after he had
been in America fifteen years, to create something really sensational. He told me that I would not be known to posterity for my
collection of paintings, but for the way he presented them to the
world in his revolutionary setting.

We had lots of parties at night in our house on the river. It was
the coolest place in New York. One night very late after a party

Max, Marcel Duchamp and John Cage, a composer of percussion music, and his wife Zenia all got undressed while Kiseler and his wife and I looked on with contempt. The object was to show how detached one could be. But Max entirely failed to attain this object, as Zenia's presence in the nude had an immediate and obvious effect on him. I am afraid Zenia took it all rather too seriously, as she wept copious tears in a bus one night soon after this, Kiesler told me, because she decided Max was not the angel she had suspected him to be.

One night after a party in our house when, having drunk quite a bit, I rushed out in search of adventure, I went to a bar on Third Avenue just as it was closing and forced my way in. Some people at a table asked me to join them and gave me drinks. I had only ten dollars on me, but I insisted on paying. One of the men said it would be safer if he kept the money for me for the rest of the night. About five o'clock we all went to Chinatown to eat. I told these people I was a governess and lived in New Rochelle. I did not ask them what they were, but it dawned on me pretty soon that they must be gangsters and up to something. They had parked their car in a dead-end street near the East River and they were arguing about something that was hidden in the rumble seat. In spite of my drunken condition I realized it was high time to leave. They wanted to drive me to New Rochelle but I declined, and I asked for my ten dollars, or at least part of it. I tried in vain to retrieve enough for a taxi or carfare, but in the end I was forced to walk home over a mile at seven in the morning. The next time I passed the bar where I had met the gangsters I went in with Max and Marcel and asked for my money back. The bartender, who I was certain had been to Chinatown with us, disclaimed all connection with these people and said he did not know them. Max's chief worry about all this was the trouble he might get into as an enemy alien if I got mixed up with gangsters.

Another night when we were having a big party for my birthday, Gypsy Rose Lee announced her engagement to an actor called Alexander Kirkland. He was very charming and handsome, but seemed hardly suitable as a husband. William Saroyan was present too. In fact there were entirely too many stars about, and there were great jealousies. Putzel took Gypsy upstairs to buy another painting of Max's. She already owned one. Jean Gorman, who was then Mrs. Carl Van Doren, went upstairs also. If I had not been so occupied with Marcel, who suddenly kissed me for the first time after knowing me for twenty years, I would have gone upstairs too and seen to it that the sale was not ruined. Jean was very tight and confused everything, and Max gave Gypsy the picture for a very modest price, and threw in another one as a wedding present. When they came down again Gypsy knew that I was annoyed and said it wasn't fair that she should get a present on my birthday. A few weeks later we motored up to Gypsy's country house, where she was to have a midnight wedding. It was a very theatrical performance and the newspaper reporters were so much in evidence, and so welcome, that they did everything short of interrupting the ceremony, which was performed by a sort of musical-comedy clergyman. Gypsy did the blushing bride stunt very well and her husband, like all bridegrooms, seemed terrified. I never knew what the marriage was about, but it did not last long, and several months later Gypsy told me it was all off. At the wedding Max was photographed by *Life* magazine sipping champagne with a South American heiress. *Life* made a dirty crack about his having married into the Guggenheim fortune, and how he was now seen drinking with another heiress, as though money were his chief preoccupation in the world. Gypsy's mother and Kirkland's mother were both present at the wedding. They took it all very seriously. Mrs. Kirkland told me she was honored to have her son enter such a distinguished family.

After Marcel kissed me I began to think we might finally consummate our suppressed desire for each other, which had been hanging fire for twenty years. One night, when Max and Marcel and I were dining together, I got terribly tight and I undressed and put on a green transparent silk rain coat and ran around the house egging Marcel on. Max asked Marcel if he wanted me and of course he had to say no. To make matters worse I said the most terrible and insulting things to Max. Max began beating me violently, and Marcel looked on with his usual detached air, not interfering in any way.

Over Labor Day we were invited to Southampton to Geoffrey and Daphne Hellman's. They were a charming couple, and I looked forward to the visit. This time Max got permission to travel. I started off well by telling Max that now that I felt he no longer desired me he could have someone else. But I am afraid I failed to maintain this self-sacrificing attitude. There was a pretty girl there called Peggy Reilly who began to flirt with Max. She played up to him as a *grand maître,* which was just what he adored. One afternoon, when we were coming home from the beach, they went ahead on bicycles and disappeared for a short time, just long enough to arouse my suspicions. I made a terrible scene. Max protested violently, saying I really went too far to think that he could make love on a bicycle. This, at any rate, completely spoiled my weekend, and I would not talk to Max for days.

I was perpetually running away from Max and going to Laurence. On one of these occasions, Max rushed downstairs and seized our dog Kachina from my arms as though she were the child in a divorce. It was a terrific anticlimax, as we were all expecting him to beat me up. Max was a great believer in revenge. He was always thinking about it. He might have walked straight out of the Old Testament. But he had a wonderful sense of humor, turning everything into a joke, and if he were hurt he never showed it. He was quite jealous of Laurence and called him "Your husband." I perpetually complained about Max to Laurence in Max's presence. It must have been very humiliating for him.

About this time Elsa Schiaparelli, whom I had known for twenty years since the days when she wore black taffeta *robes de style* and wanted to go into the antique business to make her fortune, never dreaming that she was to set the fashions for the entire western world, came to ask me to help her arrange a Surrealist show for a charity called the Coordinating Council of French Relief Societies. I sent her to Breton. With the help of Max and Marcel Duchamp, Breton organized a big exhibition, which was held in the Whitelaw Reid Mansion, an ugly, old-fashioned building. Marcel decided to cover the ceiling with strings that he criss-crossed the entire length of the room and which extended from wall to wall. It was difficult to see the paintings, but the general effect was extraordinary. At the opening I made a scene because the pictures I had lent did not have my name on them, and every other lender was acknowledged. Max's photograph was taken at this moment and, as he was standing next to beautiful Daphne Hellman, I must have appeared in the role of a jealous wife.

Kiesler did not want the Surrealist show to open before our gallery—which was nearly ready by October—but everything was late and we had to let the Surrealists get ahead of us. It made no difference, however, because ours was so special and wonderful: It was called Art of This Century, after my catalogue, and had been awaited with such curiosity that we had no rivals. Absolutely nobody knew what Kiesler had invented for my gallery. Even Max was not admitted until two days before the opening. At first he balked at having all the frames removed from his paintings, but when he saw how well all the others looked he decided not to be different. Kiesler had done a wonderful job. The publicity we got was overwhelming. Photographs appeared in all the papers and, even if the press didn't unanimously approve of Kiesler's ultra-revolutionary method of showing paintings, at least they talked about it sufficiently to bring hundreds of people a day to the gallery.

Kiesler had really created a wonderful gallery—very theatrical and extremely original. Nothing like it had ever existed before. If the pictures suffered from the fact that their setting was too spectacular and took away people's attention from them, it was at least a marvelous décor and created a terrific stir.

The only condition I had made was that the pictures should be unframed. Otherwise Kiesler had *carte blanche*. I had expected that he would insert the pictures into the walls. I was quite wrong: his ideas were much more original. The Surrealist Gallery had curved walls made of gum wood. The unframed paintings, mounted on baseball bats, which could be tilted, at any angle, protruded about a foot from the walls. Each one had its own spotlight. The lights went on and off every three seconds, to everybody's dismay, first lighting one half of the gallery and then the other. People complained and said that if they were looking at one painting on their own side of the room, they would suddenly have to stop and look at a different one in another part of the room. Putzel finally made me abandon this lighting system and keep all the lights on at the same time.

In the Abstract and Cubist Gallery, where I had my desk next to the entrance door, I was perpetually flooded in a strong fluorescent light. Two walls consisted of an ultramarine curtain which curved around the room with a wonderful sweep and resembled a circus tent. The paintings hung at right angles to it from strings. In the center of the room the paintings were clustered in triangles, hanging on strings as if they were floating in space. Little triangular wooden platforms holding sculptures were also suspended in this manner.

Kiesler had designed a chair that could be adapted for seven different purposes. It was covered in varicolored linoleum with plywood at the ends, and could serve as a rocking chair, with support for the back and was restful; or it could be turned over and used as a stand for paintings and sculpture; or as a table or a bench. You could combine it with planks of wood and make other furniture out of it. The gallery was supposed to seat ninety people, so there were also little folding chairs of blue canvas to match the wall. The floors were turquoise. Kiesler also designed an ingenious rolling storage stand, both to store paintings and to exhibit them so that you could bring them in and out when you wished to look at them. This was very ingenious and saved much space which I needed to show my large collection.

There was a beautiful daylight gallery that skirted the front on Fifty-seventh Street, and was used for current monthly shows. Here pictures could be shown in frames on plain white walls. In order to temper the light, Kiesler had put up all along the window a transparent screen made of ninon. In one corridor he placed a revolving wheel on which to show seven works of Klee. The wheel automatically went into motion when the public stepped across a beam of light. In order to view the works of Marcel Duchamp in reproduction, you looked through a hole in the wall and turned by hand a very beautiful spidery wheel. The press named this part of the gallery Coney Island.

Behind the blue canvas I had an office, which I never used, as I wanted to be in the gallery all the time to see what was going on.

My first secretary in the gallery was Jimmy Ernst. Later, when he left me, Putzel came to work with me. The first show was dedicated to my collection. Fourteen of Max's paintings and collages were on exhibition, more than those of any other painter; naturally, as I owned so many.

The opening night, October 20, 1942, was dedicated to the American Red Cross, and tickets were sold for a dollar each. Many of the invitations were lost in the mail, but hundreds of people came anyhow. It was a real gala opening. I had had a white evening dress made for the occasion, and wore one of my Tanguy earrings and one made by Calder, in order to show my impartiality between Surrealist and abstract art. The last days we worked day and night to get the gallery ready in time, but in fact workmen were still in the place when the press arrived in the afternoon before the opening.

We had great money difficulties. More and more bills kept coming in. Finally, when I realized how much Kiesler's total cost exceeded his estimate, I practically broke with him and refused to let him come to my house, but I maintained a formal museum façade. He was keen on publicity and wrote a threatening letter to one woman reporter who had given me a long interview to be syndicated all over the United States of America, insisting that his name appear too. He said he did this to protect himself as his former inventions had been stolen. She was so frightened by the letter that she would have dropped the whole article if I hadn't managed to patch up her difficulties with Kiesler just as the gallery was opening.

All this was exciting and new, and I was delighted to get away from home, where I always felt Max did not love me. He looked very happy at the opening. He was a cross between the prince regent and the museum's biggest star.

A few days after the opening he went to New Orleans, where the Gonzaleses had arranged a show for him. In New Orleans he had a much smaller audience than we did, and he was jealous of the success the museum was having.

While Max was away I was untrue to him for the first time, with Marcel, at last after twenty years. It was really too late and was almost like incest. When Max came back I was so engrossed in the gallery that I neglected him completely. He was left alone all day in our enormous house, with no lunch, as the maid came only to make dinner and there was never any food in the icebox. I would come home in the evening about six-thirty, and he was always happy to see me and made me a drink. He would open the door with a charming smile. Then we might have enjoyed what was left of the day if I had not been so boring, with my endless talking about the museum, how many people came and how many catalogues I had sold. At that time I used to sit at the desk and collect the entrance fees I had made up my mind to charge, and for which everyone hated me. Finally Putzel put a stop to this, but not before six months had gone by.

In the mornings, as I had to get up early, Max was annoyed and refused to have breakfast with me. He never came downstairs until I had left the house, although he often appeared the minute after, when I could see him through the window from the street.

Before the opening of the gallery I had decided it would also have to be a gallery where I could sell paintings for Max and young unknown artists. However a great confusion arose in the minds of the public as to what was and was not for sale, as I consistently refused to sell most of my private collection.

Soon after the gallery opened, Sindbad, Emily's son Johnnie, and Jimmy, my secretary with whom I always worked happily, all came up for the draft. Sindbad had volunteered for the E.R.C. at Columbia but had been turned down and was waiting to be drafted. Suddenly Jimmy left me, as he thought he would be in the Army soon and wanted a fortnight's holiday first. To replace him he found a friend who had once worked with him in the Museum of Modern Art. Emily's son was turned down by the Draft Board and so was Jimmy, and in the end only Sindbad was accepted. Laurence and I were terribly upset, but Sindbad took it very well. We all went down to Pennsylvania Station to see him off and suddenly he was swallowed up in a sea of unknown, tough-looking boys and disappeared. We were without news for days. Finally we had a letter saying he was in Atlantic City, and Laurence, Pegeen and I went down to see him. He looked such a baby in his uniform with his GI haircut. It nearly broke my heart to leave him.

# Chapter 14

# End of My Life with Max Ernst

One night when I had a rendezvous I told Max I was going to a concert with Putzel. He often really took me to concerts on Sunday afternoons. This particular evening Max must have suspected that I was not with Putzel because he suddenly phoned him to ask how much money he could get for a Chirico drawing that he wanted to sell. I had warned Putzel, but he had fallen asleep. When the phone rang he woke up with a start and answered it, and to his horror it was Max. Of course it was too late to do anything about it, but he pulled himself together and hung up, saying, "I will phone you later." He phoned Max back and said he had left me at the opera to go home and turn off an electric stove he had left on by mistake. When I got home I found Putzel at my streetcorner waiting for me in pajamas over which he had hastily thrown an overcoat. It was snowing. He told me what had happened, and when we got to the house Max opened the door for us and I burst out laughing. There was nothing else to do. Putzel fled.

On January 19, 1943, John Holms had been dead nine years. His anniversary still upset me very much. I generally managed to spend it with Emily if possible. But this time Edita and Ira Morris gave us a party. Late in the evening I got up and ran out in an awful state of hysteria. Ira followed, rather worried, but I told him I was going to see Emily. Once I was with her I burst out crying and told her everything between Max and me was over, and that I would never go back to him. I said I knew he was incapable of any real emotion and had nothing to do with my inner life, and that I had married him because he was a baby deposited on my doorstep. But now he no longer needed me. In the morning I went home to tell Max my decision. He was worried, as it was the first time I had been out all night. He phoned Jimmy at once to tell him I had come home. His emotion upset me and I was immediately sucked back into the family life again.

The next show of Art of This Century was an exhibition for three artists' works: Laurence Vail's decorated bottles, Joseph Cornell's Surrealist objects, and Marcel Duchamp's valise, a little pigskin suitcase he had invented to contain all the reproductions of his works. I often thought how amusing it would have been to have gone off on a weekend and brought this along, instead of the usual bag one thought one needed.

The third show was an exhibition of works by thirty-one women painters. This was an idea Marcel Duchamp had given me in Paris. The paintings submitted were judged by a jury consisting of Max, Breton, Marcel, James Sweeney, James Soby, Putzel, myself and Jimmy, who left in the middle of the session, when his girl friend came to get him. Fearing her painting would be turned down, which it was, he withdrew. Gypsy Rose Lee had done a self-portrait in collage which was very clever and which we exhibited in this show.

When Edward Alden Jewell, the art critic of *The New York Times,* came to see the show he wrote a long article in *The Times* in which he said: "The elevator man, who is tremendously interested in 'Art of This Century,' told me on the way up that he had given the place an extra-thorough cleaning (and indeed it did appear immaculate) because Gypsy Rose Lee was expected in the afternoon." The superintendent, who was very jealous, fired the elevator boy for getting this publicity. When I told Mr. Jewell what had happened he was considerably upset because he thought the boy had lost his job through him. I became very friendly with Mr. Jewell, and translating his name into French I later called him *"Mon Bijou de l'Epoque."* This was his comment on the

Surrealist gallery in *The New York Times:* ". . . it looks faintly menacing—as if in the end it might prove that the spectator would be fixed to the wall and the art would stroll around making comments, sweet or sour as the case might be."

I made Max work hard for this show. He had to go around to all the women, choose their paintings and carry them in the car to the gallery. He adored this, as he loved women, and some of them were very attractive. He was always interested in women who painted. There was one called Dorothea Tanning, a pretty girl from the Middle West. She was pretentious, boring, stupid, vulgar and dressed in the worst possible taste but was quite talented and imitated Max's painting, which flattered him immensely. She was so much on the make and pushed so hard that it was embarrassing. She wanted to be on the jury and I had to refuse her. We had met her at Julien Levy's the year before and Max had fallen for her at once. Now he became friendly with her, and as I was in the gallery all day he was happy to have a companion. She also played chess with him, which was something I could not do. He took a great interest in her painting but I was surprised that he gave her so much thought since she was vastly inferior to Leonora, who really was a creature of genius. I couldn't understand his infatuation. Max protested and said in the most pathetic manner that she was not the *fille de rien* which I accused her of being.

One night I opened a special delivery from Miss Tanning addressed to Max. It was a very silly letter written in bad French, and enclosed in it was a piece of blue silk, which she claimed to be her hair. It made me quite wild with jealousy, as she assumed that Max must be as unhappy without her as she was without him. She was somewhere in the Middle West. After reading the letter I hit Max's face several times as hard as I could. Max could not have taken this letter very seriously, because he later read it aloud to Emily and me to prove it was not a love letter. He thought it was funny.

One night Alexander Calder invited us to one of his *bals musette* in a bistro on First Avenue and Ninetieth Street. Max insisted on bringing along Miss Tanning. I was annoyed and didn't really want to go myself, because I wasn't feeling well. Max said he would go without me. I knew Calder didn't like Max, and I didn't think Miss Tanning would be an asset; anyhow I was furiously jealous and felt humiliated. I phoned Max at Miss Tanning's to tell him not to take her to the *bal musette*, threatening him that if he did I would lock him out of the house. She insisted on speaking to me herself, and told me she did not wish to make trouble between Max and me and would send him home at once. He came home, but I did not talk to him and I went out.

Another night Max was invited to a party without me and, though he had declined, I forced him to accept, as I wanted a night off to spend with Marcel. Max afterward claimed this was what broke up our marriage; since I had given him complete liberty, and for the first time he spent the whole night with Miss Tanning, as a result of which he fell in love with her. All this was for nothing, because I could not even make contact with Marcel, and went to the theatre with Pegeen instead. The next day we went to Sidney Janis' for cocktails and suddenly Max got very scared and asked if I was going to make a scene, as Miss Tanning had arrived unexpectedly. I said, "Of course not," and ignored her, as I have done ever since.

A few days later there was a Surrealist gathering at Kurt Seligmann's and Marcel Duchamp phoned Max to come. Max did everything in his power to stop me from accompanying him as Miss Tanning was to be there. I was so enraged that I left him at the door and asked him to give me the key of our house. Naturally, he went to live with Miss Tanning. But a few days later her husband came back from the Navy on furlough, and she and Max both had to flee. Max had great trouble finding a room in New York and was scared to go to any of our friends, as it would cause trouble with me.

In desperation I went to Breton. He was very much surprised by my suffering and said I must see Max and at least talk things over with him. He promised to send Max to me. He scolded me for taking the house key away from Max, and said it was a terrible thing to do to an enemy alien. I said that it was Max's fault for refusing to let me go with him to the Surrealist gathering, and that he had humiliated me too much. In the end Jimmy sent Max to see me.

When Max came I was nearly off my head and I told him that I would commit suicide if he didn't come back to me. He said it was hardly the moment for us to try to live together, and that we should both calm down first. He asked me if I would let him take

Miss Tanning to Arizona, and come back to me afterward. I nearly had a fit.

At this period I was in such a state of nerves that Pegeen had to follow me everywhere. She was worried about me, as I crossed streets without paying any attention to the traffic. One night we invited Breton to dinner and, although we hoped to make things better, everything got worse. Max, Mary and Marcel were there and some other people. We got into arguments about VVV magazine, which Marcel, Breton and Max were publishing. Max had promised me a free ad in it for my gallery and now Breton refused to let me have it. I wanted it on principle, as I felt I had done so much for the Surrealists. But Breton maintained that all his life he had sacrificed to truth, beauty and art, and he expected everyone else to do as much. Pegeen said all the Surrealists were *mesquin* because they quarreled so much. Breton was very much offended that a little girl should insult him, and he held me responsible for my daughter's doing so in my house. Max took this as an excuse to join Miss Tanning, who had been phoning him all evening. This ended our relations with Max, who disappeared for days. Pegeen did her best to patch things up between us, but she didn't suceed. The next time I saw Max I offered to give up Marcel if he would give up Miss Tanning, but he said it was too easy for me if I were tired of Marcel to ask him to give up Miss Tanning. One night he accompanied me to a dinner party and told me all about the gay life he led with her. He acted in every way as though he meant to stay with me, but after dinner he left me at home and went off to Miss Tanning. I think he merely wanted to make a public sortie with me to fool people. During all this time I spent nights with Marcel, who was sweet to me and behaved more like a nurse than a lover. I was nearly off my head and could not sleep without drugs.

Max came every day to paint in his studio. One Sunday afternoon, while Emily was with me in the house, we had tea with Max and then he went upstairs to paint again. I asked Emily to go up and talk to him for me. For some strange reason I was terrified of living alone. I asked her to tell Max that I knew the whole thing was my fault, that I didn't want to break up our marriage, and that I would wait for him to get over his affair. She began by asking him what I thought of a new painting he was doing. He said he didn't know, as I was no longer interested in his work, and that he never saw me; that I was a destructive person who had broken up our life, and that I had been in love with Marcel for twenty years. She then gave him my message and came downstairs, saying he looked impressed by it. Earlier in the winter Max had tried to get me to go to Arizona with him, but I had refused to leave the gallery, and told Emily I would rather risk breaking my marriage than give up Art of this Century.

When Max talked about Miss Tanning he was very contradictory. Sometimes he said he was not in love with her and that it was just a physical attraction. At other times he said he was like a cat who wanted to run away. Once he told me that we had had no luck, because, though he had been in love with me in Marseilles, as soon as he found Leonora again it was all over with me.

At one moment he said I should wait for him to get over his love affair, at another that it was no use because he would always want a new one. He also said I made too many scenes for him to endure our life together.

Jimmy thought I ought to be psychoanalyzed in order to straighten myself out. The only person I wanted to have for a psychoanalyst was Breton, who had been a psychiatrist in the last war. I invited him to lunch and told him all my troubles. When he heard about Marcel he said Max would never come back to me because of his pride. Breton thought I had really gone too far and had done things to Max that he himself would never endure and he wanted to know why I did not live with Marcel instead of fussing about Max. I told him Marcel had Mary Reynolds and that we could never have a serious affair. Breton said he would do anything in the world for me, but that he couldn't analyze me as he was not qualified, and that under those circumstances it would be dangerous. He told me to go away to the country and rest my nerves.

In February, 1943, Jean Hélion, who had escaped from a German prison camp and written an excellent book about his adventures, *They Shall Not Have Me,* consented to hold a retrospective show in my gallery and to come up from Virginia where he was living to give a lecture relating to some of his experiences. The show was beautiful. I bought a handsome 1934 painting and sold some others. James Johnson Sweeney wrote the preface for the catalogue and Hélion gave a very moving lecture. Over a hundred people crowded into the gallery and we turned over the proceeds to the Free French. After the opening I gave a big party in my house on the river for Hélion. He met Pegeen who was only seventeen and immediately fell in love with her. I realized it at once but Pegeen was unaware of this fact for over a year and a half; later she married him.

It was a great strain to keep the gallery going when my private life was so horrible and causing me so much misery. I was like a little girl who had torn the house down on her head, and then sat surprised among the ruins. I couldn't sleep without drugs and felt worse each day. Every morning Max came to paint in his studio. It gave him intense joy to see how awful I looked and he taunted me for getting up so late. The worst of all was that, as a result of my fighting about VVV magazine, the show I was to have had of all the originals of this review was called off, and I was left at the last moment without anything to replace it. I had to think up a new show and organize it in forty-eight hours. I used a suggestion of Jimmy's and arranged an exhibition consisting of two works each by twenty well-known painters showing what they had done twenty or thirty years before and what they were doing now. The contrast was extraordinary. I was very nerve-wracked and longed for some peace, which I soon found.

One afternoon when I came back from the gallery to get Sindbad's new address, I found Max painting in his studio. We got into an argument about pride and he said that was all women thought about. I asked him what he would do in my place. He replied he would wait until the storm blew over, which was actually what I was tryng to do. But he really took advantage of my patience as he merely used the studio to paint in, and being in the gallery all day, I never laid eyes on him. Anyhow that very afternoon I went to an opening at Julien Levy's, where I saw Miss Tanning with her hair dyed turquoise. Inserted in her blouse, which was specially cut for this purpose, were little photographs of Max. This really was too much for me. I was so disgusted that I decided I had had enough of the whole affair and, as you will see, I finally put an end to it.

In London, in 1939, Herbert Read had conceived the idea of holding a spring salon. I decided to try it in New York. I appointed a jury consisting of Alfred Barr, James Sweeney, James Soby, Piet Mondrian, Marcel Duchamp, Putzel and myself. The first year it worked exceedingly well. Out of the pickings we had a very fine show of about forty paintings. The stars who emerged were Jackson Pollock, Robert Motherwell and William Baziotes. They had all three already exhibited their work the previous month in a show of collage and *papier collé* I had organized. We all realized that they were the three best artists we had found. Soon thereafter, David Hare came to me. He had formerly been a commercial photographer but now he was entirely absorbed by his beautiful plaster sculptures. He had been very much influenced by the Surrealists and seemed to be the best sculptor since Giacometti, Calder and Moore. I promised to give him a show.

Funny things were always occurring in the gallery. Once when Putzel was there a man came and complained that one of the Cubist paintings did not resemble a man. Putzel was indignant and told him that if he wanted to see a man he should go and look at one.

Kiesler had installed a wonderful box into which you could look by raising a handle that operated the eye of a camera. Inside the box was placed a magnificent Klee painted on plaster. A woman peering in said, "I do love a peepshow, even if it's on batik."

One day a girl came from a college and said, "Will you please sign a paper for me so that I can prove to my Professor Mason that I have been here? He said I was either to get the signature of Miss Guggenheim or the Duchess." I presume she was referring to the Baroness Rebay, with whom I certainly did not like to be confused. People were forever asking me what connection I had with the Museum of Non-Objective Art. I always replied, "Not the slightest, though Mr. Guggenheim is my uncle."

On another occasion we had a visit from Mrs. Roosevelt. Unfortunately this honor was not due to her desire to see modern art. She was brought by a friend and Justine Wise Polier to view a photographic exhibition of the Negro in American Life, arranged by John Becker. Mrs. Roosevelt was extremely cordial and wrote enthusiastically about the exhibit in her column, but unfortunately in print the gallery was called "Art of This Country." Before she left I did my best to make her go into the Surrealist gallery, but she retired through the door sideways, like a crab, pleading her ignorance of modern art. My English friend, Jack Barker, had come up in the elevator with the ladies. Following them into the gallery, he mimicked the gracious high falsettos with which they greeted me. Mrs. Roosevelt, evidently amused by his behavior, turned to him smiling and bowed. The embarrassed Barker, unable to recall how well he knew this lady, whose face was so familiar, was uncertain whether to fling himself into her arms, clasp her warmly by the hand or bow back in a reserved manner. In such a dilemma he decided to ignore the whole thing and failed to return the gracious salutation.

One evening I went to Mondrian's studio to see his new paintings and hear his boogie-woogie records on the phonograph. He kept moving strips of paper with which he was planning a new canvas and asked me just how I thought it would look best. He kissed me and I was surprised to discover how young he still was at seventy-two. The last party he went to was in my gallery. He loved parties and never missed an opening. One day my cousin, Colonel Guggenheim, came to Art of This Century and when I asked him which painting he disliked least of those in my collection he said, if offered, he would accept a Mondrian. Needless to say, I did not give him one.

# Chapter 15

# Peace

I often wonder (and never found out) why this man was destined to cause such a commotion in my life, why he occupied my entire thoughts for a year, and why I bore him no grudge after all we had been through. To begin with he entered my consciousness as a myth—the sort of myth that only a very rich, irresponsible, vague and spoiled person can be; the sort of person who is so attractive and so much sought after that he never bothers to do anything he is supposed to do; who loses addresses, and never goes anywhere on time, or arrives on the wrong day, or sends telegrams full of lies and apologies. Finally I met him and he appeared to be just the opposite of what I had expected. He visited my house to buy some of Max's paintings. He had given Max an affidavit to come to America, when Mrs. Barr had asked him, so we were very curious to meet him and Max wanted to thank him. He was so handsome, so charming, so modest, so shy, that I was overcome with surprise.

The next time I saw him I sat next to him at Mozart's opera, *Don Giovanni,* and a peculiar current seemed to pass between us. He often referred to it afterward. He took me home in a taxi. Later I told Putzel that if I weren't afraid he would give me a terrible runaround I would fall in love with Kenneth. I was quite right to beware of him. Not that he meant to be evasive, he just couldn't help it. And when the time arrived and I did fall in love with him, my prophecy proved true, but in quite an unexpected way.

He came into my life when I most needed him and when he most needed me. I know now that it was inevitable. He came to me when I was very unhappy, and that was why he offered me his friendship and why I seized it, with no thought of the consequences. He immediately became my friend, and because he was over six feet tall he assumed a domination over me. The first thing he made me do was break with Max. It was so obvious that it had to be done; I don't know why I waited for Kenneth to tell me. I couldn't go on in my ridiculous situation any longer. He merely said, "The situation is absurd. It's neither one thing nor the other." I made it the other. He didn't do this from any self-interest. He just gave me the advice any sensible friend would have given me. Then he suggested I go to a lawyer and have a legal separation drawn up. Because he was used to thinking about property in a practical way, he convinced me this was necessary, and I accepted his advice.

But I am running ahead of my story. It all started this way. Everything he did was extremely practical and kind and, because he knew I was unhappy, he invited me to his house and gave a little cocktail party for me. I had been there before to large impersonal parties, but this one was quite different. At the last minute I decided to bring Max with me, and I am sure my host must have been very surprised to see us arrive together; but he did not show it, and he showed no surprise when Max left the party to join Miss Tanning. However, that was exactly what we all wanted him to do. When he left we felt much freer.

I don't know why, but Kenneth McPherson immediately gave me a sense of peace, and when I sat with his arm around me I was perfectly happy, happier than I had been for years. It is most unfortunate that I could not have been satisfied with this. If only I had been able to accept the peace and ecstasy I felt when I lay in his arms listening to music, everything would have been different. But then I am not the kind of person to accept anything as it is. I always think I can change the situation. The incredible thing is that I never believe in failure, and no one can convince me that I cannot move mountains or stop the tide until I have proved to myself that I can't. I therefore immediately set out to achieve what I was destined never to accomplish. Of course I got many other things instead, things that I hadn't dreamed of.

We went to dinner with his sister and Putzel, and then came back to my house on the river. We spent a long time on a couch behaving like undergraduates. I seem to have covered Kenneth with my lipstick, and he said he enjoyed it so much that, when his sister and Putzel returned to the room after discreetly wandering around the house, Kenneth folded his legs, saying, "Oh, dear, this seems to be very necessary." I never found out whether it was or not. Before Kenneth left he said he would take me to dinner very soon. I wanted to go home with him but his sister was staying with him and his flat was very small.

A few days later Jean Connolly was giving a big birthday party for her sister's friend Lila. I couldn't make up my mind whether or not to go. Max refused to come with me, saying, *"Je ne connais pas cette dame."* Gypsy Rose Lee telephoned to ask if she could bring a friend to our house to meet Max and to see his books and paintings. I couldn't refuse her but I felt very uncomfortable and thought I ought to explain our situation to her, it was so ambiguous. I called her back and said that I had invited Max to meet her in my house, but that we were not living together, and that I didn't know whether or not I would be home. However I hoped she would enjoy herself without me, and excuse me for not being there if I couldn't make it. I lay in bed dithering between the two possibilities for the evening. Suddenly I remembered Kenneth was a friend of Jean's. That decided me. I leaped out of bed, and got dressed and rushed to the party before Gypsy arrived.

I had a very wild and wonderful evening, a sort of independence celebration. At last I felt free of Max and spent the whole time dancing wild dances with Kenneth. I embraced him in the bathroom, where we went to wash away the smell of pickled onions that we had secretly inserted in the birthday cake. It was this night that Kenneth told me to break with Max. The next morning I phoned Max asking him to find himself a studio and not to come to the house any more. He was so outraged that he came and took Kachina without warning me, leaving our two Persian kittens Romeo and Gypsy. Kenneth had the flu at this party and couldn't tear himself away from me, but he should have been in bed. Finally a motherly soul, an old English warhorse, forced him to go home. Before leaving he invited me to dinner the following Thursday.

I was in a state of great excitement all week about my next *rencontre* with Kenneth, wondering whether or not he would forget about it. Thursday afternoon he telephoned to me and said, "Do you remember, you're having dinner with me this evening?" It would have been impossible for me to forget, but I merely replied, "Yes, I do." He came to fetch me at my house very late. I was extremely perturbed about what to wear, as I knew how much stress Kenneth laid on the appearance of anyone he was seen with in public. Of course I had nothing suitable, but I did my best and did not feel too self-conscious. I wore green gloves and a green scarf. "Now let me see, where would you like to go?" Kenneth began, and I chose a restaurant Max used to take me to. This was the only time Kenneth ever took me to a place where I had been with Max. From then on he always chose where we would eat.

Getting to know somebody suddenly is an exciting, strange and alarming factor in life, but it is even more exciting when it is something one has desired for a long time. The full impact of Kenneth's Englishness came upon me. It delighted me, even though at first I felt it was a rather conventional Englishness. He talked so much I realized at once I was merely supposed to listen. I liked that. It was easier, and it couldn't cause trouble. The only thing I remember saying was that I had been to Curzon Street (as he referred to the home of his parents-in-law in London) the day before Sindbad was born and well recollected the extreme solicitude of his mother-in-law. It gave me a pleasant feeling to be thus connected with Kenneth even so remotely. It immediately made a sort of bridge between us and, as I knew, like all the English he was very snobbish, I felt pleased to think I had been to Curzon Street.

After dinner he took me to his flat. We lay on the sofa for hours, wrapped in each other's arms, while his automatic phonograph played Mozart, Bach and Beethoven. Later in bed he told me that he was apt to get claustrophobia as his mother had made him sleep in her bed when he was a child. Therefore I took the precaution of going home as soon as he went to sleep.

Little did I know that a few hours after I had left, all this was to give him a terrible heart attack. I only learned it some days later, when he suddenly announced to me, in the middle of dinner, that he had been terribly ill and that the doctor had told him he must not drink or have a love affair. "It happened a few hours after you left, and I couldn't move, not even to get to the bathroom. But it's horrible to be ill. I don't want to talk about it." I don't know whether he realized the full psychological import of what had happened, but I felt responsible and decided we must not try to make love any more. After dinner he took my arm and walked me to his flat. We lay on the sofa in a gentle embrace for a long time, and then we went to bed and took sleeping draughts, but I lay awake all night terrified lest I disturb him. In the morning he gave me a glass of milk in just the same way he had given me the sleeping potion. He offered it the way a child offers a gift. Then he kissed me goodbye in the sweetest way. On the steps, as I went out, I met Anaminta, his little colored maid. She looked surprised to see me emerging from his flat so early in the morning.

A few days later I gave a party. Kenneth came surrounded by a lot of little young men. They were charming. Kenneth showed them my house and suddenly said it would be nice to share a big house like this with some one. He asked me how I would like to rent half of it to him, or suggested that we take another one and have a trap door between our floors. Every time, even jokingly, that he dropped a word of this kind I would seize upon it and use it to build my future.

From that day on I knew I must live with him, and indeed I never rested until I had achieved my purpose. This was comparatively easy because he was very lonely. That was why he allowed me to become a part of his life. He needed to be admired and to be loved. Partially his mentality was that of a college boy; intrigues were an important pastime to him. He liked to have a lot of people in love with him. Not that this brought him any real satisfaction, because his life was fundamentally unhappy.

Kenneth had a job with the British Intelligence Service but it never seemed to involve any work. In fact he seemed to spend most of his time listening to music. His phonograph played all day. He wasted a lot of time eating and drinking. He drank more than anyone I have ever known, except John Holms. Kenneth belonged to the eighteenth century. His surroundings, his background, his taste, his behavior were all reminiscent of a great *seigneur* of that epoch. He was so subtle and sensitive that he never missed any *finesse* or *bon mot*. Nothing escaped him, and it was a pleasure to converse with him. He would not permit me to use the word fairy. In its place he insisted on Athenian. He claimed fairy was as vulgar as the terms wop or kike. He was civilized, therefore an oasis in the American desert. However, he was much too good for himself. In a sense he never lived up to the best in him. He was dragged down to the level of his friends, who were all inferior. Possibly out of politeness, so as not to make them feel uncomfortable, he aped their inferiority. He needed someone strong to bring out his qualities. He had many friends and among them were many women. He was an ideal friend. He always made you feel that he belonged to you.

As he lived entirely for pleasure he was always anxiously awaiting the opening of the opera, concert or ballet season. He spent fortunes in the best restaurants, for he loved good food and wine; they were an essential part of his life. He wore the most elegant clothes. His suits were usually blue to match his eyes, and he had dozens of them. They were always immaculate. He was well groomed and very much made up with Max Factor's cosmetics, and his hair was bleached too blond. In his bathroom, which was more like a star's dressing room than anything else, were every kind of makeup and the most expensive perfumes from Paris. He showed me how to fix my hair. He knew how to do it much better than I did.

Because of his health Kenneth went away to the country and I was miserable and lonely. Laurence came to live in my house because he had a broken leg and could not climb the stairs to his flat. I gave a party every night for him, so that he would not have to rush around with his bad leg.

One day when I thought Kenneth was still in the country Putzel brought him to the gallery. I was just going out to lunch, although it was four o'clock, so Kenneth took me to a bar and fed me. He was very sweet, but his evasive and escapist manner became more and more noticeable. He made me feel as if he never wanted to be pinned down to anything, or counted on in any way. I think that the only reason I went on with this affair was the fact that John Holms's spirit encouraged me to, by promising me great peace from Kenneth. John himself never promised me more. The rest was left ambiguous.

Soon after this Kenneth had a thirty-ninth birthday. Jimmy Stern, not knowing I was in love with Kenneth, took me to a birthday party that was given for him by a friend. Jimmy thought he was introducing me to a new world. It was funny. Kenneth was extremely artificial and polite, the way I always hated him most.

A few days before, I had sent him a beautiful Cornell object, chosen by Putzel, as a birthday gift. My secretary, John, delivered it and came back thrilled by the glimpse of Kenneth's real life, wafted through the door to him on an aroma of whiskey. I was jealous and felt shut out of Kenneth's intimate life.

When John went into the Army, Putzel insisted on taking his job. I had resisted this catastrophe for two winters, but now I weakened, in view of the fact that this move would bring me nearer to Kenneth. They were such good friends.

I was still having a vague affair with Marcel. This never meant very much to either of us; we were almost like brother and sister, having known each other so long. I used to phone him if the spirit so moved me, or he would come to the gallery and make a rendezvous with me and take me to lunch. He was at the same time my father-confessor, and he knew all about my affair with Kenneth. It was often difficult to tear myself away from Kenneth to join Marcel, and once I phoned from a bar excusing myself on the pretext of being drunk, which I certainly was. Marcel always pretended not to care about anything. He didn't believe in emotion and certainly not in love, but he felt more than he admitted. Being with Kenneth always meant one was drinking much too much. I think Marcel understood how I felt about Kenneth and soon after broke up our affair saying his wife would hear about it because I was so indiscreet. I agreed as it was all getting to be dangerous and I was relieved when it ended, so as to be able to concentrate on Kenneth. When I didn't go to see Marcel, Kenneth asked me if I wouldn't regret it, meaning he wouldn't be able to give me what I had missed by remaining with him. But of course I didn't mind.

For the birth of the second number of VVV magazine Kiesler gave a big party. Of course I was not invited, as I would not let him come to my house since our trouble about the gallery bills. However, I was determined to go at any price, and when I could not get an invitation upon Laurence's suggestion, I dressed up as a boy and wore some of Sindbad's clothes which were left in my house. I found a beautiful blue suit and a cap, into which I stuffed my hair. I made myself up with burnt cork giving myself sideburns and a little goatee. Then I phoned Kenneth to tell him what I had done and to ask him if he would escort me. He was amused at the idea until he saw the dirty-looking little Greek boy I turned out to be. Kenneth added to my makeup, but he was ashamed to be seen with me and left me at the door and went into the party alone. He said he did not know Kiesler and therefore felt shy about bringing me. As for me, I made a great hit and no one recognized me except Max, who fled with Miss Tanning from the party the minute I arrived, as though I were the devil in person. Georges Duthuit was there and asked Jean, *"Qui est ce garçon? Il a l'air très intéressant."* Jean said, *"C'est un Grec."* *"Ah oui, je comprends,"* Duthuit replied. When Kiesler discovered who I was, he was so delighted that we made up then and there and were friendly thereafter. I thought that if ever I built a house in America Kiesler must design it.

Soon after the party our period of house hunting began. We were both looking for a place to move to in October. My house had been sold over my head and Kenneth's flat was much too small for him. It was easy for me to get lists of apartments from my old friend the agent, Warren Mark, and then share them with Kenneth. After we had visited all the places on the lists we retired to bars and spent the rest of the afternoon drinking. The gallery was abandoned to Putzel who, whenever he saw me going off to lunch with Kenneth, remarked, "I suppose you will be back by five."

I was absolutely determined to share a place with Kenneth. He wanted to live in an accessible neighborhood, so I soon realized I would have to give up the river, which was what I really preferred. Every day we were given a new list. We looked at many flats, and they were all hopeless except one duplex apartment. This was so perfect in every respect (except that it had only one kitchen) that we decided to take it. Everyone was horrified at the prospect, and all our friends warned us of the terrible dangers we would incur in the common kitchen. But, since Kenneth never ate at home except on rare occasions, we thought our friends were silly. Putzel nearly went off his head with jealousy. We had to tear down three walls to make an extra room out of four servants' rooms that were useless. When Putzel heard the conversations on the telephone about this he got all mixed up and thought we were building a wall to separate our different abodes. He did not realize what we were doing, and went quite mad when he learned that we were taking down walls instead of putting them up. He was always pushing me into Kenneth's arms and then getting furious if we became too intimate.

Our new apartment was beautiful. It consisted of two floors in two brownstone houses, so that we had twelve windows in front and twelve windows in the back overlooking terraces and gardens. The top floor, which Kenneth was to have, had a big bedroom, a sitting room, and an enormous sort of ball-room. There was a kitchen and a pantry on this floor. Below this, to which you descended by a magnificent Regency staircase, I was to live in three rooms, and the extra room I was to build out of the servants' rooms. It was inconvenient to walk upstairs to the kitchen, but on the other hand I had four bathrooms and Kenneth had only one. I made him sign the lease because he was so unreliable. I felt safer that way.

After the lease was signed we spent hours in bars thinking about the décor of our new home. There was a large entrance hall from which an elevator took you upstairs. There was no staircase up to the apartment, only the Regency one between our two floors, so we were more or less at the mercy of the elevator. The emergency staircase was not supposed to be used, except in case of fire when you had to break a door which automatically set off a fire alarm. We were preoccupied for weeks trying to think of fantastic ways of decorating the entrance hall. I was horrified by Kenneth's ideas, which were so frivolous and prewar that I really would have found it difficult to agree with them. In spite of the fact that he was politically left wing, he didn't seem to realize that a certain highly luxurious pleasure-seeking life was over and no longer fits in with our times. Fortunately he wasn't serious about anything he suggested for the hall. So instead, and with his permission, I got Jackson Pollock to paint a mural twenty-three feet wide and six feet high. Marcel Duchamp said he should put it on a canvas, otherwise it would have to be abandoned when I left the apartment. This was a splendid idea, and—for the University of Iowa—a most fortunate one, as I gave it to them when I left America. It now hangs there in the students' dining hall.

Pollock obtained a big canvas and tore down a wall in his

apartment in order to make room to hang it up. He sat in front of it, completely uninspired for days, getting more and more depressed. He then sent his wife Lee Krasner away to the country, hoping to feel more free, and that when alone he might get a fresh idea. Lee came back and found him still sitting brooding, no progress made and nothing even attempted. Then suddenly one day, after weeks of hesitation, he began wildly splashing on paint and finished the whole thing in three hours.

The mural was more abstract than Pollock's previous work. It consisted of a continuous band of abstract figures in a rhythmic dance painted in blue and white and yellow, and over this black paint was splashed in drip fashion. Max Ernst had once invented, or set up, a very primitive machine to cover his canvases with drip paint. It had shocked me terribly at the time, but now I accepted this manner of painting unhesitatingly.

We had great trouble in installing this enormous mural, which was bigger than the wall it was destined for. Pollock tried to do it himself, but not succeeding, he became quite hysterical and went up to my flat and began drinking from all the bottles I had purposely hidden, knowing his great weakness. He not only telephoned me at the gallery every few minutes to come home at once and help place the painting, but he got so drunk that he undressed and walked quite naked into a party that Jean Connolly, who was living with me, was giving in the sitting room. Finally, Marcel Duchamp and a workman came to the rescue and placed the mural. It looked very fine, but I am sure it needed much bigger space, which it has today in Iowa.

I liked the mural but Kenneth couldn't bear it. He never allowed me to light it, saying the light I had installed especially for it blew out all the fuses, so it could only be seen in the daytime or when I went down and put the lights on surreptitiously. Everybody wanted to see the mural. One rainy night James Soby stopped in on his way home from the Museum. He arrived absolutely drenched as he was not able to get a cab. I borrowed a shirt from Kenneth, fearing Soby would get a bad cold if he remained in his wet garments. However, all he accepted was a stiff highball, which he claimed saved him. Of course he loved the mural.

One day at lunch Kenneth told Putzel and me he would take a

house on Long Island and invite us. The next day he forgot all
about it, but I didn't. I immediately seized upon the plan of
renting a house with him in the country for the summer. I
tempted him with a beautiful camp in the Adirondacks, but this
turned out to be impractical, though we both wanted very much to
go there. Then I took a friend's camp in Maine, but we decided
this was too far away and gave it up. In the end we decided to go to
Connecticut to live next to Laurence on one side and Jean
Connolly on the other. (This place was on a lake where Jews were
not supposed to bathe.) I wanted Kenneth to go to see the landlord
and take the house in his name, but he rebelled and said he
couldn't talk to such a man, and finally I had to send my friend,
Paul Bowles, to take the house for me.

Before going to Connecticut I wired Sindbad to get a three-day
pass, and I flew down to Florida to see him on the Fourth of July.
He was stationed at Drew Field near Tampa. The heat was
terrific but we had a wonderful time together anyway and spent
most of it in Spanish restaurants and on beaches. I hadn't seen
Sindbad since the winter, when he was first inducted into the
Army, and it was wonderful to be with him again. We loved each
other very much and were happy to be together. After his pass was
over, I remained a few days longer, as he managed to get off in the
evening, but he was so exhausted from the heat and his long day
that it was quite a strain on him.

In the daytime I had nothing to do and a lot of time on my
hands. Kenneth had asked me to go and see an old friend of his in
the hospital at Drew Field, who had broken his hip and was
waiting for a discharge from the Army. I had met him once at a
party at Kenneth's but was afraid that he would not recognize me,
so I sent him a message that I was coming. I got lost at Drew Field
and entered the hospital by the back entrance, after wading
through hot swamps. Private Larkins, the nurse told me, was in
the tenth bed. I found him easily, but he looked very strange.
Because of his accident he was connected to contraptions, much
like Kiesler's strings in my gallery, and was half suspended from
the ceiling. He was asleep when I arrived and, not wishing to
disturb him, I sat down and waited for him to wake up. After a
long time I poked him gently with my finger. The heat was
horrible and the ward was full of the most pathetic cases of

soldiers in plaster casts with broken necks and other things. One man was not allowed to move his head and he had his eyes focused on a ball that hung from the ceiling.

Larkins seemed pleased to see me, but I felt I was bringing him out of another world and I was not certain that this was a good idea. He gave me a strange feeling that he had lain there for months with the patience of Buddha and didn't mind. I told him, in the most garrulous way, all about the duplex and our summer plans, never dreaming how he was to be the instrument of evil and destruction in my life, and that I was merely playing into his hands. Unfortunately, he too was secretly in love with Kenneth. He pretended he thought all our plans were wonderful, and he accepted my invitation to spend the summer with us if he got out of the Army in time. I went to see him twice and brought him books. Later I wrote to him from Connecticut, never dreaming what harm he was about to do me.

After I got the lease of the house in Connecticut all fixed up, Kenneth decided he wouldn't come up for the first ten days, and since we had taken it for a month, that meant he would only be there for three weeks. But there was no use in fussing. I was glad he was coming even for a short time. He helped me by going with me to buy food and lending me linen, mine being in storage; and he gave me some oil and other things I needed, and packed me in the car. I took with me an old friend, a Russian, who wanted to get out of New York for a few days, so when Kenneth arrived ten days later the whole house was in order. Maybe that was what he anticipated.

By this time I was known in the neighborhood as Mrs. Bowles, since that was the name the house was taken in. The house was horrid, but the non-Jewish lake was nice and just in front of our door. I loved sharing my life with Kenneth, and especially the feeling of sharing the responsibilities and the expenses, which made it all so domestic. He did most of the cooking, because he was so much better at it than I was. Besides being an excellent cook he was a very particular housekeeper, and fussed a lot about keeping the refrigerator clean. I washed the dishes and occasionally cooked a meal. We went shopping in my car, listened to the radio, also in the car, and did a lot of swimming and sun bathing, entertaining our neighbors and looking after my cats. I really felt as though I were married to Kenneth and was perfectly happy and peaceful for a change. Putzel came up to visit us several times as did Paul Bowles and his wife, the real Mrs. Bowles. I think Kenneth was very happy, and got restless only once and insisted on going to New York. Strangely enough, he wanted me to come along. Paul was returning to town that night, so we all went together. At this time Kenneth was quite jealous of my friendship with Paul.

When we arrived in New York, as Kenneth had a date, I asked Paul if he would put me up overnight in the big apartment he had borrowed for the summer from Virgil Thomson. We had a lovely evening. I lay on the floor on an air-mattress, wearing his African robes, while he played his compositions for me. We even made love. He is a very good modern composer. He had dozens of bottles filled with exotic perfumes which he had mixed himself, and he gave me some amber which he put on my wrists. The next day Mary, Marcel, Kenneth, Putzel, Paul and I had lunch together. Paul came in a white suit looking like a doll. He was very dainty and immaculate.

After lunch Kenneth and I went off to his flat and played the phonograph. He sat with his arm around me and, as usual under such circumstances, I was in heaven. Then we missed the train for Connecticut and spent hours drinking and eating in the bar of the Grand Central Station. We finally got home.

I lived with Kenneth during these three weeks as a wife in every respect but one. I never slept with him. One night he said I should share his bed because I was so frightened. We had come across a corpse or a crouching figure of some kind in Jean's garden. It was after a party and we were walking home. By the time we went back to fetch a light the corpse had disappeared, but not its terrifying memory.

During this period we got on so well we made all sorts of wonderful plans for the future. We decided to go to Cuba in February and leave the gallery to Putzel. Kenneth also promised to take me to Greece after the war, as I had never been there and he loved it so much.

# Chapter 16

# Life in the Duplex

On the first of September, as previously arranged, Kenneth insisted on going back to New York, although we could have remained over Labor Day. He wanted me to drive him back. It was more convenient for him, so of course I did. I then moved into the duplex alone, because Kenneth had to wait for some furniture he had in another house, which he had sublet. I think in the beginning I must have been very lonely in this enormous place, for I invited the strangest people.

Soon Jean Connolly moved into my flat for a few weeks, and stayed all winter. She was in love with Laurence and would have made him a wonderful wife, and it certainly would have been more sensible if she had lived with him rather than with me. She had been in England for years, where she had been married to Cyril Connolly, a leading English literary light. She was twenty years younger than Laurence, a handsome brunette and extremely intelligent, with a very sweet character. She was a great friend of Kenneth's but soon, without meaning to, she caused a great deal of trouble in our *ménage*.

While Kenneth was getting settled he spent all his free time in my flat. He liked to be able to escape from the confusion that existed upstairs. His ballroom floor was littered with every conceivable object, and looked more like a junk shop than anything else. It took days to put it in order. He had a lot of elaborate furniture, and spent a fortune redecorating his new apartment. I felt a strong contrast between his way of living and mine. In the beginning he loved the coziness of my home, but of course his own surroundings were what he wanted. In fact our tastes were so different that we never approved of each other's flats.

Once he got settled he instituted the closed door *régime*. He had his life with his friends. I was always made to feel most unwelcome when they were about.

Our domestic arrangements were very simple. We each had our own refrigerator. Kenneth's was in the pantry, which he considered his domain, while he gave me the kitchen where there was a larger refrigerator. I had to walk through his pantry to get to my kitchen, and he had to cook in my kitchen. I always used the back stairs to go up there, and made a lot of noise about getting ice, hoping to draw Kenneth out into the pantry. The door to his flat was sometimes mysteriously closed, or I would be invited to have a drink. He nearly always came into the pantry when he heard me there.

As he was very changeable, one never knew what to expect. Jean was very indiscreet and helped herself to everything Kenneth left about. One night she even took a bottle of Scotch. It was the only one in the house and a terrible scene followed. When Kenneth came home he came rushing downstairs to find it and bawled her out. In the mornings he would ask her to have a drink with him. He called it his first, but it was more likely his third by that time, as it was round midday. Very soon she formed the habit of going upstairs when she heard the ice rattling; she thought it was an invitation. I was in the gallery at that hour and did not partake of their little daily party. Soon Kenneth got tired of Jean's coming up uninvited every day and complained to me about it. I warned her and she stopped going. Then he missed her. Whatever he had always displeased him, and he invariably preferred what he didn't have. If a lot of people were living in my apartment he hated it, but if he were alone in the whole building he felt lonely. When Jean stopped coming up for drinks he was annoyed. He had to have a grievance of some kind in life to be happy.

At this time I became sort of a slave to Kenneth's dog, a Boxer called Imperator. The animal, neglected by his master, became greatly attached to me, and Jean named him Mr. Guggenheim. He slept on a rug next to my bed and spent all his spare time with my Persian cats, Gypsy and Romeo, whom he adored. Kenneth was very jealous of Imperator's love for me and my cats. This tremendous dog was perpetually rushing downstairs, which I must say was perfectly natural, considering how lonely and abandoned he felt upstairs, for Kenneth went out so much. I used to take Imperator to the gallery with me every day, and as he could not go in the bus I became his slave, walking him everywhere, and bringing him home for his dinner every night at six. In a way he replaced my darling Kachina. Kenneth was delighted to have found a nursemaid for Imperator, and I was delighted to be seen in public with Kenneth's dog. Kenneth certainly liked that aspect of the situation, too. Every night when he came home he called Imperator to take him out for his last walk. I always took this opportunity to ask Kenneth down for a drink. So we got in the habit of sitting up till four in the morning.

Pegeen was still in Mexico in October, where she had gone to spend her summer holiday. It was her second visit there, as she had gone the summer before with two girl friends after we were sent back from the Cape—but this time she was alone. Suddenly I got a letter of warning sent by Leonora to Mrs. Bernard Reis, telling me that Pegeen was in the most dangerous company and that I should come at once or send some one to look after her. I tried to get a reservation on an airplane but couldn't manage one for a week. In the meantime Laurence and I tried to phone Pegeen. We put in calls which were constantly delayed, and when they did get through Pegeen wouldn't come to the phone. I finally got Leonora on the phone in Mexico City and asked her if she could go to Pegeen's rescue. She said she couldn't, as it would involve too much responsibility, authority, and money to get Pegeen out of the bad hands she had fallen into. It all sounded terrifying and unreal, and we were in a state of complete hysteria. Even Kenneth tried to find out from his lawyer if he could get a visa and go with me to Mexico. (Laurence having been born abroad had to wait six weeks for one.) Suddenly we got a wire and several letters from Pegeen, saying she was fine and would be back as soon as she could get a reservation, and then a letter from

Leonora apologizing for all the trouble she had made. It was just one of her mad ideas.

I canceled my airplane reservation and was glad not to have left, as Sindbad suddenly appeared on furlough. He was surprised by my strange connection with Kenneth. Though he had to admit that he was exceedingly handsome, he could not understand what pleasure I got from this peculiar situation. Being open and free with my children, I tried to explain, and managed somehow to convey what I felt, but Sindbad thought it was very silly and inappropriate. We had a nice time while Sindbad was with us, but it was all too short. I was completely absorbed by his presence and one day when the airlines phoned me and said, "You have a reservation for Mexico City tonight" I felt as though I had fallen out of the sky, but told them it had been canceled for days. When Sindbad left he flew back to Florida. We saw him off at seven in the morning and he left by the same airline Pegeen had taken to Mexico. When my children disappeared through that cavernous door before taking a bus to La Guardia Airport I always felt as though they were being swallowed up by some dreadful monster, and that I would never see them again.

I opened the gallery in October 1943 with a wonderful show of Chirico's early works. There were about sixteen in all, borrowed from museums and private collections. Kenneth and I fell in love with *The Melancholy and Mystery of a Street* owned by Captain Resor, son of Mrs. Stanley Resor. We wanted to buy it, but he wouldn't part with it at any price. It is a most extraordinary painting. In it a little girl is rolling a hoop down a dark, deserted, north Italian street. The empty arcades and an abandoned circus wagon add to the peculiar poetic gloom of the scene.

Next came Jackson Pollock's show. The paintings were handsome and exciting and justified all my hopes. James Johnson Sweeney wrote a preface which gave the public confidence. Sweeney did so much to help me make Pollock known that I felt as though Pollock were our spiritual offspring. In a way Sweeney replaced Mr. Read in my life. He was forever giving me advice and helping me. I hate men who criticize me without dominating me. Sweeney dominated me without criticizing me. Therefore we were in perfect accord. Kenneth came and helped us hang the show and bought the best drawing. He had an incredible eye, and always knew just what he wanted. We sold quite a few Pollocks during the year and even sold one to the Museum of Modern Art. After deliberating for six months, which was their habit, they bought it. But what is certainly an unheard-of thing on their part, they bought this one without bargaining, due to Barr and Sweeney's efforts. After the opening I gave Pollock a party and we all ended up in Kenneth's apartment. He pretended to be very much annoyed, but I think he liked it.

About two in the morning I slipped on the floor and broke my ankle. I had no idea it was broken, but I would allow no one to come near me except Djuna and Kenneth, who put me to bed. I couldn't walk the next day, and I thought this was merely a repetition of what had occurred so often to me in my life. Laurence insisted on taking me to his Austrian doctor, who immediately diagnosed a broken ankle. I had an X-ray taken, and then he told me I must have broken it in the same place two months before, when I was alone in the flat, and hopped around all unsuspectingly. Dr. Kraus was a wonderful little man, and he put my foot in a plaster cast with a stirrup, which took all the weight off my ankle and permitted me to hobble around. I was therefore never laid up and was able to go to the gallery every day. I wore a blue knitted sock over my foot in place of a shoe, and everyone thought I was trying to be Surrealist and admired my color scheme. The treatment and exercises which followed upon removal of the cast entirely cured my ankle. During the treatment I could no longer exercise Imperator.

It was impossible to do anything secret in the flat, because of Imperator. I had to leave all the doors ajar for him and the cats. There was a complicated arrangement for them to go to their box through many open doors, and for Imperator to go upstairs to Kenneth when he came home. Kenneth and I were very domestic at this period, fussing about the two Persian cats and Imperator. Our life was not only boringly domestic, but it became distinctly unpleasant. To begin with the cats had their box in a little back room which was consecrated to them. It smelled rather like a jungle, in spite of the fact that the box was cleaned out every day. This awful smell used to permeate my whole flat, and even mount to the kitchen and to Kenneth's rooms. But the worst of all was the fact that Imperator, who never was sufficiently exercised by Kenneth as he was used to having lots of servants look after the dog and could no longer depend on me, became filthy. I think

Imperator was demoralized by the cats' having the privilege of using the little back room instead of having to go out-of-doors; he began to dirty the floor around the box, and from there he went further and further and finally messed up my whole apartment. In the beginning I didn't mind cleaning up after Imperator, especially as it made Kenneth actually vomit if he did it himself. But Imperator got worse and worse, and what irritated me most of all was that he never made a mess upstairs—he was too terrified Kenneth would beat him. I didn't dare beat him, as Kenneth warned me it would be dangerous. I spent all this period rushing around with a little shovel like a man between circus acts. Every time I came home I trembled at the thought of what would greet me on my exit from the elevator.

Finally we gave Gypsy to a friend of Kenneth's, and I promised Romeo to Pollock's brother. I did this partly to please Kenneth and partly because the jungle odor got me down. But giving away Romeo was too much for me. I loved him. So, after deciding to send him to the country, I wired Pollock's brother at a little country post office saying, "Cannot part with Romeo after all. Many regrets."

I then sent Romeo away to the pet shop, hoping that if he were mated he would smell less foul. For weeks he had tried to mate with Gypsy and I had done all I could to assist him, but it never came off. There was a beautiful little Persian female in the pet shop window next door, and when she came in heat the pet shop sent for Romeo, as we prearranged. This however was a great fiasco, Romeo proving to be not at all what his name implied, and he came back in disgrace. Worst of all, his habits were all changed and he now messed up my bedroom three times a night. This finally decided me to give him up.

Then only Imperator remained to torment me, but this was a much more difficult problem to solve. All Kenneth 's friends said that I should not clean up after Imperator, but make him do it. I used to send him little notes informing him how often Imperator misbehaved and finally, long after, Kenneth sent him away to the country.

Kenneth wanted so much to have people think I was his mistress that he nearly convinced me of it on many occasions. When I was in his flat on Sundays (he always cooked lunch for me on that day) and my telephone rang he used to rush down and answer it for me. He wanted people not only to know that I was upstairs with him, but that he had a proprietory right to answer my phone. He often brought his friends down to my flat and acted as though he felt as at home there, as I really longed for him to be. He wanted everyone to think I belonged to him. He was very sweet to people in trouble and was always being sent for by them and going to their rescue. That was the reason he had become so friendly with me in the beginning; though I did not need his financial help, I certainly needed his spiritual aid.

Because of Kenneth's very strong influence over me I suddenly completely changed my style of dress. I tried to stop looking like a slut and bought some expensive clothes, among them a little stonemarten coat that cost a fortune. He loved it and, as he always took good care of things, he made me raise it before I sat down. Once when I said it was a good idea, that I probably would never have another such coat in my life, he replied, "If you hang around long enough you may." He hated red so much that though it was my favorite color I entirely gave up wearing anything that approached it. I bought a little blue suit with buttons, which he adored, because he said I looked like a little boy in it. He loved what he called my *gamin* quality.

At this time Kenneth and I were very happy together. He depended on me and would have been quite lost without me. If he ever felt he was losing me, he turned on all his charm to get me back. Putzel called this putting another log on the fire. I really think that at this time Kenneth half considered me his wife.

Jean slept in my bed, and one night I made her invite Kenneth to sleep with us. The next time we tried this I realized that Jean's presence was no asset, so I asked her to sleep in the room I had had made for Pegeen. I don't think Kenneth liked my having Jean there all the time. I knew I should have sent her away. One night she was in my bed when he walked in unexpectedly to talk to me. I tried to hide her. Even though he must have known that our relationship was perfectly innocent, I felt he objected to her being there.

Our wonderful Regency staircase we never used. Jean and I always went up the back staircase into the kitchen. As most of our life seemed to depend on whether or not we met in the kitchen, Kenneth and I became sort of backstairs people. We often used to sit on the steps like servants. It was very funny, when we had this enormous and beautiful apartment, to find ourselves sitting on the backstairs.

One day I asked Max to come to the flat to take away his last remaining objects. There was practically nothing left; he had removed, one by one, his whole collection of primitive artifacts, leaving the house on the river as bare as a hospital. I also wanted to show him Kenneth's paintings. Besides several of Max's he had bought my *Toilette de l'Air* by Tanguy, a marvelous Klee, an incredible Miró, and a Picasso and a Braque. Putzel was always urging him to buy more.

When I arrived home with Max, to my great surprise I found Marcel Duchamp playing chess with Laurence Vail in my sitting room. I hadn't expected them to be there, so I burst out laughing for more reasons than one. As usual, Marcel was the detached outsider while my past, present and future were about to be assembled. I brought down Kenneth, who looked very self-conscious in the rôle of reigning prince, and made many excuses about his house costume. Max never knew exactly what my connection with Kenneth was. Probably a lot of other people didn't either—I certainly was asked enough indiscreet questions by my friends.

What Kenneth really wanted from me, and what would have made our life successful, would have been a very one-sided arrangement. He really would have liked me to live alone in my apartment and have me entirely at his disposal when it was convenient for him, and not when it wasn't. Before I had time to arrange it this way, it was all over. One weekend when Joan went away I was quite convinced of this, and I should have sent her away, but Pegeen came back from Mexico then and that complicated our life still more.

The weekend we spent alone in the flat was a very happy one. It began at lunch time when Kenneth came to fetch me at the gallery and gave me a wonderful new name, which he inscribed in the guest book. It was a combination of Max's name and his, and by changing only one letter he used both names. After lunch we went to buy a rug for our entrance hall. Then he waited for me in a bar, while I went to a necessary but boring opening of a friend's exhibition and bought a little sculpture which I soon gave to Kenneth. After that we went home. He had fo finish a quarterly article he did for an art paper. We had dinner together and went

to see *For Whom the Bell Tolls*. Afterward we went home and read
some poetry and I asked him to spend the night with me and to my
great surprise he did. The next day we had lunch together. That
night I went up and slept with him in his flat. The next day Jean
came back and everything was different.

One night at midnight, when I was in bed (resting my broken
ankle) and Kenneth was sitting talking to me, we heard the bell
ring. Kenneth was determined not to admit anyone, but finally put
his head out of the window to see who persisted so violently in
ringing. It turned out to be Pegeen, home from Mexico at last.
She wore a raincoat and carried a little bag, having lost everything
else at the frontier. She looked like such a baby, it really was
pathetic. We showed her the duplex, which she had so much
encouraged us to take in the spring, and the room which I had
built for her. She was glad to be home but quite lost in this new
setting. Complications arose at once. She was jealous of Kenneth
and he was jealous of her. That night when I went upstairs to
sleep with him he sent me back saying, "You can't do that the first
night Pegeen comes home," and when I came down, Pegeen said,
"You've been making love with Kenneth." I was caught between
two opposing forces. When I went upstairs to Kenneth's apartment Pegeen used to follow me, which was quite natural as I
provided no home life for her downstairs, being perpetually with
Kenneth in his flat at this time. When she followed me upstairs, I
invited her into Kenneth's flat, and he was annoyed that I should
take such liberties. Poor Pegeen had accepted Kenneth as a sort of
stepfather, and jokingly called him "Father," which he liked very
much. Pegeen wore high heels. They resounded mercilessly on
my uncarpeted floors, and she had a very loud voice which could
be heard all over the duplex. Added to Jean's presence, it was too
much for Kenneth to endure.

To add to the very feminine atmosphere we created, our maid,
who did our laundry, insisted on drying it in the kitchen. I must
say it was a revolting sight to see brassieres, panties, and blouses
all hanging overhead. Now that we were three females living
there, I realized it was too much for Kenneth and had the laundry
removed to one of my bathrooms.

Jean and I tried to make a home life for Pegeen. She was
miserable in New York and wanted to go back to the Mexican
family she had lived with and marry their son. Laurence and I

were against this for many reasons and we thought if she were happier in New York she would change her mind.

Jean used to cook dinner for us. She was very sweet to me when I broke my ankle and behaved like my wife. She was a good cook. Both Pegeen and Kenneth liked eating home.

A very short time after this David Larkins, whom Kenneth had been expecting for weeks, suddenly announced his arrival. The night before he came I went up to Kenneth's apartment and tried to remain all night. He had a perfect fit and turned me out saying, "How can you think of such a thing when David is coming tomorrow?" There certainly was no connection that I could see between these two facts. However it must have been an omen of the future. The next morning when I was on my way to the gallery Kenneth called me upstairs and said, "David is here. Come up and greet him." We were all pleased to see each other or pretended to be. We talked about our various broken bones, and had a drink to celebrate his arrival, and then I went off to the gallery.

David, exhausted by his trip, got a sort of relapse and went to bed for a few days. After that we all saw a lot of each other. Kenneth took us to the opera and, as usual, he and I held hands all evening. I couldn't walk very well because of the stirrup I was still wearing, and Kenneth helped me up and down the steps of the Metropolitan Opera House with great affection and care. After a few days Kenneth gave a party for David.

I had bought yards of rose taffeta with which to cover an old chair. I now decided to turn it into a dress. Kenneth cut it for me, and I got a dressmaker to sew it up. It made me look like some one in a Mozart opera. The party was not much fun. Kenneth didn't know how to mix people and the atmosphere of his flat was too formal. I invited Gypsy Rose Lee and spent most of the evening talking to her. She was extremely handsome and wore a wonderful John Fredericks costume, and all the women were jealous and rather nasty to her. Kenneth seemed to expect me to act as hostess; he assumed a possessive attitude toward me, patting the costume he had invented for me in a most intimate way.

A few days later we had our first quarrel. Kenneth went out to dinner and David came down and told me I was to get the superintendent to take Imperator out for a walk. When Kenneth returned he came to my room, where I was lying in bed and resting my ankle, surrounded by some of his friends. I asked him why he had sent me such a crazy message about the superintendent and Imperator. The superintendent had never taken the dog out in his life. Kenneth got furious and said he had not sent me such a message. Then I got boring and domestic and began nagging him about blown-out fuses and other stupid things. He suddenly turned on me and, in front of his friends, said that I had made him sign the lease in order to avoid all responsibility, that he wished he had never taken the flat, and that he hated his life in it. After he went upstairs, his best friend, Polo, apologized for him, explaining that he was drunk. This was too much for me to bear. I told Polo he need not apologize for Kenneth, that it was my affair and that he must understand I wouldn't be in such a situation if my intimacy and relationship with Kenneth didn't warrant it.

I am sure Kenneth never told his friends about his life with me. When they were around he always denied me. He was terribly hypocritical and it was often difficult for me to know what he meant. He wanted to please everyone, so he had many sides.

The next day I was very unhappy. All my peace had vanished and I felt as though I ought to leave the duplex. I had had no apology from Kenneth when I left in the morning for the gallery. Djuna came to see me and I told her what had happehed and sent her to Kenneth. He liked her very much and was always pleased to have her visit him. When I got home I found a note on my mantelpiece from Kenneth apologizing and telling me how badly he would feel if I were to leave the duplex. I rushed upstairs and fell into Kenneth's arms and we kissed and made up. Afterward Djuna told me that he had been in a bad state of nerves. I attributed it to our row, but I think I was wrong. It was already the beginning of the end.

Kenneth and I had always meant to share a big house-warming party. So far we had each given a small one. But now, suddenly, he decided to give the house-warming party on his own. I was surprised and disappointed. He said it would be compromising to put my name on the invitation because he was married. Anyhow, he wanted to give an elaborate party, not at all the kind I would have chosen, so I let it go at that. I helped him make a list of guests. We thought of all the people of importance in the art world, and of course Kenneth knew lots of other people too. He

had invitations printed. Unfortunately when the evening arrived
he and David had the flu. In the meantime we had sworn never to
fight again but to remain real friends, with emphasis on the
"friends." Kenneth always insisted that I must never expect more
than that from him. If I got more, it was either in my imagination
or because I wrung it out of him. What he most wanted was
affection.

Because Kenneth had the flu, and David was no good socially,
and I had nothing to do with the party, and because it was very
formal, and had millions of different elements and lots of Negro
performers and God knows what else, it was awful. Also the
elevator broke down under the strain and kept going to all the
wrong floors. A lot of people came down to my flat, the Sweeneys,
the Barrs, and the Sobys, and forgot, Kenneth claimed, to say
good-night to him, which upset him. He had a high fever and felt
extremely ill.

The worst of all was that, at the end of the evening, David
suddenly took it into his head to make love to me. He told me he
had fallen in love with me in the hospital at Drew Field when I
came to see him. I was very tight by this time and believed him,
and made a scene, telling Kenneth that I was sick of everything
and was going off with David. I must say Kenneth took it very well
and merely treated me like a spoiled child. David and I didn't get
very far, but we did get to bed that night and the next. After that
he told me he really couldn't feel anything about a woman, that
what he really liked was choirboys. Of course what he wanted was
Kenneth. We were both in love with him. We knew it was that
which drew us together. I am furious when I think of all the men
who have slept with me while thinking of other men who have
slept with me before.

It was bitchy of me to do this to Kenneth, though he had always
talked about it before David came and expected it to happen. I was
in my favorite rôle and making the most of it, a thorn between two
roses. I told David how much I loved Kenneth, and that I would
never leave him and that he gave me a sense of security and peace.
Never dreaming how things would turn out, I told David he would
get the worst of all this in the end. I think all my confidence about
how I felt toward Kenneth made David decide to break up our
friendship. He was jealous and afraid that I was going to marry
Kenneth. He plotted and planned very carefully to get me out of

the flat. All this time Kenneth never dreamed David was in love with him. Fate played into David's hands and, from every point of view, I was doomed. Kenneth was already tired of having so many women around and did not like to have us come up so freely to his flat.

Suddenly Kenneth got sick, and when I took his temperature and saw that it was 104, I sent for my doctor, who told me I had called him in the nick of time. He gave him some sulfa and saved his life. Two days later Kenneth got news from England that his mother had died, while he himself had been so near death. From then on he was completely under David's control. He collapsed and wouldn't see anyone else. When I finally did see him again he was very far away from me and I realized that I had lost him.

We ended with a dreadful explosion. We were in the kitchen, where I had cooked dinner for him and David, when suddenly he told me I was a dangerous woman and accused me of opening one of his letters. David had seen me open a bill from our windowcleaner which was lying on Kenneth's desk, and had reported it to make trouble. I wanted to see that the horrid little man I had engaged to do all our windows hadn't cheated Kenneth, so I had opened the bill to verify the price. The real catastrophe came when I complained about the closed-door attitude. I was playing straight into David's hands, because then Kenneth burst out and said he could not live any other way, and that if I wanted to preserve his friendship, I should leave the duplex. David egged him on and we both got more and more furious. Of course Kenneth was not in his right mind. He had been completely abnormal ever since his mother died and really had no idea what he was doing. I refused to leave the duplex and offered to take it over. David said it was more suitable for Kenneth to remain, as the lease was in his name. I said that was merely chance; anyhow, I had found the flat, had urged Kenneth to take half of it, and I really considered myself responsible for his being there. Then David said that the flat was too big for me, as I was not used to running a large establishment. This made me angry when I thought of my beautiful house on the river. David then suggested that I remain and buy all Kenneth's furniture. The more he interfered the worse things got. Naturally neither of us wanted to leave and we both felt we had a right to remain. No one left, but from then on the whole thing was over. David ruled supreme upstairs and tried to get Putzel to help him in his further efforts to have me ousted, but of course Putzel was disgusted with him. In the end David himself left, as Kenneth finally had enough of him.

Subsequently Kenneth and I became the best of friends, but that is another story. We only arrived at this, I suppose, by going through all the rest. If only we could have started where we ended, even David could not have come between us. But one lives and learns, or maybe one lives too much to learn.

# Chapter 17

## Art of This Century

As it was noncommercial, Art of This Century soon became a center for all avant-garde activities. The young American artists, much inspired by the European abstract and Surrealist artists who had taken refuge in New York, started an entirely *new* school of painting, which Robert Coates, art critic for *The New Yorker*, named Abstract Expressionism.

We had the great joy of discovering and giving first one-man shows not only to Pollock, Motherwell and Baziotes, but also to Hans Hofmann, Clyfford Still, Mark Rothko and David Hare. The group shows included Adolph Gottlieb, Hedda Sterne and Ad Reinhardt.

We also gave one-man shows to Chirico, Arp, Giacometti, Hélion, Hans Richter, Hirshfield, Theo van Doesburg, Pegeen and Laurence Vail and I. Rice Pereira. We also held several spring salons, gave another woman's show, two collage shows, and exhibited the work of various unknown artists.

After the first spring salon it became evident that Pollock was the best painter. Both Matta, the painter who was a friend of mine, and Putzel urged me to help him, as at the time he was working in my uncle's museum as a carpenter. He had once been a pupil of the well-known academic painter Thomas Hart Benton and through his terrific efforts to throw off Benton's influence had, in reaction, become what he was when I met him. From 1938 to 1942 he had worked on the WPA Federal Art Project for artists, which was part of the scheme originated by President Roosevelt for reducing unemployment.

When I first exhibited Pollock he was very much under the influence of the Surrealists and of Picasso. But he very soon overcame this influence, to become, strangely enough, the greatest painter since Picasso. As he required a fixed monthly sum in order to work in peace, I gave him a contract for one year. I promised him a hundred and fifty dollars a month and a settlement at the end of the year, if I sold more than two thousand seven hundred dollars' worth, allowing one-third to the gallery. If I lost I was to get pictures in return.

Pollock immediately became the central point of Art of This Century. From then on, 1943, until I left America in 1947, I dedicated myself to Pollock. He was very fortunate, because his wife Lee Krasner, a painter, did the same, and even gave up painting at one period, as he required her complete devotion. I welcomed a new protégé, as I had lost Max. My relationship with Pollock was purely that of artist and patron, and Lee was the intermediary. Pollock himself was rather difficult; he drank too much and became so unpleasant, one might say devilish, on these occasions. But as Lee pointed out when I complained, "He also has an angelic side," and that was true. He was like a trapped animal who never should have left Wyoming, where he was born.

As I had to find a hundred and fifty dollars a month for the Pollocks, I concentrated all my efforts on selling his pictures and neglected all the other painters in the gallery, many of whom soon left me, as Sam Kootz, the art dealer, gave them contracts, which I could not afford to do.

I felt Pollock had a deep feeling for West American-Indian sculpture, as it came out a lot in his earlier paintings, and in some of those that were to be in his first exhibition. This was held in November 1943. The introduction to the catalogue was written by James Johnson Sweeney, who helped a lot to further Pollock's career. In fact, I always referred to Pollock as our spiritual offspring. Clement Greenberg, the critic, also came to the fore and championed Pollock as the greatest painter of our time. Alfred

Barr bought the *She Wolf*, one of the best paintings in this show, for the Museum of Modern Art. Later, Dr. Morley asked for the show in her San Francisco Museum, and bought the *Guardians of the Secret*.

We did not sell many Pollock paintings, but when he gave us gouaches it was much easier. A lot of these I gave away as wedding presents to my friends. I worked hard to interest people in his work and never tired doing so, even when it involved dragging in and out his enormous canvases. One day Mrs. Harry Winston, the famous Detroit collector, came to the gallery to buy a Masson. I persuaded her to buy a Pollock instead.

In 1945, Bill Davis, the collector, who was also a fan of Pollock's, advised me to raise my contract with him to three hundred dollars a month, and in exchange, to take all Pollock's works. Pollock was very generous in giving me presents. At this time I had acute infectious mononucleosis, and during the annual Pollock show had to stay in bed. This distressed Lee Pollock very much, as she said no one could sell anything in the gallery except me, and Putzel had left to set up his own gallery in New York. Poor man, this proved to be a great tragedy, as it ended in his suicide.

Lee was so dedicated to Pollock that when I was sick in bed, she came every morning to try to persuade me to lend them two thousand dollars to buy a house on Long Island. She thought that if Pollock got out of New York he would stop drinking. Though I did not see how I could produce any extra funds I finally agreed to do so as it was the only way to get rid of Lee. Now it all makes me laugh. I had no idea then what Pollock paintings would be worth. I never sold one for more than a thousand dollars and when I left America in 1947, not one gallery would take over my contract. I offered it to them all, and in the end Betty, of the Betty Parsons Gallery, said she would give Pollock a show, but that was all she could do. Pollock himself paid the expenses of it out of one painting Bill Davis bought. All the rest were sent to me, according to the contract, at Venice, where I had gone to live. Of course, Lee had her pick of one painting a year. When the pictures got to Venice, I gave them away one by one to various museums, and now only have two of this collection left, though I also have nine earlier ones dating from 1943 to 1946. And so now Lee is a millionaire, and I think what a fool I was.

In my struggles for Pollock I also had to contend with such things as Dorothy Miller absolutely refusing to include him in an exhibition of twelve young American artists—artists who were obviously what she considered the best we had—which she did in 1946, as a traveling show for the Museum of Modern Art. I complained to Alfred Barr, but he said it was Dorothy Miller's show and nothing could be done about it. I also had great money difficulties to keep both Pollock and the gallery going, and often found myself in the position of having to sell what I called an old master. Thus, I was once forced to part with a marvelous Delaunay of 1912, called *Disks,* which I had bought from him in Grenoble, when he was a refugee from occupied Paris. This picture later turned up in the Museum of Modern Art. Its loss is one of the seven tragedies of my life as a collector.

The second was my stupidity in not availing myself of the opportunity of buying *La Terre Labourée,* by Miró, in London in 1939 for fifteen hundred dollars. Now, if it were for sale, it would be worth well over fifty thousand.

The third tragedy was selling a 1936 Kandinsky, called *Dominant Curve,* in New York during the war, because I listened to people saying it was a Fascist picture. To my great sorrow I later found it in my uncle's collection in an exhibition in Rome.

The fourth was not buying Picasso's *Pêche de Nuit à Antibes,* because I had no cash on hand, and did not have enough sense to sell some capital, which my friend and financial adviser Bernard Reis told me to do when the picture was offered to me in 1950; and now that, too, is in the Museum of Modern Art.

The fifth was having to sell a Henri Laurens sculpture and a beautiful Klee water color in order to pay Nellie van Doesburg's passage to New York; and the sixth, to have all but two of my last remaining Klees stolen from Art of This Century. But the worst mistake of all was giving away eighteen Pollocks. However, I comfort myself by thinking how terribly lucky I was to have been able to buy all my wonderful collection at a time when prices were still normal, before the whole picture world turned into an investment market.

As the gallery was a center where all the artists were welcome, they treated it as a sort of club. Mondrian was a frequent visitor, and always brought his paintings carefully wrapped up in white paper. I had bought two of his beautiful large charcoal Cubist

drawings from a gallery in New York, and these I much preferred
to his later works, of which I also had one. When I once asked
him to clean one of his own paintings, which always had to be
immaculate, he arrived with a little bag and cleaned not only his
picture, but also an Arp and a Ben Nicholson relief. He admired
Max's and Dali's paintings very much and said, "They are great
artists. Dali stands a little apart from the others, he is great in the
old tradition. I prefer the true Surrealists, especially Max Ernst.
They do not belong to the old tradition, they are sometimes
naturalists in their own way, but free from tradition. I feel nearer
in spirit to the Surrealists, except for the literary part, than to any
other kind of painting."

In the winter of 1946, I asked Alexander Calder to make me a
bedhead, which I thought would be a marvelously refreshing
change from our grandmothers' old brass ones. He said he would,
but never got around to it. One day I met him at a party and said,
"Sandy, why haven't you made my bed?" At this strange question,
Louisa, his wife, a beautiful niece of Henry James, pricked up her
ears and urged Sandy to get to work. Because of the war, the only
available material was silver, which cost more than all the work
Sandy did on it. It was not mobile, except for the fact that it had a
fish and a butterfly that swung in space from the background,
which resembled undersea plants and flowers. I am not only the
only woman in the world who sleeps in a Calder bed, but the only
one who wears his enormous mobile earrings. Every woman in
New York who is fortunate enough to be decorated by a Calder
jewel, has a brooch or a bracelet, or a necklace.

After Morris Hirshfield's death, Sidney Janis, the dealer, asked
me to give him a memorial show. It was very beautiful, and I
acquired what I consider his best painting, *Two Women in Front of
a Mirror*. It portrays the women perfuming themselves, combing
and brushing their hair and putting on lipstick. It is unre-
alistically presented, with the women seen back to front in the
mirror. They also have four bottoms, which, when the painting
was hung in my entrance hall, received many pinpricks from
sensuous admirers who were passing through the hall.

In the summer of 1945 my great friend Emily Coleman came to
see me, and brought with her a fantastic creature called Marius
Bewley. I have never met anyone like him in my life. He looked
like a priest, which he had once intended to be, and spoke with a

strange false English accent. I took to him at once, and immediately asked him to come and be my secretary in the gallery. He accepted just as readily, as he thought the idea very pleasant. Our collaboration was a great success. We became tremendous friends and remained so ever since, though Marius left me after a year to go to take a PH.D. at Columbia University. He was extremely learned and a brilliant writer, and everything he said was brilliant too. He had a marvelous sense of life and of humor. He loved modern pictures, and though he sold very few, he bought a lot from my gallery.

After Marius left me, he sent in his place a very strange young man who couldn't type and who never appeared on time—in fact, some days not at all. I was kept very busy answering the telephone for him, as his friends never stopped phoning him. The only thing he liked to do was to take my Lhasa terriers for walks, as they served as introductions to other fascinating Lhasa terriers who belonged to such distinguished people as Lily Pons, John Carradine, and Philip Barry. The original Lhasa had been given to Max Ernst, but when we were divorced he had taken it away with him. I had wanted very much to retain this darling dog, Kachina, for half the year, and wished to have this put in the divorce contract, but it was too complicated and I had to content myself, years later, with two of her puppies, which Max sold me at birth.

Much as I loved Art of This Century, I loved Europe more than America, and when the war ended I couldn't wait to go back. Also, I was exhausted by all my work in the gallery, where I had become a sort of slave. I had even given up going out to lunch. If I ever left for an hour to go to a dentist, oculist or hairdresser, some very important museum director would be sure to come in and say, "Miss Guggenheim is never here." It was not only necessary for me to sell Pollocks and other pictures from current shows, but I also had to get the paintings circulated in traveling exhibitions. The last year was the worst, when my secretary couldn't even type, and this extra burden was added to my chores. I had become a sort of prisoner and could no longer stand the strain. Levi Straus, the French cultural attaché, gave me a letter to the French consul, saying I had to go abroad to see French and European art, and with this excuse I got to Paris and then to Venice, where Mary McCarthy and her husband, Bowden Broadwater, insisted that I accompany them.

On my way there, I decided Venice would be my future home. I had always loved it more than any place on earth and felt I would be happy alone there. I set about trying to find a palace that would house my collection and provide a garden for my dogs. This was to take several years; in the meantime I had to go back to New York to close the gallery. We ended it with a retrospective show of Theo van Doesburg, which I arranged to have circulated all over the United States. Nellie van Doesburg came to New York from France as my guest, with all the pictures. I had been trying to arrange this during the war, but had not succeeded until it was too late for her to leave France.

I sold all Kiesler's fantastic furniture and inventions. There was terrific bidding for them, and to avoid complications I let them be removed by the cash and carry system. Poor Kiesler never even got one thing as a souvenir, they disappeared so quickly.

Betty Parsons fell heir to my work, spiritually, and as I said, promised Pollock a show. Happy to think that she was there to help the unknown artists, I left my collection in storage and flew to Europe with my two dogs, not to return for twelve years.

# Interlude

In 1945 the Dial Press of New York had asked me write my memoirs for publication. After I finished my manuscript Laurence Vail read it and suggested various changes and Inez Ferren typed it for me. My editor at Dial insisted on making many changes. In fact, she practically rewrote the book, and I had to put most things back the way I had originally written them. Finally the book, which was called *Out of This Century,* was published in March 1946.

Many years later John H. Davis, the author of a book called *The Guggenheims,* claimed that some of my relatives were so scandalized they sent "hordes of messengers and clerks out to the major bookstores with orders to buy up every available copy," so that in the end the only people who got a look at the book were my friends, people who bought it outside of Manhattan, "the gentle ladies who borrow from their local library; and the critics"—by which presumably he meant the book reviewers.

He was right about the reviewers, if not about much else. Many of them took the opportunity to display their own cleverness by attacking me.

*Time* was typical:

Stylistically her book is as flat and witless as a harmonica rendition of the *Liebestod,* but it does furnish a few peeks—between boudoir blackouts—at some of the men who make art a mystery.

The well-known reviewer Harry Hansen was more serious:

Sometimes her remarks are amusing, but gradually the reader feels that this book is a social document: a testimony of reckless Bohemianism, irresponsible conduct on the part of wealthy young Americans let loose in Paris and further evidence why artists shock conventional people—like ourselves. . . . The complete absence of any moral responsibility is the trademark of this sort of sophistication. Conventions, in behavior or painting, do not seem valid for the generation between-the-wars. Conduct is dictated, apparently, by caprice. Is this written for our amusement or does publicizing this life mean a catharsis for the author? The more I read this type of writing, the more I begin to understand the social and artistic usefulness of restraint.

Another approach was taken by the art reviewer Katharine Kuh:

Because Peggy Guggenheim has a distinguished and discriminating collection of contemporary art, her vulgar autobiography, "Out of this Century," is doubly offensive. For several years she has been known in art circles as a generous patron of the most advanced experimental art, especially Surrealism, and also as the founder and director of a somewhat "chi-chi" but none-the-less provocative New York gallery called Art of This Century. . . . I have no quarrel with a writer who is impelled to "tell all," if a well written book is the result, but Miss Guggenheim, unfortunately not a gifted literata, has done the cause of modern art no kindness by mixing it irrevocably with a compulsive recital of her own decadent life.

Miss Kuh concluded:

A supreme masochist, she is as relentlessly honest about herself as she is about her "friends." She leaves us with a picture of a lonely woman, too hard, too hurt, to have retained normal sensitivities.

out of this century

century

peggy guggenheim

peggy guggenheim out of this century dial

But in *View* magazine, Everett McManus wrote more positively:

> The book convinces us the way Flaubert convinces of Madame Bovary, because it is about the feelings of a woman—not necessarily of a particular woman but of a *modern* woman. . . . Miss Guggenheim should be praised for taking positive advantage of everything money could buy for her. One might criticize the author's taste, among other points, but she is never ridiculous. Most of her dignity, I would hazard, lies in her apparent awareness of the established tenet that money can not buy happiness if happiness be based, as we suppose on love. . . . Some of Miss Guggenheim's relentless critics are guilty of esthetic snobbery where her slate is clean. . . . Her book is not the autobiography of an art connoisseur or critic but of a human being. From this viewpoint, Miss Guggenheim reveals her progressive spiritualization. She passed through respective stages of infatuation with a lusty bohemian, a temperamental idealist, an enthusiastic Communist, a more or less carnal and calculating painter, and finally to a platonically minded "Athenian"; that is, in a descending scale so far as the male's carnal reaction to her went. She was always earnestly in love and regularly plunged into the despair of which she was capable. It is significant that her most frequently applied adjective for the moods of her own friends is "sad." It recurs with striking force. . . . But she has not been saddened.

In 1959, at the suggestion of Nicolas Bentley, the English editor and illustrator, I condensed *Out of This Century* into fewer than a hundred pages and added material about my life during the intervening period. As *Confessions of an Art Addict* it was published in 1960 by André Deutsch in London and the Macmillan Company in New York. The following pages (through Chapter 21) are reprinted from the latter half of that book. I seem to have written the first book as an uninhibited woman and the second one as a lady who was trying to establish her place in the history of modern art. That is perhaps why the two books read so differently. And since the Conclusion of this third book was written when I was almost 80 years old, it reads differently from the first two.

# Chapter 18

# Venice and the Biennale

One of the first people I met in Venice in 1946 was an artist called Vedova. I was in the Café Angelo at the Rialto. Not knowing anyone in Venice, I inquired of the *patron* where I might meet some modern artists. He said, "Go to the other Angelo restaurant at San Marco and ask for Vedova." I wrote this name on a matchbox and proceeded to the other Angelo. Here I received a wonderful welcome from Vedova and another Venetian artist, Santomaso, who both became my friends. They were very much interested in modern art, and knew about my uncle's collection, which surprised me. In fact, they even had the catalogue. As they spoke Venetian dialect together, I spent painful hours in their company, not understanding a word they said. But when I was alone with either of them it was better, as I could speak a little Italian.

Vedova, who painted abstractions, was an enormously tall man with a beard. He was a Communist and during the war had been a partisan. He was very young and mad about lovely young girls. Santomaso was less tall and rounder. He also had a roving eye, and a wife and child as well. He was extremely well versed in Venetian history and recounted the most fascinating things of his

great city's past. Of the two, he was the more cultivated. The
Angelo restaurant was filled with their paintings and a great many
other people's. This is a Venetian custom: painters are allowed to
eat free and give their works in return.

It was through Santomaso that I was invited to show my entire
collection at the XXIVth Biennale of Venice. He had suggested to
Rodolfo Pallucchini, the secretary-general of the Biennale, that
the collection should be exhibited, and it was agreed that it should
be shown in the Greek pavilion, which was free because of the
Greeks being at war.

The Biennale, which was started in 1895, is an international
exhibition of contemporary art, which is held every other year in
the Public Gardens at the end of Venice, on the lagoon near the
Lido. A lot of very ugly buildings put up in the time of Mussolini
give it a distinct character. The trees and the gardens are
wonderfully looked after and make a beautiful background for the
various pavilions. In the middle of June, when the Biennale
opens, the lime trees are flowering and the perfume they exhale is
overpowering. I often feel this must compete strongly with the
exhibition, as it is so much pleasanter to sit in the gardens than to
go into the terribly hot and unventilated pavilions.

The foreign countries that exhibit are each responsible for the
shows in their own pavilions, which are run under the auspices of
their various governments. In the main Italian pavilion there are
miles and miles of very boring paintings, though occasionally
something good is shown. There are also innumerable large and
small one-man shows which are supposed to be devoted to
contemporary painters, though sometimes earlier artists, such as
Delacroix, Courbet, Constable, Turner, and even Goya have
slipped in. No one knows why. Most of the Italians who exhibit go
on doing so year after year out of habit. There have also been one-
man shows of Picasso, Braque, Miró, Ernst, Arp, Giacometti,
Marini, Klee, Mondrian, Douanier Rousseau, as well as shows of
the Fauves and the Futurists. Before 1948, only Picasso and Klee
were known in Italy, apart from the Italian Futurists.

The Biennale is opened by the president of Italy, who comes in
full pomp and regalia to inaugurate it, and the Venetian state
boats of the past are brought out for the procession from the
Prefettura, the prefect's palace, to the Public Gardens.

In 1948, after so many years of disuse, the pavilions were in a bad state and there was an awful lot of repairing going on up to the last minute. My pavilion was being done over by Scarpa, who was the most modern architect in Venice. Pallucchini, the secretary-general, was not at all conversant with modern art. He was a great student of the Italian Renaissance, and it must have been very difficult for him, as well as very brave, to do his task. When he gave a lecture in my pavilion he asked me to help him distinguish the various schools; he was even unfamiliar with the painters. Unfortunately I had to go to the dentist, but he claimed that he had managed without me.

Pallucchini was very strict and tyrannical. He reminded me of an Episcopalian minister. He would not allow me into the Gardens until my pavilion was finished. I was very upset, as everyone else in Venice who was interested in modern art seemed to be getting passes. Finally I was invited to come, and was taken all over by Pallucchini's aide-de-camp, a lovely man called Umbro Apollonio. I don't know how, but while talking to him I sensed that this was the first time in his life that he was doing a job that he enjoyed, and my recognition of the fact touched him so much that we immediately became friends. Like Pallucchini, he knew nothing about modern art. In Italy, the Surrealists, Brancusi, Arp, Giacometti, Pevsner and Malevich had never been heard of. If Santomaso was conversant with what was going on outside Italy, it was only because he had been to Paris in 1945. Also, he and Vedova had both seen copies of *Minotaur* and *Cahiers d'Art,* brought clandestinely into Italy.

In 1948 the foreign pavilions were, naturally, *à la page.* But some were still very much behind the Iron Curtain, I was allowed to hang my collection three days before the Biennale opened. Actually, I wanted to go to Ravenna with Dr. Sandberg, the director of the Stedelijk Museum in Amsterdam, who had already finished his work in the Dutch pavilion. But this was out of the question, so I buckled down to work. Fortunately I was given a free hand and a lot of efficient workmen, who did not mind my perpetual changes. We managed to get the show finished in time, and though it was terribly crowded it looked gay and attractive, all on white walls—so different from Kiesler's décor for Art of This Century.

The opening of the Biennale was very formal, but, as usual, I had no hat, stockings or gloves and was in quite a dilemma. I borrowed stocking and a girdle from a friend, and instead of a hat wore enormous marguerite-flowered earrings made out of Venetian glass beads. Count Elio Zorzi, the head of the press office and the ambassador of the Biennale, who had actually extended to me the Biennale invitation, gave me strict instructions that when President Einaudi came to my pavilion I should try to explain to him as much as I could about modern art in the five minutes he would remain with me. I received exactly contrary orders from Pallucchini, who said the president was lame and would be terribly tired after visiting the whole Biennale, my pavilion being his last effort.

When His Excellency arrived he greeted me by saying, "Where is your collection?" I said, "Here," and he corrected himself and asked where it had been before. I tried to obey Count Zorzi rather than Pallucchini, and put in a few words, but luckily the photographers intervened and the entire official party was photographed with Gonella, the minister of education, the president and me under my lovely Calder mobile.

The same morning I had a visit from the American ambassador and the consular staff. The United States pavilion was not open, as the pictures had not arrived in time, and James Dunn, our ambassador, was very pleased that at least I represented the United States. Looking at one of my abstract Picassos, he seemed rather happy to note that it was "almost normal."

The introduction to the Biennale catalogue for my show was written by Professor Argan. It was very confusing, as he was all mixed up about the different trends in modern art. Upon the insistence of Bruno Alfieri, the owner of a bookshop, I had made a little catalogue of my own to sell in my pavilion, although I was included in the Biennale one. I wrote a short introduction for my own catalogue, but it was so badly translated that I became quite hysterical and even wept. I could not speak Italian well enough to cope with the situation and begged Marga Barr, Alfred's wife, who was half Italian, and who was then in Venice, to help me. But the moment I chose was on board a vaporetto and she had to get off before she could finish her task.

The two most unfortunate things that occurred at the Biennale were the theft of a little piece of bronze from a David Hare sculpture representing a baby; it must have been taken as a souvenir. And the other was Pallucchini's decision (as some

priests were coming to visit my pavilion) to take down a very
sexual Matta drawing of centaurs and nymphs. The drawing itself
was so annoyed that it fell on the ground and the glass broke into
smithereens, thus obviating its insulting removal.

A third catastrophe was avoided by Bruno Alfieri, who saved a
dismantled Calder mobile from being thrown away by the
workmen, who thought that it was bits of iron bands which had
come off the packing cases.

My exhibition had enormous publicity and the pavilion was one
of the most popular of the Biennale. I was terribly excited by all
this, but what I enjoyed most was seeing the name of Guggenheim
appearing on the maps in the Public Gardens next to the names of
Great Britain, France, Holland, Austria, Switzerland, Poland,
Palestine, Denmark, Belgium, Egypt, Czechoslovakia, Hungary,
Romania. I felt as though I were a new European country.

My next illustrious visitor was Bernard Berenson. I greeted him
as he came up my steps and told him how much I had studied his
books and how much they had meant to me. His reply was, "Then
why do you go in for this?" I knew beforehand how much he hated
modern art and said, "I couldn't afford old masters, and anyhow I
consider it one's duty to protect the art of one's time." He replied,
"You should have come to me, my dear, I would have found you
bargains." He liked best the works of Max Ernst and Pollock.
Nevertheless, he said Max's were too sexual and that he did not
like sex in art; the Pollocks, to him, were like tapestries. He was
horrified by a little bronze Moore, a reclining figure of a woman,
which he said was distorted.

The next time I saw Berenson was at I Tatti, his own home
near Florence, and I was more polite to him than he had been to
me as I admired his collection. I thought it very sad that so little
was left of all the marvelous paintings that had passed through his
hands. I begged him to visit me in Venice and promised to put
sheets over all my paintings, if that would be an inducement for
him to come. He asked me to whom I was going to leave my
collection when I died, and though he was already eighty-five at
that time, he looked at me with horror when I replied, "To you,
Mr. Berenson."

As a result of all the publicity, I was plagued by everyone who
wanted to sell me something and I couldn't come down into the
lobby of the hotel where I was staying without being accosted by

innumerable people. I asked Vittorio Carrain, a young friend, who was one of the owners of the Angelo restaurant, to protect me. As a result, he became my secretary and worked with me for years. He was intellectual, musical and very knowledgeable, and also served me as a key to the life of Venice, as I never read any newspapers. He loved the atmosphere I lived in and was exceedingly kind and a devoted friend, and a great help when we made exhibitions and catalogues.

I requested Ingeborg Eichmann, a Sudeten art historian, to give a lecture in my pavilion to explain the various trends in art. So many people came to the first lecture, on Cubism and abstract art, that we had to call off the second lecture, on Surrealism, in order to save the pictures from damage. They had all just been marvelously cleaned and refreshed by a Venetian painter called Celeghin, a charming man with enormous mustachios.

I used to go myself to the Biennale every few days and take my dogs with me. They were very well treated by a restaurant at the entrance called the Paradiso, and always given ice cream on their way in. Therefore whenever I asked them if they wished to accompany me to the Biennale, they wagged their tails and jumped with joy. They were the only dogs admitted to the exhibition, and when they were lost in this labyrinth I always found them in the Picasso exhibition; which proves how valuable their education had been at Art of This Century, where they had accompanied me every day.

At the end of the Biennale, the question arose of what to do with the pictures. I had taken it for granted that if the Biennale had brought them to Europe, paying all the expenses, at least they would be allowed to remain in Italy. But this was not the case. They had been brought in on a temporary permit and had to go out again. For several months I hesitated about what to do. I was expected to pay three per cent duty for importing them permanently into Italy. So I decided they would have to be taken out and brought back again at a lower valuation.

In the meantime the museum of Turin asked me to exhibit them there. I was delighted, but at the last minute, the day before the collection was to leave for Turin, the authorities of that city decided against showing anything so modern. A well known critic, Dr. Carlo Ragghianti, then asked me if I would show the

collection in Florence, in the Strozzina, the cellar of the Strozzi
Palace, which he was about to turn into a modern art gallery. He
wanted to have my collection to inaugurate it, and made an
excellent catalogue, which has been the basis ever since for my
Italian one.

When I arrived in Florence I was shocked by the lack of space
in the Strozzina and by some dreadful screens that resembled
shower curtains, which had been set up to make more space. Dr.
Ragghianti was very agreeable about removing these horrors, and
accepted my proposal to give three different expositions. The first
one was of Cubist and abstract art, the second Surrealist and the
third dedicated to the young painters. This idea was very
successful and permitted me to make three visits to Florence, all
of which I enjoyed immensely, staying with my friend Roloff
Beny. We had a very social life, and here I met a charming lady
poetess from Dublin, New Hampshire, called Elise Cabbot. She
was amazed by the number of my paintings shown in Florence and
said, "How did Peggy ever have time to paint them all?"

After this, I was invited to exhibit in Milan in the Palazzo
Reale. Here there was no space problem. I have never had so
many rooms at my disposal before or since. This show was such a
great success that the catalogues had to be hired out while new
ones were being printed. Francesco Flora wrote the preface to the
catalogue and the show was given for the benefit of the
Associazione Artisti d'Italia, as a result of which all the debts of
this association were paid off.

When the collection came back from Florence the problem
again arose of what to do with it. I had reached no settlement with
the authorities in Rome, though I had offered the whole collection
to Venice on my death, if the Italian government would waive the
duty they were claiming. But the old fogies in the Ministry of
Foreign Affairs were adamant and would not let me off. The
pictures in the meantime were housed in the Museum of Modern
Art in Venice, the Cà Pesaro, a beautiful seventeenth-century
building designed by Longhena, where Dr. Guido Perrocco, its
curator, kept them for me. I was allowed to borrow a few at a
time, but not too many.

A year after the Biennale exhibition Dr. Giulio Lorenzetti, the
director of the Cà Pesaro, had asked me to make an American

exhibition in two small rooms. Poor man, I am sure he was only doing his duty, as he must have hated modern art a thousand times more even than Pallucchini did.

At this same time, at the request of Michael Combe Martin, who was director of the British Institute, which was in the beautiful Palazzo Sagredo, I made a show of British painters there, so the pictures did manage to be seen.

The Palazzo Venier dei Leoni has the widest space of any palace on the Grand Canal, and at the back one of the largest gardens in Venice, with very old trees. Everyone stops in the street to look at the entrance gate, which Claire Falkenstein welded by hand and into which she inserted pieces of glass from Murano.

The view from
my roof

With Pevsner's
construction

With my Lhasa terriers and Alexander Calder's bedhead, 1956

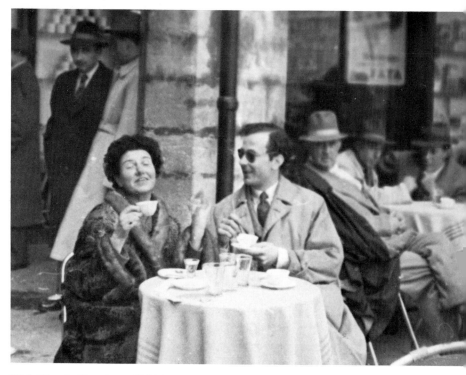

With Vittorio Carrain, c. 1954

In my gondola

The two Sir Herberts
and Raoul Gregorich

With Edmondo Bacci
and Tancredi in my
garden

The celebration of my 80th birthday, August 26, 1978

Myself in the center hall of my palazzo, 1978. On the wall is Picasso's *Girls with a Toy Boat;* on the table is Giacometti's *Piazza* (or *The Square);* Calder's *Mobile* is hung overhead.

Myself in 1978

# Chapter 19

# Palazzo Venier dei Leoni

Finally, in 1949, Flavia Paulon, secretary of Count Zorzi, found me a lovely abode. It was an unfinished palace on the Grand Canal, started in 1748 by the Veniers, a famous Venetian family who had given two doges to Venice and who were alleged to have kept lions in their garden. The front of the palace bore eighteen lions' heads, which may be the reason for the name given to it: Venier dei Leoni. It stands opposite the Prefettura, the palace of the prefect of the Veneto.

The palace was all built in white stone and covered with vines; "All" is saying a lot, as the building never exceeded one floor, and in Venice is called the *"palazzo non compiuto,"* the "unfinished palace." It had the widest space of any palace on the Grand Canal, and also had the advantage of not being regarded as a national monument, which things are sacred in Venice and cannot be altered. It was therefore perfect for the pictures. At the front entrance there was a lovely courtyard with steps going down to the Grand Canal, and at the back one of the largest gardens in Venice, with very old trees. The top of the palace formed a flat roof, perfect for sunbathing. I naturally took advantage of this, but was rather worried about the reaction of the prefect, my *vis-à-*

*vis.* However, he merely said, "When I see Mrs. Guggenheim sunbathing on the roof, I know the spring has come."

Signora Paulon got her husband to do up the place for me. Actually, it was not in very bad shape, though it had changed tenants very often since 1938. Before that, in 1910, Luisa, Marchesa Casati, a poetess, had lived in one of the wings, giving fantastic Diaghilev parties and keeping leopards instead of lions in the garden. In 1938, the Viscountess Castlerosse bought the house and spent a fortune doing over what was then practically a ruin. (I believe the Marchesa Casati barely had a roof over her head.) Lady Castlerosse installed six marble bathrooms and beautiful mosaic floors. Her taste was not the same as mine, and I had to scrape off all the Liberty stucchi from the walls. After the first year Lady Castlerosse lent the palace to Douglas Fairbanks, Jr., and then three armies of occupation, German, British and American, lived in it in turn.

In the autumn of 1949, I made an exhibition of more or less recent sculpture in the garden, and Professor Giuseppe Marchiori, a well-known critic, wrote the introduction to the catalogue. We exhibited an Arp, a Brancusi, a Calder mobile, three Giacomettis, a Lipchitz, a Moore, a Pevsner, a David Hare, from my collection, and a Mirko, a Consagra, a Salvatore and two Vianis, which we borrowed from the artists. There was also a Marino Marini, which I bought from him in Milan. I went to borrow one for the sculpture show, but ended up by buying the only thing available. It was a statue of a horse and rider, the latter with his arms spread way out in ecstasy, and to emphasize this, Marini had added a phallus in full erection. But when he had it cast in bronze for me he had the phallus made separately, so that it could be screwed in and out at leisure. Marini placed the sculpture in my courtyard on the Grand Canal, opposite the Prefettura, and named it *The Angel of the Citadel.* Herbert Read said the statue was a challenge to the prefect. The best view of it was to be seen in profile from my sitting room window. Often, peeking through it, I watched the visitors' reaction to the statue.

When the nuns came to be blessed by the Patriarch, who on special holy days, went by my house in a motorboat, I detached the phallus of the horseman and hid it in a drawer. I also did this on certain days when I had to receive stuffy visitors, but occasionally I forgot, and when confronted with this phallus

Marino Marini, *The Angel of the Citadel*

found myself in great embarrassment. The only thing to do in
such cases was to ignore it. In Venice a legend spread that I had
several phalluses of different sizes, like spare parts, which I used
on different occasions.

The sculpture show was supposed to be held in the garden, but
because Viani had brought two works in plaster they had to be

exhibited in the house. So many people came wandering into all our bedrooms that we had to cordon off the exhibition. I had a house guest, Philip Lasalle, staying with me at the time, who perpetually forgot that there was an exhibition and often found himself in the midst of strangers in his pajamas in the garden.

One of my Giacometti statues that I wanted to place in this show got stopped in the customs at Padua on its way from Milan. We went to fetch it in my open car. It was a beautiful thin figure without a head. We brought her back to Venice along the autostrada at great speed. Everyone who saw her must have thought she was a decapitated corpse. She was in very bad condition, so with the help of Pietro Consagra, a sculptor whom I knew, I got her back to her normal state and had her cast in bronze. But when the original one saw her new bronze sister, she was so scornful of her, and rightly so, as her own beauty far exceeded the other, that she remained intact ever since.

In 1950, I was asked if I would lend all my Pollocks (there were still twenty-three) to an art organization to give a show. They were supposed to get a room from the local authorities, but as they did not succeed, I came to their rescue and got old Dr. Lorenzetti to lend us the Sala Napoleonica in the Correr Museum, opposite San Marco cathedral. All that the organization did was to make a catalogue, for which I wrote an introduction and Bruno Alfieri a preface. When it came to fetching the pictures and hanging them, Vittorio Carrain and I had to do everything. The climax came when a terrible Greenwich Village-looking poster was put up, and when the catalogues gave out, they refused to print any more. I was so enraged that I took over the show, which really was mine, by all rights, and made a new catalogue, omitting Alfieri's article on Pollock. Thousands of people saw this exhibition, as it was in a room through which one had to pass in order to get into the Correr Museum. It was always lit at night, and I remember the extreme joy I had sitting in the Piazza San Marco beholding the Pollocks glowing through the open windows of the museum, and then going out on the balcony of the gallery to see San Marco in front of me, knowing that the Pollocks were behind me. It seemed to place Pollock historically where he belonged as one of the greatest painters of our time, who had every right to be exhibited in this wonderful setting. All the young painters were very much influenced by this show.

A Giacometti statue in my open car

Encouraged by the Pollock exhibition, I got Dr. Lorenzetti to lend me the Sala degli Specchi in the Palazzo Giustinian, the headquarters of the Biennale, for an exhibition I wanted to give Jean Hélion, my son-in-law. Everything went wrong from beginning to end. It was an ill-fated show. First of all, Christian Zervos, who edits *Cahiers d'Art,* took ages to write the introduction to the catalogue. When it arrived, it was much too long and I had to cut it and have it translated, and then Hélion was displeased by my cutting it. The pictures got stuck in the customs, as always happens in Italy, and we nearly had to call the show off. Finally, Vittorio Carrain overcame all these difficulties, only to find new ones creeping up. Two days before the show was to open, the brocade that covered the walls of the Sala degli Specchi was removed by the person who owned it, and we were forced to replace it with some sacking. Then, as though the gods were against us, a terrible storm came and rain dripped from the crimson banner we had placed in the street to announce the show and ruined the dress of a girl passing beneath it. After that, the wind blew down the banner altogether. It really was a triumph that we held the exhibition at all.

Hélion showed three periods of his work, his early naturalistic paintings, his abstract period, and his new period, which began in 1943, portraying men with umbrellas, nudes, men with newspapers, and *natures mortes* with bread. People were very much interested to see these various transitions and how he was getting around to complete realism, which he now does.

As a result of all our troubles in connection with this show, I decided never again to do anything with works from abroad, or ever again to ask the authorities for a gallery. My own troubles with the customs had not been solved, and Dr. Sandberg, of the Stedelijk museum, suggested taking my collection to Amsterdam for an exhibition, and then sending it on to the Brussels Palais des Beaux-Arts and to the Zurich Kunsthaus, thus giving me a proper excuse to reintroduce it into Italy. This was done very successfully. After the three shows, the pictures were brought back from Zurich and finally I was allowed to pay the least possible amount of duty.

I was so happy to have my collection back again, and at last to be able to hang it in my palazzo; but the next problem was one of space. I got three architects in Milan, Belgioioso, Peressutti and Rogers, to draw up plans to make a penthouse on my roof. They were very much under the influence of Le Corbusier, and thought of an arrangement that reminded one of him, namely a two-story gallery elevated from my roof on pillars twenty feet high. The front was to resemble the Doge's Palace, and in their minds they conceived something that they thought would be a link between the past and the present. I found it very ugly and I was certain the Belle Arti of Venice, the authority that controls all rebuilding in the city, would never have allowed it to be built. It would have cost sixty thousand dollars, only a bit less than I paid for the whole *palazzo,* and I could not afford it. In fact, I was only able to buy the *palazzo* because Bernard Reis broke one of my trusts for me. Peressutti was terribly disappointed, and asked me if I could not sell a picture in order to find the money. Had I liked the scheme, and had prices been what they are today. I could easily have parted with one painting to have built this museum.

Finally, in order to create space, I began turning all the downstairs rooms, where the servants lived and the laundry was done, into galleries. Some of these rooms had been used as studios, which I had lent to various artists. Matta helped me transform the enormous laundry into a beautiful gallery, and then one by one the other rooms followed suit, till finally the servants got pushed into smaller quarters and the laundry had to be done in a basin at the entrance to the waterfront.

Since 1952, I had been sponsoring a young Italian painter from Feltre, whom Bill Congdon had asked me to help. His name was Tancredi Parmeggiani, but he used only his Christian name, dropping the one that so much resembled the cheese. I promised him seventy-five dollars a month in exchange for two gouaches. His first ones were very geometrical and resembled Theo van Doesburg's (which greatly pleased Nellie, his widow), but gradually he evoked a Pollock style, and then finally his own. He was what is called in Italy a *spazialista,* a spatial artist. His gouaches soon filled my house. They were so delicate and airy, and were very easy to sell after the first year, when I had given them away as presents. As there was no room other than a guest room to show and sell them in, they had to be piled up on a bed. When James Sweeney came to Venice and saw them, he at once said, "Get that boy canvas and paints and let him expand, he needs space." I did as I was told, and then my spatial problem grew to such an extent that I no longer knew where to show the canvases. Tancredi had one of the studios in the cellar for several years, but it was a great relief when he finally left, as he used to drive the servants crazy by walking all over the house with his feet covered in paint of every conceivable color. When at last he left, it took four days to remove this mess from the floor of his studio. This room has now become a Pollock museum, and for a time Tancredi's paintings were sold in the room that used to be the laundry.

My second protégé was Edmondo Bacci, a very lyrical painter in his mid-forties, whose work was inspired by Kandinsky. He had a very organized way of life and with him everything went calmly and successfully. Tancredi, on the other hand, who was in his early thirties, was madly temperamental and perpetually made rows. Often he removed all his paintings, only to bring them back in a few days. As I gave him the money (keeping no commission other than the pictures he gave me, which in turn I gave to museums) he threw it all away, only to come back for more. When I tried to give him a weekly allowance he went around Venice saying he would sue me for having ruined his career. Bacci and Tancredi were the two painters in Italy whose works gave me most pleasure, and I had my private apartments filled with them. I also admire Vedova's work and own two of his paintings.

Apart from this, and opening my house to the public three afternoons a week, I have not done much in Italy. Santomaso was madly disappointed, as he thought I was about to become a new dynamic and cultural center for Italian art. But I was so uninspired by what I found in Italy that little by little I lost interest. The painting in the Biennale gets worse every year. Everybody just copies the people who did interesting things forty years ago, and so it goes on down the line, getting more and more stereotyped and more and more boring. I have continued buying whenever possible, but infinitely prefer contemporary sculpture to painting.

Since my collection has been opened to the public, people come from all over the world to see it, and as I also hold a salon for intellectuals, a great confusion arises. Anyone is welcome to visit the gallery on public days, but some people, not understanding this, think that I should be included as a sight. I get phone calls from many persons whom I do not know, who begin by saying, "You don't know me, but I once met your sister Hazel in California." or "Your friend Paul Bowles told me to phone you," or "We have just arrived in Venice and have a letter of introduction to you, and would like to invite you to lunch or dinner or a drink." On one occasion a young American, in Italy on a Guggenheim musical fellowship, even wrote and asked if I had a piano, as he would like to come and practice on it. I was happy to be able to say I hadn't got one. I would never dare phone a stranger on such flimsy pretenses. If I had a letter of introduction,

I would send it round and wait to be invited. People don't know how to behave any more. Oh, for the good old days, when they still had manners!

My salon is most informal, provided you have been invited, but my museum days are strictly for art lovers. All my personal guests are requested to write in my guest-book, and if they are poets or artists they may add a poem or a drawing, which is more than welcome.

When Mrs. Clare Boothe Luce, whom I had met occasionally at consular parties, was the U.S. ambassador in Italy, I invited her to come and see my collection, which she did very late one night, followed by a train of people. I felt that none of them were much interested in art, but Mrs. Luce, as usual, was very polite and charming, and of course marvelously dressed, looking younger and more glamorous than ever. She seemed to like best my daughter Pegeen's paintings, though when I made the observation that the people in Pegeen's paintings, strangely enough, never seem to be engaged in any conversation with each other, all going their own ways, Mrs. Luce replied, "Maybe they have nothing to say." When Mrs. Luce went into my dining room she encountered three young Italian painters, Dova, Tancredi and Crippa. In her true ambassadorial manner, she asked them whom they considered the best painter in Italy. Each of the three at once answered, "I."

Mrs. Luce complained that my corridors were not sufficiently lit to view the paintings properly. I must admit she was quite right, and I afterward installed strong fluorescent lights for which idea I am very grateful to Mrs.. Luce. This suggestion gave me occasion to make a good Italian pun, as "la Luce" (as Mrs. Luce was called in Italy) thus brought *"la luce"* to my house, *"luce"* in Italian meaning light.

Count Zorzi, who ran the Biennale review, and who now, to my sorrow, is dead, was one of the few remaining grand seigneurs of Venice. He was, quite fittingly, the descendent of a doge, and one of the few people in Venice with elegant manners and a sense of humor. The Biennale always consulted him about protocol. But that wasn't the only thing he knew about. He ran their bimonthly review extremely well, and always encouraged me to write for it. He wanted an article on Pollock, but I never felt up to it. But I did write one, which he also asked for, about how I became a collector. Then I wrote one on my painter-daughter, Pegeen, and one on Bill Congdon. In this article I claimed that he was the first painter since Turner who had understood the soul of Venice, and in the article on Pegeen I expounded Herbert Read's theory that she remained as fresh and pure in her painting, and still brought the same magical, innocent touch to her work, as she did at the age of eleven.

In the article on how I started to be a collector, I related a story about a woman who went around an art show grumbling bitterly all the time. I approached her and asked why she bothered to come and look at painting that seemed so much to displease her. She replied that she wished to learn what modern art was all about. I warned her how dangerous it was to do so, as she might become an addict.

After my show at the Biennale, they were perpetually asking me to lend them pictures for their successive exhibitions. In the beginning I complied with their requests, but later there were so many demands from everyone that when my house was opened to the public it became impossible to lend any more. Pallucchini took offense at this and wrote me a very unpleasant letter, scolding me and telling me how ungrateful I was for all the Biennale had done for me. I wrote back and said, on the contrary, they should be grateful to me for having lent them my collection, which turned out to be the most popular show in the Biennale of 1948, and that therefore we were quits. He was so infuriated by this that he had my name withdrawn from the list of people who were invited to the opening of the Biennale, and in 1952 I had to accept Santomaso's kind offer of his invitation in order to get into the opening.

When Count Zorzi died, Pallucchini wrote a beautiful obituary in the Biennale magazine. I was so moved by this that I felt it incumbent upon me to write to Pallucchini telling him so, and thanking him. This brought about our reconciliation, and my name was put back on the invitation list.

At one time I considered buying the United States pavilion at the Biennale, which belonged to the Grand Central Art Galleries, who wished to part with it for about twenty thousand dollars. But I felt it would have been an awful responsibility, and also one that I could not afford. It would have meant going to New York every two years to choose the shows, and then incurring all the expense of transport and insurance. It obviously was a museum's job, if not a government one. All the other foreign pavilions of the Biennale are under the auspices of organizations sponsored or supported by their governments. But we in the United States had no government subsidy for the Biennale. Luckily, in 1954, the Museum of Modern Art bought the pavilion, which was more fitting.

In 1950, Alfred Frankfurter, editor of *Art News*, arranged an American show in this pavilion, in which Pollock was represented by three paintings. By far the best in the whole Biennale was one of his called *N I 1948*, owned by the Museum of Modern Art. This magnificent painting, which several years later was one of the few to suffer in the museum fire, stood out beyond everything in the whole Biennale, even though there were shows of the Douanier Rousseau, Matisse and Kandinsky. I remember at the time my infinite surprise at having been convinced of this fact, because it was always difficult for me to accept Pollock's greatness.

In 1950 also, the Biennale made a very small mixed sculpture exhibition in a ridiculously inadequate space, not in the main hall of the Italian pavilion, where it should have been held, but in an outside one. The exhibitors were Arp, Zadkine and Laurens. Giacometti refused to exhibit because Laurens had such a bad *salle*. Arp had been warned that he was very badly shown, and when he arrived in the central hall, where there was a Viani show, he said with joy, "Oh, I haven't such a bad place at all."

In 1954 Arp had a beautiful show at the Biennale. So did Max Ernst. They each received the most important prize. On this occasion Max came to my home and wrote in my guest-book: "An old friend is come back forever and ever and ever." And so finally peace was made.

The prizes given at the Biennale always cause great excitement. A lot of politics are involved and no one is ever pleased. The four most important prizes, two for painting and two for sculpture, are given by the Presidenza del Consiglio dei Ministri, which gives two for two million lire each, and by the Commune of Venice, which gives two for one million five hundred thousand lire each. Innumerable other small prizes are given by all sorts of people and business firms, not only in Venice but all over Italy. Among these there is one given by the Angelo restaurant, which belongs to my ex-secretary, Vittorio Carrain. The Angelo is much frequented by artists and the walls are covered witn contemporary paintings, an idea started by Vittorio's brother, Renato, who died in a car accident. He also catered for rugby players as well as artists, and it was very odd to see these two completely different elements equally at home in this restaurant, which serves delicious food and where I ate daily for years before I found my *palazzo*.

In 1956, the Museum of Modern Art lent their Biennale pavilion to the Chicago Art Institute, and Katharine Kuh, who was then a curator of the Institute, made an exhibition called "The American Painters and the City." Katharine came to my house to buy a Bacci, and was very much impressed with my two maids, whom she called my curators, who helped drag enormous canvases in and out. These two Italian country girls acted as hostesses on Mondays, Wednesdays and Fridays, the days on which my house is open to the public. I usually hide on these occasions. Afterward, they often related to me what had happened during the course of the afternoon. Once they told me with great horror that a Cubist Braque had been pointed out to a group of students as a Picasso. I said, "Why didn't you correct this?" and they replied, "Oh no, we couldn't, because it was a professor." Besides making my maids into curators, I also taught my two gondoliers to be expert picture hangers.

One day, in 1948, when I was walking through the Campo Manin, I noticed a very exciting painting in the window of a little art gallery. My first reaction was to take it for a Pollock. I went in and met the artist, who turned out to be Alan Davie, a tall Scotsman with a red beard. He had a blonde, equally Scottish wife called Billie. I bought a painting at once and we became great friends. Later his father, a clergyman, wrote me the sweetest letter, thanking me for the interest I took in his son. Alan Davie developed his own style very quickly, and though his work was not bought by anyone except me for years, he is one of the best British painters. Now, like everyone else as good, he has finally been recognized in England and New York, where he has been a great success, though for years he had to support his wife and baby by making jewelry.

In 1950 I met Dr. Eugene Colp, the curator of the museum of Tel Aviv. He asked me to lend him a large number of pictures to show there. At that time, my basement was stacked with the overflow of my collection, and as the cellar was very damp, I began giving away pictures, including Pollocks, in all directions, which, as I have already said, I now very much regret. My friend Bernard Reis said that instead of lending Dr. Colp the pictures I should give them to him, so I gave him thirty-four, and later some more. Dr. Colp was very much infatuated by me, and one day when he asked me what there was between us I replied, "Nothing, except thirty-four paintings."

My cellar was also stacked with all the paintings I had bought during Art of This Century shows, such as those of Baziotes, Motherwell, Still, Virginia Admiral, Pousette-Dart, Laurence Vail, Pegeen, Kenneth Scott, Janet Sobel, Rothko, Hirshfield and Gorky. In 1953, Walter Shaw and Jean Guerin, old friends of mine, who lived in Bordighera, asked me to lend them all these paintings to make an American show there. It was under the auspices of the Commune, and therefore rather official. Cocteau wrote the introduction to the catalogue. I accepted, and went there with Laurence Vail and a friend of mine called Raoul. The luncheon that Walter and Jean gave for Cocteau and for us was very amusing, but the long-drawn-out official dinner party bored Raoul, and he left as soon as it was over. To my surprise, we were all three the guests of the city of Bordighera and were given three lovely rooms in a hotel. Raoul, who was interested only in motor cars (in one of which he was so soon after to meet his untimely death) never took much interest in art, but he was, as Herbert Read called him, quite a "philosopher." Raoul always maintained that I would go down in history, which statement, though quite exaggerated, I found very touching.

I had a dog named Sir Herbert, after Mr. Read (as he then was), though the dog was knighted by me long before Herbert. When I phoned Raoul to tell him about the real Herbert Read's knighthood he said, "Do you mean the dog?" The same thing always happened in my home when Sir Herbert was my guest. The servants invariably asked, "Do you mean the dog or the man?"

After I left New York, Pollock had a very unsuccessful show at Betty Parsons' gallery. A few months later my contract with Pollock expired, and he remained with Betty without a contract until 1952, when he went to Sidney Janis's gallery. Not being in New York, I had no idea what was happening, but soon I began to realize that little by little everything I had done for Pollock was being either minimized or completely forgotten. Catalogues and articles began to appear, ignoring me or speaking of me in inadequate terms, as in the case of Sam Hunter, later curator of the Minneapolis Museum, who referred to me in his introduction to a traveling Pollock show as Pollock's "first dealer." In the São Paulo catalogue and in the New York catalogue of the Museum of Modern Art, Sweeney's introduction to my first Pollock show was attributed to my uncle's museum (where I knew Pollock had merely worked as a carpenter). In the biographies in the São Paulo catalogue I was completely ignored. Everyone gave credit to the Fachetti studio in Paris for Pollock's first European show, ignoring the ones that were held in Venice by me, and one in Milan, for which I had lent my pictures. Worst of all was an article that appeared in *Time* magazine, accusing Pollock of having followed up his success at the Biennale by coming to Europe to further his career by showing in the Correr Museum in Venice, and in Milan. Pollock was furious and wrote a letter to deny this, saying he had never left the United States. My name was not mentioned in the article, nor in Pollock's reply, and my great friend Truman Capote, who was very indignant, said someone should have written another letter with the true facts, but no one did. I complained to Alfred Barr and to Sam Hunter, and Barr did his best to straighten things out, but I was taking no chances, and when Pollock's pictures were shown in Rome, I was very careful to write all the facts to Giovanni Carandente, assistant to the museum director. At least in Italy I wished to have things straight.

In 1956 Rudi Blesh, who had exhibited his paintings in Art of This Century, wrote a book about modern art called *Modern Art U.S.A.* He knew all about my gallery and wrote the truth as he saw it, and as it was. I believe this made the book very unpopular among those who were pretending to have discovered Pollock. Some of the facts I referred to occurred before Pollock's death and gave me reason to believe that Pollock had been very ungrateful, so when in the summer of 1956 Lee Pollock arrived in France and phoned to ask if I would find her a room in Venice, I said that Venice was absolutely full up. A few days later, I received a cable from Clement Greenberg telling me to break the news of Pollock's death in a car accident to Lee Pollock, who was supposed to have been with me. Imagine how I felt. Maybe it would have been a fitting end to the Pollock cycle if Lee and I had been together at this moment. But we were not, and that is why.

Actually, when I went to Rome for the Pollock show in the Museum of Modern Art in 1958, I was terribly moved, seeing all the early enormous canvases that for years I had dragged in and out and encouraged, if not forced, people to buy. It certainly had been the most interesting and important time of my life, since 1934, and I think by far my most honorable achievement.

At this point I must go back to certain events that occurred in 1948, in order to lead up to the Museum of Modern Art in Rome. After I accepted Count Zorzi's invitation to the Biennale, I went to Capri for the winter. In the spring, Italy was to have a general election, and everyone was terrified that it would go Communist and that Tito would immediately walk into Italy. The atmosphere in Capri was very hysterical and some of my friends made me so nervous that I began to regret my promise to the Biennale. I thought the collection was safer in storage in New York. However, I decided to consult the head of the United States Information Service (USIS) in Naples. He sent me on to Rome to Dr. Morey, who was the cultural attaché at the United States Embassy. What a charming and distinguished man he was! He immediately reassured me so much (being convinced himself that Italy would not go Communist) that I decided to let the Biennale have my pictures. Not only that, he also sent me to Dr. Palma Bucarelli, the director of the Museum of Modern Art in Rome, to arrange to show my collection there, under the auspices of the United States government, after the Biennale. Dr. Palma Bucarelli accepted with joy, as the United States was to pay all the expenses. Unfortunately when the time came the government had withdrawn a greater part of the funds from the new budget of USIS, and the project had to be relinquished.

Dr. Palma Bucarelli was a very beautiful woman. She had an aquiline nose, wavy chestnut hair, mauve eyes with superbly long eyelashes, and very white skin. She was petite and slim and very elegantly dressed, and had known many Fascists, thus acquiring this wonderful position. She knew nothing about modern art, but she worked very hard in later years to make her dreadful morgue of a museum give good exhibitions and buy pictures. She held Mondrian, Modigliani, Malevich, Kandinsky and Pollock shows, besides one of my uncle's collection. She did behave a little bit as though she had discovered modern art, but she must be excused as, with her assistant Carandente, she really did wonders for Italy.

My most famous house guests were Giacometti and Truman Capote. Giacometti, when he married Annette, came to spend his honeymoon in my house. Nancy Cunard was in Venice at that time and often came to visit me. Giacometti said she resembled a marvelous race horse. At that time or later Giacometti offered me his six Venetian statues for a million French francs. Of course I accepted. However I never got them, though he thought, being Venetian, they belonged in my collection. I think his dealer, Pierre Matisse, must have objected.

Truman Capote I first met in my entrance hall. A little man in carpet slippers huffling around. We became very good friends and later he spent two months as my house guest writing *The Muses Are Heard*. He was very keen on keeping his line and made me diet also. Every night he took me to Harry's Bar and made me eat fish. He only allowed me a very light lunch of eggs. He is always madly amusing and I loved having him stay with me.

# Chapter 20

# Ceylon, India and Venice Again

In the fall of 1954, after Raoul's death, I decided to get out of Italy and try to think of something else. Paul Bowles had invited me to Ceylon, where he had bought a little island. It was fantastically beautiful and luxuriant, with every conceivable flower and exotic plant from the east. The house resembled the Taj Mahal, as it was built in octagonal form. We all lived there together in separate rooms divided by curtains, we being Paul, his wife Jane, Ahmed, a young Arab primitive painter of great talent, and an Arab chauffeur, who seemed rather sad without the Jaguar car, which had been left behind in Tangiers, Paul's other home.

In order to get to the island one had to pick up one's skirts and wade through the Indian Ocean. There was no bridge or boat. The waves usually wet one's bottom, even though the distance one walked could be done in one minute and a half. It was terribly unpleasant to go about all day with a wet bottom, but there was no other way. The beauty of the surroundings made up for all the inconveniences, which were many. There was no water on the island and the servants had to carry it over on their heads. This made bathing, apart from sea-bathing, virtually impossible. But there was a raft just below the house and the swimming was superb. The beach opposite was skirted with coconut palms, and there were narrow fishing craft with beautiful Singhalese fishermen riding them astride. It was another dream world, so different from Venice.

As Ceylon was such a small island, I was received with enthusiasm and written up in the papers as a great art authority and asked to broadcast. I was even consulted by the wife of the chief of police, who begged me to tell her if her twelve-year-old son should be encouraged to paint. His father very much disapproved of his artistic child's pursuits, which were fostered by the adoring mother. Actually, the child was an infant prodigy, and I had to admit it to the father, with the reservation that often children who began painting well lose all their freshness when they grow up.

Reading from my diary I find the following entry:"Yesterday I was invited to go and see the paintings of a child genius, son of the chief of police. His father does not want him to paint, except as a hobby, the mother is fostering the child's genius. An angelic little creature of twelve, who showed me all his pets, dogs, puppies and white mice. His paintings are as mature as a man of twenty-five. He has an extraordinary talent amounting to genius. His style is not formed, sometimes it resembles Matisse or Bonnard, but he has great force and sense of color and design. A direct, simple and pure approach, and at the same time quite sophisticated. His mother was a beautifully dressed little elegant Singhalese, with oriental jewelry and wearing an occidentalized sari. The house was a little gem, all opening on to lovely cinnamon gardens. My infant prodigy had exquisite hands. He showed me all his art books, Egyptian, Japanese, Dufy, Picasso, etc. The child had wonderful taste and perception in pointing out details. The mother spends all her money on his paints and art books.

"There was another infant prodigy, a cellist, a protégé of Casals. He belonged to a very distinguished family and his uncle, Darangale, is one of the best painters of Ceylon, but I fear too much influenced by Tchelichef. This infant prodigy was much older, about sixteen, and already well known as a cellist. He also had an adoring mother, who lived only to further his career. But she seemed as worried as the wife of the chief of police. Neither of these ladies seemed to be entirely convinced that they were doing the right thing."

After five weeks in Ceylon, I set off alone for India. My trip was planned by Thakore Saheb, the Indian ambassador in Colombo. He had formerly been in Washington and was married to the sister of the Maharajah of Mysore. He must have had a very exaggerated idea about the speed of American travelers, which I grant can be rather racy, as the itinerary he prepared for me would have killed a far stronger person than I was. I had to cut out about half of it, though I managed to visit over twenty cities in forty-eight days. In Colombo I was told by a journalist not to miss the paintings of Jaminy Roy, in Calcutta. When I got to Mysore, where I went to visit the maharajah, I went to the art museum. Faced with a painting that resembled a Brauner, my mind began to wander and I tried to remember the name of the painter whom I was supposed to look up in Calcutta. I was very upset because I did not succeed. I thought I must send a wire to the person in Colombo who had told me about him. Suddenly I looked up at the painting I was standing in front of, and realized that it was a Jaminy Roy.

When I got to Calcutta the publicity agent of the West Bengal government, to whom I had a letter of introduction from the Indian ambassador, took me, upon my request, to visit Jaminy Roy, to whom he presented me as an art critic. In my diary I find the following entry: "Went to visit Jaminy Roy, a saintly man of sixty. Lives in a beautiful white modern house, where he shows his paintings. They are all mythological subjects, even the Christian ones. He has exhibited in New York and London, but has never left India."

Jaminy Roy painted a lot on a woven papyrus, but I bought a picture for seventy-five rupees which was on paper, as it was easier to pack. The picture depicts the abduction of Siva by Ravana. The demon King Jataya wanted to stop Ravana, a fight ensued and Jataya, the valiant bird, was killed. This is an episode from the Ramayana, the great Hindu mythology. Jaminy Roy had copied a few European painters from reproductions. One was Campigli and another was Van Gogh. His own work resembled Victor Brauner's, except that all his eyes are shaped like little boats or almonds. He had a primitive quality, like the Arab Ahmed. He did not approve of three-dimensional painting. His was quite flat. I felt he was a wise man and quite unspoilt.

When I got to New Delhi, exhausted by all my travels, trying to

keep up with the itinerary of Thakore Saheb, I was rescued by
Paxton Haddow, a lovely girl in the American Embassy, who
worked for USIS. She invited me to live with her in a beautiful
house, and thus for a while I forgot I was a tourist.

Pax drove me to Chandigarh, a city which took the place of
Lahore, the former capital of the Punjab, which belongs to
Pakistan, since the division of India. The following entry is in my
diary: "Went . . . to Chandigarh, where we arrived a few hours
after the Prime Minister had held the official opening of the
supreme court, the masterpiece of Le Corbusier, a very fine
monument, much resembling his apartment house in Marseilles,
but of course much less domestic. The whole town of Chandigarh, laid out by Le Corbusier, is an amazing example of modern
town planning, all built within his theory of Man's proportions.
The head, the body, the arms must all be represented approx-
imately. It was amazing to see Chandigarh after seeing Fatehpur-
Sikri, the dead city near Agra. There are twenty-six sectors in all,
with huge highways for fast traffic and roads for pedestrians . . .
Few sectors are finished, but those which are contain houses all
alike, in straight rows, to be rented by government officials at ten
per cent of their salaries. So everybody knows by your house-rent
what your salary is. All the people who are judges live in one row,
etc., down to the coolies, who have their own houses. As a
venture, this is stupendous, but the other buildings, designed by
Maxwell Fry and Jane Drew, are not so nice. Le Corbusier
designed some of the official buildings, engineering college,
schools (each sector is to have one), hospital, printing office, etc.
There are few trees, and the whole effect so far is very desert-like
and monotonous. In ten or twenty years it will be interesting to
see. Now, everything is makeshift, the schools being used for
assembly halls, local dispensaries for hospitals, etc.

"A very charming woman, wife of a judge, accompanied us, and
though she knew much less than Pax, who had been there once
before, she knew more of the practical side of living in Chandigarh. She had chosen a house that she already regretted, as a
huge building was going up opposite, though she had especially
chosen the house for its privacy. She lamented her dining-room,
which served as a corridor. There was no portico over the
entrance to protect her from the rain, which is devastating in
Chandigarh. Her garage was behind the house, as were the

servant's quarters; all very bad for the monsoon time, which causes floods. Her house, being one of the first to be built, was already out of date. The new ones had benefited by all the mistakes made in building the others, and were much nicer, as we saw for ourselves.

"We stayed in a Le Corbusier hotel. It was quite comfortable. Le Corbusier had made lattice-work cement walls everywhere to keep out the sun and let in the wind. This idea, though seemingly his invention, is an old Indian custom, so everyone is happy. The city is not beautiful, and never will be, because the houses are too regular, similar and uninspired. Anyhow, the idea is to raise the standard of living of the poor. It is quite socialistic. We saw one cinema in one sector that is finished. This sector resembled a town in the United States . . . The whole enterprise must give great satisfaction to Le Corbusier, who is the only person in the whole world ever entrusted with such a commission. In his office there is a plan on the wall, which you are supposed to view before you see the town. The workmen of Chandigarh have been honored by having the streets lined with poles bearing the colorful bowls which carry earth and cement, the symbols of their work. The worst houses looked like women's knitting or embroidery. There were one or two rows of very handsome houses, but nothing really wonderful or stately. However, the enterprise was not supposed to be anything else. Too bad. It could have been much better, even within these limits."

Modern art in India was very disappointing, as it was in Ceylon, where George Keytes was considered the best modern painter. He decorated temples in semi-realistic style with Buddhist myths as subjects. I could find nothing to buy besides my Jaminy Roy, except one very lovely primitive painting I saw in an all-Indian show in New Delhi. This depicted a village scene of peasants seated at night around a table. It had tremendous atmosphere and, though it was not at all realistic, gave one a great sense of Indian life. I wished to buy it, but when Pax went with the money she was just too late, as Nehru had given it as a present to Nasser.

What I lost in painting I made up for in earrings, coming home with a great many bought all over India, and even some from Tibet. These I found in Darjeeling, where I went to look for Lhasa terriers, endeavoring to put an end to the inbreeding of my

numerous dog family. I went to visit Tenzing Norkay, the sherpa
who climbed Mount Everest with Hillary. Tenzing had six Lhasas
who walked with him daily in the Himalayas, but he would not
part with any of them.

Princess Pignatelli once said to me, "If you would only throw all
those awful pictures into the Grand Canal, you would have the
most beautiful house in Venice." And so it was considered. But no
Venetian approved of my modern décor. However, I had to have a
suitable modern décor for the collection, which was exhibited all
over the house for lack of space. In place of a Venetian glass
chandelier, I hung a Calder mobile, made out of broken glass and
china that might have come out of a garbage pail. I had sofas and
chairs covered in white plastic that could be washed every
morning, as my large family of dogs felt most at home in the best
seats. (My two darling Lhasa terriers had mated with a gentleman
dog specially brought for this purpose from America by Mrs.
Bernard Reis, and had produced fifty-seven puppies in my home.
About six usually remained in residence.) Over the sofas I placed
black-and-white striped fur rugs, which the dogs adored to lick.
This was also un-Venetian.

Most Venetian, and at the same time un-Venetian, is a *forcole*,
or gondolier's oar-rest, which Alfred Barr presented me with for
my garden. Those who don't know what it is admire it as a
wonderful piece of modern sculpture, which is just what Alfred
intended.

Originally the entire house was open to the public on museum
days. My poor guests—how they suffered! I remember once the
painter Matta locking himself up in his room in order to take a
siesta. The lock was so seldom used that we had to get a locksmith
to release him. I did not even have the privacy of my own
bedroom, as it contained my Calder bed, which, strangely enough,
against my turquoise walls looked as though it had been made for
its ultimate destination—Venice. There is also a painting by
Francis Bacon, the only one of his I have ever seen that didn't
frighten me. It depicts a very sympathetic ape seated on a chest,
guarding a treasure; the background is all done in fuchsia-colored
pastel, which goes admirably with my turquoise walls, and with a
curtain made out of an Indian sari and a marabou bedcover of the
same color. The rest of the walls are decorated by my collection of

earrings, a hundred pairs or more, collected from all over the world. In addition to this, the room has Venetian mirrors and Laurence Vail's decorated bottles and Cornell's Surrealist "objects." Everything combined makes a fantastic atmosphere.

It was difficult to exclude the public from all this, but in the end I had to. Now, only friends, or visitors who specially ask to see it, are allowed to. My dining room, hung with Cubist paintings, has to be open to the public. This room has fifteenth-century Venetian furniture which I bought in Venice years ago, and brought back to its original home, after having lived with it in the South of France, Paris and Sussex, my previous homes. The Cubist pictures look admirable with the old furniture.

When all the spatial possibilities of the *palazzo* were exhausted I decided to build a pavilion in the garden. At least there was plenty of room. Next came the tree problem. In Venice no one is allowed to cut down trees, not even their own. I therefore decided to build along a wall which I shared with my neighbors, the American Consulate, the State Department having bought this property a few years previously. (This turned out to be a blessing in disguise, as I was guarded by soldiers night and day for many years thereafter.) This was the only part of the garden where there were no trees. I now required the permission of the State Department. It seemed very odd, living in Italy, to need this. However, it was no problem. Permission was soon granted. After that, I had to have the permission of the Belle Arti. My architect submitted our plans to the Commune of Venice who, thinking they were pleasing the American consul, never presented the plans, but hid them in a drawer and hung me up all winter. In the end I had to write to the mayor of Venice to have them released. Finally the commission of the Belle Arti came to inspect my garden and passed the project.

During this time I had changed my plans several times. At first, I had wished to build a pavilion that would have resembled a painting by Giorgio de Chirico, called *Melancholy and Mystery of a Street,* but Vittorio Carrain warned me that my building with all its arches might turn out to look too Fascist. My friend Martyn Coleman, who always gave me the best advice in matters of taste, told me to make a loggia outside the building. I copied as closely as possible the wing of the Palladian villa Emo at Fanzole. However, my loggia had to be much smaller, as there was room for only six arches, instead of eleven. The Belle Arti consented to this plan, with the exception of one vital point: a lady architect called Renata Trincanato insisted on preserving intact a little lost corner of the garden and would not allow this very necessary space to be used. Therefore I could not join up the new wing with my house, which I should have done in order to make a real *barchessa* (as such wings were called in Veneto, where they were and still are used for storing grain and hay). So my architect, Vincenzo Passero, had to modify the plans. There was no time to waste. The Biennale was to open in two months, and my *barchessa* had to be finished by then.

The opening of the Biennale is of great importance in Venice. The entire art world comes for a week—not only all the organizers of the different exhibitions, and the architects of the new pavilions, but all the artists who are invited, or failing that, the ones who can afford to, as well as many others. It is a big fair, and a tremendous amount of salesmanship goes on. All the art critics come too, and all the gallery owners who have any exhibition on. As I am a collector, and as I made a point, as long as I could, of buying something at the Biennale, everyone focuses their attention on me. Also the art collectors come, and all this means innumerable parties continuously for a whole week. I usually give a very big cocktail party in my garden, so the *barchessa* had to be finished in time, and it was. But not only had the *barchessa* to be finished, but the whole garden, which I had let grow wild for ten years, had to be put in order. However, this was finally accomplished too, and the garden looked larger than before, which surprised everyone. In the *barchessa* I made an exhibition of all the younger artists' work that I had bought in the last few years. It really looked lovely, and I called it "my Biennale."

In the fall the builder, against the wishes of the architect, took matters in his own hands and said we could finish the *barchessa* as it had been originally planned without getting the permission of the Belle Arti. We persuaded the architect to proceed, and then disregarding Renata Trincanato's admonition, built the second half of the pavilion, which was much prettier than the first, on her sacred spot, leaving just a fragment of the garden in the very background. This time we connected the *barchessa* with the *palazzo,* and it was an immense improvement.

The workmen had been very nice all the time they worked in

the garden, in spite of the fact that they had completely upset our life. We were in perpetual danger of falling into pits, being covered in dust, or being deafened by the noise of machines. A fifteenth-century well came to light during the excavations, as did also part of a house of the last century. Wanting to show my appreciation of the workmen, I asked the builder what I should do for them, and he said that at the termination of the building operations I should give them what is called a *granzega,* meaning a dinner party. It was a great success, held in June in the garden of my favorite restaurant near the Accademia. We were eighteen to twenty people, and the architect's wife and I were the only women present. We drank a lot and got very gay. I moved from one guest to another in order to talk to them all. They sang songs and one played a mandolin. Suddenly I remembered my guest-book, and sent home for it. When it came, they all signed their names, and the partner of the builder turned out to be a poet and wrote a lovely poem for me, in which he called me the Lioness, in honor of the name of my *palazzo.* The architect, Passero, made a lovely drawing of the *barchessa.* The next morning, when I woke and looked in my guest-book, I found my addition to all my guests' signatures. The following words were written in a very wobbly handwriting: "The nicest night of my life in Venice, 1948–58, Peggy G."

I gave a second *granzega* in the fall, at the termination of the second building. It was held in the same restaurant but because of the season was not in the garden. Maybe for this reason it was not so pleasant. In fact, it was a complete letdown. I presume one cannot repeat such a marvelous soirée. But if the second party was not such a success, the second building definitely was. The *barchessa* was now large enough to permit me to place all my Surrealist paintings and sculptures in it. I removed them from a very overcrowded corridor in my *palazzo,* and also took this occasion to rehang everything in my home, as well as finally deciding not to admit the public to my library and sitting room any more. I painted both rooms white, instead of the dirty dark blue I had suffered for ten years, and felt that a new life was commencing.

# Chapter 21

# New York Revisited

I had many times put off returning to America, where I had not been for twelve years. Instead I had been to Sicily, Malta, Cyprus, India, Ceylon, Lebanon, Syria, Greece, Corfu, Turkey, Ireland, England, Holland, Belgium, Yugoslavia, Austria, France, Switzerland, Germany, Spain and Tangiers. I had always said I would return to New York for the opening of my Uncle Solomon's museum. When my uncle died, several years later, his nephew, Harry Guggenheim, took over the museum and the Baroness Rebay, the former curator, was replaced by my great friend James Johnson Sweeney. This was a great blessing for the museum. I had been expecting it to open sometime in the winter of 1959, and was prepared to go to New York at any moment. However, at Christmas my friends, the Cardiffs, invited me to visit them in Mexico, where Maurice Cardiff was stationed as cultural attaché to the British Embassy. I had met them in Italy, in 1948, when he was posted in Milan, and once followed them to Cyprus. I now was delighted to go to see them in Mexico, which was much more exciting than New York, though I intended to go there on my way home.

It was a most marvelous trip. Maurice and I went to Yucatan, where we saw the most fantastic ruins at Palenque, which is set deep in the jungle and really seems to be out of this world. It was so inaccessible we could go there only by helicopter, which took us forty minutes. Then we had to make an enormous climb up many steep steps. Of everything that.I saw in this one month, Palenque was by far the most exciting. The setting was wild and beautiful and the sculpture and the architecture thrilling. In fact, the ruins were more beautiful than any I have seen anywhere. After this, I went to Oaxaca, Puebla, Acapulco, Taxco, Cuernavaca and many other places. However, this is not the place to write about my trip, as I must confine myself to modern art.

Let me first of all say how much I hate the enormous frescoes of Diego Rivera, Orozco and Siqueiros that one sees in all official buildings in Mexico—and how much I like Tamayo, but even better, two remarkable women painters, Frida Kahlo, Diego Rivera's wife, and Leonora Carrington, who lived in Mexico City. She was still very beautiful, and was married to a Hungarian photographer and had two lovely little sons. She was by now quite a well-established painter and her work had greatly developed. She still painted animals and birds rather resembling Bosch's, but nevertheless her work was very personal. There were no other painters of interest, though all the galleries in Mexico seemed to be flourishing.

Frida Kahlo was dead and her home had been turned into a museum. I was familiar with her work, having included her in my women's shows, realizing how gifted she was in the true Surrealist tradition. Her museum was very touching and very sad. One felt how much she must have suffered in this home, where she was to die in 1954 from a spinal injury caused in a motor accident in her youth, which had practically invalided her for life. Many of her pictures dealt with physical sufferings and her various operations to cure her spinal condition, none of which were successful. We felt an atmosphere of tragedy on another plane. We saw her invalid's chair, in which she painted to the end. There could have been no love between Diego Rivera and Frida at the end of her life.

Diego Rivera, at his death, left no money to his children, who nevertheless continued to adore him. Instead, he left a fortune to be used to build a monument to himself designed by himself. It was in the suburbs of Mexico City, in a forlorn spot surrounded by houses of poor squatters. In this pyramid, which was a bad imitation of a Mayan ruin, were to be placed not only Rivera's bones, but also many of his paintings and his collection of pre-Columbian art.

When I got to New York, it was still too soon for the opening of the Guggenheim Museum. Sweeney had warned me of this, but I decided to go anyway, on my way back to Venice. Sweeney asked my cousin Harry Guggenheim to show me over the museum. I had not seen him for thirty-five years and was delighted to have this occasion to do so. I was also delighted, when I got back from Venice, to receive a letter in which he said:

> Before your arrival, and before we had a chance to become reacquainted after all these years, I had the general feeling that perhaps some day you might want to leave your collection to the Foundation to be housed in the new Frank Lloyd Wright Museum. However, after thinking the matter through, I most sincerely believe that your Foundation and your palace, which has, thanks to your initiative, become world-renowned, should, after your death, be bequeathed, as you have planned, to Italy. I think that is the appropriate place for it, and I think from the family point of view—which I confess is always uppermost in my mind, this plan would be the most beneficial. I do hope while you were over here you were able to make progress with your plans.
>
> May you continue, in great success, in your life dedicated to the progress of art, and also get lots of pleasure and fun from it.

Harry seemed to take his responsibilities very seriously and obviously had had great difficulties as a buffer between what he referred to as "two egotistical geniuses," Sweeney and Wright, the latter then a very old man. I did not envy Harry his position, but I completely sided with Sweeney against Wright who, I am certain, like Kiesler, was not interested in the pictures, but only in his architecture.

Two people could not have been more at loggerheads than Sweeney and Wright. Poor Sweeney, who inherited this millstone along with his job as director of the museum, was an absolute purist about display—in fact, he was a fanatic. The interior of his home resembled a Mondrian painting. Luckily Wright died while I was in New York, and I presume this cleared the air and left Sweeney with fewer difficulties.

The museum resembles a huge garage. It is built on a site that is inadequate for its size and looks very cramped, suffering from its nearness to adjacent buildings. It should have been placed on a hill in the Park; instead it is on the wrong side of Fifth Avenue. Around an enormous space intended for sculpture displays, the rising ramp, Wright's famous invention, coils like an evil serpent. The walls bend backward, and a cement platform keeps one at a respectful distance from the pictures. Nothing could be more difficult than viewing them at this angle. Eventually they were to be placed on brackets extending from the walls. It is amazing how Kiesler's ideas have been copied. The colors were very ugly, beige in some places, white in others. But I felt, somehow, that Sweeney with his genius would eventually overcome all the difficulties and the museum would be all right. Nevertheless, I much preferred my modest *barchessa* in Venice, and for the first time I did not regret the enormous fortune I had lost when my father left his brothers to go into his own business, a few years before he was drowned on the *Titanic*.

My best day in America was spent visiting the Barnes collection and the Philadelphia Museum, ending up for cocktails in the modern apartment of Ben Heller, the art collector. Rather a heavy program for one day, which also included a midnight party.

I was escorted to the Barnes Foundation by my friend Robert Brady, who had once been a pupil there. He obtained a special invitation for me, as I was leaving in a few days. He was not admitted with me, as his invitation was for a fortnight later. It was the first time that I had asked to visit the collection. The house, situated in a lovely park, is not very large or modern, but this marvelous collection is unbelievable. The place is not in any way considered as a museum. The pictures are intended to be shown only to art students and are taken down from the walls when being studied. Miss Violette de Mazia presided as hostess and teacher. She was very kind and hospitable, but when I asked her for a catalogue she seemed very shocked. It took half an hour to get used to the arrangement of the pictures. I have never seen so many masterpieces assembled in such confusion, at times five rows deep. There were about twenty small rooms, apart from the large hall. Here, in a gallery above, there was a large series of paintings by Matisse, done specially for the space. One had to concentrate with all one's will power to look at each picture in turn, as the surrounding ones were so close. There were about two hundred and forty Renoirs, one hundred and twenty Cézannes, forty-three Matisses, thirty Picassos, twenty Douanier Rousseaus, twelve Seurats, twenty-five Soutines, as well as paintings by Modigliani, Manet, Monet, Daumier, Van Gogh, Courbet, Klee, Vlaminck, Degas, Jean Hugo, Laurens, Utrillo, Braque and Derain. There were also some old masters, like Titian, Tintoretto, Cranach, Van de Velde and Franz Hals. Another room contained old American furniture, and another was filled with pre-Columbian sculpture and jewelry. The walls were dotted everywhere with early-American wrought-iron arabesques. I was permitted to remain two hours, though I could have stayed a month. I went around two or three times, and at the end Robert Brady slipped in unnoticed.

Completely exhausted and overwhelmed by what I had seen, I nevertheless proceeded to the Philadelphia Museum to see the Arensberg and Gallatin collections in their new setting. I was enormously impressed by Henry Clifford's installation. Apart from this, the museum had innumerable other treasures and I wandered around through a part of the Indian temple of Madura, a Chinese palace hall, a Japanese teahouse, a Japanese scholar's study, the cloister of St. Michel de Cuxa, from Toulouse, the fountain of St. Genis des Fontaines, as well as Italian, French and English interiors, all brought to America like the Scottish castle in the Robert Donat movie, *The Ghost Goes West.*

After such a day, it seemed a fitting climax to take cocktails surrounded by Pollocks, Philip Gustons, Stamoses, Rothkos, in the home of Mr. and Mrs. Ben Heller and in the company of Mr. and Mrs. Bernard Reis, outstanding collectors themselves, and with Lee Pollock. The Hellers' apartment was dedicated to their collection. They had taken down walls in order to make space for Pollock's fabulous painting called *Blue Poles.* In fact, they moved from a lovelier place, because here, on Central Park West, they had more room. The flat was so bare that it looked halfway between a sanctuary and a hospital. This is the prescribed way of life for those who dedicate themselves to modern art, and the Hellers were not the only victims.

In the twelve years I had been away from New York everything had changed. I was thunderstruck, the entire art movement had become an enormous business venture. Only a few persons really cared for paintings. The rest bought them from snobbishness or to avoid taxation, presenting pictures to museums and being allowed to keep them until their death, a way of having your cake and eating it. Some painters could not afford to sell more than a few paintings a year, as now they were the people to be taxed. Prices were unheard of. People only bought what was the most expensive, having no faith in anything else. Some bought merely for investment, placing pictures in storage without even seeing them, phoning their gallery every day for the latest quotation, as though they were waiting to sell stock at the most advantageous moment. Painters whose work I had sold with difficulty for six hundred dollars now received twelve thousand. Someone even tried to sell me a Brancusi head for forty-five thousand dollars. Lee Pollock kept all Pollock's paintings in storage and did not even want to sell to museums.

I could not afford to buy anything that I wanted, so I turned to another field, that is, after a few artists were very kind to me and made me special prices. I began buying pre-Columbian and primitive art. In the next few weeks I found myself the proud possessor of twelve fantastic artifacts, consisting of masks and sculptures from New Guinea, the Belgian Congo, the French Sudan, Peru, Brazil, Mexico, and New Ireland. It reminded me, in reverse, of the days after Max had left our home, when he came back in the afternoons, while I was in the gallery, and removed his treasures one by one from the walls. Now they all seemed to be returning. I even succumbed to the dangerous little Mr. Carlebach, who had formerly sold so many things to Max in New York, and who now had a magnificent gallery on Madison Avenue. His prices had doubled, but at least they were still possible.

For several years Clement Greenberg had said that when I came back to New York he would like to make a show called "Hommage à Peggy," to include all my "war babies," as I called the painters I had discovered during the war. It was to have been a huge exhibition launched with a champagne party. But I had to decline. Greenberg had become artistic adviser to French and Company, where it would have to have been held, but I did not like what they exhibited in their galleries, nor what most of my "war babies" were now painting. In fact, I do not like art today. I think it has gone to hell, as a result of the financial attitude. People blame me for what is painted today because I had encouraged and helped this new movement to be born. I am not responsible. In the early 1940s there was a pure pioneering spirit in America. A new art had to be born—Abstract Expressionism. I fostered it. I do not regret it. It produced Pollock, or rather, Pollock produced it. This alone justifies my efforts. As to the others, I don't know what got into them. Some people say that I got stuck. Maybe it is true. I think this century has seen many great movements, but the one which undoubtedly stands out way beyond all the others is the Cubist movement. The face of art has been transformed. It is natural that this should have come about, as a result of the industrial revolution. Art mirrors its age, therefore it had to change completely, as the world changed so vastly and so quickly. One cannot expect every decade to produce genius. The twentieth century has already produced enough. We should not expect any more. A field must lie fallow every now and then. Artists try too hard to be original. That is why we have all this painting that isn't painting any more. For the moment we should content ourselves with what the twentieth century has produced—Picasso, Matisse, Mondrian, Kandinsky, Klee, Léger, Braque, Gris, Ernst, Miró, Brancusi, Arp, Giacometti, Lipchitz, Calder, Pevsner, Moore and Pollock. Today is the age of collecting, not of creation. Let us at least preserve and present to the masses all the great treasures we have.

# Conclusion

In 1956, Carlo Cardazzo asked me to write a short and amusing book of anecdotes, one of a series. Laurence Vail named it *Una Collezionista Ricorda* (which the publisher rendered on the copyright page as *A Collectioner Remembers*). On the cover was a fabulous photograph of me under by Calder bedhead with my eight Lhasa terriers.

In 1960, an Italian publisher called Ugo Mursia asked me to write an introduction to a book called *Invitation to Venice*. The photographs were by Ugo Mulas and the text by Michelangelo Murare. I never thought I could do it, but Mursia insisted so much that I finally did. The introduction turned out to be quite full of fantasy and very unlike *Out of This Century*, which I thought was the only way I could write, and the text is reprinted as an appendix to this book.

That same year, I went to Japan with John Cage. He was invited by the Master of Flowers to give concerts in different cities. I followed him everywhere. I can't say I like his music, but I went to every concert. Yoko Ono was our guide and translator and also took part in one of the performances. She was terribly efficient and nice and we became great friends. She was followed

everywhere by an American boy called Tony Cox who had come to
Japan to find her, never having met her. He came on all our trips,
even though her husband, a fine composer, was also with us. We
were a large party and had our own private photographer. I
allowed this Tony to come and sleep in the room I shared with
Yoko. The result was a beautiful half-Japanese half-American
baby whom Tony later stole when Yoko was married to John
Lennon, having meanwhile married and divorced Tony.

What I liked best in Japan was Kyoto, but I never managed to
see enough temples as John Cage was not interested in sightseeing
and would not let us out of his sight. He spent a whole afternoon
looking for a special tie he had had made in Japan years before.
Everything we saw we had to do by stealing away from him. I
managed to get away and went along to Bangkok, Hong Kong and
Angkor Wat. At last I was free to see everything I wanted. I could
remain in Angkor Wat only forty-eight hours but managed to visit
nearly all the temples. The combination of the jungle and the
ruins is a most impressive sight and reminded me of Palenque. It
certainly is one of the most marvelous places I have ever seen.

In 1960, or about then, André Malraux came to Venice. The
French consul brought him to visit me and the collection.
Malraux was quite fascinated by Pegeen and insisted on explaining her own paintings to her. She did not understand a word of
what he said but was very pleased to have his attention. Several
days later he sent me photographs of two masks that he owned.
They were very beautiful, but I never knew why he sent them to
me unless he might have thought I would be interested in case he
wanted to sell them. Later on, Pegeen made use of his friendship
to ask his help to get two of her fairy photographer friends out of
trouble. Of course Malraux thought one of these men was her
lover. At the same time I asked his advice about whether or not I
should allow my pictures to be shown in Paris in the Ville de Patis
side of the Musée de l'Art Moderne where I had been invited.
Nellie van Doesburg said it was not at all a suitable place for me as
it was not important enough. Malraux said if I would show there
they would make it just as nice as the other side of the Museum,
which was the national side. However, I did not take his advice
and luckily waited until my collection was shown in the Orangerie
years later. During the time my show was at the Orangerie, I
happened to meet Malraux at a luncheon in the country near

Paris and wondered if he remembered all this and maybe was vexed, because he did not talk to me very much on this occasion. I did not know him at all well, but when he died I really felt very sad.

In 1961, I had a visit from a man called Egidio Constantini, who sought my help to execute glass sculptures from the many designs he had from all the most famous artists. He had no money to produce the glass and was quite desperate. He even wept. As I cannot bear to see a man cry, I promised to help him. Anyhow, I thought it a very good project and was always looking for someone to help. He made the most beautiful glass sculptures from designs by Picasso, Arp, Max Ernst, Cocteau, Calder, Le Corbusier, Chagall, Matta, Kokoschka and many others. Cocteau named the enterprise *La Fucina degli Angelli*. My house is now filled with these sculptures and I have given a great many to museums in America. I launched this man, sold a lot of his works and even obtained an exhibition for him at the Museum of Modern Art in New York. Constantini has been eternally grateful to me, which is more than I can say of a great many other artists.

Also in 1961, I asked Claire Falkenstein to make me new gates for the entrance to my palace. I had seen photographs of beautiful ones she had made for somebody on the Adriatic Coast and admired them so much I thought she would be just the person to do this. With bands of iron, which she personally welded by hand, a tremendous job for a woman, she inserted discarded pieces of glass from Murano. The result was stunning. Everyone stops in the street to look at the gates. Herbert Read was afraid they would not be strong enough, but they were. Perry Rathbone, director of the Boston Museum of Fine Arts, was all for them. I used to say to Claire, "Now go home and do your knitting," referring to her welding. When she had a show, I wrote in the catalogue: "Claire presented herself at the Gates of Heaven. St. Peter said, 'What are you doing here, my child? You may not be admitted.' And Claire replied, 'But I made these gates myself.' 'In that case,' said St. Peter, 'you may come in.'"

Alan Ansen, an American poet, wrote and produced two lovely masques in my garden, acted by all our friends. After he left Venice and went to live in Athens, he came back on a short visit every year on his way to Auden in Austria. On one of these occasions when I was giving Ansen his usual cocktail party,

Norton Simon phoned that he was in Venice and wanted to come at once. We said we could not receive him then as we were having a party for a Greek poet. Norton Simon insisted, saying that the appointment had been made by the American Embassy. I, too, insisted that he had come one day too soon, but finally we gave in. He turned out to be charming, not a bit like a millionaire, and fitted very well into our Bohemian party. The next day he came to lunch alone and asked me if I would leave my collection to the University of California, Berkeley. I said I would on one condition, that he would save Venice, and that, I am afraid, was the end of it.

I was at last made an honorary citizen of Venice in 1962. My dear friend Count Elio Zorzi wrote a speech for me to make. The mayor made a speech also written by someone else, and so did a third person. Thus all our speeches were not our own. This occurred in the Town Hall. I was presented with a beautiful bouquet and a parchment. Drinks were served and later all my artist friends gave me a luncheon at the Angelo restaurant.

About this time Joseph Losey asked me if I would act in the film *Eve* he was making with Jeanne Moreau. Actually, all I had to do was to sit at a gambling table and play baccarat. I had no idea how to play baccarat, but a very nice man who sat next to me, whom I suspected of being a gondolier dressed up in very fashionable cheap clothes, showed me how to play or played for me. I don't really see what I was paid for—some enormous sum—except that I had to get up very early in the morning to get to the Casino in time.

One of the worst gaffes since I have been in Venice was when I met Prince Philip, who was telling us how he attended a ball in my house given by Lady Castlerosse, and he had a great flirt with a young woman, who since then had married and become the mother of four children. At this time Princess Elizabeth and Prince Philip had only two children. I perked up and replied, "Ah, she did better than you, then." Everybody surrounding us was silent with horror.

My other bad gaffe occurred when I first met Tennessee Williams. I did not know which was he and which was his boy friend. After talking to him for quite a while I decided he must be a writer and I said to him, "You don't write, by any chance, do you?"

One day I had a visit from Amilcare Fanfani, the president of the Italian Senate. He came with two detectives and his wife and Giovanni Carandente, who gave him a lecture tour of my collection. He seemed not at all interested in what he saw and made no comments. Signora Fanfani was very charming and told me her husband was a painter and invited me to Rome to lunch to see his work. I imagine that Signor Fanfani thus had hopes of being in my collection and that was the purpose of his visit.

In 1965, I was invited to show nearly my entire collection at the Tate Gallery in London. A tremendous fuss was made over this. The Tate's chief restorer came to prepare the paintings to travel. I felt very guilty to think how much I had neglected them and how badly they were in need of restoration. The Tate Gallery hoped to inherit the collection. They gave a big dinner party for me in one of the galleries, borrowing old silver for the occasion. I was allowed to hang the pictures; this was the last time I ever did so. We had a very impressive opening. I went around on the arm of the new director, Norman Reed, receiving the guests. The show was a terrific success, with people queuing up all the way down the steps of the Tate and along the Embankment. My only rival was Churchill's funeral. After the show, which was prolonged two weeks, they restored lots of paintings for me.

In 1966, we had a most terrible flood in Venice. The city was completely under water for twenty-four hours and when the tide receded, it left behind the most filthy brown oil which covered everything and even got on the faces of my lions' heads. For the second time my basement was flooded, but the pictures were safe as they were all packed ready to go to Stockholm, and were outside in the *barchessa,* which was too high for the water to penetrate. Actually, my house is on the highest land in Venice, called Dorso Duro, so the flood reached only the basement.

So much damage was done by this flood that it was necessary to think of restoring Venice. Many committees were formed, CRIA being the first, But that was mostly to help Florence, and was started by Fred Licht, who was then director of the Florida State University Center in Florence and later became director of the Princeton University Art Museum. Soon after, many different countries formed their own committees. First was the United States and then came Great Britain, France, Germany and Australia. They have all done wonders of restoration, which

Venice so badly needed even before the flood, and certainly much more after. I myself became an honorary member of Save Venice and have given lots of money every year to John MacAndrew, its former chairman. There is, of course, the possibility of Venice sinking, which would make all this useless, but we all hope that some solution will be found to prevent this terrible catastrophe from occurring.

One year after the Tate Gallery show, I was asked by Pontus Hulten to show in his gallery, the Modern Museum of Stockholm. King Gustaf Adolf opened the exhibition, and I had to show him around. I fear he was much more interested in excavations and Chinese art than in modern art.

While I was in Stockholm, Knud Jensen came from Louisiana, the beautiful museum outside of Copenhagen, to ask me if I would allow the collection to go there after the show in Stockholm ended. He invited me and Pegeen to come and visit in Copenhagen so that we could see Louisiana. Even before seeing it I had decided I would show there, but we had three lovely days in Denmark, almost my happiest and last days with Pegeen, who was to die a few months later. Sam Kaner, who runs the Royal Gallery in Copenhagen and who is a painter, showed us around and took great care of us. Copenhagen is a delightful city. I had not thought so when I visited it before. I did not go to my show, as I went to visit Robert Brady in Mexico, and that is where I was when I got the tragic news of Pegeen's death. My darling Pegeen, who was not only a daughter, but also a mother, a friend and a sister to me. We seemed also to have had a perpetual love affair. Her untimely and mysterious death left me quite desolate. There was no one in the world I loved so much. I felt all the light had gone out of my life. Pegeen was a most talented primitive painter. For years I had fostered her talent and sold her paintings. She was just beginning to have a real success, having shows that winter in Canada, Stockholm and Philadelphia.

In 1967, I decided to enlarge my museum. I had so many new paintings and sculptures, in spite of the fact that I had given a vast amount to museums in America, that I found it necessary to have more space. This, of course, was all accomplished in my basement. Some old caretakers had left, which left me their apartments free, so I added four more rooms. This was just after Pegeen's death, so having started the work before, I consecrated one room to Pegeen. As I was no longer to sell her paintings, I closed my sales gallery. Pegeen's room was very lovely, with about twleve of her paintings from all ages, beginning with one done when she was twelve. Constantini gave me a present of a lovely glass she had executed with him. This was the high spot of the room. It was in twelve parts and looked just like her paintings. He said he would never repeat it for anyone else so that I should have the only one in existence. I also placed in the room a photograph of Pegeen sitting in my Byzantine throne in the garden and her biography on a beautiful parchment. To me this was Pegeen's tomb.

Also in 1967, I was made a commendatore of the Italian Republic, which deserved another ceremony. But because of Pegeen's death I did not wish to have one. This time I was given a parchment and a medal, which I never wear but which I expose on a glass shelf. It makes me feel like the old lady shows her medals. There are, I believe, only two other lady commendatores in Italy.

In 1968, I accompanied Roloff Beny, the photographer, to India. He was a state guest, as he was doing a book on that country. We went everywhere, driving over a thousand miles. I went almost mad waiting for Roloff to photograph everything in sight. His photographs are all works of art, each one looks like a painting. We went to the most marvelous places quite off the beaten track where I felt no one had ever been before. This was quite unlike my previous trip to India which was quite touristy. We stayed almost every night in a different place, and what places they were. Terrible government hostels with practically no conveniences. But it was marvelously worthwhile considering all the fantastic things we saw.

In 1969, the Guggenheim Museum of New York invited me to give a show. A great fuss was made over this, as they wanted to inherit my collection. I had had the same idea, so I was like someone who was longing to be proposed to by someone who was longing to marry her. Harry Guggenheim, my cousin, the president of the museum in New York, was in hospital where I went to visit him, and we drew up an agreement. The terms were that the collection remain in Venice intact in my name to be administered by them. Nothing was to be removed.

The museum gave wonderful parties for me in New York, and

so did everyone else. It was an exhausting time. I was put in charge of Robin Greene, their publicity manager, who took wonderful care of me and my publicity, so the show was a great success. I became devoted to Robin as he was to me. I never dreamt, after all the rows I had with my uncle Solomon, that I would one day see my collection descending the ramp of the Guggenheim Museum like Marcel Duchamp's nude descending the stairs. It was a great relief to have the collection's future settled.

While I was in America I stayed with my friends Bernard and Rebecca Reis and with darling Marius Bewley in Staten Island, Jim Moon in North Carolina, Barbara Obroe, my cousin, in South Carolina, and John Goodwin in Santa Fe. I also visited Perry Rathbone in Boston, where I was robbed on the Common—not mugged, thank goodness. When I came back to New York I stayed with my friends the Garnetts next door to the Museum. I have never liked the museum and called it my uncle's garage. I did not think my collection looked well there, especially seen across the ramp, where the paintings looked like postage stamps. One day, when passing the museum in a bus, I had forgotten the collection was there and had such a shock to find it there.

Since I have been back in Venice, I have given first the *palazzo* and after that the entire collection to the Guggenheim Museum with the condition that I can live here until I die and administer the collection myself until then.

In 1971, Virginia Dorazio asked me if I would allow her to write a book about me. I accepted gladly and helped her as much as I could, putting at her disposal all my library of documents, catalogues, newspaper clippings, photographs etc. She obtained a contract with the Viking Press, but the book is still not finished.

In 1973, John Hohnsbeen, an old friend, whom I asked to help me with the gallery as it was all getting too much for me alone, came to stay with me every summer as a house guest. He took charge of selling the catalogues. The entrance is free, but the catalogues are for sale. He also does all my errands for me in the morning and writes my letters, but spends all the rest of the day at Cipriani's pool. He is the most social person I have ever met and the telephone rings for him all day long. He adores going to parties, but always comes home disillusioned. Besides the new friends he makes at the pool, he seems to know everybody. He never stays with me, but goes out for all his meals. I don't think he can bear being at home, but he is very kind and helpful and when I broke my wrist was an angel of kindness. I depend on him very much.

In recent years the kindness and devotion of Jane Rylands and her husband Philip have been beyond all I could imagine.

In the winter of 1972 fifteen of my very valuable small paintings were stolen. They were taken out of my house by the front and probably deposited next door in an empty house. The thieves broke through a window in the Pollock galleries. The chief of police here is a very active man, who makes friends with the underworld to help his work. After two weeks he recovered all of the paintings where they were, rolled up and buried in the mud near Mestre. An insurance agent had come from Milan to offer his services to help me find the paintings. The very next day the chief of police found them. He could brook no rival. The next robbery occurred ten months later. The Guggenheim Museum in New York had been promising to send someone to see about installing an alarm system. They delayed so long that I wrote them that if they did not hurry, it would be too late. And so it was. That very night thieves broke through the thick iron grill on one of the windows of my sitting room on the Grand Canal and stole sixteen small paintings. It was a very foggy night when the visibility was practically nil. This time I was in the house and the dogs barked like mad, but I thought they were barking at a cat. There was no trace of the paintings for months and I was beginning to get very worried. Finally, I pretended that the insurance agent from Milan had come back to offer his services. The next day all the pictures were returned. Now I have an alarm system that goes off often without any provocation.

Downstairs in a long corridor of my *palazzo* there are many drawings and gouaches. One day a visitor held out a bag to someone next to him, and said, "Hold this." Whereupon he took a Tanguy gouache off the wall and put it in the bag, departing with it. Luckily, this was observed by another visitor who came up to John Hohnsbeen and told him. He rushed after the thief and got back the Tanguy without any trouble. The man neither resisted nor fled. In fact, he docilely came back to the house with John and waited for the police to come and take him away. He must have been drugged.

In 1975, I was invited to show my collection in the Orangerie of the Louvre. This was a great honor and also my revenge for the time when the Louvre had refused to save it in 1940. The newspapers made a great point of this, so I was rather pleased. Unfortunately, Jean Leymarie, who did the show, placed my two Brancusis in front of the windows, where you could not see them because of the light. I asked to have them moved and never have I been treated with so little courtesy at any of my shows. Leymarie said he had placed them there because there were trees outside and he felt my birds belonged in the trees. Everyone else was terribly disagreeable and treated me as though I had no right to make this modest demand. They all knew much better than I did. However, in the end I won my battle by sheer force of will. This show was prolonged because of its popularity, as the one in the Tate Gallery had been. There were 120,000 visitors.

In 1976, Dr. Ezio Gribaudo, the publisher of my catalogue and of the book on my collection by Nicolas and Elena Calas, asked me to show my collection in Turin in the Modern Museum where he was a trustee. In 1949, the city of Turin had invited me to have a show there, but at the very last minute called it off for no reason except that my collection was too modern for them at the time. This was another revenge for me. This time they had two modern architects to set up the collection. However, their idea of being modern was to place all the sculptures helter-skelter on tables covered with turquoise linoleum, large and small all mixed up. They even placed the two tall Giacomettis on these tables. I did succeed in having them put on the ground. They were very polite and nice to me—not like the Orangerie. Turin is a very Communist city and the mayor, who is a Communist, received me most charmingly, giving me caviar and smoked salmon sandwiches and a big box of orchids and a book on the art treasures of the Piedmont. I told him I was so happy that the Communists had gotten in with the recent regional elections. He looked rather surprised to hear this from an American, but understood that I preferred the Communists to the Christian Democrats, who have ruined Italy. All the time I was in Turin I was escorted everywhere by the Communist cultural *assessore*, Giorgio Balmas, and followed everywhere by two policemen in a car. Dr. Balmas explained that this was not the kind of show that the new government planned to give, but that it was too good to refuse, and

that they wanted to make it very polemic, in order, I suppose, to
be more Communist. The show had 80,000 visitors and was also
prolonged two weeks. In 1967, Madame Agnelli had asked me to
lend her my Surrealist paintings for a show she was giving there
in the Modern Museum. At the time she wrote me that my
paintings had made the show. So this was the second time they
were exhibited in Turin. In the entrance they put a photo
enlargement of my Marino Marini sculpture, which was too big to
travel, and also an enormous photograph of me by Man Ray, taken
in the early twenties, wearing a Poiret dress and a headdress by
Vera Stravinsky. They also made a vitrine of photographs and
documents from my life.

When I was in Turin I was the guest of the city and was invited
back again for the end of the show. Unfortunately, I did not
accept, as I could not bear to see the blue linoleum again. Instead
I remained in Venice, where, without knowing it, I had a blood
pressure of 300 and fainted, breaking eight ribs and remaining in
the Ospedale Civile seventeen days. The nurses were terribly nice
and kind, but as there were only two of them to forty patients, it
was almost impossible to be bathed. The bed pan, to my horror,
was brought by male orderlies. I seem to have survived all this,
being overwhelmed by visitors and flowers, fruits, wines and
sweets.

I used to have a lovely Fiat car with a beautiful Ghia body, a
motorboat, which I had made to order by the famous Oscar, and a
gondola. I gave up everything except the gondola, my last
remaining joy. My gondola was made to order and is beautifully
carved with lions. The *cavalli* are Golden Lions. First I used it to
go to parties and to do errands in and to shop, like a car. Then I
had it at my disposal all day and sometimes at night. After that I
used it only four hours a day, and now I am reduced to two, which
is really quite enough and very expensive, as the price of a
gondolier is now excessive. When I had the motorboat the
chauffeur served as a second gondolier, but now I am reduced to
one. So every afternoon during the warmer months, at sunset
time I go for a two-hour ride which is sacred and with which
nothing must interfere. Sometimes I take friends to see churches,
if they do it briefly enough, as every hour is so precious that I
can't bear to interrupt the ride. Mine is the last private gondola in
Venice, as all the Venetians, and there were about twenty, have

given up their gondolas in favor of motorboats. Having a car was really unnecessary and worried me a lot, as I never used it and I felt I had to exercise it like a horse at least once a week. The motorboat I gave up when my darling Guido, whom I had for twelve years, left me with one day's notice, as he was given a taxi to drive. This is the great ambition of every driver in Venice and Guido was extremely lucky to get it. I have seen him only once in all these years and he is very happy.

In May 1977, Giovanni Carandente gave a lecture about me and the collection at the Athenee. It was very comprehensive and complete with slides, nearly all of which were shown upside down. Then he gave two lectures in my house for the Friends of the Museum. After the lecture, Countess Zavagli gave a big dinner party in my honor. While we were at dinner, we suddenly saw everything swinging from the curtains to the chandeliers. It was very exciting but did not in the least frighten me, as I did not believe that Venice could suffer a real earthquake. This was the tail end of the Friuli earthquake and frightened most people so much that they spent the night in the street. Not me, however, as I went peacefully to bed and to sleep.

In 1978, Jacqueline Bograd wrote me that Holt, Rinehart and Winston had asked her to write my biography. She came to Venice and was a charming girl and we got on beautifully. I was so pleased that she could then put right all the awful things John Davis had written about me in his book *The Guggenheims: An American Epic.* He wrote, for example, that I had given a garage to Raoul Gregorich. In fact, I gave him exactly three cars. Raoul did not murder a man; the man died long after. Davis wrote that Tancredi was my lover. In fact, he was strictly a protégé. Davis wrote that Pegeen was deprived of seeing her children after her divorce from Jean Hélion. That is not true. She saw them constantly. I gave a large regular allowance to Pegeen and Sindbad and sold many paintings for Pegeen in my gallery. If she was short of money it was because her husband Ralph Rumney provided nothing and spent fortunes. Sindbad did not trudge the streets for his insurance company. He had two cars which he could use. There is no proof that Pegeen committed suicide. The doctor who performed the autopsy said that she died from her lungs. I think she must have suffocated from her vomit. When married to Kay

Boyle, Laurence Vail did not lead a promiscuous life but a very domestic one. Finally, I resent particularly Mr. Davis's question, "What to do after fifteen years in and out of various, ultimately worthless beds?" since at that time I had had only one husband and two lovers.

After writing *Confessions of an Art Addict* and the introduction to *Invitation to Venice*, I stopped writing altogether for sixteen years. A few years ago, Fred Licht had an offer from his publisher Louis Barron of Universe Books for me to combine *Out of This Century* and *Confessions of an Art Addict*, bringing my memoirs up to date. At the time I did not feel like it, but now several years later I came round to thinking of it. It came about in this way: The French consul, André Tronc, wanted to do a best-selling book of my memoirs with me on a tape-recording machine. It turned out to be a complete fiasco. He had a very good publisher, who wanted to give me $15,000, but luckily I hesitated about signing the contract. Nothing ever came of this. I disappointed Mr. Tronc thoroughly. I could not produce anything he wanted, I was so much in love with *Out of This Century*. He said I should read it again to get new ideas, but I got only old ones. Mr. Tronc said the French would not like *Out of This Century;* it was for an English public, and anyhow he could not give them a translation, it would not be fair. I got hold of Mrs. Jenny Bradley in Paris and asked her to be my agent. But in the meantime, I was worried about what the French consul would produce, so I went and told her I could not sign the contract until I saw his version. She quite agreed with me, which was terribly nice of her, considering all the money she was about to lose. Anyhow, I came back to Venice with the idea of doing my own book. The French consul also wanted to get rid of me, but he never said so. We just drifted apart and this book is the result of the failed Franco-American effort.

To end my memoirs I think it appropriate to add that on August 26, 1978, to celebrate my eightieth birthday, Dr. Passante, the director of the Gritti Hotel, gave a dinner party for me and twenty-two of my chosen guests. My son Sindbad made an impromptu speech, and other speeches were made by the British consul Ray Jacques, by the film director Joseph Losey, and by Dr. Guido Perocco, director of the Museum of Modern Art of Venice. There was a banner with my name on it and "To the Ultima

Dogaressa," wishing me a happy birthday, and a beautiful sugar model of my *palazzo*, an exact replica lit from the inside. The American and Italian flags on the wall and millions of photographers greeted me as I descended from my gondola. The evening ended with all of us watching me on television. Altogether a memorable occasion.

# Appendix
# Venice

It is always assumed that Venice is the ideal place for a honeymoon. This is a grave error. To live in Venice or even to visit it means that you fall in love with the city itself. There is nothing left over in your heart for anyone else. After your first visit you are destined to return at every possible chance or with every possible excuse. There is no staying away for long. You are inevitably drawn back as though by magic. As to the Venetians themselves, they are all in love with Venice. With sighs they recount their undying passion for their beloved city. With the rising tide their love mounts and with the receding tide it gently diminishes only to surge forth again when the sea pours back its waters. When Venice is flooded it is even more truly beloved. Then a new ecstasy comes over the inhabitants, as they sweep out the waters from their ground floors, in order to be able to proceed with their daily lives and normal existence. Normal existence is a *façon de parler*. There is no normal life in Venice. Here everything and everyone floats. Not only the gondolas, launches, barges, vaporettos and *sandolos* but also the buildings and the people float.

Reprinted, with permission, from *Invito a Venezia,* wih a text by Michelangelo Muraro and photographs by Ugo Mulas, published by Ugo Mursia Editore, Milan, 1962.

One floats in and out of restaurants, shops, cinemas, theaters, museums, churches and hotels. One floats luxuriously with such a sense of freedom, never tormented by traffic or even disturbed by the sound of a klaxon. It is this floatingness which is the essential quality of Venice. As the tide rises and recedes twice a day one has the impression of the entire city being in perpetual motion. The buildings seem to rise and sink with the tide. Sometimes Venice partly disappears under the sea for a few hours. In very high tides it can be submerged a whole meter. But this does not greatly alter its character. It merely makes one even more conscious of how much it is a city sprung from the sea and living in it.

Here no sense of time exists. One is barely aware of the passing of the hours. The only thing that makes one realize time is the change of the light.

Church bells ring all day long, but one becomes so accustomed to them that one does not relate the chimes to time. The only hour of the day of which one is definitely conscious is noon. Then all the church bells of the entire city ring out at once in chorus, with an extra force, and added to this, a mysterious cannon goes off.

Every hour of the day is a miracle of light. In summer with daybreak the rising sun produces such a tender magic on the water that it nearly breaks one's heart. As the hours progress the light becomes more and more violet until it envelops the city with a diamond-like haze. Then it commences slowly to sink into the magic sunset, the *capolavoro* of the day. This is the moment to be on the water. It is imperative. The canals lure you, call you, cry to you to come and embrace them from a gondola. More pity to those who cannot afford this poetic luxury. In this brief hour all of Venice's intoxicating charm is poured forth on its waters. It is an experience never to be forgotten. Day after day one is drawn from *terraferma* to float in the lagoon, to watch the sunset, or to go gently past the palaces seeing their images reflected in the canal. The reflections are like paintings more beautiful than any painted by the greatest masters. The striped *pali,* when seen in the water, deny their functional use and appear like colored snakes. If anything can rival Venice in its beauty, it must be its reflection at sunset in the Grand Canal.

Though this is the irresistible hour to be in a gondola the nights also have their own special fascination and mystery. The people look quite different in the dimly lit city. One can barely distinguish their modern costumes. One can imagine these semi-invisible figures, as they were once dressed in all their splendor and glory, in their velvets and brocades and sables with their swords and jewels and even masqued in carnival time. To go out in a gondola at night is to reconstruct in one's imagination the true Venice, the Venice of the past alive with romance, elopements, abductions, revenged passions, intrigues, adulteries, denounce-ments, unaccountable deaths, gambling, lute playing and singing.

To evoke the Venice of the past one must keep away from the Grand Canal with its trumped-up tourist serenades, sheer mock-eries of the past, and float through small dark canals, past dimly lit crumbling palaces, under bridges, where lovers nightly plight their troth, past gondolas with Japanese lanterns and harmonica players, past *fondamentas* with *bistros,* where gondoliers assemble to drink wine, past warehouses and closed shops and rats and floating garbage.

I have never been in a city that gave me the same sense of freedom as Venice. The extraordinary enjoyment experienced from walking about without being tormented by the dangers of traffic is only rivaled by the sense of freedom one enjoys in choosing one's attire. Here one can wear almost anything and not appear ridiculous. On the contrary, the more exaggerated one's clothes, the more suitable they appear in this city, where carnival once reigned supreme.

The bourgeois ladies, who go about donned in suits, small hats with veils, gloves and handbags seem ridiculously out of place. In this fantastic city only fantastic clothes should be worn.

Venice is not only the city of freedom and fantasy but it is also the city of pleasure and joy. I have never seen anyone cry here except at a funeral. But to a Venetian a funeral without tears would not be a real funeral. A Venetian funeral is still a completely medieval spectacle. The large black barge with four gondoliers in ancient black costumes, the coffin buried under a mass of gigantic wreaths, is one of the most impressive sights on the Grand Canal. But apart from death there is no sorrow here. One notices great patience and a sort of resignation in the people, who take all unpleasant things for granted. They do not worry. They have a *dolce far niente* attitude.

One spends most of one's life in Venice waiting for things that either do or do not occur. One accepts this, as part of the Venetian tempo. No Venetian has any sense of time. He is never on time, comes to appointments late or appears days after he was expected, showing no sense of guilt. One waits hours, days, weeks, even months for the most trivial or even the most important things. And so one drifts along barely aware of anything new happening or of any changes of the seasons.

A book was once published called *Venice Without Water*. This was a great surprise to many people, who believed that Venice is a city without streets and that one circulates only by boat. This is completely false. To get about with haste one must walk. If you know your way through this labyrinth you can, by making short cuts, get on foot from any given point of the city to any other in twenty minutes. This might involve crossing the Grand Canal two or three times as it winds its serpentine route through the city.

If you go on foot you discover quite a different Venice to the one you have seen from a gondola. The entrances to the houses are from the streets and not from the canals, often through gardens with big trees and lovely flowers enlivened by the sweet songs of birds. The gardens are enclosed by brick walls and one is amazed by their quantity.

Apart from the gardens one sees flowers everywhere in window boxes. They mostly are various shades of pink and red geraniums. This is a great relief from the austerity of the city. Wherever one walks, one's eye is confronted with sculptures and carvings, not only of lions, but also of camels and dwarfs and madonnas with Christs, crusaders, people in boats and numerous other subjects. One's eyes can never rest. There at every point some fascinating surprise.

On one's strolls one passes from campo to campo each with its own church and café, and often with a market. One winds in and out of narrow *calles* so narrow that two umbrellas cannot be held at the same level. One comes to dead ends either in mysterious courtyards or at a canal. If there are a great many gardens in Venice there are even more courtyards with wells and beautiful gothic staircases with balustrades ornamented by carved lions. There are innumerable cloisters which bring one back to the Middle Ages. One passes buildings of every century in the last thousand years, all so harmonious that there appears no difference in the times when they were built. Venice is the most oriental of European cities, not only in architecture but also in its tempo. The people unexpectedly are very blond, the result of their having intermarried with the Germans and Austrians. One rather would expect to find dark Turkish visages. One finds here everywhere *altanas*, little pergolas on the top floors of houses, where ladies used to bleach their hair. This combined with the beautiful chimney pots and the lovely crooked old tiled roofs cause one to be looking upward continuously. One is perpetually walking up and down bridges. In fact there are so many that they are used as landmarks to give directions; one says *over the next bridge to the left,* or *at the foot of the bridge* or *three bridges away!* People stand for hours on the bridges watching the traffic go by. Women also are forever gazing out of their windows, as though they were expecting some important event to take place, though they know only too well that nothing will occur. Maybe they are looking for a fiancé or for some charming young man to pass by. But I think more likely they go to mass for this purpose.

The Venetian nobles used to keep horses and not only rode over the city and its bridges but also up the winding staircases to their high palaces. The steps were built especially for the horses to mount with perfect ease. Gone are the days of the horses and sadly enough now we find only lions, and stone ones at that. As the lion was the symbol of Venice one finds him everywhere. My own palace has eight lion heads on the front. They look as though they were about to spout water into the Grand Canal. Most of the lions of Venice look very fierce and most of them have a certain resemblance to each other. Many have wings. But there is one little creature at the Arsenale, who was brought here from Delos, who bears no resemblance to the other nine which adorn this beautiful building. In fact he looks quite melancholy, rather lost and extremely pathetic, as though he were longing to go home to his Greek isle and leave all the other lions to roar here without him.

There are no other animals here today except thousands of cats and a few dogs. Most of the cats are homeless and are fed in the *calles* by so-called charitable people, who bring filthy little packages of leftovers, which they leave about in the streets and which they even have the effrontery to toss into private gardens, where the cats come to eat. It is amazing that the cats have survived this poisonous form of charity. During the war all the cats were eaten as rabbits, but now they seem to have been reborn. Dogs, in Venice, are supposed to be muzzled or kept on a lead. A few years ago, failing this, they were seized and carried off to the stockyards, or more often their owners were merely fined. Now the authorities are more indulgent, and there seems to be no more control exerted over the happy creatures, who are so fortunate as to live in a trafficless city. At least they should be allowed to benefit by this blessing. The best *maison de coiffeur* in Venice is called Casa del Cane. They perform such miracles of hairstyling that I often with I were a dog myself to benefit from their services.

Venice has become so popular lately that in the summer months it is almost impossible to walk in the streets or to ride on a vaporetto or even to circulate in a gondola. In November everyone has gone home again and left the city to its loneliness and poverty. The summers are rich with tourists. Money pours in. The glass business thrives. The gondoliers overcharge in order to make enough money to last during the winter months, when people huddle together around brasiers, their throats wrapped in woollen scarves, their only protection against cold. The city is covered in a deep fog until January, when the weather becomes crisper and colder. In February it snows once, which transforms the city into a complete fairyland. The outer lagoons freeze but the canals never, as there is a perpetual movement of the water from the tides. There is plenty of sun in January and February, and in March suddenly the spring appears. But November and December are cast in gloom. Saint Mark's is barely recognizable. It rises through the fog like a ghost with no resemblance to itself, or rather completely distinguishable from its summer sister. Possibly a much more beautiful San Marco than the real one, which is over-gaudy, ornamented by hideous 19th-century mosaics on its front. Piazza San Marco, Napoleon's ballroom, is no longer a ballroom. Gone are the open-air cafés with their music, each band rivaling one opposite. Gone are the open-air concerts playing beautiful Wagnerian operas. Gone are postcard vendors and photographers and the grain merchants leaving the starved pigeons to the inadequate public feedings of the Commune. One walks under the arcades, not daring to face the rain and the slippery wet stones underfoot.

There are practically no gondolas in circulation except the public ones at the traghettos, and a very few that are hired with their *felze,* the winter cabin, which protects one from the wind and cold but which must give the passengers claustrophobia. On the other hand, the *felze* has the advantage of affording a certain privacy, which is entirely lacking in summer when everyone stares at you and takes your photograph.

Many people prefer Venice in winter. Not only the Venetians themselves but also some of the foreigners, who live here permanently. They say, at last we have it to ourselves. But to me the poor city seems to be reduced to the lowest level of gloom, cold, ice, fog and rain. Most of all one misses the society of stimulating visitors, who come from all corners of the earth. This is very important, as they serve as a link with the rest of the world, which one is so prone to forget when one lives in this island of lotus eaters.

If the summer tourists ruin Venice, at least they serve to keep it alive. Without them it could not exist. Its life is in the past and its beauties, like those of a museum, are preserved for those who care to come and admire them. Venice is kept alive only by this means and would perish entirely were the tourists to cease their pilgrimages. Ten centuries of magnificent architecture must be maintained. A city as beautiful, as unique as Venice must not die. The paintings of Vivarini, Mantegna, Crivelli, Bellini, Antonello, Carpaccio, Cima, Giorgione, Sebastiano, Lotto, Tiziano, Palma, Pordenone, Bassano, Tintoretto, Veronese, Tiepolo, Canaletto and Guardi belong here and must be preserved as part of this miraculous city, Venice, which must be eternal.

# Index

An asterisk before a name indicates that the person or work of art is illustrated in this book. Page references for illustrations are in italics.

Abbott, Berenice, 67, 267
Abruzzi, 108
Admiral, Virginia, 345
Agnelli, Mme, 375
Ahmed, 349
Albert (butler), 120
Alfieri, Bruno, 328, 329, 336
Algiers, 77
Allen, Jay, 111
Allenhurst, N.J., 14-15
Amalfi, 43
American Tragedy, An (Dreiser), 104
Amsterdam, 338
Anaminta (maid), 291
Anderson, Margaret, 22
Andorra, 68
Angelo café, Venice, 325
Angelo restaurant, Venice, 325, 330, 343
* Angel of the Citadel, The (Marini), 334, 335, 375
Angkor Wat, 366
Annecy (lake and town), 109, 209, 221, 223
Ansen, Alan, 367
Anticoli, 54
* Anti-Pope, The (Max Ernst), 261–62, between 268 and 269
Antwerp, 106
Apollonio, Umbro, 327
Aquila, 108
Aquitania, 60, 71
Aragon, Louis, 41, 174
Arcachon, 208, 214
Arensberg collection, 252, 255–56, 362
Argan, G. C., 328
Arizona (Max Ernst), 260
Arlington, Va., 264
* Arp, Jean, 162, 163, 172, 193, between 204 and 205, 219, 221, 223, 226, 250, 262, 314, 318, 326, 327, 334, 343, 367
Arp, Sophie Taeuber, 162, 172
Art Digest, 253
Art Institute of Chicago, 344
Art News, 343

Art of This Century (book), 262–63
* Art of This Century (gallery), between 204 and 205, 273–77, 279–80, 283–86, 292, 303, 314-20, 330, 346
Ascot, 16
Assisi, 108, 109, 110
Astor, John Jacob, 17
Aswan, 46
Auden, W. H., 367
Austria, 52-53, 95, 96, 117
Avignon, 86
Avila, 111
Azores, 245, 247

* Bacci, Edmondo, between 332 and 333, 340, 344
Bacon, Francis, 354
Bad Reichenhall, 95-97
Balmas, Giorgio, 374-75
Barcelona, 68
barchessa, 356-57, 361, 369
Barcelonnette, 74
Barker, Jack, 285-86
* Barnes, Djuna, 28, 37, 110, 112, 114-20, 147, 150, 166, 180, 188, 197, 198, 203, between 204 and 205, 266, 304, 310, 346
Barnes Foundation, 361-62
Barr, Alfred H., Jr., 7, 190, 250, 259, 260, 266, 284, 311, 314-15, 317, 354
Barr, Daisy (or Marga), 260, 286, 311, 328
Barry, Philip, 319
Bauer, Rudolf, 169-70, 197, 250, 251
Baziotes, William, 285, 314, 345
Beaumont, Comte Etienne de, 51
Becker, John, 285
Beckett, Samuel, between 140 and 141, 162-68, 175-79, 184, 187, 193, 194, 208
Bedales boarding school, 154
Beekman Place house (Hale House), 258-60, 270-72, 294
Belgioso (architect), 338
Belle Arti, Venice, 338, 355-56
Bénedité, Daniel and Theo, 227
Benenson, Fira, 25, 28-29, 38
Benno, B. G., 193
Bentley, Nicolas, 324
Benton, Thomas Hart, 315

Beny, Roloff, 331, 371
Berchtesgaden, 96
Berenson, Bernard, 25, 329
Berenson's seven points, 34
Berkman, Alexander, 76, 82
Berlin, 91
Bermuda, 245
Bettiri Balta, 103
Bewley, Marius, 318-19, 372
Biddle, George, 255
Biennale, Venice, 326-30, 340, 341-44, 347, 356
Bill, 219-20
* *Bird in Space* (Brancusi), 211-12, *213*, 250
* *Birth of Liquid Desires, The* (Dali), *214*
Blesh, Rudi, 346
Blisset (butler), 136
*Blue Poles* (Pollock), 362
*Boeuf sur le toit*, 31, 50, 51
Bograd, Jacqueline, 376
Bolzano, 53
Bonnechose, M. de, 103, 109
Bordighera, 345
Boston, Mass., 269-70, 372
Bouché, Louis and Marion, 120-21, 250
*boules*, 70
Boulogne, 179
Bowles, Jane, 349
Bowles, Paul, 297, 299, 349
Boyle, Kay, 93-94, 110, 111, 117, 140, 143, 145, 147, 155, 201, 205, 217, 231-33, 237, 238-39, 240, 241, 244, 253, 377
Boyse, Vera, 116, 120
Bradley, Jennie, 377
Brady, Robert, 361-62, 370
* Brancusi, Constantin, *between 140 and 141*, 161, 172, 174, 208, 210-12, *213*, 219, 250, 256, 327, 334, 363, 364, 374
Braque, Georges, 105, 205, 219, 251, 326, 362
* Brauner, Victor, *between 140 and 141*, 183, 186-87, *187*, 210, 219, 227, 230-31, 232, 236, 351
* *Break of Day* (Delvaux), 191
Breton, André, 160, 182-83, 188-89, 226, 227, 235, 249-50, 252, 254, 262-63, 266-67, 273, 279, 281, 282-83
Breton, Aube, 189, 227
* Breton, Jacqueline, *between 140 and 141*, 189, 227
Brittany, 102-3
Broadwater, Bowden, 319
*Broom*, 31
brothels, 66, 76
Bryant, Louise, 52
Bucarelli, Palma, 347-48
Buckfastleigh, 117

Bullitt, William C., 52
Bush, Albert, 254, 255
Butts, Camilla, 73
Butts, Mary, 73
Buxbaum, Dr., 9

Cabbot, Elise, 331
Cafés: Angelo, 325; Dôme, 27; Harry's Bar, 348; Leão d'Ouro, 238, 240; Rotonde, 27
* Cage, John, *between 204 and 205*, 271, 365-66
Cage, Zenia, 271
*Cahiers d'Art*, 327, 337
Cairo, 43-44, 47
Calas, Elena, 374
Calas, Nicolas, 260, 267, 374
Calcutta, 351
Calder, Alexander, 172, 250, 275, 280, 318, 329, 334, 354, 367; bedhead and *Mobile*, *between 332 and 333*
Calder, Louisa, 318
*Calendar of Modern Letters*, 140, 145, 198
*Call of Night, The* (Delvaux), 191
Cambon, Vicomte de, 48
Campbell, Roy and Mary, 134, 153
Canada, 19
Cannan, Gilbert, 23
Cannell, Kitty, 31, 41, 76-77
Cannes, 203
Capote, Truman, 346, 348
Capri, 30, 31-34, 41-43, 347
*Captain's Doll, The* (D. H. Lawrence), 96
Carandente, Giovanni, 346, 348, 369, 376
Cardazzo, Carlo, 365
Cardiff, Maurice, 358-59
Carlebach, 263, 363
Carlozza, Dr., 75
Capaccio, Vittore, 154, 215
*Carpathia*, 13
Carradine, John, 319
Carrain, Renato, 344
* Carrain, Vittorio, 330, *between 332 and 333*, 336, 338, 344, 355
* Carrington, Leonora, *between 204 and 205*, 216, 228-29, 231, 237, 238-39, 240, 244, 245, 249, 251-52, 260, 261, 266, 267, 280, 302-3, 359
Casati, Marchesa Lucia, 31, 334
Cascais, 241-43
Cassis, 70, 178, 233, 234
Castlerosse, Lady, 334, 368
Castle Stewart, Arthur Stuart, Earl of, 36
cats, 152; Anthony, 225; Giorgio, 210; Gypsy, 289, 302, 304-5; Romeo, 289, 302, 304-5; Sans Lendemain, 210
Cavalaire, 103
Cavalière, 63

Celeghin, 330
Central Park, New York, 7-9
Ceylon, 349-50
Cézanne, Paul, 362
Chagall, Marc, 235, 251, 367
Châlons, 76
Chandigarh, 352-53
Chaplin, Charles, 254
Cheltenham, 117
Chemaillère, 200
Chicago, 21, 267
Chirico, Giorgio de, 219, 256, 303, 314, 355
Chuto (pig), 70
Cincinnati, 22
Cintra, 244
Cipriani's pool, 372
Ciro's, 254
Clark, Lady Elizabeth, 199
Clark, Sir Kenneth, 199-200
Clarke, Mary Mowbray, 23
Clash by Night (Odets), 267-68
Clifford, Henry, 362
Coates, Elsa, 64, 76
Coates, Robert M., 37-38, 64, 76, 251, 314
cockroaches, 257
Cocteau, Jean, 58, 161, 164, 165-66, 166, 345, 367
Coffey, Brian, 167-68, 171
Cogolin, 59
Col de Voza, 217
* Coleman, Emily, 78-79, 87, 98, 103, 104-5, 106, 108, 109, 110-11, 113-22, 123, 125-27, 135, between 140 and 141, 145, 147, 155, 158, 159-60, 256, 262, 279, 280, 282-83, 318
Coleman, John, 98, 111, 115, 118, 135, 277
Coleman, Loyd Ring ("Deke"), 79, 106
Coleman, Martyn, 355
Collobrières, 69
Colp, Eugene, 344-45
Communism, 151-57, 161, 174, 374-75
Concepção, 243-44
Connecticut, 72, 258, 297-99
Connolly, Jean, 289, 296, 297, 300, 301, 306, 307, 308
Consagra, Pietro, 334, 336
Constable, John, 326
Constantini, Egidio, 367, 371
cooking, 148-49, 209, 255, 259, 298, 301
Copenhagen, 94, 370
Cornell, Joseph, 279, 293, 355
Correr Museum, Venice, 336, 346
Corsica, 91
Cotswolds, 118, 195
Courbet, Gustave, 262, 326
Courvoisier Gallery, San Francisco, 252
Cox, Tony, 366

Cranach, Lucas, 362
Crane, Hart, 72
cricket, 142, 144, 154, 184
Crippa, Roberto, 341
Crosby, Caresse, 255
Cunard, Nancy, 183, 348
Curzon Street, 290

Dali, Gala, 144-45, 208, 214
Dali, Salvador, 208, 214, 219, 250, 256, between 268 and 269, 318
Dame de Pique, La, 37
Darangale, 350
Darjeeling, 353
Dartmoor, 112, 114, 121
Daumier, Honoré, 362
Davenport, John, 195-96
Davie, Alan, 344
Davie, Billie, 344
Davis, Bill, 316
Davis, John H., 321, 376-77
Dawson, Peter, 179-81, 190
Degas, Edgar, 362
Delacroix, Eugène, 326
Delaunay, Robert, 219, 225, 250, 251, 256, 317
Delaunay, Sonia Terk, 225
Delvaux, Paul, 191, between 268 and 269
Dembo, Boris, 30, 65
Derain, André, 362
Deutsch, André, 324
Dial Press, 321
Diavolezza (glacier), 53
Dieppe, 183
Dietrich, Marlene, 118
Dijon, 86-87, 179
Disks (Delaunay), 317
divorces, 86-89, 146
Doesburg, Nellie (Petra) van, 198, 200-206, 208, 209, 210, 212, 216, 220-26, 236, 259, 268, 320, 339, 366
Doesburg, Theo van, 200, 219, 314, 320, 339
dogs, 319, 320, 330, between 332 and 333, 353-54, 373; Borotra, 136, 152; Imperator, 302, 304-5, 309-10; Kachina, 261, 273, 289, 319; Lola, 63, 69, 94, 95, 97, 98; Lulu, 69; Robin, 136, 148, 152; * Sir Herbert, 345; Troendjen, 95, 97
Domela, César, 250
Dominguez, Oscar, 186
Dominant Curve (Kandinsky), 317
Don Giovanni (Mozart), 106, 287
Dorazio, Virginia, 372
Doris (nurse), 68, 70, 71, 72, 73, 74, 87, 89, 92, 94, 102, 103, 104, 106, 107, 112, 113, 117, 120, 128, 134
Dova, Gianni, 341

Draguignan, 88-89
Drew, Jane, 352
Drew Field, Florida, 297
Dreyfus, Valerie, 24, 29, 31, 36
Driberg, Tom, 174
*Duchamp, Marcel, 50-51, 65-66, *between*
   *140 and 141,* 160-62, 165-67, 198, *between*
   *204 and 205,* 208, 209, 216, 232, 233, 256,
   271-72, 273, 276, 279, 281-84, 293, 295,
   296, 299, 307
Duchamp-Villon, Raymond, 172
Dudensing, Valentine (gallery), 260, 267
Dudley, Dorothy, 144
Duncan, Isadora, 73
Dunn, James, 328
duplex apartment, 294-96, 300-313
Duthuit, Georges, 294


Earp, Thomas W., 39
earrings, 43, 50, 77, 193, *194,* 263, 275-76,
   318, 353, 354
Edward the Seventh (porter), 241, 244
Edward VIII, 155
Egypt, 43-47
Eichmann, Ingeborg, 330
Eiffel Tower, 29, 50
Einaudi, Luigi, 328
Eliot, T. S., 198
Ellis Island, 247-48
Eluard, Paul, 189, 249
Emanu-El, Temple, New York, 1, 14
Epstein, Sir Jacob, 172
Epstein, Kitty (Mrs. Wyn Godley), 139, 141,
   149
*Ernst, Jimmy, *between 204 and 205,* 246-58
   *passim,* 268, 273, 277, 279, 281, 283, 284
*Ernst, Max, 106, 193, *between 204 and 205,*
   216, 218, 219, 227-29, 230-83 *passim,*
   *between 268 and 269,* 287-89, 294, 296,
   307, 318, 319, 326, 329, 343, 363, 367
Estoril, 243
*Eve* (film), 368


Fairbanks, Douglas, Jr., 334
Falkenstein, Claire, 367; door, *between* 332
   *and* 333
Fanfani, Amilcare, 369
Fanny (Mary Reynolds's maid), 208, 209
Farcy, André, 224-26
*Fata Morgana* (Breton), 249
Favai, 54-55
FBI, 269-70
Ferren, Inez, 246, 262, 321
Ferren, John, 250, 256
fights, 36-37, 38, 41, 51, 52, 57-58, 61,

   65-66, 75, 82-83, 84, 156, 171-72, 184-86,
   233, 260, 264-65, 272
Finch Junior College, 258
Fini, Leonor, 235
*Finnegans Wake* (Joyce), 168
Fitzgerald, Eleanor (Fitzi), 77, 82
Fleischman, Helen Kastor, 23, 24, 25, 28, 29,
   30, 99. *See also* Joyce, Helen
Fleischman, Leon, 23, 24, 25, 28, 29
Flora, Francesco, 331
Florence, 331
Font Romeu, 68
*forcole,* 354
Ford, Charles Henri, 260, 267
Ford, Gordon Onslow, 200, 201
Forêt du Dom, 69
*fourière,* 98
*France,* 59-60
Frank, Ethel, 19, 20
Frankfurter, Alfred, 343
Fréjus, 87
French Lick, Indiana, 22
Freud, Lucien, 190
Freund, Giselle, 197
Fry, Maxwell, 352
Fry, Varian, 227-28, 231, 235-36, 270

Gabo, Naum, 317
Gallatin collection, 251, 362
Gargellen, 117-18
Garman, Deborah (Mrs. William Chattaway),
   120, 135, 139-49 *passim,* 154, 156, 160,
   161, 182
*Garman, Douglas, 118-28 *passim,* 130-57
   *passim, between 140 and 141,* 268
Garman, Helen (Mrs. Sarfatti), 144
Garman, Jean Sophie Hewitt (the first Mrs.
   Douglas Garman), 146, 161
Garman, Marjorie Frances McGill (Douglas
   Garman's mother), 132, 138, 141, 149
Garman, Paddy (the second Mrs. Douglas
   Garman), 156-57, 161, 174
Garman family, 133-34, 144, 147
Garnetts, 372
Gavarnie, 104
Gerhardi, William, 116, 123, 125, 128, 153
Giacometti, Alberto, 214-15, 219, 314, 326,
   327, *between 332 and 333,* 334, 336, 337,
   343, 348, 374
Giglio, Victor, 13
Gillette, William, 9
*Girls with a Toy Boat* (Picasso), *between* 332
   *and* 333
Gleizes, Albert, 204, 219, 251, 256
Gogh, Vincent van, 362
Gold, Mary Jayne, 227

*Goldman, Emma, 76-77, 78-79, 83, 87, 104, between 140 and 141
gondola, between 332 and 333, 374-76
Gonella, Dr. (minister of education), 328
Gonzaleses, 255, 257, 276
Goodwin, John, 372
Gorky, Arshile, 345
Gorman, Herbert, 107, 168
Gorman, Jean (later Mrs. Carl Van Doren), 107
Gottlieb, Adolph, 314
Goya, Francisco, 326
Grand Canyon, 21, 256
Grand Central Art Galleries, 342
granzega, 357
Grasse, 201-3
Greenberg, Clement, 314, 346, 363
Greene, Robin, 372
Greenwich, 182
*Gregorich, Raoul, 345, 349, 376
Grenoble, 224-28, 231
Greta (Douglas Garman's friend), 156-57
Gribaudo, Ezio, 374
Grimaud, 87
Gris, Juan, 219, 250
Guardians of the Secret (Pollock), 316
Guerin, Jean, 345
*Guggenheim, Benita (Mrs. Edward B. Mayer), 4, 6, 7, 8, 9, 11, 16, 17, 19, 20, 21, 31, 35, 38, 39, 41, 46, 51-54, 57, 61, 71-72, 73-75, between 77 and 78, 136
Guggenheim, Benjamin, 2, 5, 6, 9, 10-14
Guggenheim, Daniel, 13
Guggenheim, Eleanor May, Lady Castle Stewart, 35, 36, 41
*Guggenheim, Florette Seligman, 2, 5-6, 8, 10-12, 14, 18, 19, 21, 23, 24, 28, 29, 30, 39, 49-50, 51-52, 60, 67, 75, 76, 99, 120, between 140 and 141, 145, 154, 157-58, 159, 161
Guggenheim, Harry F., 286, 358, 360, 371
*Guggenheim, Hazel (Mrs. Charles McKinley), 4, 6, 7, 10, 21, 25, 31, 38, between 77 and 78, 167, 179-80, 181-82, 184, 252, 253-56
Guggenheim, Irene (Mrs. Solomon R. Guggenheim), 35, 197, 251
Guggenheim, Meyer, 1-4, 15
Guggenheim, Rose, 34
Guggenheim, Solomon R., 169-70, 197, 251, 285, 358, 372
Guggenheim family, 1-4, 13-15, 20, 23, 34
Guggenheim house, 4-7
Guggenheim Jeune (gallery), 165-66, 170, 171-74, 176, 180, 189-93, 196, 197, 199; contemporary sculpture exhibition, 173; Van Velde catalogue, 177
Guggenheim Museum, New York, 250-51,

285, 346, 358, 360-61, 371-72, 373
Guggenheimer, Mrs. Randolph, 17
Guggenheims, The (Davis), 321, 376-77
Guido, 376
Gustaf Adolf VI, 370
Guston, Philip, 362

Haddow, Paxton, 352-53
Hadley, Dr., 35, 39, 40
Hale House. See Beekman Place house
Hals, Franz, 362
Hampstead, London, 134, 161, 180, 191
Hansen, Harry, 322
Hare, David, 285, 314, 328, 334
Harris, Jed, 93
Harry's Bar, Venice, 348
Hartley, Marsden, 23
Hartman, Mrs., 10-11
Hayford Hall, 113-22
Hayling Island, 135
Hélion, Jean, 212-14, between 268 and 269, 283-84, 314, 337-38, 376
Heller, Ben, 361, 362
Hellman, Daphne, 272, 273
Hellman, Geoffrey T., 272
Henderson, Ion, 175
Henderson, Nigel, 175
Henderson, Wyn, 120, 123, 130, 161, 171, 174-75, 180-81, 182, 196
Heye Foundation, 251, 320
Hirshfield, Morris, between 268 and 269, 314, 318, 345
Hoare, Sir Samuel, 117-18, 120, 123, 130, 135, 206
Hofmann, Hans, 314
Hohnsbeen, John, 372-73
Holbrook, Miss, 20
Hollywood, 21, 254
Holms, Beatrix, 117, 127
Holms, Dorothy, 79-88, 91, 92, 95-96, 99, 117, 118, 123, 127-28, 143, 147
*Holms, John, 79-129 passim, between 140 and 141, 143, 149, 198, 244-45, 278, 292
Hopkinson, Tom, 116
Horses, 152; Katie, 115, 121; Starlight, 115
Horses of Lord Candlestick, The (Carrington), 216
Hotels: Beau Rivage, Ouchy, 60-62; Belmont-Plaza, New York, 246-47, 248; Bourgogne et Montana, Paris, 97; Brevoort, New York, 59, 250; Crillon, Paris, 160-61; Frankfort-Rocio, Lisbon, 237, 240; Great Northern, New York, 245, 258, 259; Gritti, Venice, 377; Kensington, La Croix, 202; Lutétia, Paris, 37, 48, 65, 73; Mena House, Giza, 44; Pardigon, London, 88; Plaza, New York, 251; Plaza Athénée,

Paris, 26, 29, 30, 31, 36; Quisana, Capri, 42; Ritz, Paris, 49; Royal Condé, Paris, 105; St. Regis, New York, 23; Shelton, New York, 248-49
Howard, Charles, 252
Hugo, Jean, 362
Hulten, Pontus, 370
Humes, Betty, 31, 75
Hunter, Sam, 346
Huon de Bordeaux (Gaston Paris), 188
Hyères, 68, 70, 84-85

Ile de France, 145
Ile St. Louis, 167, 209
India, 351-54, 371
injuries, 8-9, 140, 208, 217, 243, 292, 304
Iowa, University of, 295, 296
Ismay, Bruce, 12

Jack (gardener), 142-43, 144, 148-49, 155
Jacoby School, 16-17; graduating class of 1915, between 77 and 78
Jacques, Ray, 377
Jaded Blossoms, 60
Janis, Sidney, 253, 262, 267, 281, 318, 345
Japan, 365-66
Jeanneret, Charles-Edouard, 265. See also Le Corbusier
*Jennings, Humphrey, between 140 and 141, 159-60, 161, 178, 250
Jensen, Knud, 370
Jerusalem, 47
Jesus Concepção, 243-44
Jeu de la vérité, 266-67
Jewell, Edward Alden, 279-80
John (secretary), 293
John, Augustus, 194
Jolas, Eugene, 120
Jolas, Maria, 107, 120, 122, 168, 190, 219
Jones, Phyllis, 143, 147, 154, 156, 157, 199
Joseph (gardener), 63-64, 70, 84
Joyce, Giorgio, 99, 103, 109-10, 120, 186, 207-8, 209, 210, 211, 223
Joyce, Helen Fleischman, 103, 109-10, 163, 168, 207-8, 209-10. See also Fleishman, Helen
Joyce, James, 41, 99, 110, 162, 163, 165, 168, 194, 207, 211; *postcard, 169
Joyce, Nora, 41, 99, 110, 164, 180
Joyce, Lucia, 41, 99, 162, 175

Kahlo, Frida, 359
Kairouan, 77
Kandinsky, Nina, 168, 170, 202
Kandinsky, Wassily, 168-70, 202, 208, 219, 250, 251, 256, 340, 343, 347
Kaner, Sam, 370

Kapital, Das (Marx), 142
Karesee, 52-53
Kastor, Robert, 208, 268
Kempner, Sigmund, 25
Keytes, George, 353
*Kiesler, Frederick, between 204 and 205, 270-71, 273-76, 285, 293-94, 320, 360, 361
Kiki, 41, 49
Kimombo Temple, 46
Kingsmill, Hugh, 80, 100, 102, 123, 127, 128, 143
Kirkland, Alexander, 271-72
Kitty (cook), 148-49
Kitty (Garman's niece). See Epstein, Kitty
Kitzbühl, 132, 136, 139-40
Klee, Paul, 219, 225, 251, 256, 326, 362
Kohn, Lucile, 18-19, 22, 63
Kokoschka, Oskar, 357
Kootz, Sam, 315
Krasner, Lee. See Pollock, Lee
Kraus, Dr., 304
Kuh, Katharine, 322, 344
Kuhn family, 221-23
Kunsthaus, Zurich, 338

La Croix Fleurie, 58-59
La Fierte, 98
Lakewood, N.J., 8
Lanvin, 11
*Large Volumes (Hélion), between 268 and 269
Larkins, David, 297-98, 309-13
Lasalle, Philip, 336
La Tourelle, 202
Laurens, Henri, 172, 219, 343, 362
Leão d'Ouro, Lisbon, 238, 240
Le Bourg, Elaine, 34
Le Canadel, 58, 63, 69, 75, 93, 202
Le Corbusier, 338, 352-53, 361
Lee, Gypsy Rose, 271-72, 279, 289, 309
Lefèvre Foinet, René, 226-29, 231, 233
Léger, Fernand, 218, 219, 250
Le Lavandou, 63, 67, 68, 71
Lenbach, Franz von, 7
Lengnau, 1
Lennon, John, 366
Lenox High School, 258
Léon, Paul, 162
Le Rayol, 111
Les Baux, 204
Le Trayas, 38
Le Veyrier, 221
Levy, Julien, 247, 252, 256, 260, 267, 280, 284
Lewisohn, Adele, 17-18
Lewisohn, Fay, 17-18
Leymarie, Jean, 374
Licht, Fred, 369, 377

*Life*, 272
Lila, 289
Lilly (nurse), 41, 46, 47, 56, 61, 71
Lipchitz, Jacques, 219, 334
Lisbon, 237-45
Lissitzky, El, 251
*Little Review*, 22
*Little Women* (Alcott play), 17
Llewellyn, 194-95, 197
Llewellyn, Mrs., 195, 197
*Locus Solus* (Roussel), 37
Loeb, Charles, 29-30
Loeb, Edwin, 40
Loeb, Harold, 23, 31-32, 41, 107, 263
Loeb, Mary Frank, 74, 136
Loeb, Willard, 136
London, 10, 35, 38-41, 88, 112, 118, 119,
    123-32, 134, 143, 154, 157, 165, 176, 179,
    188, 194
*London Bulletin*, 178
London Gallery, 178
Lorenzetti, Giulio, 331-32, 336, 337
Los Angeles, 253-56
Losey, Joseph, 368, 377
*Lost Girl, A* (D. H. Lawrence), 109
Louise, 120
Louisiana, Copenhagen, 370
Louvre, 28, 219, 374
Lowengard, Armand, 24-25
Loy, Faby, 64
Loy, Joella, 64, 67
Loy, Mina, 41, 60, 64, 67, 71
Luce, Clare Boothe, 341
Luxor, 45
Lyons, 62, 232
Lysol, 2, 31, 38

Mabille, Dr. Pierre, 227
McAlmon, Robert, 39, 52, 255
MacAndrew, James, 370
McCarthy, Mary, 319
Mack, Mrs., 20
Mackenzie, Compton, 31
McKinley, Charles Everett, Jr., 253, 255
McManus, Everett, 324
Macmillan Company, 324
* McPherson, Kenneth, *between 208 and 209,*
    287-311
Madeleine (maid), 117, 120
Magritte, René, 219
*Maiastra* (Brancusi), 211-12
Malevich, Kazimir, 259, 327, 347
Malibu, 253
Maloja, 82
Malraux, André, 366-67
Manet, Edouard, 362
Manson, J. B., 172-73

Marchiori, Giuseppe, 334
Marcoussis, Louis, 219, 225
Marie (cook), 117, 120
Marini, Marino, 326, 334, *335,* 375
Mark, Warren, 294
Marseilles, 178-79, 227-36, 248
Martigues, 144
Martin, Michael Combe, 332
Marx, Karl, 142, 151
Masson, André, 67, 316
Matisse, Henri, 343, 361-62
Matisse, Pierre, 348
Matta (Roberto Sebastian Antonio Matta
    Echaurren), 268-69, 314, 329, 339, 354,
    367
Mayer, Edward B., 21, 35, 38, 39, 51-54
Mazia, Violette de, 361
Mégève, 76, 161, 183, 188, 201, 205, 209,
    217, 220-21, 231-32
*Melancholy and Mystery of a Street* (Chirico),
    303, 355
* Mesens, Edouard L. T., *between 140 and*
    *141,* 176-78, 180, 190, 191, 199, 216
Meudon, 162, 201, 204-5, 221
Mexico, 302, 358-60
Meyer, Edgar, 17
Milan, 331, 346
Miller, Dorothy, 317
Miller, Henry, 267
Minneapolis Institute of Fine Arts, 346
*Minotaur*, 327
*Miracle, The* (Brancusi), 250
Mirko (Basaldella), 334
Mirmande, 109, 111-12
Miró, Joan, 219, 256, 317, 326
*mistral*, 70
* *Mobile* (Calder), 328, *between 332 and 333*
*Modern Art U.S.A.* (Blesh), 346
Modigliani, Amedeo, 347, 362
Moises, 50
* Mondrian, Piet, 190-91 *between 204 and*
    205, 219, 262, 284, 317-18, 326, 347
Monet, Claude, 362
Monmartre, 107, 189
Monte Estoril, 239-41
Montparnasse, 27, 51, 65, 107
Montsouris, 145
Monzie, M. de (minister of education), 206
Moon, Jim, 372
* Moore, Henry, *between 140 and 141,* 192-93,
    219, 329, 334
Moreau, Jeanne, 368
Moreton-in-Marsh, 118
Morey, Charles R., 347
Morley, Grace McCann, 252-53, 315
Morris, Cedric, 40, 171-72
Morris, Charlotte and Ronnie, 129

Morris, Ira and Edita, 140, 147, 188, 278-79
Morris, Ivan, 140
Motherwell, Robert, 285, 314, 345
Muir, Edwin, 80, 99-102, 123, 127, 128, 147
Muir, Willa, 99, 100, 147
Mulas, Ugo, 365
Munich, 97
* Mural (Pollock), 295-96
Murare, Michelangelo, 365
Murat, Princess, 93
Murder! Murder! (Laurence Vail), 68, 72
Murphy (Beckett), 164
Murphy, Esther (Mrs. Chester Arthur III), 59-60
Murphy, Katherine, 52
Mursia, Ugo, 365
Muses Are Heard, The (Capote), 348
Museum of Modern Art: New York, 247-48, 250, 259, 260, 265, 304, 317, 343, 344, 346, 367; Rome, 346-47; Stockholm, 370; Turin, 374-75; Venice (Cà Pesaro), 331-32
Museum of Natural History, New York, 251
Museum of the American Indian, New York, 251, 320
Mysore Art Museum, 351
* Mystic Marriage, The (renamed The Anti-Pope) (Max Ernst), 261-62, between 268 and 269

Nasser, Gamal Abdel, 353
Neagoe, Peter, 109, 111
Nehru, Jawaharlal, 353
Neuilly, 107, 149, 208
Neumann, J. B., 267
New Delhi, 352
Newhaven, 183, 184
New Orleans, 257-58
New York, 1-24 passim, 35, 59-60, 67, 71, 245-52, 258-68, 270-320 passim, 358, 360-61, 362-63, 371-72
N I 1948 (Pollock), 343
Nicholson, Ben, 318
Nierendorf, Carl, 200-201
Nightwood (Barnes), 27, 114, 116
Nina, 132
Norcia, 108-9
Norfork broads, 145
Norman (Mary Reynolds's friend), 28, 38-39
Norway, 94-95

Oblomov, 166-67
O'Brien, Edward, 188
Obroe, Barbara, 372
Octobon, Mme, 58, 63, 69, 84, 93, 202
Odets, Clifford, 267-68
O'Keeffe, Georgia, 24
Ono, Yoko, 365-66

Orangerie, Paris, 366, 374
Orazi, 188
Orchard Poyle, 123
Orozco, José Clemente, 359
Oslo, 90
Ouchy, 60-62
Out of This Century (Dial edition), 321-24; * Jackson Pollock's book jacket, 323
Ozenfant, Amédáe, 105, 265
Ozenfant, Marthe, 265

Palais des Beaux-Arts, Brussels, 338
* Palais Promontoire (Tanguy), 180, 181, 203
Palazzo Giustinian, Venice, 337-38
Palazzo Reale, Milan, 331
* Palazzo Venier dei Leoni, Venice, between 332 and 333, 333-36, 354-57, 367, 370-72, 375-76, 379-85
Palenque, 359
Palestine, 47
Pallucchini, Rodolfo, 326, 327, 328, 329, 342
Pamplona, 104
Pan-American Airways, 245-47
Papi, 87
Paradiso restaurant, Venice, 330
Paris, 10, 11-12, 25-31, 36-38, 41, 47-52, 64-67, 70, 72-73, 75-76, 92, 93, 97-99, 105-8, 109, 119, 122, 128-29, 144-45, 154, 156, 160-65, 167-68, 175, 178, 183, 184-88, 193; 200-201, 204-5, 209-20
Parmeggiani, Tancredi. See Tancredi
Parsons, Betty, 316, 320, 345
Passante, Dr., 377
Passero, Vincenzo, 356-57
Patuni, Captain, 41-43
Pau, 205-6, 209
Paulon, Flavia, 333, 334
Peacock, 81
Peacock and Waller, 142
Pêche de Nuit à Antibes (Picasso), 317
Pegeen. See Vail, Pegeen
Peggy. See Waldman, Peggy
Penrose, Sir Roland, 180, 190, 191, 192, 193, 199, 216, 250
Pereira, I. Rice, 314
Perressutti, Enrico, 338, 339
Perocco, Guido, 331, 377
Petersfield, 139, 147, 149, 154, 159, 176, 179-80, 181, 188, 189, 195, 199, 201. See also Yew Tree Cottage
* Peur donnant ailes au Courage, Le (Cocteau), 166
* Pevsner, Antoine, 172, between 204 and 205, 216-17, 219, between 232 and 233, 251, 327, 334 ·
Phalaes Temple, 46
Philadelphia Museum, 361, 362

Philip, Prince, Duke of Edinburgh, 368
* *Piazza* (or *The Square*) (Giacometti), *between 332 and 333*
Picabia, Francis, 51, 219
Picabia, Gabrielle, 63, 105
Picasso, Pablo, 250, 251, 256, 315, 317, 326, 328, 330, 362, 367
*Pied Piper of Hamelin, The,* 149
Pignatelli, Princess, 354
Plant, Wilson, 147
*Plastique,* 162
Poiret, Paul, 38, 48, 50; *dress, *between 77 and 78*
Poissonnière (art dealer), 214
Polier, Justine Wise, 285
Pollitt, Harry, 151, 157, 174
Pollock, Jackson, *between 268 and 269,* 285, 295-96, 303-4, 314-17, 319-20, 323, 329, 336, 339, 341, 343, 344, 345-47, 362, 363, 364
Pollock, Lee, 296, 315, 316, 346-47, 362, 363
Polo, 310
Pompeii, 26
ponies, 114-15
Ponisovsky, Alec, 207
Pons, Lily, 319
Popoff, Dr., 97-98
Porquerolles, 91-92
* *Portrait of Peggy Guggenheim* (Tanguy), 185
Portugal, 237-45
*Possessed, The* (Dostoevsky), 136
Pound, Ezra, 57-58
Pousette-Dart, Richard, 345
Pramousquier, 62-64, 66, 67, 68-71, 73-74, 76, 81, 97, 98, 202
Prefettura, Venice, 326,.333, 334
pregnancies, 37-39, 57, 60, 71-72, 195-96
Proust, Marcel, 142
Provincetown, Mass., 268-70
Prunier's restaurant, Paris, 31
* *PSI* (Tunnard), 190, *between 268 and 269*
Putzel, Howard J., 215-16, 217, 225, 246, 252, 265, 267, 270, 273, 276, 278, 279, 284, 285, 287, 289, 292, 293, 294-95, 296, 299, 306, 307, 313, 314, 316
Pyrenees, 67-68, 103, 104

Quaife, Mrs., 17

Radiguet, Raymond, 58
Ragghianti, Carlo Ludovico, 330-31
Ramatuelle, 82
Rapallo, 57
Rathbone, Perry, 367, 372
rats, 153
Ratton, Charles, 180-81
Ravello, 43

Ravenna, 327
Ray, Man, 41, 48, 49, 218, 255, 375
* Read, Sir Herbert, *between 140 and 141,* 193, 196-200, 206, 245, 251, 262, 284, *between 332 and 333,* 334, 342, 345, 367
Read, Mrs. Herbert, 199, 206
Reavey, George, 176
Rebay, Baroness Hilla, 170-71, 197, 285, 358
Reed, Norman, 369
Reilly, Peggy, 273
Reinhardt, Ad, 314
Reis, Bernard, 317, 339, 345, 362, 372
Reis, Rebecca, 266, 302, 354, 362, 372
Reno, Nevada, 252
Renoir, Pierre Auguste, 362
Resor, Captain, 303
* Reynolds, Mary, 28, 29, 38-40, 41, 42, 50-51, 54, 108, 125, 131, *between 140 and 141,* 145, 147, 154, 161, 163, 165, 178, 186, 208, 209, 214, 216, 218, 282, 283, 299
Richter, Hans, 314
Rickword, Edgell, 140, 145-46, 147, 153, 174
Rickword, Jackie, 145-46, 147, 153
riding, 114-15, 152
Rivera, Diego, 359-60
Robert, Henri, 72
Robin (Thelma Wood), 27
Rockefeller family, 4
Rogers (architect), 338
Rome, 31-32
Roosevelt, Eleanor, 285-86
Rossbach, Max, 8
Rostrom, Captain, 13
Rothko, Mark, 314, 345, 362
Rouen, 29, 183
Rousseau, Henri, 250, 326, 343, 362
Roux, Gaston Louis, 67
Roy, Jaminy, 351, 353
Rudi, 11
Rumney, Ralph, 376
Rumpelmeyer's, Paris, 11
Russell, Bertrand, 147-48
Russell, Dora, 190
*Ryder* (Barnes), 118-19, 143
Rylands, Jane and Philip, 373

Sadleir, Sir Michael, 169
Sage, Kay (Mrs. Yves Tanguy), 203, 209, 227, 249, 250
Saheb, Thakore, 351, 352
sailing, 145-46
St. Gallen, 234
St-Gerand-le-puy, 219
St. Jean de Luz, 103, 109-10
St. Maxime, 103
St. Martin d'Ardèche, 231, 244

St. Moritz, 29, 34-35, 53
St. Raphael, 85
St. Rémy, 204
St. Tropez, 70, 78, 81, 82, 87
Salvatore, 334
Salzburg, 96-97
San Francisco, 252
San Francisco Museum, 252-53, 316
Sandberg, P. J. H. B., 327, 338
Santomaso, Giuseppe, 325-26, 327, 340, 342
São Paulo, 346
Saroyan, William, 271
Save Venice, 370
Scarpa, Carlo, 327
Schiaparelli, Elsa, 207, 273
Schiffrin, Jacques, 31, 37, 236
Scoby, Dr., 22-23
Scott, Evelyn, 70
Scott, Kenneth, 345
Seaton, Devon, 144
Secret Service, 9
* Self-Portrait (Brauner), 187
Seligman, Sir Charles, 15
Seligman, James, 1, 6, 14, 15, 19
Seligman family, 1-3, 10, 16, 30
Seligmann, Kurt, 281
Seurat, Georges, 251, 362
Severini, Gino, 219
Shaw, Walter, 345
She Wolf (Pollock), 316
Sides, Mr., 201-3
Silvertoe (architect), 171-72
Simon, Norton, 367-68
Simpson, Wallis Warfield, 155
Singer, Freddy, 16
Siqueiros, David Alfaro, 359
Sobel, Janet, 345
Soby, James T., 260, 267, 279, 284, 296, 311
Soirées de Paris, 51
* Soleil dans son écrin, Le (Tanguy), 180,
    between 268 and 269
Southampton, N.Y., 272
South Harting, 133, 134, 136, 143, 182
Soutine, Chaim, 362
Spain, 110-11, 236-37
Spanish Relief Committee, 194-95
Stamos, Theodoros, 362
Stedelijk Museum, Amsterdam, 327, 338
Stelvio (pass), 52-53
Stern, James, 266, 293
Sterne, Hedda, 314
Stieglitz, Alfred, 24
Stijl, De, 200
Still, Clyfford, 314, 345
Stillman family, 4
Stockholm, 95, 370
Straus, Isidor, 13

Straus, Levi, 319
Stravinsky, Vera, 48, 375
Strozzina, Florence, 331
Suchon, Dr. Marion, 257-58
Sulzberger, Dulcie, 6
Sulzberger, Marion, 6, 29
Sunwise Turn Bookshop, 23
Sussex downs, 147
Surrealism and Surrealists, 67, 149-50,
    182-83, 184-86, 189, 191, 200, 219, 227,
    249-50, 254, 262, 266, 273-74, 281, 282,
    318, 327, 330
Swanage, Dorset, 157
Sweden, 95
Sweeney, James Johnson, 279, 283, 284, 303,
    311, 314, 339, 346, 358, 360, 361

Tamayo, Rufino, 359
* Tancredi (Parmeggiani), between 332 and
    333, 339, 340, 341, 376
Tanguy, Kay Sage. See Sage, Kay
*Tanguy, Yves, between 140 and 141, 160,
    179-88, 181, 185, 191-92, 193-94, 194,
    200, 203, between 204 and 205, 209, 210,
    219, 250, 256, between 268 and 269, 307,
    373
Tanguy, Mme Yves, 179-88, 203
Tate Gallery, London, 172, 369
Taverny, Countess, 11-12
Tchelitchew, Pavel, 350
Tel Aviv Museum, 344
Tennessee, 258
tennis, 147
Tenzing Norkay, 354
Teresina, 34
Terre Labourée, La (Miró), 317
Thayer, John B., 317
They Shall Not Have Me (Hélion), 283
Thomson, Virgil, 217-18
Time, 321-22, 346
Tintoretto, 362
Tirelli, Signor (lawyer), 42-43
Titanic, 12-13, 14
Titian, 362
Toilette de l'Air (Tanguy), 307
Toledo, 111
Torquay, 117
Toulon, 70, 73, 74, 75, 83-84
toys, 7
transition, 120
Tremezzo, 53-54
Treviso, 55
Trevor Square, London, 119
Trieste, 99
Trincanato, Renata, 356
Tronc, André, 377
Trondheim, 95, 96

Trouville, 11
*Tunnard, John, *between 140 and 141*, 190, *between 268 and 269*
Turin, 330, 374-75
Turkel, Pauline, 68
Turner, J. M. W., 326
*Two Women in Front of a Mirror (Hirshfield), 318, *between 268 and 269*
Tyrol, 52-53, 95, 96

Utrillo, Maurice, 362

Vail, Clotilde, 26, 30-43 *passim*, 51-54 *passim*, 57, 61, 64, 67, 73-74, 76, 82, 149
Vail, Eugene, 26, 27, 54, 55, 60, 149
Vail, Gertrude, 26, 27, 29, 30, 33, 35, 49, 52, 53, 60, 67, 93, 183, 240
*Vail, Laurence, 23-77 *passim*, between 77 and 78, 81-84, 97, 103-4, 109-112 *passim*, 117, 125, 132-33, 136, 143-44, 145, 147, 149, 153, 183, 188, 190, 193, 201, 203, 205, 217, 219-20, 225, 231-34, 251, 252, 253, 258, 263, 265, 273, 277, 279, 292, 293, 297, 300, 302, 304, 307, 308-9, 314, 321, 345, 355, 365, 377
*Vail, Pegeen, 4, 60-62, 67, 68, 70, *between 77 and 78*, 87, 92-93, 94, 95-99, 102, 103, 104, 106, 107, 109, 110, 113-22, 124, 127-28, 132-33, 134, 136, 138, 139-49 *passim*, *between 140 and 141*, 154-55, 161, 179-80, 182, 183, 192, 217, 221, 232, 237, 241, 245, 252-58, 262, 263-64, 268, *between 268 and 269*, 277, 281, 282, 284, 302, 307, 308-9, 314, 341, 342, 345, 366, 370-71, 376
*Vail, Sindbad, 40, 41, 46, 47, 53-54, 56, 59, 62, 64, 67, 68, 70, *between 77 and 78*, 87, 89, 93-94, 98, 103-4, 109, 110, 111, 115, 116, 124-25, 132, 135, 136, 140, *between 140 and 141*, 142, 143-44, 145, 153-55, 183, 184, 188, 192, 195, 201, 202-3, 205-6, 209, 217, 221, 237-38, 241, 252, 277, 297, 303, 376, 377
Vail children, 241
Vantongerloo, Georges, 219
*Van Velde, Geer, *between 140 and 141*, 163-64, 176-77, 178-79
Vedova, Emilio, 325, 327
Velde, Willem van de, 362
Venice, 51, 54-57, 109, 153-54, 320, 325-48, 354-57, 366-70, 375-76
Venier dei Leoni. *See* Palazzo Venier dei Leoni
Ventadour, Jacqueline (Mrs. Jean Hélion), 217, 232, 236-37, 241, 258
Viani, Alberto, 334, 335-36, 343
Vieira de Sylva, 225

Vienna, 89, 91
*View*, 267, 322-24
Villerville, 41
Virginia, 264
Vitrac, Roger, 76-77
Vlaminck, Maurice de, 362
VVV, 282, 284, 293-94

Wadi Halfa, 46
Wahab, 148
Wailing Wall, 47
*Waiting for Lefty* (Odets), 268
*Waldman, Milton, 38, 82, 116, 119, 123, 125-27, 135, 136, *between 140 and 141*
*Waldman, Peggy (Marguerite David), 21, 40-41, 43, 74, 75, 82, 85, 87, 89, 93, 117, 123, 125-27, 136, *between 140 and 141*, 159
Wales, 136-37, 144
Warblington Castle, 134-36
Warwick Castle, 137
Washington, D.C., 263-64
weddings, 30, 264, 272
Weinstein, Pierre, 25
Welles, Sumner, 268
Wellfleet, Mass., 268
Wengen, 64
Wessel, Harold, 21-22
West End, N.J., 15
White, Antonia, 116, 135
White Star Line, 12-13
Wichita Falls, Texas, 257
Widener, Harry Elkins, 17
Wiegand, Charmion, 262
Williams, Tennessee, 368
Wimbledon boarding school, 180
*Winnipeg*, 233
Winston, Mrs. Harry, 316
Wishart, Ernest, 132, 133, 145, 147, 153
Wishart, Lorna, 133, 147, 153
Woburn Square, London, 123-34
*Woman with a Cut Throat* (Giacometti), 215
*Women and Children* (Laurence Vail), 67
Wood, Thelma, 27
Woodbridge, Sussex, 146
Wright, Frank Lloyd, 360-61

Yarrow, Katherine, 246
Yeats, Jack, 163-64
Yew Tree Cottage, 139-58. *See also* Petersfield

Zadkine, Ossip, 343
Zavagli Ricciardelli, Countess Lucia, 376
Zervos, Christian, 337
Zorzi, Count Elio, 328, 341, 342, 347, 368
Zurich, 132
Zweig, Stefan, 97